S0-BWX-727

COMPUTER LITERACY

COMPUTER LITERACY

SECOND EDITION

Helene G. Kershner
State University of New York at Buffalo

D. C. Heath and Company
Lexington, Massachusetts   Toronto

Address editorial correspondence to:
D. C. Heath
125 Spring Street
Lexington, MA 02173

Cover: Joanna Steinkeller *(design),* Slide Graphics *(photograph)*

Copyright © 1992 by D. C. Heath and Company.
Previous edition copyright © 1990 by D. C. Heath and Company, under the title *Introduction to Computer Literacy.*

All rights reserved. No part of this publication may be reproduced or transmitted in any form or by any means, electronic or mechanical, including photocopy, recording, or any information storage or retrieval system, without permission in writing from the publisher.

Published simultaneously in Canada.

Printed in the United States of America.

International Standard Book Number: 0-669-27998-6

Library of Congress Catalog Number: 91–75382

10   9   8   7   6   5   4   3

This text is dedicated to Josh and Libby,

without whose love and attention

this book would have taken half the time,

and to Bruce,

whose love made all this possible.

AUGUSTANA UNIVERSITY COLLEGE
LIBRARY

Preface

Computers are an essential part of our daily lives. We often use them without even knowing we are doing so, as when we get cash from an automatic teller machine or program a VCR. These activities do not require an understanding of how computers work. Yet to tap a computer's resources fully, it is important to understand how its components work together to store and process information. To be effective users, we must understand the potential and limitations of the hardware, the process of problem solving, the capabilities of today's software, and much more.

Computer Literacy is designed to meet this need. The purpose of this book is to develop students' literacy in all aspects of computers, and, by so doing, to make them comfortable in the computer age. The text removes the mystery of computers by giving readers a firm foundation in hardware, software, and the vocabulary of computers. All major types of computers, from microcomputers to mainframes and from notebook computers to supercomputers, are discussed. The text also features comprehensive coverage of common applications that students will encounter, including word processors, spreadsheets, data bases, and graphics and telecommunications packages, in both IBM and Macintosh versions. In addition, ethics and problem solving are highlighted throughout. The information provides students with an essential understanding of computers and their uses that prepares them for further study.

TEXT CONTENT AND ORGANIZATION

Computer Literacy's topical coverage, flexible organization, writing style, pedagogical features, and supporting materials have been designed to assist students and instructors alike in achieving computer literacy.

Variety

The table of contents outlines the many topics covered. Beginning with an overview and a brief history of computers, the book deals with both the computer hardware and the applications software that transform the machine into a tool for problem solving. The text develops the problem-solving technique of designing algorithms. This top-down technique is applicable not only to the design of programs but to general problem solving. The text directly applies this approach to applications software such as spreadsheets and data base systems.

Chapters are crafted to give students a solid grounding in the uses and potential of computers. The increasingly important area of computer communications and networking receives extensive coverage featuring practical examples, including E-mail and on-line information services as well as academic and business networks. The often neglected topic of ethical use of the computer is discussed throughout the text, with an emphasis on the individual's responsibility for ethical use. Discussions here include criminal use of the computer and the computer's impact on personal privacy. Some additional topics explored in the text are programming languages, artificial intelligence, management information systems, and the very practical issue of how to buy computers and software.

Flexibility

An important feature of any text is how adaptable it is to the needs of various instructors. This text uses a generic approach to software. Computer screen examples are drawn from the most popular packages, but discussion is not limited to specific packages. This text's flexibility makes it ideal as a core text or, when paired with the Heath Laboratory Course Series, as part of a lecture/lab sequence. After Chapter 1, "An Overview of Computers," the chapters may be covered in order or rearranged to conform to the various needs of almost all instructors.

Readability

Written in a clear, engaging style and at a highly accessible level, this text makes sometimes difficult concepts easily understandable.

Chapter Preview

Because repetition is one of the keys to learning, each chapter begins with a preview of the main topics that will be presented.

Examples

To demonstrate the great value of computers to society and individuals, the text draws examples from situations students typically experience in everyday life.

Boxed Features

"On Line" boxes illuminate how computers solve problems and meet needs in the real world. Demonstrating that computers are a vital part of everyday life, the articles reflect current technology and issues of widespread interest.

Design and Illustrations

Textbooks that are well designed and contain ample illustrations hold students' interest. This text liberally uses illustrations, including photographs and line art. High-resolution pictures of computer screens and program examples prepare students for the data displays encountered when working with the computer. Three special sections of color photographs focus on key subjects.

End-of-Chapter Material

Carefully graded review materials are provided at the end of each chapter to reinforce understanding. A comprehensive yet concise summary reviews the chapter's major points. "Key Words" lists include important terms along with page references. (These terms appear in boldface type within the chapter.) "Test Your Knowledge" questions help students review the chapter, and "Expand Your Knowledge" questions challenge them to apply the facts to realistic situations. The exercises stress hands-on experience to reinforce the learning process.

Glossary

A complete glossary includes definitions (with chapter references) for the boldface terms in the text.

SUPPLEMENTS

Extensive packages of software and programming supplements are offered with the text to help both student and instructor cover the material. Each supplement has been prepared by experienced teacher/authors.

Software Supplements

The Heath Laboratory Course Series teaches students to use applications packages productively. Many of the most popular applications packages are included in the series. A listing of the Heath Laboratory Course Series appears on the back cover of this text.

Programming Supplements

For courses with a programming language component, comprehensive programming supplements are available.

- *An Introduction to Structured Microsoft BASIC Programming* by Thomas W. Doyle and Jeremy I. Clark.

- *Programming in Pascal* and *Programming in Pascal with an Early Intro-duction to Procedures* by Nell Dale, The University of Texas at Austin.

Instructor's Supplements

The supplements designed for instructors include an Instructor's Guide and computerized testing for the IBM PC.

- *Instructor's Guide.* The Instructor's Guide includes a wealth of materials for busy instructors. For each chapter, learning objectives, a chapter overview, annotated lecture outlines, answers to text questions, additional classroom and lecture materials, transparency masters, and test items are provided.
- *Computerized testing.* Computerized testing for microcomputers is also available. Instructors can produce chapter tests, midterms, and final exams easily and accurately.

ACKNOWLEDGMENTS

A book such as this is not produced in a vacuum. Communicating complex ideas and perspectives clearly and accessibly requires a supportive and stimulating environment. A special debt is owed to Kulbir Arora for his contribution of the assembly language, TeX, and LISP examples. Thanks go to Patricia J. Eberlein, former chairman of computer science at the State University of New York at Buffalo, for urging me to begin this endeavor. I owe further thanks to Jacquelynn Kud for her work on the screen snapshots that add another dimension to the applications chapters.

I would like to thank my colleagues who reviewed the manuscript, including Virginia T. Anderson, University of North Dakota; Joseph Frasca, Sonoma State University; Kate Goelz, Rutgers University; Lee R. Janczak, Lackawanna Junior College; Marilyn Meyer, Fresno City College; James L. Noyes, Wittenberg University; LoriLee Sadler, Indiana University; and Liang Chee Wee, University of Arizona.

Three other people must be acknowledged. To Barbara Sherman go my special thanks for her constant support and advice, particularly during development of the MIS chapter. To David C. Brown at the University of Wisconsin–Madison I give my heartfelt appreciation for reading every word, making corrections where needed, and listening to my frustration when writing became difficult. To Susan Bundy-Myrow I send a unique thank-you, for keeping me sane when everything around me threatened to fall apart.

I also must thank my husband, Bruce. Not only did his support at home allow me the time I needed to craft this text, but his love, support, and editorial skills made the impossible a reality.

H. G. K.

ABOUT THE AUTHOR

Helene G. Kershner is the assistant chairman of computer science at the State University of New York at Buffalo. She is an award-winning teacher, recognized for her ability to make complex concepts understandable. During her eighteen years as a teacher and administrator, she has developed a strong appreciation for the needs and concerns of the nontechnical computer user. In addition to teaching, she oversees the instructional laboratories that are used to introduce computing to more than 800 students each semester. She has appeared on radio and television and has given numerous workshops and talks on computer literacy, the importance of computers, and computer science as a discipline. Kershner received her B.A. in mathematics from Queens College–CUNY, her M.S.E. in computer and information systems from the University of Pennsylvania, and completed advanced graduate work in educational psychology at the University of Connecticut–Storrs. Before coming to the State University of New York at Buffalo, she was the departmental administrator for computer science at the University of Wisconsin–Madison.

Brief Contents

Contents

3   The Central Processing Unit   73

8   Programming Languages   213

9   Ethics and Responsibilities   235

10   Software   255

11   Word Processing   285

12   Spreadsheets   313

15 Computer Communications and Networking   391

16 Artificial Intelligence   421

17   Management Information Systems   445

18   Evaluating Computers and Software   471

COMPUTER LITERACY

1

An Overview of Computers

CHAPTER OUTLINE

Computers are an essential part of our lives. We find them in our cars, our markets, and our schools. They are, in fact, almost everywhere and affect nearly everything we do. Yet most of us have no idea of *what* they do and even less of an idea of how they work. The study of computers, like the study of any other subject, whether car repair or medicine, has a language all its own. This is not surprising. Talking with a car mechanic is often like conversing in a foreign language. We expect to understand what the mechanic is saying, but most often that is not the case. Talking to a doctor is even more like a visit to an exotic country. The physician discusses our medical problems, but to the average person, the words and the described procedures might just as well be a foreign language.

Learning about computers can be equally confusing and difficult until you know the jargon, the vocabulary. When working with computers, common words such as *data, bug,* or *bit* take on unique meanings. Some computer jargon, such as *input, network,* and *down,* has become part of our everyday language.

This text will familiarize you with the concepts upon which computers are based as well as the vocabulary used. When you have completed this text, computers will be familiar territory, not a foreign country. You will understand how the components that make up the computer work and how computers are changing the world. In addition, you will understand how programs are written and how they are used. You will speak the language of computers and be comfortable with these machines.

After studying this chapter, you will be able to:

- Understand the difference between data and information.
- Identify the basic components of all computer systems.
- Understand the binary number system, bits, bytes, and words.
- Distinguish between digital and analog computers.
- Identify the different classes of computers.
- Distinguish between microcomputers, minicomputers, and mainframes.
- Understand how workstations, superminis, and supercomputers are complicating the classification system used to describe computers.

UNDERSTANDING THE MACHINE

To understand how computers work, we must start with the basic vocabulary. We need to comprehend the language being "spoken" before we can even begin to understand the machine. The first computer-related words to learn focus on what the computer does. We have heard that computers "crunch numbers." What computers really do—and just about the only thing they do—is *process data*. In this chapter we will discuss the meaning of these two words. Then we will see how computers do their work—and do it very well indeed.

Data Versus Information

In common speech, we use the words *data* and *information* interchangeably. However, these terms have different meanings. In everyday conversation these differences are not too important, but for computers this difference is critical.

Data are raw facts. Raw facts can be collected from any number of sources. For example, every 10 years the U.S. Census Bureau collects facts, such as the number of bathrooms, the ages of family members, and the first names of the children in America's households. Taken alone, these facts are not informative. It is impossible to draw meaningful conclusions about anything from this collection of data.

Information, on the other hand, is the result of data that have been transformed. The data have been processed in some ways so that meaningful conclusions can be drawn. For example, it is interesting to know that *J* names, such as Jeremy, Jennifer, and Joshua, are very popular among the children of the baby-boom generation, or that the average American family today has 1.5 children. This is information.

Why is the difference between data and information so important for computers? Computers have become the agents that transform data into information. The computer is used to collect, organize, sort, and transform raw facts into meaningful information from which logical conclusions can be drawn. For example, when registering for college, the following 10 students indicated their grade level:

Penny Lofers	Freshman
Frank N. Stein	Freshman
Inna Pickle	Freshman
Sandy Beaches	Sophomore
Phil Errupp	Freshman
Polly Nomial	Junior
Said A. Mint	Sophomore
Telly Graham	Freshman
Willie Maykitt	Senior
Senior Itis	Freshman

In its current form we can draw few conclusions from this data. However, if we organize the data alphabetically we can easily find the status of an individual. Furthermore, if we sort the data by academic year we can make inferences about these students.

Phil Errupp	Freshman
Telly Graham	Freshman

Senior Itis	Freshman
Penny Lofers	Freshman
Inna Pickle	Freshman
Frank N. Stein	Freshman
Sandy Beaches	Sophomore
Said A. Mint	Sophomore
Polly Nomial	Junior
Willie Maykitt	Senior

We might conclude that most of these students are freshmen, but all classes are represented.

Computers are data transformers. They assist us in organizing raw facts so that we can draw meaningful conclusions from them.

The "Basic" Computer

To explain the actual work—processing—done by a computer, we must first look at the parts that make up every computer. All computers, from the smallest home computer to the largest supercomputer used by the military, are made up of the same basic components (see Figure 1.1).

Input represents the starting data—the raw facts—that are entered into the computer. Every computer requires a means of receiving input; this hardware is called an **input device**. The *processor*, **central processing unit (CPU)**, is the data transformer. Inside the CPU, electronic circuits change the initial data in some way. Often, input data are combined with other data in the CPU to produce information. All computer processors have some **memory,** or **storage.** These are special electronic circuits that store data and the results of processing that will be needed later. Memory functions as an electronic storage cabinet. Information isn't useful if no one knows about it. Therefore, **output** is the necessary result of processing. To be useful, a computer needs a component that can output data. The ways in which we use the information produced by a computer

---

Figure 1.1   Simplified "General" All-Purpose Computer.

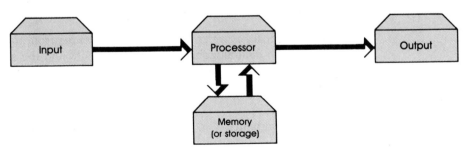

depend on the form of the output. The form of the output depends, in turn, on the **output device** we use. To send a letter to our congressman, we would need a printer. To simply view text, we would need a monitor.

Computers need storage devices to supplement the relatively small amount of memory built into the processor if people are to use them as effective tools. Notice that the storage box in Figure 1.1 is outside the processor. Here, storage represents memory added onto the computer. This added memory makes it possible for the computer to remember and to retrieve large amounts of both data and information. For example, census data can be stored in this additional memory, as well as the instructions that will analyze the data and the results of that analysis.

All computers have all of these components. However, the components are designed differently in different computers, as Figure 1.2 shows.

Instructing the Machine

How is initial data changed into output? A computer will do only what it is told; it must be given instructions. It cannot do anything on its own. In a sense, computers need directions. They need to follow these directions carefully, making all the correct turns and looking for all the appropriate landmarks, in order to arrive at the destination and produce the required output.

More specifically, a program is used to tell the computer how to transform data. A **program** is the step-by-step set of instructions in a language understandable to the computer that directs the computer to perform specific tasks

Figure 1.2   (a) The Apple Macintosh Classic Microcomputer and (b) the Cray Y-MP4E Supercomputer. All computers have similar components, although the design and power can differ markedly.

(a)   (b)

(process facts) and to solve specific problems (create information). Programs used for problem solving or for directing the operations of the machine (coordinating its many parts) are called **software. Hardware,** on the other hand, is the set of physical components that make up the computer. Just as a stereo system is made up of components, including the compact-disk player and speakers, so a computer is made up of components, including the CPU, monitor, keyboard, memory, and perhaps a printer.

Despite all the jargon, we must keep one thing in mind: A computer is a machine. It is a tool designed to assist people in solving problems. *Computers do not think.* They do exactly and only what they are told. They are not psychic; they cannot figure out what you meant or what you implied. They follow only the specific instructions they are given. *They do what you say, not what you mean.*

Computers can do amazing things and accomplish a considerable amount of processing, however. Computers are used in sorting, comparing, listing, updating, ordering, calculating, and much more. By doing such lower-level processing, they free us to do more complex tasks.

So far, we have learned the difference between data and information and have looked at the main parts of every computer. Now we will learn some computer jargon relating to *how* a computer stores information.

THE BINARY MACHINE—BITS AND BYTES

Computers don't really understand the data and instructions we put into them. All they really understand is two states: on or off. We can talk about the *on* state as being positive, or existing in the presence of electric current. We can talk about the *off* state as being negative, or existing in the absence of electric current.

These two electronic states are numerically represented as 1's (on, positive, electrical current present) and 0's (off, negative, no current). These two states can be represented by the base 2, or **binary number system.** In this system the base is 2, not 10 as in our decimal system. Combinations of only two unique digits, 1 and 0, are used to represent all numbers, letters, and special characters.

Most of us learned arithmetic and process mathematical data in the decimal number system, or base 10. It seems reasonable to assume that our decimal system developed from our 10 fingers. The decimal system uses 10 unique symbols, or digits: 0, 1, 2, 3, 4, 5, 6, 7, 8, 9. All the remaining numbers in the decimal system are combinations of these 10 unique symbols.

When we enter numbers into a computer we do so in the decimal system. To be usable by the computer, however, these numbers must be converted into binary form. Referring to the short table that follows, we see how the decimal number 5 is translated into its binary equivalent, 101.

Decimal	Binary
0	000
1	001
2	010
3	011
4	100
*5	101
6	110
7	111

Each 0 or 1 in the binary system is called a **bit** (for **bi**nary dig**it**) when used with computers. The bit forms the simplest unit of data stored in the computer's memory. A single bit, though, does not tell a computer very much. By combining bits into groups, we can represent more complex things. A **byte** is a group of bits (usually eight). Each byte represents one character of data, such as a number, letter, or special symbol (%, $, and so on). Numbers, letters, and special symbols are the forms *we* use to represent information.

A computer **word** is the number of bits that can be processed at one time by the CPU. An 8-bit computer has a word length of one byte, or a single character. The Apple IIGS is an 8-bit computer. The word length of a 16-bit machine is two characters or bytes. IBM's PC-class machines and IBM's PS/1 are 16-bit machines. In general, a 16-bit machine will process twice as much information over a fixed period of time as an 8-bit machine. Other computers use word lengths of 32 and 64 bits and process information significantly faster than 8- or 16-bit machines. Apple's Macintoshs and most IBM PS/2s are 32-bit machines.

Computers are frequently described in terms of the amount of memory that is associated with their processors. Computer memory is measured by the number of bytes it contains. This is usually expressed in terms of K bytes or kilobytes. K is often used to mean 1000 bytes, although technically it is equal to 1024 bytes. For example, an inexpensive IBM class machine may come with 640K, while Apple's Macintosh II-class machines come with a minimum of 2 megabytes of memory (**megabyte** = 1000K bytes or 1 million bytes). This list could go on and on.

Although all computers have great similarities, they are not all the same. Such terms as *digital* and *analog, mini, mainframe,* and *micro* are also part of today's computer vocabulary. These words all describe different kinds of machines. Let us look at these machines and examine their differences.

DIFFERENT GOALS, DIFFERENT MACHINES

There are two basic categories of computers. The two designs reflect two different ways in which we can look at or analyze our world. When we gather data for input to a computer, we can represent mathematical values obtained by simply counting, such as the number of students or change from a dollar; or we can use continuous direct measurement, such as gauging voltage, car speed, or body temperature.

Digital Computers

The computers described throughout this text are **digital computers,** which are by far the most popular and common of all computing devices. They assist in problem solving by organizing data into countable units or digits; that is, combinations of zeros and ones.

Digital computers have large and easily expandable memory capacity. By storing the programs and data in memory they are capable of solving many different kinds of problems. Digital computers are highly flexible machines.

Analog Computers

Analog computers operate with quantities such as voltage, pressure, and rotation. Since the input data of analog computers are directly measured in the real world, they are used to simulate or model problems. In analog computers the program is built directly into the hardware. Since processing a new program requires rewiring the machine, they are less flexible than digital machines.

The difference between analog and digital devices can be seen in the following example. A watch with a circular dial is an analog device. An hour is represented by the dial, and the movement of the hands simulates the passage of time. The time of day must be approximated by reading the position of the hands. With a digital watch, however, the time of day is accurately expressed as a number of digits. The digits themselves can represent many things. When they appear in a clock we interpret them as representing time.

Hybrid Computers

Hybrid computers combine the input/output design of analog computers with the digital computer's ability to store instructions and perform highly accurate mathematical calculations. Examples of hybrid machines include those used in air traffic control and hospital intensive care units (ICUs). In an ICU for example, a patient's heart rate, temperature, blood pressure, and other vital signs are measured using analog devices. These direct measurements are converted into numeric quantities and are used as input to a digital computer, which continually checks them against established standards and issues a warning if dangerous readings occur.

Special-Purpose Computers

Special-purpose computers are designed to solve specific problems. The program instructions are built directly into the computer's hardware. For this

Figure 1.3   The Special-Purpose Computer: Special-purpose computers are designed to
solve a single problem, such as (a) this Boeing navigational computer and (b)
this NASA computer system used in space shuttle flights.

(a)

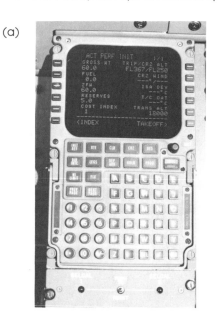

(b)

reason, special-purpose computers are said to be **preprogrammed.** If the special-purpose machine is an analog device, the layout and organization of the computer components comprise the program. If it is a digital device, the instructions are built directly into the processor (see Chapter 3). Such computers, whether analog or digital, can do only what their hardware or built-in instructions tell them to do (see Figure 1.3).

Special-purpose computers are used for blood analysis devices, automobile cruise controls, video arcade games, dishwasher and microwave memory panels,

---

Figure 1.4   General-Purpose Computers: These flexible machines include (a) microcomputers such as the Compaq Deskpro 486/25 and (b) mainframe computers such as the IBM ES/9000.

(a)

(b)

and navigational controls on spacecraft. Video arcade games use digital computers; cruise controls are analog devices.

General-Purpose Computers

General-purpose computers are designed to solve a variety of problems. They are not preprogrammed. These machines are flexible, so the same hardware can receive many kinds of instructions and can be used to solve different problems (see Figure 1.4).

In general, most digital computers are general-purpose machines, and most analog computers are used as special-purpose machines. We must be careful with generalizations, however, because both digital and analog computers are used in other ways as well.

MACHINES AND THEIR SIZE

Today's digital computers vary in cost, size, internal design, computing power, and speed. They perform a vast array of tasks, from monitoring patient health and supporting humans in space to providing entertainment and remembering dishwasher settings (see Figure 1.5).

Miniaturized computers can be as small as your fingernail. Such tiny computers are found in car engines, dishwashers, and microwave ovens. At the other extreme, room-size supercomputers are used to control and simulate space flights, to assist in nuclear research, and to forecast the weather nationwide or even worldwide. As computers of various sizes were developed over the last decade, the following three logical groups became apparent:

MICROCOMPUTERS

relatively small
inexpensive ($500–$15,000)
single user
microprocessor based
processes 1000–6000 instructions/second

MINICOMPUTERS

middle sized
medium priced ($25,000–$500,000)
multiple users (2–40 users at once)
processes up to 20,000 instructions/second

MAINFRAMES

large to very large
very expensive (more than $500,000)
multiple users (more than 40 users at once)
processes millions of instructions/second

Figure 1.5   Computers in Household Equipment: Many appliances now have built-in microprocessors to control their operation and ease troubleshooting for repair.

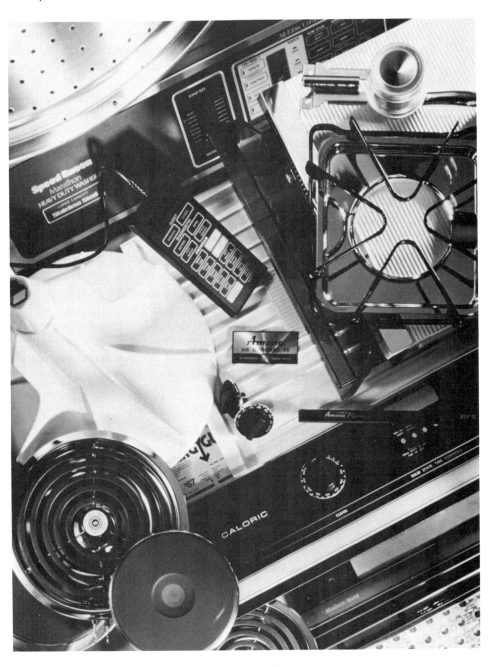

It is quite fortunate (although confusing) that the world of computers is not static. Despite our desire to categorize computers, they cannot be divided into clear-cut groups. At best, terms such as *micro, mini,* and *mainframe* can be used only as general guidelines. Microcomputers are slower, smaller, and less expensive than minicomputers and mainframes. However, where one class of machine ends and another begins is increasingly difficult to distinguish. The rest of this chapter examines various types of computers, from microcomputers to supercomputers, exploring their differences and similarities.

Microcomputers

Microcomputers, or **micros,** are often called computers on a chip. The CPU of these machines is a **microprocessor,** a tiny processor designed to fit on a single chip smaller than a fingernail (see Figure 1.6).

However, micros consist of more than just processors, as Figure 1.7 shows. Like all computers, micros require input devices, so a keyboard is usually added. Since they need a way to communicate their results to us (output), a special monitor and a printer are added.

Figure 1.6   The Microprocessor: A powerful device in a tiny package, all of the electrical connections of this Motorola 68030 microprocessor are etched onto a chip of silicon.

Figure 1.7   A Computer System: The microprocessor chip is part of a complete system with input, storage, and output devices.

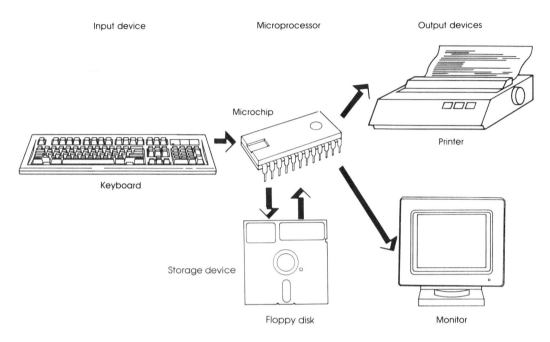

Floppy disk drives are attached to microcomputers as external memory. Hard disks are also available for micros at affordable prices. As microcomputer users have become more sophisticated (using more complex programs and analyzing more data), they have demanded machines with more and more internal memory. Today's micros, such as those in Figure 1.8, provide space to expand the machine's internal memory and add communication devices.

Microcomputers come in 8-bit (Apple IIGS), 16-bit (IBM PC), and 32-bit (Apple Macintosh) varieties, depending upon the design of the microprocessor chip that forms the machine's core. Two manufacturers developed most of the microprocessors currently on the market: Motorola, whose chips find their way into Apple's vast Macintosh line, and Intel, whose current chips include the popular 80286, 80386, and 80486 (often called simply 286, 386, 486). These chips make their way into most other machines.

Intel's 286-chip uses a 16-bit design and is common in many low-cost machines. Its processing speed is quite sufficient for running most standard tasks. The most complex tasks and operating environments require chips that use a 32-bit design that processes information much faster. Examples include Motorola's 68030 chips used in Apple's fastest Macintoshs, and Intel's 486-chip used by microcomputer manufacturers such as IBM, Compaq, and Toshiba.

Figure 1.8   Powerful Microcomputers: (a) The IBM Personal System/2 and (b) the Apple Macintosh IIci are powerful and flexible computers whose speed and power rival yesterday's room-sized machines.

(a)   (b)

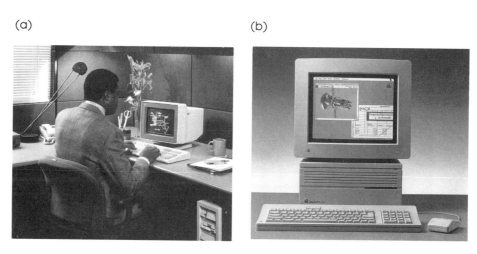

The amount of memory and the complexity of add-ons cause micros to vary widely in capabilities and price. Some very simple micros cost as little as $500, whereas sophisticated and complicated setups can cost as much as $15,000.

Since the core of the microcomputer is the size of your fingernail, manufacturers can design micros to fit the needs and wants of their users. Within the major category of micro, several subgroups can be identified.

Personal Computers   The term *personal computer,* or *PC,* was coined by IBM to describe its microcomputer. As with other words that originated as brand names (such as Kleenex for tissues and Xerox for photocopier), **personal computer,** or **PC,** has come to refer to a flexible and memory-rich microcomputer. Personal computers are relatively inexpensive, single-user machines most often found in business settings. A single-user computer is a machine used by only one person at a time. Increasingly, they are used in the home, often as extensions of the modern office. They can solve very sophisticated problems. Microcomputers process between 1000 and 6000 instructions per second, depending upon processor design and layout. With the regular release of newer processors, these speeds will continue to increase. Personal computers usually include additional internal memory, often as high as 10 megabytes, one or more floppy disk drives, and a large hard disk (80–100 megabytes). Personal computers frequently have color monitors and a laser printer attached.

Home computers are micros that are used predominantly in the home for nonbusiness tasks. Some machines such as IBM's PS/1 were designed specifically for home use, but all types of machines, ranging from the Apple IIGS to complex 486-based machines, are used at home.

Software dictates the machine's use in the home. Entertainment packages ranging from video-arcade-style games to interactive-fiction games such as Space Quest to thought-provoking simulations like Sim World are very popular.

Software is available to assist in maintaining family finances, printing greeting cards and posters, and studying math and spelling. Word processing programs and printers have replaced typewriters, and data base programs and computer files help organize family records. Income tax, check balancing, and investment programs are increasingly popular. Learning games that reinforce math and reading skills have also found widespread acceptance (see Figure 1.9).

Portable Computers   **Portable computers** are complete microcomputers that are designed to be carried easily from place to place. Essentially, portable com-

---

Figure 1.9   Home Computing: Games, personal financial planning, as well as educational use continue to fuel sales of microcomputers such as this Apple IIGS.

On Line

COMPUTING AT HOME

Are we bringing our computers home? The Census Bureau recently surveyed American homes and found that, yes, the computer was coming home.

The survey indicated that in the five years from 1984 to 1989 the percentage of homes with computers grew 9 percent. The credit for such growth is given to the general lowering of computer hardware prices during the period and to improvements in easy-to-use applications packages including word processing and desktop publishing, data base systems, and electronic mail.

Census Bureau researchers found that two types of people were most responsible for the increased purchases in computers for the home: individuals who had become comfortable with computers in the workplace and saw applications for them at home, and parents who

wished to give their children an educational and technological edge into the future.

The survey found that in 1989, almost 50 percent of young Americans, 17 years old or less, reported using computers. This represented an increase of almost 20 percent since 1984. Of the population 18 and over, 28 percent reported using computers. This reflects a 10 percent increase in five years. Similar increases were reported among working Americans. In 1989, 37 percent of workers used a computer on the job as compared to 25 percent who used them in 1984.

As computers become easier to use, similar increases can be expected in both home and work use in the years to come.

Source: "Computers Hitting Home," *New York Newsday*, March 31, 1991, p. 62.

puters come in two varieties:

- **Hand-held Portables** are battery-powered computers that are tiny and light. They look much like hand calculators, with miniature keys not designed for typing, and have tiny screens (see Figure 1.10). They have limited memory, although BASIC is usually built in. Cassette tapes are used to store data. Despite their small size, devices such as printers and modems are available.

- **Notebook Portables** are small enough to fit comfortably into a briefcase. They have a typewriter-sized keyboard and a monitor with an average dimension of $8\frac{1}{2}$ inches by 11 inches—the size of a standard notebook (see Figure 1.11). Their height is often less than 2 inches, and they weigh less than 7 pounds. Internal memory capacity is comparable to desktop models, and peripheral devices include floppy and hard disk drives, as well as modems and printers.

Portable computers are "go anywhere" machines, giving people the flexibility of taking their computers wherever they go. Now computing can be done in

Figure 1.10   Hand-Held Portable Computer by Radio Shack.

Figure 1.11   Notebook Portable by Toshiba.

the office, on the road, or at home. Portables allow for on-site data collection and analysis. Portability can be a real advantage in our fast-paced world.

Minicomputers

In the late 1960s, Digital Equipment Corp. (DEC) marketed a new line of computers that differed significantly from earlier machines. They were called **minicomputers** or just **minis** because they were smaller, less sophisticated, and much less expensive than existing standards (mainframes).

Today's minis range in price from $25,000 to $500,000 and are usually 32-bit machines. Early models were 16-bit machines. They serve a portion of the computer market, mostly businesses that do not require the speed or immense storage capacity of a mainframe but require more computer power than the small,

Figure 1.12   Minicomputers and Superminicomputers: Ideal for medium-sized firms and scientific and engineering applications, minis and superminis such as these from Digital Equipment Corp. offer flexibility rivaling more expensive mainframe computers.

single-user micro or group of micros can provide. Minicomputers are **multiuser** machines—computers that serve two or more users. Minis serve between 2 and 40 people at one time, each with his or her own monitor and keyboard. Mini-computers can process as many as 20,000 instructions per second and their speed is steadily increasing as newer, faster processors are developed. They can handle large, complex programs and can support many sophisticated computer languages. Significant amounts of external memory can be attached.

With advances in computer technology and a rapid decline in the price of hardware, the minicomputer industry is increasingly being squeezed by its mainframe and micro competitors. As microcomputer companies add features and memory to their machines, minicomputer companies are forced to do the same. The result is minicomputers that look more and more like mainframes. A number of computer manufacturers, such as Digital Equipment Corp. (DEC), Prime, and Hewlett-Packard, produce computers that are classed as **supermini,** (extrapowerful minicomputers) and are hardly distinguishable in their abilities from other manufacturers' mainframes (see Figure 1.12).

Workstations

When applied to computers, the term *workstation* has more than one meaning, two of which we discuss here. First, the most popular application of the word —the way it is commonly used in businesses and offices—defines a **workstation** as the physical layout of furniture and computer equipment designed to make using computers both comfortable and efficient.

Such a workstation includes a personal or single-user computer placed at an appropriate height for comfortable use, a printer, and desk space (often at a different height) for preparing documents. In addition, the computer that makes up the workstation is generally part of a group of interconnected yet independent computers called a *local area network (LAN),* which is discussed further in Chapter 15. The connected equipment is directly wired together (hard-wired) within a restricted location, usually a building or group of buildings located close to one another (see Figure 1.13).

In this environment, the personal or single-user computer is usually connected to a larger machine. Such an arrangement allows individuals to take advantage of a variety of machines. The specialized, user-friendly software available for personal computers is accessible, as is the superior storage and calculating capacity of larger computers. Of equal importance, individuals are not isolated. They are interconnected with one another and can communicate using **electronic mail,** or **E-mail,** in which computer users exchange electronic messages that are temporarily stored on the machine. Electronic mail will be discussed in greater detail in Chapter 15. The users also have access to data and information stored on the larger machines. From their own desks, individual users can tap into large data bases, transfer material to other users, and work with large programs or data too extensive for small machines.

Figure 1.13   Networked Computer Workstations: Operator comfort and the ability to communicate with other users or a larger computer have made this concept popular.

Increasingly, a second type of computer workstation is gaining popularity. This workstation is a highly sophisticated desktop <u>mini</u>computer including a large monitor for graphics, a pointing device (such as a mouse), and software that enables its user to run several programs at the same time (see Figure 1.14). Such systems are used in environments where processing power or graphics

Figure 1.14 The Workstation: More powerful than a microcomputer but requiring little more space, the SPARC station by Sun Microsystems is very popular.

capacity is a critical consideration, such as architecture, engineering, computer graphics, and artificial intelligence research.

The large screen can be divided into a number of often overlapping sections, or **windows,** each of which displays a different computer process. As with the business workstation described previously, this system is usually networked to other computers so that data, information, and processors can be shared. Some systems are so sophisticated that different windows can actually display operations occurring on different machines.

These systems range in price from $1,000 to $25,000, depending upon the CPU's processing speed, the amount of memory available, and whether a color monitor is required. The price of such systems is decreasing, and they are increasingly replacing microcomputers as desktop machines.

Equally important, the distinction between such workstations and minicomputers becomes more blurred by the day. Professionals typically differentiate a minicomputer from a workstation by its intended use since the CPUs may be the same. The device is a workstation if it sits on someone's desk, uses windows, has a somewhat large screen capable of doing detailed graphics, and is used for tasks such as document preparation and computer graphics. The device is a minicomputer if it is used by multiple users, has a very large amount of external memory, and usually sits in a special machine room.

Mainframes

In general, **mainframes** are large, very fast 32- to 64-bit multiuser machines (see Figure 1.15). They are typically used in environments with large, centralized processing needs, such as major business organizations, and for research and development. They can service more than 40 users at the same time. For example, using automated teller machines, bank customers rely on mainframes to make bank transactions simultaneously in dozens of locations.

Mainframes process at speeds greater than 10 million instructions per second, and cost more than $500,000. They are designed to support both complex input/output systems and massive amounts of internal and external storage. The availability of specialized hardware and software makes mainframes ideal for

Figure 1.15   The Mainframe Computer: Ideal for the needs of a large firm or government agency, mainframe computers such as this IBM AS/400 are capable of processing enormous amounts of data.

the solution of complex problems that involve complicated sequences of mathematical manipulations, or **number crunching.** Common applications include data processing by large department store chains, income tax processing by the Internal Revenue Service, information storage and retrieval by colleges and universities, and manufacturing control and forecasting.

Increasingly, mainframes such as ENCORE's Multimax are parallel machines. That is, these machines contain multiple CPUs and associated memory that can process instructions simultaneously. In such environments, different parts of large complex programs can be processed at the same time by different CPUs. These same machines can also process multiple programs at once.

Supercomputers

As the complexity of our problems grew, so computers have grown to assist in solving them. Today, computers are being developed that dwarf the standard mainframes in terms of speed. These ultrafast computers, or **supercomputers,** are designed to process hundreds of millions of instructions per second and store and retrieve millions of data items (see Figure 1.16). Supercomputers service hundreds of users and cost millions of dollars to operate.

Figure 1.16   The Supercomputer: The complex calculations and numerous variables involved in weather forecasting, aircraft design, and space exploration require ultrafast machines such as this Cray Y-MP8E supercomputer.

Traditional supercomputers, built by companies such as Cray Research in the United States and NEC of Japan, arrange the billions of calculations to be processed as a list. Each calculation is performed at incredible speed, in order, by one of at most a handful of very complex and expensive processors. A new breed of supercomputers distributes a problem's calculations to hundreds or thousands of independent, inexpensive processors. Supercomputers are discussed more fully in Chapter 3.

To date, supercomputers have been purchased principally by governments, large research universities, corporate think tanks, and industries to solve complex problems involving massive mathematical calculations. The demand for these powerful machines has risen dramatically in the last few years. Researchers nationwide increasingly require access to supercomputers for their work. Unfortunately, these machines are not only incredibly expensive to purchase, but also very expensive and difficult to manage and operate. In an effort to make such resources available to all the nation's researchers, the National Science Foundation (NSF) has built a network of interconnected supercomputers called NSFnet, which will be discussed further in Chapter 15. The computers are located in centers across the country. By linking universities, government agencies, and research corporations in such a network, supercomputer facilities can be available to all who need them, and data and ideas can be shared as well.

We have seen that learning about computers requires an understanding of computer jargon. In addition, computers, like people, come in different shapes and sizes. The capacity of a computer to store and process information is reflected in its use. Computers are used just about everywhere, from intensive care units to spacecraft, from the entertainment industry to the weather service. Despite outward differences, they all require a processor, memory, and input/output devices to communicate with people. Furthermore, regardless of how complex the problem they are solving, they still follow the instructions given by people. If computers seem to have the capacity to change the world, it is so because they are the unique handiwork of humans.

SUMMARY

Computers process data. **Data** are raw facts collected from any number of sources. When data have been processed so that meaningful conclusions can be drawn, the result is **information.**

All computers have four basic components: an input device, a processor, memory, and an output device. **Input** represents the starting data, the raw facts that are entered into the computer. An **input device** is used to enter the data into the computer. The processor, or **central processing unit** (CPU), is the electronic circuitry that changes the initial data in some way to produce information. **Memory** is the special electronic circuitry that stores data, instructions, and the results of processing. **Output** is the result of processing. An **output device,** such as a printer, is needed to present this output to people.

A **program** is the step-by-step set of instructions, written in a computer language, that directs the computer to perform specific tasks and solve specific problems. Programs are used for problem solving or directing the operations of the machine and are called **software.** The physical components that combine to make up the computer are **hardware.**

All data and instructions used by a computer must be converted to the electronic states of on and off. These two states can be represented by the 1's and 0's of the base 2, or **binary number system.** Combinations of these two digits represent all numbers, letters, and special characters. Each 1 or 0 is called a **bit** and forms the simplest unit of data stored in the computer's memory. A **byte** is a group of bits representing a character of data. A **word** is the number of bits that can be processed at once. Computers are frequently described in terms of the amount of memory that is associated with their processors. Computer memory is represented in terms of K (approximately 1000) bytes. A **megabyte** of memory (MB) is one million bytes.

Computers fall into two basic categories. **Digital computers** use mathematical values obtained by counting for input. **Analog computers** use continuous direct measurement of dimensions such as voltage and temperature as input. **Hybrid computers** combine the input/output design of analog computers with the ability to store instructions and perform highly accurate calculations found in digital machines. **Special-purpose computers** are designed to solve specific problems, while **general-purpose machines** are used to solve a variety of problems.

Digital computers come in a wide variety of sizes, costs, and computing capacity. **Microcomputers** are single-user machines based on the microprocessor. Microcomputers have processors that come in 8-, 16-, and 32-bit varieties. They range in price from $500 to $15,000. Microcomputers that are used predominantly in the home for nonbusiness tasks are often called **home computers;** those frequently found in businesses and offices are called **personal computers. Portable computers** are complete microcomputers that can be carried easily from place to place.

Minicomputers are **multiuser** systems designed to serve those organizations that do not require the speed or immense storage capacity of a mainframe, but cannot be served by the small, single-user micro. Such computers are usually 32-bit machines and range in price from $25,000 to $500,000.

When used in most business environments, the term *workstation* refers to the physical layout of furniture and computer equipment designed to make using computers comfortable and efficient. However, **workstation** also can refer to a highly sophisticated desktop minicomputer. Such a machine includes a large graphic monitor, pointing device, and software that enables it to run several programs at once and display each simultaneously in different windows on the monitor. These workstations range in price from $1,000 to $25,000.

Mainframes are large, very fast, 32- to 64-bit multiuser computers costing more than $500,000. They are designed to support complex input/output systems and process millions of instructions per second. Increasingly, many are parallel machines designed to process multiple instructions at once. The largest of these machines, called **supercomputers,** have the capacity to process hundreds of millions of instructions per second and store and retrieve millions of data items.

Key Words

As an extra review of the chapter, try defining the following terms. If you have trouble with any of them, refer to the page number listed.

analog computer *(8)*	microcomputer (micro) *(13)*
binary number system *(6)*	microprocessor *(13)*
bit *(7)*	minicomputer (mini) *(19)*
byte *(7)*	multiuser *(20)*
central processing unit (CPU) *(4)*	notebook portable *(17)*
data *(3)*	number crunching *(24)*
digital computer *(8)*	output *(4)*
electronic mail (E-mail) *(20)*	output device *(5)*
general-purpose computer *(11)*	personal computer (PC) *(15)*
hand-held portable *(17)*	portable computer *(16)*
hardware *(6)*	preprogrammed *(10)*
home computer *(15)*	program *(5)*
hybrid computer *(8)*	software *(6)*
information *(3)*	special-purpose computer *(8)*
input *(4)*	supercomputer *(24)*
input device *(4)*	supermini *(20)*
mainframe *(23)*	window *(22)*
megabyte *(7)*	word *(7)*
memory (storage) *(4)*	workstation *(20,21)*

Test Your Knowledge

1. Explain the difference between data and information.

2. List the four components that make up all computers. Explain the function of each component.

3. What is a program?

4. What is the difference between hardware and software?

5. Why must all data and instructions be converted to binary numbers before they can be understood by the computer?

6. How do bits, bytes, and words differ?

7. What is a megabyte?

8. Describe the differences between the input used in analog and digital computers.

9. What is a hybrid computer?

10. Define *preprogrammed* and explain how such programming is applied to a special-purpose computer.

11. Describe a microcomputer.

12. How does a home computer differ from a personal computer?

13. Identify the two kinds of portable computers. How are they different?

14. Describe a minicomputer.

15. Workstation can mean two different things. Describe the office workstation. Describe the desktop workstation.

16. Describe a mainframe.

17. How do mainframes and supercomputers differ?

18. Discuss number crunching.

19. What is NSFnet?

20. Describe the two different designs of supercomputers.

Expand Your Knowledge

1. Go to your campus computing center and find out what kinds of computers (micros, mainframes, etc.) are available for student use on your campus. Make a list of these machines and their locations. How does a student get access to these machines? By whom are they manufactured?

2. Find out if your college has a discount purchase arrangement with microcomputer manufacturers. If so, what machines are available at a discount? How do students take advantage of these discounts? How much is the discount? If students have problems with machines purchased under this discount program, whom do they contact?

3. Using the pattern of binary and decimal digits displayed in this chapter, write out the binary equivalent of the decimal numbers 9 through 15. Each binary number will have four digits. The decimal number 1 = 0001, 7 = 0111, and 8 = 1000.

4. When designing an office workstation, *ergonomics* is the key. What does ergonomics mean? Talk with friends and family members who work in an office. What factors do they consider important in a workstation? Look into a few of the offices on campus that have computers. Have the factors you identified been considered? If not, find out why.

5. A number of microcomputer manufacturers including IBM, Apple, and Sun Microsystems have developed machines they consider workstations. Go to a computer store and find out how such systems differ from standard micros. Who is expected to purchase these machines? What kind of specialized software is available on these systems?

2

The History of Computers

CHAPTER OUTLINE

THE DEVELOPMENT OF COMPUTING MACHINES

No invention springs forth from the human mind fully formed. Technological advances are the result of an evolving process. Existing products are continually being improved. The computer is an example of one such product. Since our prehistoric ancestors first stood upright, people have needed counting tools. The computer is an incredibly fast counting device with a long history.

Since the computer is a machine, it would be easy to focus on the technological changes alone that eventually produced it. However, machines are the physical results of the ideas, needs, and fascinations of people. This chapter looks at the people and ideas, as well as the machines, that in combination led to the development of the modern computer.

After studying this chapter, you will be able to:

- Trace the development of early calculating devices.
- Recognize the individuals who invented computing devices.
- Understand the theoretical contributions of Babbage and von Neumann.
- Explain the evolution of computers and the high-tech industry.
- Identify and analyze the characteristics of the computer generations.
- Trace the development of microcomputers.

THE PRE-COMPUTER AGE

Our earliest ancestors used their fingers and toes as counting aids. It was not long before these built-in human tools gave way to more expandable devices. Groups of tiny stones or knots tied in strings became early counting devices. Counting evolved into mathematics. The ancient Egyptians and Aztecs performed complex calculations to design and build their pyramids. The Phoenicians employed mathematics to keep track of their vast commercial activities and to navigate the seas.

The Abacus

As the world became more complex, the use of mathematics increased. Calculations needed to be performed accurately and quickly. The earliest calculating device, the **abacus**, has seen approximately 7000 years of continuous use. Although its invention is credited to the Chinese (the ancient Orient) around 5000 B.C., different forms of this device were also used in ancient Babylon, Rome, and Japan.

Calculations on the abacus are performed by manipulating strings of beads. With the abacus, still commonly used in China, adept users can perform calculations with remarkable speed. The abacus is a fast, inexpensive, highly portable nonelectronic calculator (see Figure 2.1).

Oughtred's Slide Rule

Many centuries passed, and in 1621 an English cleric and mathematician named William Oughtred invented the **slide rule.** A slide rule consists of two movable rulers fixed so that one will slide against the other (see Figure 2.2). Both rules are marked so that the distances of the marking from the ends are mathematically proportional. Oughtred's device was successful because it was accurate, easy to use, and inexpensive to make. It continued to be widely used until the 1970s when, unlike the abacus, it was replaced almost overnight by the hand calculator.

Pascal's Calculator

In 1642, a Frenchman named Blaise Pascal, then 19 years old, invented what is often considered the first adding machine (see Figure 2.3). Pascal would later

Figure 2.1   The Abacus: A fast, inexpensive, and ancient calculating device.

Figure 2.2   The Slide Rule: Sales of this popular calculating device ended almost overnight with the advent of inexpensive hand-held electronic calculators.

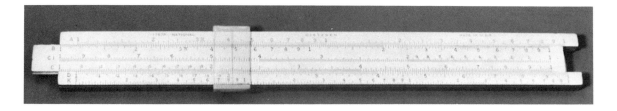

On Line

THE SLIDE RULE'S DOWNWARD SLIDE

Until the 1970s, it was easy to spot engineering students on college campuses. The engineers were the ones with a 12-to-18 inch scabbard hanging from their belts. At a moment's notice, they would pull their slide rule from its case with a swoosh and begin solving mathematical problems.

Before 1972, the slide rule was a mainstay in science and engineering classrooms. Carefully crafted models made of mahogany were available for around $100. Then the death knell sounded. In 1972, Hewlett-Packard released the HP35 hand-held calculator. Even at the asking price of $395, the HP35 was so easy to use that demand outpaced availability. Within a month, Texas Instruments released the SR-10, which sold for less than $150 and could perform most of the slide rule's mathematical functions.

By 1976 most slide rule companies had ended production. Only one company continued to produce a small number of slide rules annually, priced between $10 and $25 each. A year later the hand-held calculator had completely replaced the slide rule. Technology had killed the slide rule almost overnight.

Some scientists and engineers continue to use their slide rules because it's second nature for them. They can't imagine using anything else. Some feel that students who use calculators are taking the easy way out and performing calculations without understanding the underlying mathematical principles. Some of these concerns are valid. Calculators are so easy to use that they can provide a false sense of security. Students need to scrutinize their work. An answer displayed by a calculator is not guaranteed to be correct.

Keep in mind that both the slide rule and the calculator are operated by people. They are only as accurate as the people using them.

Source: David Gates and Frank Bruns. "Sliding Towards Oblivion," *Newsweek,* July 23, 1984, p. 11A.

become a noted mathematician, and a computer language would bear his name. One historical legend tells us that Pascal invented the device to assist his father, a tax collector, with the time-consuming task of adding and subtracting long columns of numbers. The device consisted of a series of gears or wheels moved with a pointed object. The basic functions of modern adding machines were found in Pascal's model. His invention, known as the Pascaline, had the following features:

- The *carry* (in addition) and the *borrow* (in subtraction) were performed automatically.

- Subtraction was performed by reversing the gears.

- Multiplication and division were performed as a series of repeated additions or subtractions.

Figure 2.3   Blaise Pascal and his calculator, the Pascaline.

Unfortunately, building Pascal's machines required a higher level of technical expertise than was generally available in his day. The calculators broke easily
because of poorly cut gears. As a result, only eight of the approximately 50 calculators Pascal had built have survived.

Leibniz's Multiplier

In 1673, the German Baron Gottfried Wilhelm von Leibniz expanded upon Pascal's calculator and produced a machine that could directly multiply and divide.
Leibniz's multiplier contained features found in modern calculators. Notably, all
the digits of a number could be entered at once. As with Pascal's device, the
limits of technical engineering continued to influence computer history. Leibniz's invention also broke easily because it was fashioned from poorly tooled
parts (see Figure 2.4).

PROGRAMMING AND EXPANDING THE MACHINE

The signposts of computer history mark ideas as well as physical inventions.
The Industrial Revolution of the 1800s saw an incredible chain of evolving ideas
and devices. Inventors often get their ideas from unlikely places, and computer

Figure 2.4   Gottfried Wilhelm von Leibniz and his calculator.

inventors were no exception. Indeed, the weaving loom technology spawned ideas critical to the development of modern computers.

Jacquard's Loom

In 1804, a Frenchman named Joseph Jacquard invented an attachment to the mechanical loom for weaving cloth. Jacquard recognized that the design found in woven cloth followed a fixed, repetitive pattern (a program). By punching holes at specific intervals in cards attached to the loom, he could control the threads reproducing the desired pattern. Jacquard's improved loom automated the weaving industry and revolutionized cloth production (see Figure 2.5).

Charles Babbage

If punched cards could be used to store information and instructions for one device, it was only a matter of time before they were put to similar use in other devices.

Charles Babbage, a wealthy, eccentric British mathematician and inventor, is often considered the father of modern computers. Disturbed by the inaccuracies he found in the hand-calculated mathematical tables that scientists of his day used, he designed a machine to calculate these tables accurately and automatically.

Figure 2.5   Joseph Jacquard and his loom.

In 1822, he presented a paper to the Royal Astronomical Society proposing to build such a machine. The Difference Engine, as this device was called, was named after the method Babbage used to perform the calculations (Figure 2.6a).

The British government was convinced that the accurate calculations produced by this machine would be a great help in navigation and ballistics. Armed with government financial aid that was one of the first research grants, Babbage hired the finest tool makers to construct his machine.

Figure 2.6   (a) Babbage's Difference Engine: a special-purpose calculating machine and (b) Babbage's Analytical Engine: a more sophisticated, general-purpose computing device.

(a)

(b)

Although a scale model was built, difficulties between Babbage and the craftsmen over precision and design hindered the completion of the Difference Engine. As with Pascal and Leibniz before him, Babbage found the engineering techniques of the day inadequate. To complicate matters further, Babbage lost interest in the project when he became intrigued with more complex ideas. He was not discouraged by his failure to complete the Difference Engine. The British government, however, held a different view and refused to fund his next project.

In 1833, Babbage designed a steam-powered device he called the Analytical Engine (Figure 2.6b). Although the Difference Engine was a special-purpose machine that could perform specific calculations, his Analytical Engine was a far more sophisticated, general-purpose computing device. It included five of the key components that form the basis of modern computers:

1. *An input device* using punched cards that contained instructions and data.

2. *A processor* or calculator, called a *mill*, where all calculations were performed.

3. *A memory unit,* called a *store*, where data and intermediate calculations could be stored.

4. *A control unit* that controlled the sequence in which operations were performed.

5. *An output device.*

Babbage's input device incorporated the idea of punched cards invented by Jacquard for his loom. Babbage had the active support of Lady Ada Augusta, the Countess of Lovelace and daughter of poet Lord Byron (see Figure 2.7).

Ada Lovelace was not only a gifted mathematician who saw the machine's potential, but also Babbage's friend, providing the emotional support he needed to continue his work. She contributed by developing the problem-solving instructions the engine would follow when doing calculations. Since she developed sample programs for the Analytical Engine, she is often referred to as history's first programmer. The programming language Ada is named after her. Ada Lovelace published notes discussing her work on the Analytical Engine. In them she remarked, "We may say most aptly that the Analytical Engine weaves algebraic patterns just as the Jacquard-loom weaves flowers and leaves."

While Babbage never lived to see the Analytical Engine built, it was a prototype for current computers. Using modern engineering techniques and Babbage's plans, his son built a successful electrical version of the Analytical Engine.

The Industrial Revolution radically altered the way people lived and worked. People moved from farms and villages to the cities. Mechanization and industrialization changed the farms and created factories. The steam engine made long-distance transportation possible. Populations grew, and businesses and governments found that they needed to process information more rapidly. Hand calculations simply could not keep pace. Information processing needed to be mechanized.

Figure 2.7   Lady Ada Augusta, the Countess of Lovelace, the first programmer and Babbage's co-worker.

Hollerith's Census Machine

One example of a huge information processing project is conducting a census. The U.S. Constitution requires that a census be taken every 10 years. The 1880 census, complicated by a rapid surge in the population owing to a flood of immigration, took almost eight years to complete. The Census Bureau recognized that dramatic changes were needed if the 1890 census was to be completed before 1900. Tabulators could not perform their calculations by hand. To stimulate the invention of a machine to tabulate census data, the Census Bureau ran a contest. The winner would be awarded the contract to tabulate the 1890 census. The contest's winner was Dr. Herman Hollerith, a Census Bureau employee, who developed a machine that automated the tabulating process. Hollerith's 1887 Census Machine combined electricity with Jacquard's method of storing information on punched cards (see Figure 2.8). Holes representing census infor-

Figure 2.8   (a) Hollerith's Tabulating Machine combined Jacquard's method of storing information on (b) punched cards with electricity.

(a)

(b)

mation were punched in stiff paper cards, and rods were passed through the holes. This completed electric circuits, causing clocklike devices (electromagnetic counters) to tabulate the information on the card.

The punched cards used by Hollerith measured $3\frac{1}{4}$ by $6\frac{5}{8}$ inches. This odd size exactly matches that of the 1890 U.S. one dollar bill. Some historians believe that Hollerith chose this size because people were familiar with it. Current computer cards are approximately the size of Hollerith's original. Using Hollerith's machine, the data from the 1890 census were completely tabulated in less than three years.

Recognizing the immense commercial potential of his machine, Hollerith left the Census Bureau to found the Tabulating Machine Company. The company tabulated the 1900 census as well, but its largest client was the fast-expanding railroad industry. Hollerith's machine kept track of the passengers and goods moved by the railroad. In 1911, the Tabulating Machine Company merged with a number of other companies to become the Computing, Tabulating, and Recording Company (CTR). In 1924, five years before Hollerith's death, CTR changed its name to International Business Machines, or IBM. At the time the company was under the leadership of Thomas Watson.

In preparation for the 1910 census, John Powers, an engineer and inventor employed by the Census Bureau, developed an automatic card-punching ma-

---

Figure 2.9   The Burroughs Adding and Listing Machine and William Seward Burroughs.

chine along with a variation of Hollerith's tabulating machine. Powers' machines further reduced the time required to tabulate census data. Like Hollerith before him, Powers recognized the value of his equipment and left the Census Bureau to start his own company. This company was awarded the contract to tabulate the 1910 census. Powers' company was later purchased by Remington Rand Corporation, which eventually became UNISYS. As one might expect, Hollerith and Powers were not alone in recognizing the demand for calculating devices.

Burroughs' Adding and Listing Machine

In the latter half of the 1800s, the U.S. Patent Office did a booming business in desktop calculating devices. William Burroughs patented the most famous of these in 1888. Burroughs invented the first adding and listing machine. His machine differed from others of his day by the addition of a device to list or print out the numbers entered into the machine and the calculated results. The calculator had a full numeric keyboard and was operated by a hand crank (see Figure 2.9). Burroughs founded the corporation that bears his name.

THE COMPUTER AGE

The increasing complexity of the devices and systems just discussed improved the efficiency of processing information in the sciences and business. The next major wave of development in computing devices was spurred and funded by the World War II efforts of Britain, Germany, and the United States. However, research was headed toward the development of such machines even without the war.

During the late 1930s, scientists and engineers in all three countries began building digital computers. Computer technology was heavily influenced by the communications industry. As scientists tinkered with components while building their machines, they debated the comparative values of different types of hardware. The debate centered on the machines' internal components. Should the reliable electromagnetic relays found in telephone systems be used, or the newer electronic relays called vacuum tubes? **Vacuum tubes** operated hundreds of times faster than electromagnetic telephone relays, but they were not as reliable. Vacuum tubes were also more expensive and required huge amounts of electricity to operate.

Atanasoff's ABC

In the late 1930s, John V. Atanasoff and some of his graduate students at Iowa State University began working on a computing machine. Atanasoff designed a memory drum and unit to perform arithmetic. In 1942, with the help of a student named Clifford Berry, a prototype of this special-purpose machine was built. It was called ABC (Atanasoff-Berry Computer). The ABC used vacuum tubes for internal components and punched cards for input. Although a full-scale version of the computer was never assembled, the discoveries made by Atanasoff were incorporated into later machines (see Figure 2.10).

As the war intensified, scientific interaction decreased because of wartime security measures. As a result scientific teams made similar discoveries independently.

Germany's Wartime Computer

As Atanasoff was developing the ABC, a German named Konrad Zuse started building computer components in his parents' kitchen. Since the cost of electronic relays (vacuum tubes) was prohibitive, Zuse designed his machine around electromagnetic relays used in telephone systems.

In the early 1940s, Zuse sought support from Hitler's government based on the promise his device held for the war effort. Zuse's request was initially refused because the German government believed that the war was essentially over. In late 1943, however, the German government reconsidered and began to

---

Figure 2.10   John V. Atanasoff and the Atanasoff-Berry Computer.

support Zuse's project. As German scientists worked on the development of missiles, Zuse's project was seen as leading to a quick, reliable, accurate means of calculating the paths of these missiles. While prototypes were built, most of the plans and hardware were destroyed in the Allied bombings. Some consider the 1941 prototype the first computer.

England's Wartime Computer

In the early 1940s, a weak, isolated England stood against the powerful German war machine. What the British lacked in military power, however, they made up for in sheer willpower and military research. For example, radar was invented to provide an early-warning system for the Royal Air Force. To assist the British military in analyzing information gathered about the German war effort, COLOSSUS was developed with the help of mathematician Alan Turing (see Figure 2.11). In December 1943, under total secrecy, COLOSSUS became the first practical, single-purpose electronic computer.

Figure 2.11   COLOSSUS, an early vacuum tube computer built by the British, deciphered German codes during World War II.

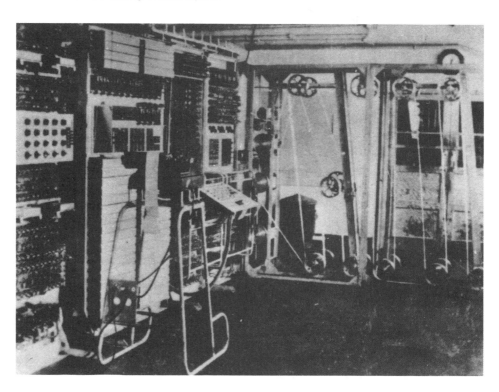

COLOSSUS was a room-sized machine, designed exclusively to break German codes. While much of the research into COLOSSUS is still clouded in the secrecy of Britain's Official Secrets Act, it is known that more than 1800 vacuum tubes were used, and that paper tape acted as input. Ten machines were built and were invaluable to the Allied war effort. Although historians agree that COLOSSUS was one of the first digital machines, it was designed to solve a specific problem. It could not solve other problems without major alterations to its physical design.

America's Wartime Computer Research

Unlike England, the United States did not have the German army sitting on its front steps. Consequently, America's wartime computer effort moved at a slower pace and was more diverse.

Harvard Mark I   Prior to the war, Harvard professor Howard H. Aiken developed the plans for a general-purpose computer (see Figure 2.12). Aiken realized that such a machine would require very strong financial backing. The story is told that Aiken approached Thomas J. Watson, the ruler of IBM, who impulsively decided to back Aiken's research and invest $1 million. When the United States' war effort began, the Aiken-IBM computer became a secret U.S. Navy project.

Figure 2.12   The Harvard Mark I computer.

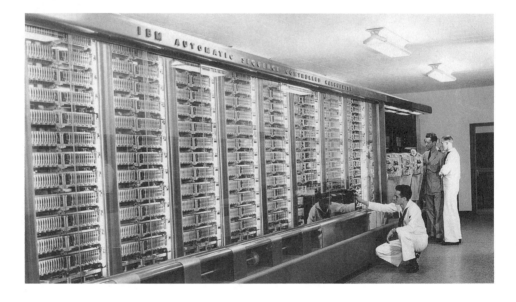

In late 1943, the Harvard Mark I developed by Aiken was born. Although Aiken did not know of Babbage's work, the Mark I contained many of the features that Babbage had included in his Analytical Engine. Aiken's machine used electromagnetic telephone relays, choosing reliability over speed. The Harvard Mark I received instructions via punched paper tape and could perform addition or subtraction in 0.3 second. The Harvard Mark I did not have a memory, however. It was extremely noisy and slow compared to other machines of the period such as COLOSSUS, and was not particularly reliable despite its use of telephone relays. These relays made it so noisy that people remarked that hearing it operate was "like listening to a roomful of old ladies knitting away with steel needles." After the war, IBM mounted a publicity campaign with the Harvard Mark I, which helped make IBM a powerful name in the growing computer industry.

ENIAC   During the war, John W. Mauchly and J. Presper Eckert, Jr., at the University of Pennsylvania's Moore School of Electrical Engineering, in association with the U.S. government's Aberdeen Proving Ground, began development

---

Figure 2.13   J. Presper Eckert, Jr. (left) and John W. Mauchley (center) with their ENIAC computer.

of a general-purpose electronic computer. In 1946, ENIAC (Electronic Numerical Integrator and Calculator) was unveiled (see Figure 2.13).

While based in part on the earlier ABC machine, ENIAC was larger in scale and complexity than anything Atanasoff imagined. More than 18,000 vacuum tubes were used as internal components in this room-sized computer. ENIAC had independent circuits for storing numbers and program instructions. Several mathematical operations could be performed at once. By modern standards, it had a very limited storage capacity of only twenty 10-digit numbers. However, when compared with the Harvard Mark I, limited memory is significantly better than no memory. ENIAC did not store instructions as modern computers can. Instead, each new program required rewiring of its program circuits. It could multiply two numbers in 0.003 second.

ENIAC's major drawback was its insatiable appetite for electrical power to activate its 18,000 vacuum tubes. Some people claimed that whenever ENIAC was turned on, all the lights in Philadelphia dimmed. These tubes also generated tremendous heat, which caused them to burn out rapidly. In addition, ENIAC was difficult and time-consuming to program because each new program required a complete rewiring of the program circuitry.

Von Neumann's Logical Computer

Research continued at the Moore School and around the world. In 1944, John von Neumann added his talents to the ENIAC team. Even before ENIAC was completed, scientists recognized its limitations and set out to design a machine that was easier to program, more powerful, and compact at the same time (see Figure 2.14).

Von Neumann was a mathematician, not an engineer like Mauchly and Eckert. As such, he dealt with ideas and not the reality or limitations of technology. As a result, he was able to develop the logical framework around which computers have been built.

Von Neumann developed the concept of storing a program in the computer's memory, called the *stored program concept*. Before this, all computers, including Babbage's Analytical Engine, stored only the numbers with which they worked. The program to process these numbers was part of the circuitry. Each new program required that the computer be rewired.

Von Neumann's theory converted each program instruction into a numeric code. These codes, which were binary digits, could be stored directly in the computer's memory as if they were data. Von Neumann also reorganized the hardware of the computer. Rather than being a single, powerful unit, von Neumann's computer was broken into components. Each of these components performed a specific task and could be called upon repeatedly to perform its function.

The six components of von Neumann's theoretical computer bear a remarkable resemblance to the basic components found in Babbage's Analytical Engine.

Figure 2.14   John von Neumann, a mathematician, developed the logical framework of computers.

The components were:

1. *An arithmetic unit* for basic computation.
2. *A logic unit* where decisions and comparisons could be performed.
3. *An input device* designed to accept coded instructions and numeric data.
4. *A memory unit* for storing instructions and data.
5. *A control unit* for interpreting the coded instructions and controlling the flow of data.
6. *An output unit* to communicate the results.

Von Neumann's theories, presented in lectures and papers, were well received. A number of stored-program computers were built around his design.

EDSAC   After attending von Neumann's lectures at the Moore School, Maurice Wilkes and his associates completed EDSAC (Electronic Delay Storage Automatic Calculator) at Cambridge University in England in 1949. This was the first computer to incorporate the stored-program idea. EDSAC used letters as input and converted them to binary digits. In addition, the EDSAC group created a library of small programs that could be used by the machine when problem solving.

EDVAC   While the British were working on EDSAC, von Neumann and Moore School engineers were developing EDVAC (Electronic Delay Variable Automatic Computer). It was a stored-program machine that used a unique code of zeros

On Line

THE COMPUTER MUSEUM

In a refurbished warehouse on Museum Wharf in downtown Boston stands the world's only computer museum. Although it specializes in devices less than 50 years old, the technological changes in computers and computing devices over that period have been dramatic.

Exhibits span the computer's history from first-generation vacuum-tube devices of monstrous proportions to fourth-generation microcomputers. Displays include computers used in business and the military, as well as personal machines. Visitors can try their hand at flying a plane on a computer-based flight simulator, or they can explore computer art and animation. Physical devices that no longer exist have been preserved on film. Whenever possible, the computers have been repaired and they remain operational.

To give visitors a tour inside a computer, the Museum includes a two-story, Walk-Through Computer. This model includes a color monitor that measures 12 by 9 feet, a 25-foot long by 10-foot wide keyboard with 10 working keys, 4 foot-high RAM chips, and a working trackball that measures 9 feet. Visitors can walk along the motherboard whose layout is modeled after a real desktop machine. Special lighting powered by a minicomputer simulates the flow of current through the board. The keyboard and monitor are powered by hidden microcomputers. Most of the Walk-Through Computer's components are 50 times larger than the real thing.

The microcomputer gallery includes examples of the earliest micros, such as the Altair 8800, which was built from a kit, and the Commodore PET. Current models are also displayed. Visitors can explore paint packages and computer graphics. They can experiment with machines that talk and others that understand the spoken word.

The Computer Museum provides a hands-on learning environment. Visitors are encouraged to touch, examine, and experiment with the computers around them.

Sources: "Museum unveils giant computer," *MacWeek,* June 26, 1990, p. 4. "PC Leaves A Large Footprint," *Personal Computing,* June 29, 1990, p. 46.

and ones developed for it by von Neumann. EDVAC's hardware directly reflected the distinct components he described.

The money-making potential of these early computers was not lost on their inventors. Computers quickly moved out of the laboratories and into big business.

Eckert and Mauchly left the Moore School for private enterprise, taking many of the ideas behind ENIAC and EDVAC with them. They founded Eckert-Mauchly Computing Corporation (EMCC). Low on capital, EMCC struggled for a number of years in an attempt to build and market the Universal Automatic Computer or UNIVAC, a commercial version of ENIAC. In 1950, just as John Powers' company before it, EMCC was purchased by Remington Rand. A sound financial base for the development of the UNIVAC I was assured.

UNIVAC I In 1951, the first UNIVAC I was delivered to the U.S. Census Bureau to assist in compiling the 1950 census data. UNIVAC I, containing only 5000 vacuum tubes, was relatively compact when compared with ENIAC. It was a stored-program machine, and revolutionary in its use of a magnetizable tape, similar to audio tape, for input and output. It could read 7200 digits per second. The UNIVAC I was the first computer designed and marketed for busi-

Figure 2.15   UNIVAC I: CBS News used the UNIVAC I to predict the election of Dwight Eisenhower in 1952. Newsman Walter Cronkite (right) and other CBS staff members are shown with the computer.

ness computing rather than military or research use. In 1952, CBS News used a UNIVAC I to predict the election of Dwight Eisenhower to the presidency over Adlai Stevenson, and ushered the computer age into America's living rooms (see Figure 2.15).

IBM 650 During this time, IBM was not sitting idly by. Thomas Watson, Jr. recognized the potential business demand for computers and persuaded his father to put money into computer research (see Figure 2.16). IBM set out to build a relatively inexpensive business computer.

In late 1954, IBM began selling a computer designed specifically for the business community. Like the UNIVAC I, it was a stored-program, vacuum-tube machine. IBM executives expected to produce 50 of these IBM 650's (see Figure 2.17). Much to their surprise, they sold more than 1000. IBM's experience in selling typewriters helped sell computers. In its sales strategy, the company emphasized customer service along with research and development. As a result, IBM became the undisputed leader in the computer industry.

Figure 2.16   Thomas J. Watson, Jr.

Figure 2.17 The IBM 650: Designed for the business community, the IBM 650 started the company on its road to success.

For computers to be truly useful, it rapidly became clear that the method of programming them would have to be simplified. Instructions coded as binary digits were too cumbersome and inflexible. In 1952, Grace Murray Hopper (see Figure 2.18) developed the first translator program. Her program took instructions coded as groups of letters and translated them into the zeros and ones (machine language) that the computer could understand. This advance made programming easier and more efficient. In 1959, after working for many years with the UNIVAC team, she led the way in the development of COBOL, the first business language. COBOL, which stands for COmmon Business Oriented Language, used English phrases rather than letters or binary codes. COBOL was designed to run on a variety of machines with few if any changes.

A COMPUTER GENEALOGY

Research into newer, faster, smaller computers did not stop with UNIVAC I or the IBM 650. Computer components have decreased in size since the 1950s, while remaining basically faithful to John von Neumann's ideas. Computer

Figure 2.18   Experiences with cumbersome program-input methods such as this manual tape punch may have encouraged Grace Murray Hopper, shown in this 1944 photograph, to develop better methods of programming,

generations, like human generations, are marked by the "birth" of new family members. Each new computer generation has distinguished itself from its predecessor by a further miniaturization of the machine's internal components.

First-Generation Computers (1951–1958)

First-generation computers were epitomized by the UNIVAC I and the IBM 650. Remington Rand (UNIVAC) and IBM were by no means the only computer companies of the period, however. Honeywell, Burroughs, General Electric, and others also built first-generation machines.

What is a first-generation computer? First-generation computers have several characteristics: They used vacuum-tube technology. Input and output of data and instructions were done using punched cards, although some machines, such as the UNIVAC I, used magnetic tape. While these machines were programmable—that is, stored-program machines—their use of numeric codes called machine language (see Chapter 8) made programming them very time-consuming. Computer memory consisted of magnetic core (see Chapter 3), which continued to be popular for 20 years.

As with anything truly new, first-generation machines were beset by problems, which only the advancing technology of the next generations could solve. These first computers were room-sized monsters with huge price tags. Their thousands of vacuum tubes generated tremendous heat, frequently resulting in blown tubes. Since tube burnout made the machines unreliable, keeping these monsters cool became a major engineering effort. First-generation machines also were energy hungry, since massive amounts of electricity were required to power the thousands of vacuum tubes. The focus of the research efforts that created the next generation of machines was on finding a device that would make vacuum tubes obsolete.

Second-Generation Computers (1959–1964)

In 1948, John Bardeen, Walter Brattain, and William Shockley, working at Bell Labs, invented the transistor (see Figure 2.19). In 1956, they were awarded the Nobel Prize in Physics for their efforts. Transistors were being produced in volume at relatively low cost by 1959.

Figure 2.19   (a) John Bardeen, William Shockley, and Walter Brattain (left to right) invented the transistor in 1948. (b) The first transistors (left) were about 1/100th the size of a vacuum tube.

(a)

(b)

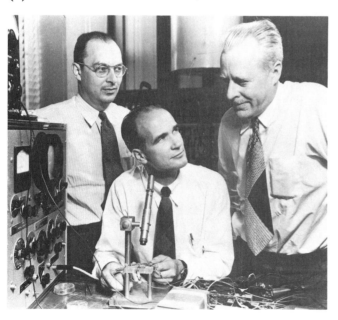

Just as a vacuum tube is a switch, a **transistor** is a tiny electronic switch. It relays electronic messages, yet it is built as a solid unit with no moving parts **(solid state).** The first transistors were approximately 1/100th the size of a vacuum tube.

The second computer generation saw the replacement of vacuum tubes by transistors. These new machines were at once smaller, faster, and more reliable than first-generation machines (see Figure 2.20). Second-generation computers used solid-state technology, which required no warm-up time and eliminated troublesome tube burnout. They were also more rugged and energy efficient. In these newer and more powerful computers, binary codes or *machine language* was replaced by the easier-to-program *assembly language*. Instructions were coded as letters, such as *A* for ADD or *L* for LOAD. Further developments resulted in English-like languages, such as FORTRAN (FORmula TRANslation) and COBOL (COmmon Business-Oriented Language). Programming languages are explained more fully in Chapter 8.

Figure 2.20   Second-generation computers, such as this IBM 1401, used transistors instead of vacuum tubes.

Miniaturization continued. In the early 1960s, when IBM announced its revolutionary computer family—the IBM System/360—the third generation of computers was born.

Third-Generation Computers (1965–early 1970s)

In the IBM System/360, transistors had been reduced in size so that hundreds of them could be embedded in small pieces, or chips, of silicon (see Figure 2.21).

Figure 2.21   (a) Much smaller than vacuum tubes, (b) this IBM/360 chip could hold hundreds of electronic circuits.

(a)

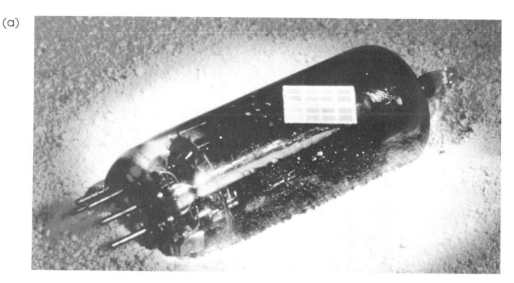

(b)

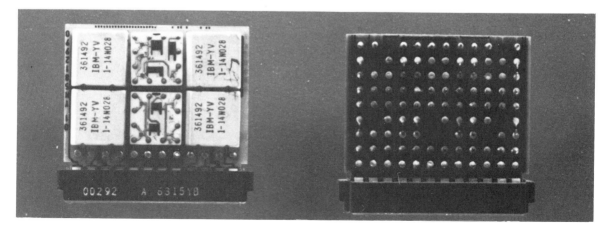

By etching these tiny silicon chips with the appropriate electronic circuitry, a new, miniaturized solid-state technology of **integrated circuits (IC)** was formed. The term *integrated* is used because all the parts are built as a single, integrated unit. While integrated circuit technology was invented at Bell Labs as early as 1955, little use was made of it until IBM took the plunge and designed an entire machine around it.

Third-generation computers were smaller and even more reliable than their second-generation parents. With the significant reduction in size and raw materials came a considerable reduction in power usage and an astronomical reduction in cost. Now small and middle-sized companies and organizations could afford computers. Digital Equipment Corp. designed a line of minicomputers to suit the needs of these smaller organizations.

Figure 2.22   Smaller and more reliable, third-generation computers such as this Digital Equipment Corp. 8800 were also less costly.

Throughout the third generation, the number of circuits squeezed onto chips grew from approximately 1000 per chip in 1965 to more than 15,000 by the early 1970s. This circuit squeezing is called **large-scale integration (LSI)**. Large-scale integration not only reduced machine size but improved the computer's speed (the time involved in solving problems) by reducing the distance current had to travel. As a result, computers were more powerful and less expensive (see Figure 2.22).

The computer industry was evolving in other ways during the third generation, with IBM leading the way. In addition to building cheaper, faster computers, IBM developed new and improved storage and input/output devices (peripheral devices) designed specifically for the business market. The IBM System/360 advertised 40 add-on devices. It came in a variety of models, each designed to serve different segments of the business community. Other manufacturers followed suit. A wide range of programming languages and prewritten software made third-generation machines more usable than earlier machines. Computers began to revolutionize business and industry.

Fourth-Generation Computers (early 1970s – present)

In the fourth generation, as more and more circuits continued to be packed onto chips, technology moved from large-scale integration to **very large-scale integration (VLSI)**. With this advance, hundreds of thousands of transistors and circuits are now being packed onto silicon chips (see Figure 2.23). Along with this incredible reduction in size came a computer with an entirely new design.

In the early 1970s, the microprocessor, or computer on a chip, was developed. As discussed in Chapter 1, a microprocessor chip is a central processing unit (CPU) condensed onto a single chip. Until recently, an Intel Corp. engineer named Ted Hoff was credited with its invention. In August 1990, the U.S. Patent Office awarded Gilbert P. Hyatt a patent for the microprocessor chip based on a prototype built in 1968. Hoff claims that Hyatt's design could not have been built as a full-scale model. The "who is the inventor" debate continues.

With the invention of the microprocessor, computers could now fit anywhere, since the entire CPU was no larger than a fingernail. With this microprocessor chip, the desktop microcomputer was born. The generations of computer development are depicted in Figure 2.24.

In addition to a highly compact CPU, peripheral devices were designed to make computers easier to use. These improvements included compact storage devices (floppy or optical disks), color graphic screens, and a wide variety of input devices. In addition to the development of small desktop computers, the fourth generation also witnessed the development of supercomputers. Using VLSI design, supercomputers have vast storage and processing capacity. Such machines are used to perform complex mathematical tasks. Compact chip technology also brought about the development of parallel computers. These computers use multiple processors working simultaneously to solve problems.

AUGUSTANA UNIVERSITY COLLEGE
LIBRARY

Figure 2.23   Hundreds of thousands of transistors and circuits are now packed onto silicon chips such as this Motorola MC88200.

Hardware advances were followed closely by a software explosion. Prewritten software is now available for all sizes of machines. Packages for micros make up the largest segment of this multibillion dollar industry (see Figure 2.25).

THE RISE OF THE MICROCOMPUTER

In barely 50 years, the computer revolution has changed the way we live. The microcomputer, often considered the leading edge of this revolution, is much younger, however. Its birth is marked from the invention of the microprocessor. The microcomputer revolution began in the early 1970s when Intel Corp. successfully marketed the first microprocessor chip.

Figure 2.24   Generations of Computers.

First-Generation Computers (1951–1958)
- vacuum tube technology
- punched card or magnetic tape
- machine language
- magnetic core
- examples: UNIVAC I, IBM 650

Second-Generation Computers (1959–1964)
- transistor
- solid-state technology
- punched card or magnetic tape
- assembly language and some high-level languages
- magnetic core
- examples: IBM 1401, GE 235

Third-Generation Computers (1965–early 1970s)
- integrated circuit (IC) technology
- silicon chips
- large-scale integration (LSI)
- punched cards, magnetic tape, magnetic disks
- magnetic core, some semiconductor memory
- examples: IBM System/360, DEC PDP 8

Fourth-Generation Computers (early 1970s–present)
- very large-scale integration (VLSI)
- microprocessor chip
- magnetic disks, floppy disks, etc.
- high-level languages
- user-friendly software
- semiconductor memory
- examples: IBM SYSTEM/370, Apple Macintosh, SPARC II workstation

Computers from a Kit

The microprocessor chip made it possible to design and build a computer compact enough to sit on a desk and fit in a small box. In 1975, the first personal computer was advertised in *Popular Electronics* magazine by Ed Roberts. The

Figure 2.25   Microcomputer software makes up the largest segment of the software industry.

Altair 8800 was an 8-bit, $400 microcomputer designed for the hobbyist. The buyer had to put it together, because it was available only in kit form. The Altair 8800 was a huge success—hundreds were sold.

Success bred competition. Steven Jobs and Stephen Wozniak, working out of Jobs' garage, created and released the Apple I in 1976. The 8-bit Apple I, easy to use, easy to assemble, and inexpensive, was designed with the nonhobbyist in mind. The first Apple showed there was a strong market for assembled machines, so in 1977 Jobs and Wozniak released an improved, fully assembled version, the Apple II (see Figure 2.26).

The Birth of the Personal Computer

Jobs and Wozniak understood that the future of their creations would depend on the tasks that the machines could be made to do. Since they were essentially computer designers, they encouraged other companies to develop software and accessory hardware, such as printers and tape and disk drives, that would work with their machines. In 1979, the first business accounting software package, VisiCalc (VISIble CALCulator), was released commercially. VisiCalc was written and designed on an Apple II. Sales of both products skyrocketed because most

Figure 2.26   Apple president John Scully, flanked by co-founders of Apple Steve Jobs (left) and Steve Wozniak (right).

purchasers bought them together. Meanwhile, dozens of other companies, including Radio Shack (Tandy), Atari, and Commodore, had entered the microcomputer market.

The infant microcomputer industry was dominated by companies as new as the products they sold. In 1981, all that changed. IBM, the world's largest manufacturer of computer hardware, released its 16-bit microcomputer, called simply the PC (Personal Computer). Breaking its historical pattern of developing and marketing only its own hardware and software products, IBM followed Apple's lead and encouraged other companies to develop software and accessory hardware for the IBM PC. In less than two years, IBM was the dominant force in the microcomputer market. Even now, it is unclear whether it was the superior design of the PC or simply IBM's reputation for reliability that sold its machines.

The success of IBM's microcomputer had two significant effects. First, almost immediately, IBM became the "standard" machine for which software and accessory hardware were designed. Second, competitors started building microcomputers that could do most of, or more than, what an IBM PC could do. Such machines were called **compatibles.** They were able to run much of the extensive software designed for the IBM PC (see Figure 2.27).

Some of these microcomputers went even further. They were virtual look-alikes, or **clones,** of the IBM PC. Clones and compatibles are quite attractive to customers because they usually cost less than IBM's product. Legally, competitors cannot build exact duplicates of IBM's machines. Thus, each of the compatibles or clones differs from IBM's machines in some way. Standard equipment on such machines often includes graphics monitors, additional internal memory, and redesigned microprocessor chips that work faster than those built into IBM products. IBM computers are known for their remarkable reliability, easy-to-upgrade-and-maintain hardware as well as innovation.

The IBM PC and later related models, among them the IBM XT and IBM AT, are all based on 16-bit chips from Intel. The compatibles are based on the same inexpensive and readily available Intel microprocessors. Some compatibles, such as AT&T's 6300 and Compaq, improved upon IBM's hardware design.

Figure 2.27   Compatibles: IBM-compatible computers such as this Compaq Deskpro 386/20e use the same software and have most of the capabilities of the IBM PC.

Toward a User-Friendly Machine

In 1984, Apple responded to IBM's dominance by releasing the Macintosh (see Figure 2.28). This was a 32-bit machine designed to be easy to use and advertised as the computer "for the rest of us." It featured on-screen pictures called **icons** to represent common computer tasks. The user pointed to an icon with a special pointing device called a mouse, which will be more fully discussed in Chapter 5 (see Figure 2.29).

The Macintosh also introduced a more user-friendly way of issuing commands. When the user pointed to one of a group of words at the top of the screen, a box or window would appear. This window, which covered only a small portion of the screen, would display available commands. The user then pointed to the desired command, and it was performed. Many people found that using a mouse to point to icons and open windows was an easy, enjoyable way to use a computer.

In 1987, both IBM and Apple released new microcomputer systems. The IBM Personal System/2 and Apple Macintosh II are families of powerful machines. They are designed to run much of the existing software developed for earlier

---

Figure 2.28   The Macintosh: Apple Computer released the Macintosh in 1984 in response to IBM's domination of the microcomputer market.

Figure 2.29   Macintosh icons including hard disk (Enterprise), applications software (Word, SAM), and the trash can for erasing files.

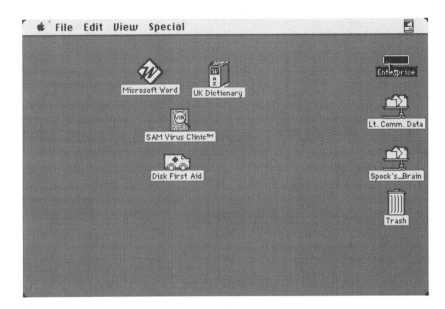

models, as well as new and improved packages. As with the IBM PC before it, the IBM PS/2 family of machines spawned an entire industry of compatibles. By 1991, with the development by Intel of a new class of powerful but inexpensive microprocessor chips (the 80286, 80386, 80486), IBM had lost its dominance in the microcomputer market as competitors built comparable machines.

In 1988, NeXT Corp., founded by Steven Jobs (formerly head of Apple Corp.), released the NeXT Machine. It combined state-of-the-art processor chips with high-fidelity sound, incredible graphics hardware, and a revolutionary optical storage device. Like the Macintosh, a mouse is used to open windows, point to icons, and activate the stereo sound system. At $6,500–$10,000, this NeXT Machine was too high priced for the traditional microcomputer user. By 1990, however, NeXT had released new, improved, and less expensive models that caught the attention of users (see Figure 2.30).

In late 1990, Apple took a bold step and released a redesigned product line. To compete with the low cost machines of vendors such as IBM, Apple released the Macintosh Classic with a purchase price as low as $700. The rest of the product line is dominated by remarkable color displays.

Despite differences in internal design, microcomputer manufacturers, with the support of software vendors, are producing machines that have remarkably

Figure 2.30   The NeXT machine contains features that may become standard in future microcomputers.

similar features. Mice, color graphics, and windows are increasingly popular on all microcomputers. Many popular software packages, such as WordPerfect and Excel, run on machines like the IBM PS/2 as well as the Macintosh. Until recently, sharing data across machines was impossible. While it is still difficult, the machines are acting more and more alike. With the new Macintosh super-drive, and special Apple software, users can read information created on IBM-class machines and transfer it to their Macintoshs. In addition, a program called SoftPC makes it possible for software designed for IBM and compatible equipment to be run on Macintosh and NeXT computers.

BEYOND THE FOURTH GENERATION

What will fifth-generation computers be like? Without a crystal ball, it is impossible to say with certainty. Using current research in the United States and Japan as a starting point, the next generation of computers is likely to have

Figure 2.31   Timeline showing the major events in computer history.

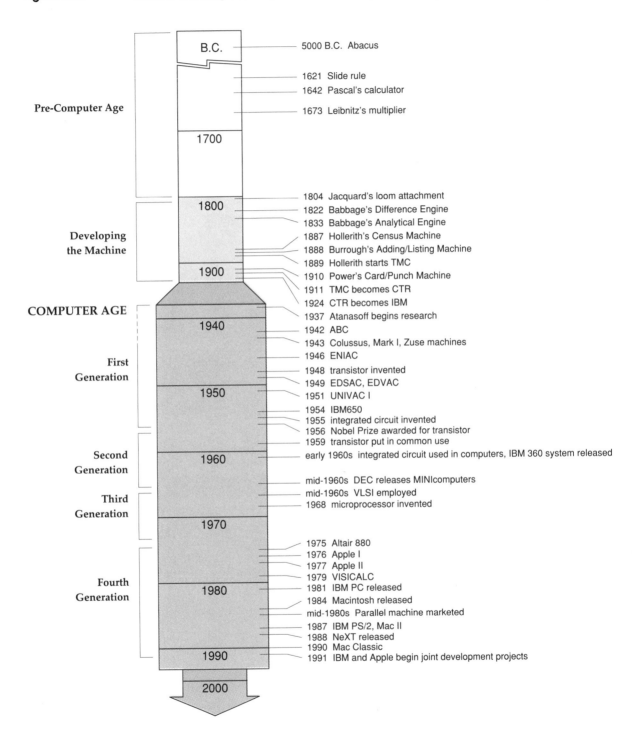

common features. They may be:

1. *More compact.* Their hardware will be more compact, based on "super chips" composed of thousands of already compact, smaller chips linked together.

2. *Faster.* They will operate and calculate hundreds if not thousands of times faster than current machines. Computers are rapidly moving away from the von Neumann model of processing information one piece at a time. Parallel processing will be incorporated into smaller and smaller machines.

3. *Smarter.* These machines will be considerably more "intelligent" than modern computers. Computer programs designed to make decisions in a human-like fashion will be more capable of assisting people in decision making.

4. *Friendlier.* Software will make these new computers even more user-friendly. In other words, people will find computers easier to use and operate because the software will require less technical expertise.

5. *Closer to natural language.* Software will make greater use of natural or spoken language.

Computers, whatever their form, will link our homes with all kinds of services, from banking and shopping to education and entertainment. Our offices will become increasingly "paperless," and more and more people will work from home by dialing into the office.

Although the computer in its present form is only 50 years old, two things should be clear. First, people have been engaged in the increasingly complex development of computing devices for hundreds if not thousands of years. (Figure 2.31 shows the major events in this development). Second, the computers available 20 years from now are likely to be as radically different from the machines in popular use today as the Apple Macintosh is from ENIAC.

SUMMARY

The earliest computing tool was the **abacus,** which uses strings of beads to perform computations. The 1600s saw the development of many calculating devices. The **slide rule,** using specially marked rulers, was introduced in 1621 and continued in popular use until the 1970s. Blaise Pascal invented a mechanical calculator in 1642, and Gottfried Leibniz introduced a multiplier in 1673.

The Industrial Revolution not only produced greatly improved calculating devices but began the process of designing machines that were programmable. Jacquard's use of punched cards to store the pattern woven in cloth directly influenced the designers of calculating devices. In 1833, Charles Babbage's Analytical Engine was designed. It was a complete computer containing punched card input, an output device, a processor, and memory. Although this machine was not completed in Babbage's lifetime, his ideas assisted future scientists.

In the 1800s, computing devices found practical applications. Herman Hollerith invented a Census Machine that assisted in tabulating the 1890 and 1900 censuses. The railroad industry used it to keep track of passengers and goods shipped. William Burroughs' 1888 invention of an adding/listing machine found widespread application.

The pattern of devices from the 1600s through the early 1900s led directly to the development of calculating machines that contained memory and were programmable. The research environment of World War II hastened the development of computing machines, including the ABC, Harvard Mark I, and ENIAC. Recognizing the deficiencies of these machines, John von Neumann devised a means of storing program instructions in memory using numeric (binary) codes. His theoretical machine consisted of single function components, which form the basis of the majority of today's machines. Von Neumann's ideas were first implemented in the EDSAC (1949) and EDVAC (1951) computers. Because of the commercial viability of these new machines, the UNIVAC I and IBM 650 were introduced in the early 1950s.

From the 1950s to the present, computer hardware has changed very rapidly. Hardware and software advances mark the computer generations. First-generation computers used **vacuum-tube** technology and were programmed in machine language. The transistor marks the transition into the second computer generation. Transistors made computers smaller and more reliable. While assembly language was popular, both FORTRAN and COBOL were created during the second generation.

Miniaturization packed hundreds of **transistors** on a tiny silicon chip, bringing about the third computer generation. A wide variety of devices were invented that could be added to computers, making them easier to use. English-like programming languages and prewritten packages were the popular software. The fourth generation found manufacturers squeezing all of the components found in a CPU onto a single chip (microprocessor). Fourth-generation machines come in a vast array of sizes. Prewritten software has made these machines available to all of us.

Microprocessor-based microcomputers first became available in the early 1970s in kit form. In 1977, Steven Jobs and Stephen Wozniak released the Apple II, the first fully assembled microcomputer. Packaged software such as VisiCalc made microcomputers useful to people without a programming background. In 1981, IBM released its Personal Computer (PC) and encouraged other hardware and software manufacturers to develop products that could be used with it. In a short period of time, it was the industry standard. Compatible computers are machines that run most of the software designed originally for IBM's microcomputers. Apple's 1984 Macintosh featured a pointing device called a mouse, and **icons** representing common computer tasks, making the computer easy to use. Both IBM and Apple released new computers in 1987 that featured color graphic displays, mice, and compact memory. The IBM machines spawned a new class of compatibles. In 1988 the NeXT Machine was released. It was designed to be a powerful workstation that appealed to the microcomputer user. Improved chip design and easy-to-use software marked machine changes in the early 1990s.

Key Words

As an extra review of the chapter, try defining the following terms. If you have trouble with any of them, refer to the page number listed.

abacus *(32)*
clones *(64)*
compatibles *(64)*
icons *(65)*
integrated circuit (IC) *(58)*
large-scale integration (LSI) *(59)*

slide rule *(33)*
solid state *(56)*
transistor *(56)*
vacuum tube *(43)*
very large-scale integration
(VLSI) *(59)*

Test Your Knowledge

1. Briefly describe the components of an abacus.

2. How do Pascal's calculator and Leibniz's multiplier differ?

3. What contribution did Jacquard's loom make toward the development of computers?

4. Why is Charles Babbage called the father of the modern computer?

5. Why is Ada Lovelace called the first programmer?

6. What was the Census Machine? Why was it important?

7. What was COLOSSUS? What did it do?

8. Why is the Harvard Mark I <u>not</u> considered a complete computer?

9. John von Neumann revolutionized the way computers work. Explain his two major contributions.

10. How did ENIAC differ from EDVAC?

11. The UNIVAC I and IBM 650 were both important computer firsts. Explain this statement.

12. What contributions did Grace Hopper make to the computer industry?

13. List the basic features of first-generation computers.

14. List the basic features of second-generation computers.

15. List the basic features of third-generation computers.

16. What distinguishes fourth-generation machines from those built in the third generation?

17. How did the Apple II differ from the Apple I?

18. What company coined the term *personal computer*? How is the PC different from the Apple II?

19. What are compatibles?

20. What basic differences distinguished the Macintosh and the PC?

21. What features are common to the newest microcomputers?

Expand Your Knowledge

1. Locate either a slide rule or an abacus. Learn how it works. Demonstrate its use to your class.

2. Write a three-page paper on Napier's "bones." They are considered a precursor to the slide rule. Include what the bones were and how they worked. Use at least two sources.

3. Research the Atanasoff versus ENIAC case. Write a short (three- to five-page) paper detailing your opinion on this question: Should ENIAC have been patented? Support your viewpoint, using at least three sources of information.

4. Grace Hopper made critical contributions to the development of second-generation computers. Write a brief three-page paper describing her contributions. Be sure to focus on why her work was critical to the computer industry.

5. What is Japan's Fifth-Generation Project? Write a short (three- to five-page) paper on this project. Use at least three sources of information.

6. Go to a local computer store and compare the machines based on Intel's 386 and 486 chips with the Macintosh II family of machines. Identify key similarities and differences. Include a list of prices. If money were not an issue, which machine would you buy? Defend your position.

3

The Central Processing Unit

For many people, the computer is like a magician's "black box," an incredible machine that works mysteriously. For these individuals, how the data are altered inside the computer is of no consequence. All that matters is that the results are consistent and accurate. If we opened this black box and found mice running around inside touching levers and pushing buttons, that would be fine. The process is less important than the results.

Many of us relate to our cars in the same way. We care only that when we turn the key the car starts. Although a car or a computer can be operated with limited knowledge, when we think this way we are unable to handle or avoid problems. Driving and maintaining a car requires some knowledge of how a car operates. It is important to understand that the muffler is part of the exhaust system, that the radiator assists in cooling the engine, and that the lights and starter require a working battery. Similarly, to remove the mystery of the computer, we should understand how the components work together to store and process information effectively. With such knowledge, we can better understand what the computer can and cannot do. Just as an uninformed driver cannot competently discuss the safety features of cars, an uninformed computer user cannot effectively understand the power of computers.

After studying this chapter, you will be able to:

- Understand the components of the CPU.

- Explain the relationship between primary memory and the CPU.

- Illustrate how data are stored and addressed in memory.

- Relate the steps involved in executing instructions.

- Understand how EBCDIC and ASCII are used.

- Demonstrate the use of parity bits for error checking.

- Identify the basic types of primary memory.

- Relate the differences between RAM and ROM.

- Discuss new CPU and primary memory technologies.

THE CENTRAL PROCESSING UNIT (CPU)

We saw in Chapter 1 that all computers, regardless of size, cost, or manufacturer, have four basic components: input devices, a processor, memory, and output devices.

The "brains," or processor, of the computer consists of the central processing unit (CPU) and the primary memory associated with it (see Figure 3.1). The CPU, you will recall, is the electronic circuitry responsible for interpreting and issuing instructions to the rest of the machine so that the necessary operations

Figure 3.1   General ''All-Purpose'' Computer.

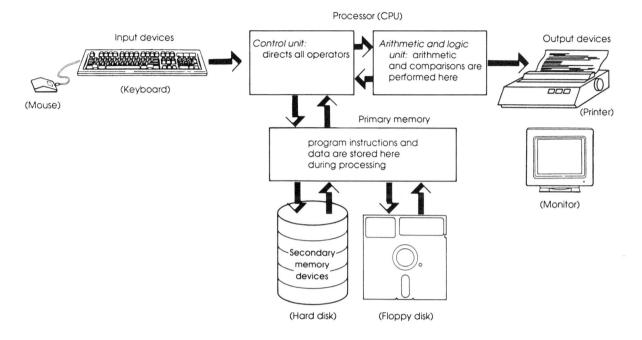

will be carried out. The CPU has two components: the arithmetic and logic unit, and the control unit.

The Arithmetic and Logic Unit

Computers are very fast calculating devices, and it is the **arithmetic and logic unit (ALU)** that performs these calculations. The ALU has two functions. First, its circuitry is responsible for performing the arithmetic operations of addition, subtraction, multiplication, and division. Second, it can make simple "decisions" by comparing two alternatives and choosing between them. In choosing, the computer uses the mathematical operations of less than ($<$), greater than ($>$), and equal to ($=$). When making decisions, the computer can be thought of as using an extremely exacting scale, as represented in Figure 3.2. By balancing two values, a computer can decide if one number is greater than another, or if they are exactly the same.

Computers are more precise than people. When comparing the numbers 8.999999999 and 9, for almost all purposes we would regard them as essentially the same. For example, 8.999999999 pounds of potatoes is the "same" as 9

Figure 3.2   Logical Comparisons Using a Scale.

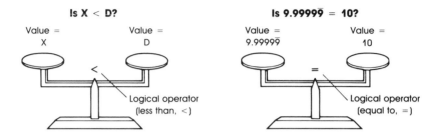

pounds of potatoes. To a computer, they are distinctly different. Numbers that are *essentially* the same are *not* equal.

8.999999999 < 9

Mathematical comparisons containing less than, greater than, and equal to are called *logical* operations resulting in the component's name, logic unit. Computers can be designed to perform more complex comparisons, such as greater than or equal to, by combining the standard operations.

The Control Unit

While the arithmetic and logic unit is responsible for mathematical calculations and comparisons, the **control unit** is the computer's internal police officer. This CPU component maintains order and controls all the internal activities of the machine. The control unit sends out electronic signals directing the computer to perform specific tasks such as moving data between memory and the CPU, activating the ALU, receiving data, and sending information. The control unit manages the flow of data throughout the machine based on the instructions it receives from programs. No instructions are processed by the control unit. Rather, it directs other parts of the computer to perform their functions in a specific order, at a specific time.

Registers

The CPU contains a small number of superfast memory devices called registers. Each **register** temporarily holds a data item, an instruction, or a piece of information about to be transferred between the control unit and the ALU or processed by the ALU. The CPU can process only one instruction or use one item of data at a time. Registers are designed to temporarily hold the necessary information. Registers also hold the intermediate values used in calculations and comparisons. The final results of computations made by the CPU are transferred from registers to primary memory. To facilitate processing, the following registers are used by the CPU:

- *Accumulator.* This register holds the result of the operations performed by the ALU.

- *Storage register.* This register holds information just received from internal memory or just processed by the ALU and about to be sent to internal memory.

- *Address register.* This register holds the location of data about to be transferred from internal memory.

- *General-purpose register.* This register can store data, addresses, or instructions.

Memory

Although primary memory is not technically a part of the CPU, it stores the data and instructions required during processing. Without memory, the CPU could not effectively perform its duties. As shown in Figure 3.1, computers use two forms of memory: primary memory, directly associated with the CPU; and secondary, long-term memory, which is discussed in Chapter 4. The name *primary memory* was not chosen casually. *Primary* means first; primary memory is the first memory used by the machine to store data and information and therefore its most important memory. It is designed for high speed and easy access. However, data and program instructions are stored only temporarily in primary memory. As long as a program or file is being processed or worked on, it resides in primary memory. Information that is not currently in use but which we wish to retain for later use is placed in long-term storage (secondary memory).

Both primary memory and the memory not associated with the CPU go under a host of different names. The common names used for primary memory are:

primary memory or primary storage
hard memory (hard-wired, built-in)
main memory
internal memory
core memory

The names given to the memory not associated with the CPU are:

auxiliary memory or auxiliary storage
secondary memory or secondary storage
mass storage
external memory or external storage

The Bus

For data and instructions to flow between the CPU, memory, and other parts of the computer, a pathway or connection must exist between the various devices. A **bus** is a group of shared wires that link the components of a computer. Instructions, operational commands, and data pass along the bus just as cars, trucks, and motorcycles might share a multilane highway. Just as laws govern the use of a highway, built-in rules control the order in which devices send messages along the bus, and control the situations where routine messages may need to be interrupted for high-priority messages. Microcomputers commonly use bus technology, and complex parallel systems are finding buses useful as well.

CODING INFORMATION

As indicated in Chapter 1, computers do not understand words or decimal system numbers. All data and instructions must be converted to binary digits (bits)—combinations of zeros and ones—to be understood by the machine. Humans, however, are not machines. For people to use data, they need to be organized so that conclusions can be drawn and decisions made. No matter how effective our computers are, people ultimately have to do the decision making. Not only do we break down facts into data so they can be fed into a computer, but by writing programs we guide the computer in organizing the data to suit our needs.

While people can deal with information in the form of zeros and ones, we are far more comfortable manipulating information in the form of *characters* found in natural languages such as English. There are three types of characters:

1. Alphabetic: A, B, C, D. . . a, b, c, d. . .

2. Numeric: 0, 1, 2, 3, 4, 5, 6, 7, 8, 9

3. Special: +, =, -, /, &, , $, *, etc.

Over the years, a number of coding schemes have been developed to translate characters into a series of bits. Taken together, these bits form a byte, so that one character is stored as a single byte of memory.

The two most popular coding schemes that computers use are the **Extended Binary Coded Decimal Interchange Code,** or **EBCDIC** (pronounced *EB-see-dick*), and the **American Standard Code for Information Interchange,** or **ASCII** (pronounced *AS-key*). These coding schemes translate the characters people are comfortable with into the zeros and ones the computer can understand. Figure 3.3 gives examples of these two codes.

Figure 3.3   ASCII and EBCDIC codes. Many computer users prefer ASCII to EBCDIC, feeling that it uses a more rational bit pattern.

```
EBCDIC    character    ASCII

(8-bits)              (7-bits)
1100 0001    A        100 0001
1100 0010    B        100 0010
1100 0011    C        100 0011
1100 0100    D        100 0100
1100 0101    E        100 0101
1100 0110    F        100 0110
1100 0111    G        100 0111
1100 1000    H        100 1000
1100 1001    I        100 1001
1101 0001    J        100 1010
1101 0010    K        100 1011
1101 0011    L        100 1100
1101 0100    M        100 1101
1101 0101    N        100 1110
1101 0110    O        100 1111
1101 0111    P        101 0000
1101 1000    Q        101 0001
1101 1001    R        101 0010
1110 0010    S        101 0011
1110 0011    T        101 0100
1110 0100    U        101 0101
1110 0101    V        101 0110
1110 0110    W        101 0111
1110 0111    X        101 1000
1110 1000    Y        101 1001
1110 1001    Z        101 1010

1111 0000    0        011 0000
1111 0001    1        011 0001
1111 0010    2        011 0010
1111 0011    3        011 0011
1111 0100    4        011 0100
1111 0101    5        011 0101
1111 0110    6        011 0110
1111 0111    7        011 0111
1111 1000    8        011 1000
1111 1001    9        011 1001
```

EBCDIC

EBCDIC was developed by IBM to code information on its mainframes. Using 8-bits, which allows for 256 unique combinations, each character is coded into its binary equivalent. In addition to ordering the coded numbers, so that 1 (1111 0001) is less than 2 (1111 0010), the letters are also ordered so that comparisons can be made. *D*, for example, is less than *E* when their binary equivalents are compared.

$$1 < 2 \quad \text{since} \quad 11110001 < 11110010$$

and

$$D < E \quad \text{because} \quad 11000100 < 11000101$$

ASCII

ASCII was developed as a combined effort by a group of computer manufacturers who hoped it would become the standard for all machines. Although it has become the standard for microcomputers, including IBM, and is extensively used by minicomputer manufacturers and many mainframes, IBM continues to use EBCDIC on its mainframes. Like EBCDIC, ASCII codes each character into a series of bits. However, this scheme uses a 7-bit code rather than 8, while maintaining the natural ordering within letters and numbers. Through such coding schemes, not only numeric quantities but also characters can be compared and manipulated by the computer. As we can see from Figure 3.3, letters, and the words they form, can be placed in alphabetic order using the logical operations of less than (<), greater than (>), or equal to (=) when comparing their ASCII or EBCDIC codes.

Parity

With information constantly being transmitted both within the computer and between machines, it is essential to guarantee that information is accurately transferred. Each coded character, whether EBCDIC or ASCII, has a bit added to it prior to transmission. The added bit is called the **parity,** or **check bit.**

Odd and Even Parity *Coding the Byte.* To demonstrate the use of parity bits, let us start with an initial character, code it into EBCDIC and ASCII, and then add the appropriate bit used in an *even-parity* system.

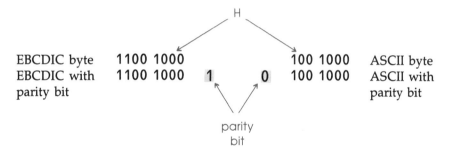

In both cases, all the bits in the string were added. In binary, summing a string of digits produces the same result as counting the number of 1's in the string. In the EBCDIC system, the result was 3, which is an odd number. To produce even parity, prior to transmission an additional 1 is added, making the sum even. In ASCII, the sum was 2, which is even, so a 0 is added. In EBCDIC the parity bit is the rightmost bit, while in ASCII the parity bit is the leftmost bit. In the circuitry used to test for odd parity, the digits of the transmitted byte, including the parity bit, are added together. If the result is an odd number (an odd number of 1-bits), it is assumed that the byte was transmitted correctly. Even-parity circuitry tests for an even number of 1-bits.

Testing for Accurate Transmission. In transmitting the word *HELLO* between two machines using the ASCII code and an even-parity system, an error occurred. The following example demonstrates how the error is detected:

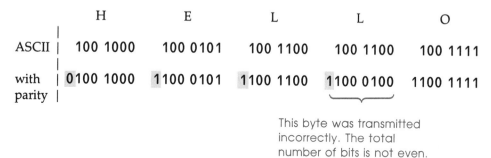

The computer, being unable to determine which bit within the byte was transmitted incorrectly, knows only that an error has occurred. To correct the error, the entire byte is retransmitted.

If a 1-bit was lost or changed during transmission, the parity of the byte would change, indicating a transmission error. This is not an infallible system, as it is possible to lose or incorrectly transmit more than a single bit. The chances of transmitting two bits incorrectly in a single byte are very small, however, so the method works for most practical purposes.

ADDRESSES: LOCATING INFORMATION

Primary memory contains thousands of electronic circuits designed to store a single piece of data as a series of zeros and ones (binary digits). As von Neumann suggested, instructions are also coded by the machine as binary digits. For the computer to process data into information, it must be able to locate the required data and instructions. Each memory location has a unique **address.** Just as your home address uniquely identifies where you live, so an address in computer memory uniquely identifies its location.

A memory location is similar to a mailbox (see Figure 3.4). A mailbox is uniquely identified on the outside by an address and the last names of those living at that address. The address on the mailbox remains the same regardless of the contents of the box, which might change every day. Some days it might contain letters; on other days, a magazine or a package. Memory works in much the same way. Each location has a unique numeric address that identifies it. The address of each location is fixed, but the contents or *value* of memory can change. Each location can contain data or instructions. Contemporary English-like programming languages do not use numeric addresses when referring to

Figure 3.4   Addresses: Each memory location has an identifying address.

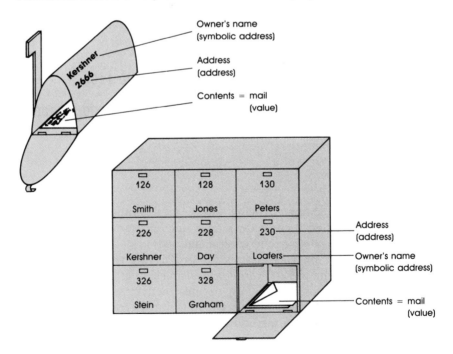

memory. They use symbolic addresses, English-like words that more clearly describe the contents of memory. Such programs refer to memory by using names such as PayRate, Total, InitialValue, or StoreNumber. A symbolic address is similar to the name on the outside of a mailbox. The name on the outside of the mailbox identifies whose mail is inside. The computer associates a unique numeric address with each of these symbolic addresses.

A memory location can store only one item at a time. When new information is stored, the old contents are destroyed. This occurs because memory locations are collections of switches that turn on or off to represent stored data. When the contents of a memory location change, the switches are reset and the previous settings are lost. One could compare this to a mailbox that could hold only a single letter or a single issue of a magazine. If a second letter is pushed into the mailbox, the first falls out the back and is lost. However, when retrieving information, the mailbox analogy breaks down. When mail is retrieved from a mailbox, the mailbox is empty. When information is retrieved from memory, a copy of the contents is made and this copy is used. The stored information remains intact. Such unique addressing enables the CPU to retrieve information very rapidly.

EXECUTING INSTRUCTIONS

For a computer to process, or *execute*, a program, the control unit must copy and move instructions and data from primary memory to the CPU's registers and then return the results to memory. Most modern computers can perform only a single calculation or comparison at once. Programs are executed one instruction at a time, in sequence. For each instruction, the following steps are followed:

1. *Copy.* The control unit copies, or *fetches*, an instruction from primary memory and stores it in one of its registers.

2. *Decode.* The instruction is decoded by the control unit. If data are required they are fetched from memory. The decoded instruction and any required data are sent to the ALU.

3. *Calculate or compare.* The ALU performs or executes the required calculation or comparison.

4. *Store.* The control unit stores the results of the ALU's operation in primary memory or, if the result is to be used immediately, in another register.

This procedure is followed over and over again until all instructions have been executed. Steps 1 and 2 together are referred to as **I-time,** or **instruction time,** which is the time required to interpret an instruction. Steps 3 and 4 make up **E-time,** or **execution time,** the time required to execute an instruction. All four steps require only a small fraction of a second to complete.

PRIMARY MEMORY

To be used effectively by the CPU, main memory must offer fast, easy access to data. Unfortunately, the faster a memory technology, the more expensive. Information that is not needed for processing is stored on less expensive secondary storage devices. Primary memory provides direct access to all information. Since each memory location has a unique address, all information can be located in the same amount of time. It is left to the computer to "remember" exactly where each item of data is stored so that it can be retrieved.

Magnetic Core Memory

The primary memory technology of second- and third-generation computers was **magnetic core memory,** often referred to simply as **core.** Core consisted of tiny (1/100 inch) iron oxide (ferrite) rings with several wires threaded through each ring (see Figure 3.5).

If enough current passed through the wires, the rings were magnetized in either a clockwise (representing 1) or a counterclockwise (representing 0) direction. Since each core remained magnetized when the electric current was no

Figure 3.5   Magnetic Cores: (a) A magnetic core memory and (b) a closeup of a magnetic core memory.

(a)

(b)

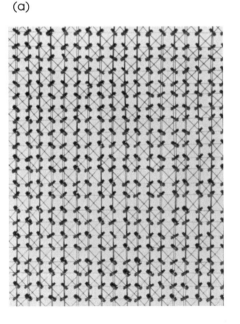
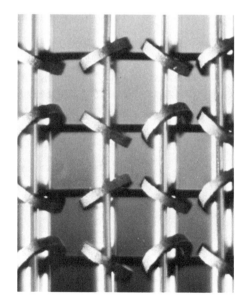

longer present, it was called *nonvolatile*. Core memory was very reliable and reasonably fast. However, when compared to more recent technologies, it was rather bulky, required a significant amount of power to create the directional charges, and was expensive to assemble.

Semiconductor Memory

Semiconductor memory is the common memory technology of current machines. Its size and design make it faster and less expensive than core memory. Semiconductor memory consists of thousands of microscopic integrated circuits etched onto chips of silicon (see Figure 3.6).

These circuits, acting as switches, either allow electric current to pass over a given path or they stop the current. The presence of current is represented by a 1, and the absence of current is represented by a 0. Semiconductor memory is very compact, making it very fast. It is reliable, uses low power, and is relatively inexpensive.

However, unlike magnetic core, semiconductor memory is *volatile*. Continuous electric current is required to store data. If the current is interrupted, even briefly, all stored information is irretrievably lost. For this reason, today's computer users should regularly save, or copy, the information they have stored in

Figure 3.6   Semiconductor Memory: Today's computer makes use of microscopic, integrated circuits etched onto silicon chips.

primary memory into secondary storage. In this way, if a power failure occurs, only a small amount of very recent information is lost.

RAM and ROM

Semiconductor memory comes in two forms: random access memory (RAM) and read only memory (ROM). **Random access memory (RAM)** is general-purpose memory. It is used to store program instructions, data, and intermediate and final results from programs. RAM is easily and directly accessed by the CPU, acting as the machine's work space or scratch pad. It is user-programmable memory. A user can store information in RAM and read what is there, or erase the information as desired. RAM is volatile memory; information is stored there temporarily. The information is available only when electrical current is present or as long as the user is actively working on a larger machine.

The capacity of a computer, especially a microcomputer, is often determined by the amount of RAM it has available. The more RAM, the larger the programs and data that can be stored and processed. Early microcomputers contained between 4K and 16K of RAM. Many of today's micros come standard with 640K to 8 megabytes (8000K) of RAM.

If all the primary memory associated with the CPU were RAM, every time the machine was turned off or the power was interrupted the instructions required by the machine for its operation would be lost. As a result, a portion of primary memory containing vital operating instructions is protected on special chips. This portion of the primary memory is called **read only memory (ROM)** and is preprogrammed or manufacturer defined. The information placed in ROM is determined by the vendor and is part of the computer when it is manufactured. The user can read or gain access to the information stored in ROM but unlike RAM, cannot change it. ROM is often called *firmware*, because programs are held firm in memory and cannot be altered by the computer user. ROM chips are nonvolatile, require fewer circuits, and are faster and less expensive than RAM. In addition to governing the computer's start-up procedures, many microcomputers also include ROM chips that contain the BASIC programming language.

Some computer engineers and programmers need to store special programs in ROM. **Programmable read only memory,** or **PROM,** chips are designed for this purpose. PROM chips can be programmed only once. Once programmed, they act like standard ROM chips in that their information cannot be changed. If the program placed on a PROM chip contains an error, the error cannot be corrected without replacing the chip. To overcome this problem, some erasable PROM chips have been developed. **Erasable and programmable read only memory (EPROM)** chips must be removed from the computer and specially treated to remove the embedded instructions. Some EPROM chips are treated with ultraviolet light, and others are electronically erased. When these chips are inside a computer, they are nonvolatile and act like other ROM chips.

On Line

SUPERCONDUCTING TRANSISTORS

Researchers experimenting with superconductors (ceramic compounds that conduct electricity without a loss of energy) have been working hard to invent devices that could revolutionize the computer industry. Until the 1980s, super-conduction occurred only if the materials in question were cooled to temperatures approaching −460 degrees Fahrenheit. At this temperature the resistance and heat usually associated with the flow of electricity are virtually eliminated. To produce these low temperatures, materials must be supercooled by surrounding them with liquid helium.

In 1987, scientists experimenting with ceramic compounds rather than metallic alloys, found that superconduction could be produced at higher and higher temperatures (−283 degrees Fahrenheit). At these temperatures, super-conductive devices became feasible because liquid nitrogen can replace liquid helium, and liquid nitrogen is very inexpensive and long lasting. Using ceramic materials, high-temperature superconductors transmit electricity without resistance. Conventional electrical transmissions lose 20 percent of their energy to heat.

Researchers, however, have been frustrated by a phenomenon called magnetic flux creep. When superconducting materials are subjected to the strong magnetic fields needed to control the flow of electrical current, the magnetic flux drift unexpectedly, creating electrical resistance and destroying the superconducting nature of the materials.

Researchers at Sandia National Laboratories, in association with the University of Wisconsin-Madison, have incorporated this flux drift into newly designed circuits creating high-speed transistors. These new transistors performed better than traditional devices in recent tests. The new devices are called superconducting flux flow transistors (SFFT).

Sandia researchers have built a number of electronic devices using this technique. While they currently are quite large (measuring several feet on each side) scientists hope to make them more compact so that they can be replaced by a single small chip.

It is believed that the SFFT might provide the link between traditional electronic circuits and the Josephson Junction. Josephson Junctions are super-high–speed superconducting electronic "switches" designed in the 1980s by British Nobel Prize winner Brian Josephson.

Sources: Tim Beardsley, "Superconducting transistors show their speed," *Scientific American,* February 1991, p. 28. Michael D. Lemonick, "Superconductors!," *Time,* May 11, 1987, pp. 65–67.

NEW AND CHANGING TECHNOLOGIES

Scientists are constantly experimenting with ways of improving the CPU and primary memory. Despite the low cost and compact size of semiconductor technology, other systems are always being examined.

Parallel Computing

Most modern computers following the von Neumann design contain a single ALU and can perform only a single calculation or comparison at one time. Because the ALU performs its function with incredible speed, this limitation is generally not a problem. However, people working on very large and complex problems ranging from weather prediction to weapons research, which require vast numbers of computations and comparisons, find that this restriction hinders problem solving. Executing one instruction at a time is called the von Neumann bottleneck.

Computers containing more than one CPU can execute multiple instructions simultaneously. In some designs, each CPU has its own primary memory. In other systems, the multiple CPUs share a single large primary memory. In either case, such computers require very complex control units to keep track of their operations. Considerable research is going on in this field, which is called **parallel computing.**

Until recently, parallel computers, most often supercomputers, arranged the calculations to be performed as a list. Calculations are sent sequentially to a few very complex and expensive processors that work at incredible speeds. Companies such as Cray Research and NEC commonly build this type of supercomputer. Such parallel machines have been successfully used in aircraft design, oil and mineral exploration, long-range weather forecasting, computer circuit design and research, and the development and implementation of the military's laser weapons.

A new design called **massively parallel computers** distributes a problem's calculations across a very large number of independent, low-cost processors (similar to existing microprocessors). By carefully coordinating the processors, these new supercomputers can solve problems that seemed impossible only a few years ago. Massively parallel computers are produced by companies such as Thinking Machines Corp., Intel, and NCube (see Figure 3.7).

The popularity of these machines has led companies such as Cray Research to actively explore this new technology. Researchers feel that massively parallel computers could be used to simulate the human body's reaction to drugs, examine the effects of pollution on the environment, and understand natural or spoken language.

Optical Computing

As chip designers have placed more and more circuits onto their chips, they have come to realize that compaction has limits. The etched pathways must be large enough for electrons (the basic component of electricity) to move freely along the circuits. In addition, circuits must have sufficient insulation so that the charge along one pathway does not interfere with that on a nearby path. These limitations have stimulated considerable research into the use of optics (light) rather than electronics as the basis of future computer technology.

Figure 3.7   Thinking Machines' Connection Machine Model CM-200 uses thousands of processors operating in parallel to achieve peak processing speeds.

Optical computing could have a number of advantages. Light can move faster than electricity, making optical computing faster than electronic computing. Unlike electrons, photons (light's equivalent of electrons) do not react with each other. As a result, with optical systems there are no charged interactions between nearby pathways. Light circuits do not require insulation, so chips containing them can be more compact. Research indicates that thousands of light beams could travel through a lens at once. This would create a natural environment for massively parallel machines. In addition, light requires less energy to transmit data than electricity, and no heat is produced as a by-product.

AT&T's Bell Laboratories has made significant progress in optical computer technology. In 1987 Bell scientists developed the first optical switch or transistor called S-SEED (for Symmetric Self-Electro-optic Effects Device). Not only can this device be used to represent *bits* of information, it can also control the passage of information between existing electronic processors. In 1990, Bell scientists built the first **optical processor** using 128 S-SEED transistors and optical circuits (see Figure 3.8).

Figure 3.8   An optical computer will use light rather than electricity to process information. The AT&T prototype represents a new direction for computers.

Although this prototype could perform only very limited calculations, it could do so at speeds much faster than conventional electronic processors. While research into a fully functional optical processor continues, AT&T is focusing its current efforts on designing hybrid components. They hope to combine optical circuits that can transmit vast amounts of data very rapidly with electronic processors.

Optical mass storage devices are already changing the way information is stored on current electronic machines. These devices are discussed in Chapter 4.

As research continues, it is certain that optical components will be incorporated into computer technology with increasing frequency. By combining optics and electronics, computers will indeed help light the future.

Biological Chips

Researchers from diverse scientific disciplines are investigating the possibility of designing molecular chips using organic (molecules produced by living organisms) and inorganic (not from plants or animals) molecules. Molecular circuits would be significantly smaller (perhaps 1000 times smaller) than solid-state electronic circuits.

Building molecular chips would involve a considerable extension of current genetic engineering. Current research in the area has developed a molecular switch made of an inorganic substance that can change its electrical and optical properties when hit with a laser. This molecular switch would act like an electronic switch and store a single bit of data.

It is somewhat fanciful to imagine a time when enough is known about the structure of genes and the development of molecules that a self-assembling, possibly self-reproducing biological chip could be developed. Although such research makes us wonder about the future, it is a long way from changing the face of modern computers.

SUMMARY

The processor of a computer is made up of the central processing unit (CPU) and primary memory. The CPU consists of an **arithmetic and logic unit** (ALU) and a control unit.

The ALU performs the basic arithmetic functions of addition, subtraction, multiplication, and division. It is here that logical decisions using the mathematical operations of less than ($<$), greater than ($>$), and equal to ($=$) are performed. The **control unit** coordinates the internal activities of the computer.

Registers are very fast, mini-memory devices directly embedded in the CPU. They are used by the control unit and the ALU for temporary storage during the execution of instructions. There are four kinds of registers: accumulators, storage registers, address registers, and general-purpose registers.

Primary memory is associated with the CPU and stores instructions and data during processing. Secondary memory is outside the processor and is used for longer-term storage.

All characters must be coded in binary form before the computer can use them. The two most popular coding schemes are **ASCII (American Standard Code for Information Interchange)** and **EBCDIC (Extended Binary Coded Decimal Interchange Code)**. ASCII, a 7-bit code, is the standard for most minicomputers and all microcomputers. EBCDIC, an 8-bit code, is used on IBM mainframes. To ensure accurate transmission of data, a **parity** or check bit is added to ASCII and EBCDIC codes.

Each storage location in memory has a unique **address** that identifies its location. The contents or value of memory is the data stored at a particular address. Each memory location can store only a single item of data or a single instruction.

Programs are executed one instruction at a time. Four steps are required to execute each instruction: (1) the instruction is fetched from memory, (2) it is decoded, (3) the ALU performs the required operation, and (4) the results are stored in a memory device. The time required to perform steps 1 and 2 is **I-time**, or **instruction time,** and steps 3 and 4 comprise **E-time**, or **execution time.**

Early primary memory consisted of **magnetic core.** Although it was a nonvolatile storage medium, it was bulky and expensive to assemble. Current primary memory uses **semiconductor memory (RAM,** for **random access memory)** and consists of thousands of microscopic integrated circuits etched on a silicon chip. It is volatile, requiring continuous current to retain stored information. A portion of primary memory called **ROM,** for **read-only memory,** is composed of special nonvolatile chips containing vital operational instructions for the computer.

Computer technology is constantly changing. **Optical processors** are likely to alter the internal structure of the CPU, and molecular chips may alter the nature of primary memory. **Parallel computing,** which enables multiple instructions to be processed simultaneously, is altering the way instructions are processed.

Key Words

As an extra review of the chapter, try defining the following terms. If you have trouble with any of them, refer to the page number listed.

address *(82)*
American Standard Code for Information Interchange (ASCII) *(78)*
arithmetic and logic unit (ALU) *(75)*
bus *(78)*
control unit *(76)*
E-time (execution time) *(83)*
erasable and programmable read only memory (EPROM) *(86)*
Extended Binary Coded Decimal Interchange Code (EBCDIC) *(78)*
I-time (instruction time) *(83)*

magnetic core memory (core) *(84)*
massively parallel computer *(88)*
optical processor *(89)*
parallel computing *(88)*
parity (check bit) *(80)*
programmable read only memory (PROM) *(86)*
random access memory (RAM) *(86)*
read only memory (ROM) *(86)*
register *(76)*
semiconductor memory *(85)*

Test Your Knowledge

1. Name the four basic components of all computer systems.

2. What do the letters *CPU* stand for?

3. What is the function of the control unit?

4. List the four logical operations performed by the arithmetic and logic unit (ALU).

5. In addition to comparisons, what other operations does the ALU perform?

6. List three alternative names for primary memory.

7. List two of the names given to the memory not associated with the CPU.

8. How are registers different from primary memory?

9. How is a memory location like a mailbox? How does it differ?

10. Briefly describe the four steps involved in processing every computer instruction.

11. What are I-time and E-time?

12. Why were EBCDIC and ASCII developed?

13. Explain how a computer uses the parity bit to check for accurate data transmissions.

14. Using ASCII in an odd-parity system, code the letter *H* for transmission.

15. Using EBCDIC in an even-parity system, code the letter *I* for transmission.

16. Describe magnetic core memory.

17. Why is semiconductor memory volatile?

18. What is RAM? What is ROM?

19. Explain how PROM and EPROM chips differ from ROM chips.

20. How does parallel computing differ from more traditional computing?

Expand Your Knowledge

1. Research the ASCII system and determine the codes for all 128 characters. List each character and its corresponding code.
   (a) How many nonprinting symbols are coded?
   (b) Are uppercase characters less than or greater than lowercase characters?
   (c) How many printable, special characters are coded? What are they?

2. An early computer coding system was called Binary Coded Decimal (BCD) and it used a 4-bit code.
   (a) What was the system able to code? List the characters and the corresponding code.

(b) Why do you think it was necessary to increase the number of bits from 4 to 7 or 8?

(c) Is there a relationship between BCD and EBCDIC? If so what is it?

3. In the early 1980s, a number of toxic-waste sites were discovered in Silicon Valley in California. Write a short paper describing how Silicon Valley became polluted and what has been done to clean up the sites.

4. Write a short paper on the development of the superchip using wafer-scale integration.

5. Write a short paper on massively parallel computing. Focus on how this new architecture varies from the traditional von Neumann machine and how it differs from earlier parallel designs.

4

External Memory

CHAPTER OUTLINE

Most computers today contain both primary and secondary memory. You will recall from Chapter 3 that primary memory is linked directly to the CPU. It provides extremely fast access to information and very compact storage, but the expense of these two factors limits its usefulness. Computer manufacturers today must balance hardware costs against storage capability. As a result, primary memory is normally restricted to temporary storage of information.

External memory, or mass storage, is less expensive but provides slower access to information than primary memory. There is another difference as well. External memory is designed to store vast amounts of information for much longer periods of time. Capacity is critically important in external memory. This chapter examines external memory in detail.

After studying this chapter, you will be able to:

- Understand how computer files are organized.
- Be familiar with punched media.
- Identify the types of magnetic tape.
- Understand how data are stored and organized on magnetic media.
- Distinguish the different types of magnetic disks.
- Understand the importance of backup on computer systems.
- Discuss future storage technologies.

ORGANIZING INFORMATION

We are all familiar with storing information in a file cabinet. A file cabinet is filled with folders, each containing papers, records, or other kinds of related information. Each folder is labeled on the outside with a brief description of the contents. The folders are organized in some logical way so they can be located. They may be organized alphabetically based on the folder's label, or they may be stored by some key, such as the date on which the folder was created.

Information stored in a computer must also be organized so that it can be located when needed. A **data item** is a combination of characters, such as names, numbers, addresses, and dollar amounts, that, taken together, have meaning for people. Data items, often called **fields,** are combined to form larger units of meaningful information called **records,** such as mailing addresses or a student's grade report for a given semester. Records combine to form **files,** which are frequently read and processed as a single unit. In general then, information is stored in the computer's memory in the form of files (see Figure 4.1).

Files on a computer, just like files in a filing cabinet, are large units of information grouped together on the basis of similar characteristics. Examples of files are all student grades for a given semester, all cake recipes, or all tax information about a particular corporation.

Figure 4.1   Files are composed of smaller units of information such as records, which in turn contain data items (fields).

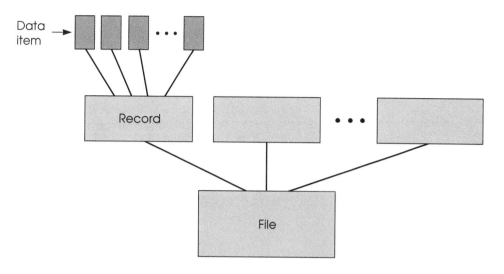

Just as there are different ways to organize file folders in a file cabinet—such as alphabetic, chronological, and geographic—there are different methods of organizing files on a computer. The three most popular methods are: sequential file organization, direct access file organization, and indexed file organization.

Sequential File Organization

This method stores information in some predetermined order. Records can be ordered by a key, such as a social security number or an ID number, or information can be stored as it becomes available. To find a given record, the entire file must be searched in order or sequence from the beginning. Each stored item must be checked until the requested record is located. Magnetic tape is the most popular medium for sequential storage, although magnetic disks can be used. This technique is very efficient for files that are processed at regular intervals or when most of the stored information can be processed at once. Examples include payroll processing, in which every employee is issued a paycheck at regular intervals, and student billing, in which bills are issued to most students each semester.

Direct Access File Organization

Using this method, information can be stored in any order, including sequentially. Each record has a unique address, enabling the computer to locate each record in the same amount of time. Information can be located directly without the user's having to examine other records. Magnetic disks are the common media used for storing such files. Direct access file organization is critical when instant access to information is important. For example, airline reservation systems require quick access to stored information, as do course registration programs and programs that let customers check their current bank balances.

Indexed File Organization

Indexed file organization combines both sequential and direct access storage techniques. Information is stored sequentially, and each record has a key or index associated with it. Each key is linked with an address that can be used to locate the record directly. This method allows files to be processed either sequentially or directly. For example, insurance companies use sequential files to process customer bills at regular intervals. To handle customer inquiries properly, these firms need direct access to the stored information. They use magnetic disks to locate records directly.

PAPER MEDIA

The oldest form of mass storage is the **computer (punched) card** shown in Figure 4.2. Sometimes called IBM cards or Hollerith cards, they use a data storage device attributed to Herman Hollerith, who created a punched card tabulating machine (see Chapter 2). These cards continued in popular use until the late 1970s.

Each card is 80 columns long, and each column can record a single character. Digits and uppercase letters are represented by one or more holes punched in each column. Characters punched in a given column can be printed in the space above the column so that people, as well as computers, can read the information. Many second- and third-generation programming languages such as FORTRAN and BASIC restricted their statements to 80 columns or less, reflecting their card-oriented origins. When cards were popular, they were relatively inexpensive and provided virtually unlimited storage capacity, but they were not only very slow to read and punch but also bulky and easily damaged.

Another kind of paper medium, **punched paper tape,** was used in the 1940s and even later with teletype machines. Paper tape was experimented with as an input, output, and storage device for computers in the 1960s and early 1970s. The tape was a one-inch-wide continuous strip of paper on which information could be stored as a unique pattern of holes punched across the tape's width. Paper tape did not restrict information to a fixed number of characters and could be viewed as an infinitely long punched card. While paper tape was inexpensive, it was not as durable as cards, and correcting errors was very difficult.

Figure 4.2   The Computer Card: This data storage device remained in popular use until the late 1970s.

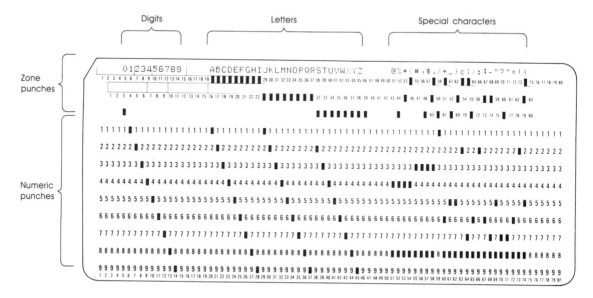

A paper medium stores data sequentially. To retrieve data stored in the middle of a stack of cards or a roll of paper tape, all preceding material must be read into the computer, and the data are compared to the requested data. When no match occurs, the data are ignored. The primary drawback of paper medium was its slow processing speed. Input/output (I/O) speeds were very slow when sequential storage was combined with the very low storage density of the data. The CPU sat idle for significant periods of time while waiting for data to enter and exit the machine. Additional disadvantages stemmed from the paper itself: the punched medium was easily damaged, cumbersome, and not reusable.

MAGNETIC TAPE

Magnetic tape is used to store data in much the same way that audio tape records sound. Magnetic data tapes vary from $\frac{1}{2}$ to $\frac{1}{8}$ inch in width and come in different designs, a number of which are shown in Figure 4.3.

1. *Reel-to-reel tape.* This tape is usually $\frac{1}{2}$ inch in width, is used predominantly on mainframes, and typically stores 1600 characters per inch.

2. *Cartridge tape.* This tape is usually $\frac{1}{4}$ inch in width, is used mostly on minicomputers, and stores approximately 400 characters per inch.

Figure 4.3 Two Varieties of Magnetic Tape: (a) reel-to-reel tape and (b) cartridge tape.

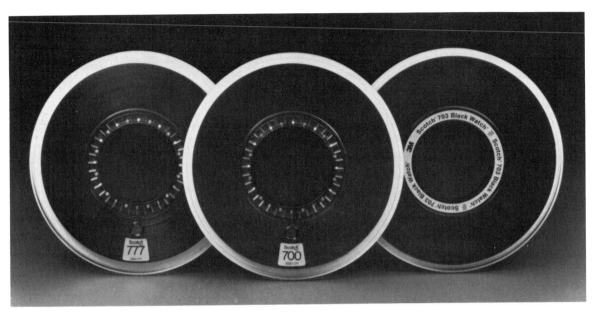

(a)

(b)

Hardware

Computer Systems

The IBM PS/2 Model L40 SX is a briefcase-sized laptop as powerful as a desktop computer. (IBM)

The SPARCstation. (Sun Microsystems, Inc.)

The Mac IIFX uses the Macintosh operating system. (Apple Computer, Inc.)

The IBM PS/2 Model 90XP 486 can run under DOS or OS/2. (IBM)

The DEC VAX 9000 minicomputer, sometimes called a supermini.

(Digital Equipment Corp.)

The IBM ES/9000 mainframe computer can serve hundreds of users at one time. (IBM)

The Connection Machine is a massively parallel supercomputer that can execute billions of instructions per second.

(Thinking Machines Corp.)

Input Devices

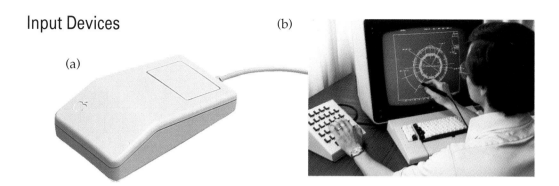

(a)

(b)

Some graphic input devices are (a) the mouse, used to drag images across the screen (Apple Computer, Inc.); (b) a lightpen, used to draw images directly on the screen (IBM); (c) a digitizer (IBM); and (d) a graphics tablet, used to transfer images from a surface to the screen (IBM).

(c)

(d)

Printers

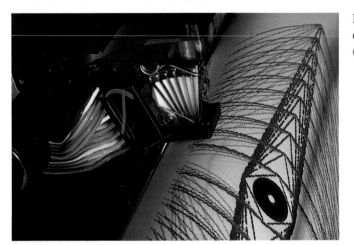

Inkjet plotters spray "jets" of ink onto paper.
(Ken Whitmore/BASF)

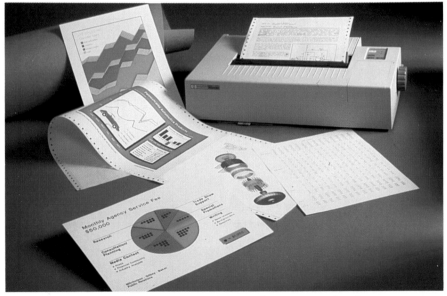

Laser printers are the most advanced type of printing technology.
(Hewlett Packard)

3. *Cassette tape.* This tape is identical to cassette audio tape, is usually ⅛ inch in width, is used on some microcomputers, and stores 200 characters per inch.

4. *8mm (Exabyte) tape.* This tape uses VHS videotape technology, is heavily used on minicomputers and workstations, and stores 2.3 *gigabytes* (2.3 billion bytes or characters) of data on a single tape.

5. *Digital Audio Tape (DAT).* DAT tapes use the same technology as DAT audio tapes and store 1 gigabyte of data. DATs provide the most reliable tape storage technology currently available.

Magnetic tape is made of a strong plastic (Mylar) coated on one side with an iron oxide that can be magnetized. Data are stored as microscopic magnetized dots that are created, read, or erased by a magnetic tape unit, or recorder.

Data Organization

Magnetic tape is divided along its length into parallel *tracks,* or *channels,* and across its width into *frames,* as Figure 4.4 shows.

Figure 4.4   Magnetic Tape: Data are stored on magnetic tape in tracks and frames. Here, arrows pointing up represent binary ones, arrows down represent zeroes.

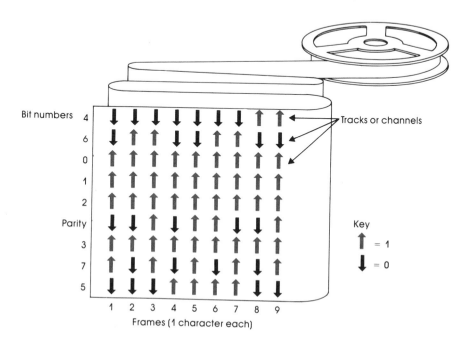

Each frame stores a single character (or byte) using one of the standard coding schemes such as EBCDIC or ASCII (see Chapter 3). Combinations of characters form fields, while related fields combine to form **logical records.** A logical record, for example, could contain information about a particular student: name, social security number, local address, and student ID number. Records can vary in size, reflecting the nature of the information stored. A piece of blank tape called an **interrecord gap (IRG)** is used to separate logical records

---

Figure 4.5   Records and Blocks: Logical records must be separated by interrecord gaps (IRGs) or interblock gaps (IBGs) on magnetic tape to be individually accessible.

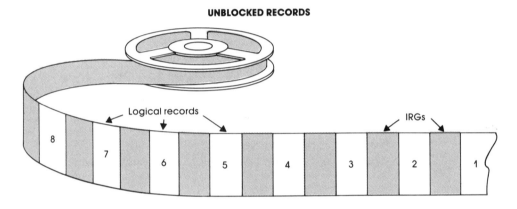

for processing. However, these gaps result in a great deal of unused tape and considerably increase processing time. Whenever an IRG is encountered, reading stops so that the record can be processed.

To increase data storage and decrease processing time, a number of logical records are usually combined to form a **physical record,** or **block.** A block is a group of logical records that are read and processed at once. Once read in, software divides the blocks into logical records. Each block is separated by a section of blank tape called an **interblock gap (IBG),** as shown in Figure 4.5.

Like paper medium, magnetic tape is sequential storage, and searching for information stored on the tape can be time consuming. Unlike paper, however, magnetic tape is compact and highly portable. It is relatively inexpensive and is best suited to data that are processed sequentially such as payroll, billing, and computer backup. Magnetic tape can easily be erased and reused. However, it is subject to damage by frequent handling and environmental conditions such as humidity and dust.

MAGNETIC DISKS

The most widespread form of mass storage is the **magnetic disk** or **hard disk,** which is a direct access storage device. It was first marketed by IBM in 1956 but did not come into common use until the mid 1960s. Its popularity stems from its large storage capacity and the computer's ability to get information to and from the disk very rapidly. Information can be retrieved from disk in less than 0.001 second. Because of their retrieval speeds, magnetic disks are popular for most computer applications. They are especially useful when speed is necessary, as in making airline reservations, conducting banking operations, and forecasting the weather.

A magnetic disk is a flat plate made of plastic or metal that looks somewhat like a phonograph record. Hard disks range in size from 14 inches down to 3 inches in diameter. A **disk pack** is a number of disks stacked together on a single spindle, similar to phonograph records. The number of disks in a disk pack varies from 2 to 12.

Both sides (surfaces) of the disk are coated with a magnetizable compound on which (like magnetic tape) data are stored as magnetized dots. Disk drives have movable **access arms,** which read information from the disks. These arms are similar to the playing arm of a phonograph, which holds the needle. Disk packs have multiple access arms that extend between the disks. Each access arm has a separate read/write head for each recording surface. A **read/write head** is a tiny electromagnet that can create, read, or erase the magnetic dots that store information on the surface of a disk. The topmost and bottommost surfaces of the stacked disks are often unused when recording information because they are easily damaged (see Figure 4.6).

Figure 4.6   Read/Write Heads and Access Arms.

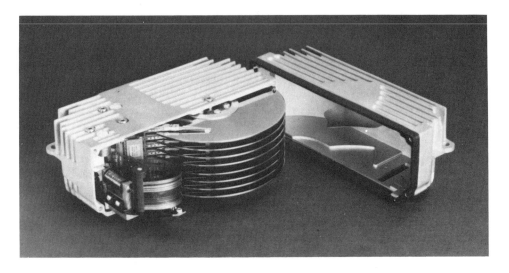

Data Organization

Each disk surface is divided into tracks similar to a phonograph record. However, a phonograph record has one continuous track running from the outer edge to the center, whereas magnetic disks are divided into a series of concentric circles (one inside the other), each of which is a separate track. The magnetized dots representing ones and zeros are stored along the tracks. Standard coding schemes such as ASCII or EBCDIC are used to code characters. Data stored on magnetic disks are **addressable,** which means that each record has its own unique storage location or address, similar to a street address. For example, a family living at 23 Main Street, Clearfield, has an address that describes the location of their residence. They reside in the community of Clearfield and at the house numbered 23 on Main Street. In much the same way, a disk address uniquely describes the location of a record. The two common disk addressing methods are the sector method and the cylinder method.

The Sector Method   The most common sector technique divides each track into an equal number of pieces or *sectors,* much like slices of a pie.

Each sector holds an equal number of characters. The tracks closest to the center are smaller than those near the outer edge, and the number of characters in each sector is limited by the centermost sectors. This technique wastes valuable storage space. An alternative technique uses equal-sized sectors, with different tracks having different numbers of sectors.

Figure 4.7   The Sector Method of Disk Addressing.

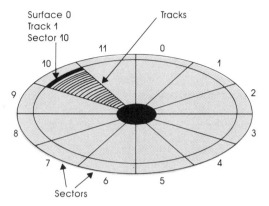

Surface 0
Track 1
Sector 10

Tracks

Sectors

The sector method makes storing and retrieving information straightforward. An address is defined by a surface number, track number, and sector number. This method is used on single disks, diskettes, and some disk packs (see Figure 4.7).

The Cylinder Method   The cylinder method was developed to reduce **seek time,** the time it takes to find information on a disk, using the sector method. On all disk packs, all the disks revolve around the spindle at the same rate, all the tracks are aligned so that track 101 on surface 4 is directly above track 101 on surface 6, and all the access arms move in unison. Rather than recording information track-by-track on one surface before moving on to the next surface, information is stored on a track on one disk surface, then on the same track on the next surface, and so on, until every disk surface has the same track filled. Only then does the access arm move on to fill the next track out (see Figure 4.8).

The effect is to create a cylinder of stored information. Because of the positioning of all the read/write heads, a single movement of the access arms makes significantly more information available. Thus seek time is reduced. Using the cylinder method, information can be retrieved without the constant, time-consuming motion of the access arms. An address is defined in the cylinder method by a cylinder number, a surface number, and a record number. This method is used on most hard disk systems.

FLOPPY DISKS

A second direct access storage device is the **floppy disk,** or **diskette,** a small, single disk used mostly with microcomputers. When first released in the early

Figure 4.8   The Cylinder Method of Disk Addressing.

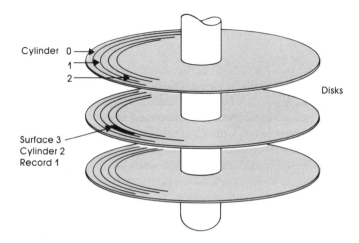

1970s, it was 8 inches in diameter. Today floppy disks are commonly available in $5\frac{1}{4}$-inch and in $3\frac{1}{2}$-inch diameter. Both are manufactured in standard and high-density varieties (more compact, larger capacity storage on the same size disk). The $5\frac{1}{4}$-inch variety looks like a 45 RPM audio record encased in a flexible plastic envelope (see Figure 4.9). If held by a corner and shaken slightly, it flops or bends without being damaged. This is how the diskettes got their name. The $3\frac{1}{2}$-inch disks come in a hard plastic case for protection. They do not flop.

Floppy disks are popular because they are reliable and inexpensive, costing less than half a dollar each if purchased in bulk. The $5\frac{1}{4}$-inch disks are already being replaced by the $3\frac{1}{2}$-inch disks, which store more data in a safer, more reliable package.

WINCHESTER DISKS

The **Winchester disk** was developed by IBM in the 1970s and is said to be named for the famed Winchester rifle. In Winchester technology, the disks, access arms, and read/write heads are sealed in an airtight container. This feature keeps the components free from dust, moisture, and other airborne contaminants and increases the disks' reliability. Since Winchester technology is more precise than other disk technology, storage and retrieval speeds and storage capacity are increased. Winchester disks are usually fixed, which means they

Figure 4.9   Floppy Disks: (a) Floppy disks are mass storage devices that come in different sizes (3½-inch and 5¼-inch) and (b) have various parts.

(a)

(b)

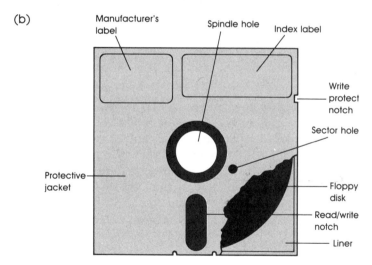

cannot be removed from their drives. The drive is the hardware that spins the disk and includes the read/write heads and arms. Recent advances have developed cartridgelike Winchester disks that can be removed along with the access arms. Removable Winchester disks are very expensive, however. Winchester disks are direct access storage devices originally designed to be used with minicomputers and mainframes (14-inch disks). Their storage capacity continues to increase as their price declines. Winchester disks, often simply called hard

Figure 4.10   Winchester Disks: A direct access mass storage device. This $2\frac{1}{2}$-inch disk is so compact that it fits inside a Faberge egg.

disks, are now the storage device of choice on all microcomputers. Manufacturers have developed large capacity $5\frac{1}{4}$- and $3\frac{1}{2}$-inch varieties (see Figure 4.10).

Until the early 1980s, most disk systems used removable disk packs with retractable access arms. Winchester disks had replaced most other hard disk technologies by 1987, largely because they are more reliable and less expensive.

On Line

*T*HE NeXT COMPUTER

Without a crystal ball, few people would try to predict what computers will be like through the 1990s. Yet, in late 1988, Steven Jobs did just that. He introduced a computer he called "the machine for the '90s."

Jobs is a cofounder of Apple Computer. In 1985, he was pressured to leave Apple, where he had been the moving force behind the development of the Apple II and the Macintosh. Jobs started a new computer company called NeXT and began working on his vision of the computer of the future.

The NeXT machine, fondly called The Cube, is a workstation based on a state-of-the-art Motorola microprocessor chip. Added to this is a high-speed math chip to help process decimals, and specially designed VLSI chips to control input and output. Primary memory consists of eight megabytes of RAM. Initially, the Cube's mass storage device was the first application of an erasable, removable, replaceable *optical* disk capable of storing 256 megabytes of data, equivalent to more than 300 floppy disks.

All this power is housed in a one-foot by one-foot cube designed to sit on the floor or on a nearby shelf. The Cube is connected to a keyboard by a long cable. The Cube also contains a full-featured stereo sound system.

Impressive in-house developed software accompanies The Cube's dramatic hardware. The NeXT computer uses the UNIX operating system. Since many people find UNIX hard to use, Jobs has created a Macintosh-like graphical interface making it friendlier. Applications software includes a word processor, a personal data base, the Sound and Music Kit, an electronic (including voice) mail system, an electronic dictionary, a thesaurus, a book of quotations, and the complete works of Shakespeare.

Despite all of its impressive hardware and vendor-supplied software, initial sales of the NeXT Machine were poor. At an original asking price of between $6,500–$10,000 the "black box" couldn't make inroads into the student market where microcomputers could be purchased under $2,000. They weren't as flashy, but they did the job. Users found the optical drive much too slow, and the lack of floppy drives or a standard hard drive made backups and developing software difficult. Many of these drawbacks have since been corrected.

Many still view Jobs' vision as a pipe-dream. As *PC WEEK* describes it, "The vision simply was to build a big black cube, a cube that would do everything one would expect such a magical box to do: paint, talk, sing, unfurl the great literature of the world at a finger's touch, crunch numbers . . . , simplify the art of programming and spawn effortless connections with other networks and computers." Yet, Jobs has been a miracle worker before. The first Macintosh, like the initial NeXT, was an idea in search of a market. For many the Macintosh has become the "computer for the rest of us," as Jobs described it.

The release of the NeXT Dimension color workstation may change Jobs' tarnished image. Its graphics processor is far superior to that of any other microcomputer. Adobe is working on a NeXT version of its image-editing program PhotoShop. Lotus 1-2-3 has a special version of its famous spreadsheet that makes use of the power and potential of the Cube, called Improv. Similarly, WordPerfect, FrameMaker, WingZ, and Adobe Illustrator are already available. For users who cannot easily do without their DOS environment, SoftPC, a DOS emulation package, is available for the NeXT as it is for the Macintosh.

It may take time yet before Jobs' "black box" is "the machine for the '90s." But no significant advance comes without a price. Slow sales on early NeXT machines may be the price for innovation, and the re-invention of the personal computer.

Sources: Fred David, "Market Problems Aside, the NeXT Cube Is a Visionary Product," *PC WEEK*, April 29, 1991, p. 138. T. Thompson and N. Baran, "The NeXT Computer," *Byte*, November 1988, pp. 158–175.

OPTICAL STORAGE

Since the arrival of the home video disk in the late 1970s, significant research has focused on developing a similar optical technology for use with computers. Optical disks have a number of advantages over their magnetic cousins. Optical technology provides high-capacity data storage, storing hundreds of times more data than comparably sized magnetic disks. Billions of characters can be stored on each recording surface. Because only light touches the surface of optical disks, they are relatively insensitive to such environmental factors as dust, moisture, and localized magnetic fields that would damage magnetic media and their drives.

Although optical storage is a fairly recent invention, it already has had three distinct "generations." Like computer history, each generation is identified by a significant change in the overall technology. The first-generation format was read only. The next phase produced disks that were write-once. Once written by the user, they became read only. Recent developments (third generation) have produced an optical storage method that, like the more popular magnetic medium, is truly a read/write design.

Optical technology holds the promise of revolutionizing mass storage in much the way it has revolutionized the recording industry.

CD-ROM (Compact Disc Read Only Memory)

The first stage in the development of optical storage came about in the late 1970s. Philips, the Dutch electronics firm, in association with Sony, produced a *read only* medium that uses the same technology found in audio compact disc players. Called **CD-ROM,** for **Compact Disc Read Only Memory,** this is a highly compact, removable, optical storage medium, storing up to 660 MB (megabytes) per disk. (See Figure 4.11.)

On CD-ROMs, information is unchangeable and thus highly secure. Unfortunately, because updates are impossible, the medium's usefulness is limited.

To produce CD-ROM disks, a master disk is first prepared. Using a high-powered laser, bubbles or pits are formed on a reflecting surface. From the master, a mold is produced. This mold is used to stamp out copies on plastic disks. These plastic disks are then coated with a thin layer of aluminum and encased in clear glass or plastic for protection. To read the data, a low-power laser beam moves across the disk and is deflected differently when pits, bubbles, or other surface changes are encountered. These surface changes can be interpreted as bits.

CD-ROM disks are such a compact form of storage that the entire *Encyclopedia Britannica* can be stored on a single disk. When produced in volume, CD-ROMs are very economical. Many computer manufacturers use them to distribute operating systems and other system software. NYNEX has made the New York City metropolitan area white pages available in this format. Hundreds of

Figure 4.11   Optical Disks: Inexpensive optical disks such as this from Sony can hold 250,000 pages of data.

commercial CD-ROMs are available, including dictionaries, encyclopedias, financial publications, and computer games. Potential storage possibilities for CD-ROM appear limitless. Distributors of large data bases are seriously considering this medium. It presents an enormous potential for storing and retrieving a combination of text, graphics, and photographic images.

WORM (Write Once Read Many)

A number of American, Japanese, and European companies have developed *write once* and then *read only* optical computer disks. This advance represents the second generation in optical disk technology. The user is provided with the ability to determine what is stored on the disk. **WORMs** use the same technology as CD-ROM except that the WORM drive contains both the high-power laser used in burning the pits in the disk's surface and the low-power laser used in reading them.

WORMs have an extremely high-density storage capacity. They are especially well suited for storing such information as archival files and the accounting and tax information generated by large businesses and government agencies. In general, the use of this medium is limited to the storage of fairly permanent information. The large capacity of WORMs, and their write once feature, enables users to add data to the disk to reflect changes.

Although WORM storage is somewhat more flexible than CD-ROM, it is much more expensive because such disks are not mass reproduced as part of a distribution process. WORMs are used only where the amount of data to be stored makes the less expensive, but less compact, magnetic medium somewhat inappropriate.

Magneto-Optical Technology

The third generation of optical storage is the **magneto-optical disk.** This technology combines lasers with a magnetic recording medium. To record data on a disk, a high-powered laser momentarily heats a spot on the disk's metal surface without burning a pit. Simultaneously, a magnet causes the surface of the heat-sensitive disk to be charged in one of two directions representing a bit of data. These bits are read by passing a low-powered laser, much like those used by CD-ROM drives, over the disk. This low-powered laser can identify the charged spots. Writing, rewriting, and erasing are done by repeating this procedure.

Reusable optical computer disks have potentially widespread applications. Matsushita Electric, 3M Corp., and other companies have developed rewritable,

Figure 4.12   Magneto-optical disks are reusable, removable disks that combine lasers with a magnetic recording surface. Shown is a model by NeXT that is no longer in production.

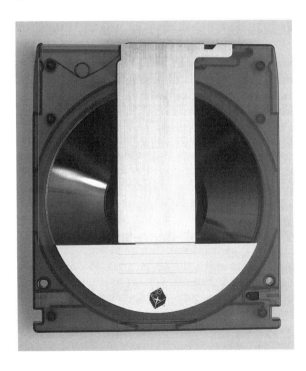

removable optical disks. These disks have important advantages over traditional magnetic disks. Winchester disks are fixed and cannot be easily removed. This limits storage capacity. Magneto-optical disks are designed to be removed and exchanged. This provides essentially unlimited storage capacity, while enabling data to be shared between machines. Furthermore, magneto-optical disks are high-density disks storing as much as 650 megabytes of data on a single sealed cartridge. Very large-capacity Winchester disks store only 120 megabytes. Like CD-ROM, magneto-optical disks are exceptionally reliable because nothing touches the disk except light.

However, magneto-optical disks have limitations. Although magneto-optical drives retrieve data at speeds as much as five times faster than CD-ROM drives, they are four to six times slower than traditional Winchester technology. Moreover, magneto-optical technology remains quite expensive, so users favor the much less expensive magnetic medium. It is expected that improvements in speed and price will make this optical technology appealing. However, magnetic disks are also expected to improve. NeXT Corporation is so enthusiastic about this technology that early NeXT machines came equipped with a removable, magneto-optical disk drive (see Figure 4.12). NeXT makes disks available to its customers at very reasonable prices. The speed of the magneto-optical drive has been one of the primary drawbacks of the NeXT machine, and NeXT has been forced to make traditional hard disks available.

Magneto-optical technology has significant potential and may eventually become a significant player in the mass-storage market. In situations where large amounts of removable storage are essential, magneto-optical disks will play a significant role.

BACKUP

When computers break down or lose power, or when their software fails to operate as expected, data are lost. To reduce the risk of losing large amounts of information, **backup,** or duplicate, copies of the information stored in memory are periodically made. Backup is a safety measure. The more critical the information stored on a computer, the more frequently backup copies need to be made. A **full backup** is a complete copy of all the data stored in memory at a given time. A **partial backup** is a copy of those data items that have changed over a given period of time. If the computer does **crash,** or break down, the information stored in memory prior to the crash can be reproduced by using the backup files. Some data may be lost because backup copies are not always current, but the last and the most recent items entered are generally the easiest to re-create.

The most popular medium for backup is magnetic tape. Here its sequential nature is not a disadvantage, because everything stored on the backup tape will be needed to restore the lost information to memory. Easy storage, low cost, and reusability are added advantages. WORM storage is also used for *archiving* data that needs to be retained for long periods.

Information stored on microcomputer disks can just as easily, if not more easily, be lost than that found on the mass storage devices of larger systems. Making duplicates of floppy disks and using tape or floppy disks to back up hard disks are essential if microcomputer programs and data are to be protected from unexpected losses.

NEAR-FUTURE TECHNOLOGIES

Despite the incredible speeds and storage capacities of today's computers, current hardware research is seeking to increase significantly both the storage capacity and the operating speeds of computers.

Perpendicular Recording

Current disk technology stores information as magnetic dots along tracks on the surface of the disk. These magnetic dots (microscopic magnets) are oblong in shape and are stored end-to-end in a straight line. Japanese and American researchers, such as those at Toshiba, have developed **perpendicular recording** techniques for reorienting the tiny magnets so that they lie perpendicular to the recording surface (see Figure 4.13).

By turning the magnetized dots 90 degrees, up to 100 times more data can be stored. Finding magnetic materials that will allow data to be recorded in this form has been difficult. Barium ferrite, often used in the manufacture of permanent magnets, has proved an effective and reasonably priced magnetic mate-

Figure 4.13   Magnetic Storage: (a) In traditional magnetic storage, oblong dots are stored end to end. (b) In perpendicular magnetic storage, dots lie perpendicular to the recording surface, and 100 times more information can be stored.

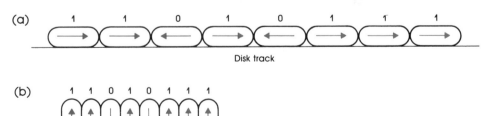

rial. Production costs are dropping, and in 1990 Toshiba released a $3\frac{1}{2}$-inch extra-high density disk that records data perpendicularly. This disk can store up to four times more data than a standard floppy disk. This technology continues to be expensive. Since such disks are not yet common, perpendicular disk technology holds the promise of smaller, more compact magnetic disks.

Holographic Storage

Holography is a method of storing data by making a two- or three-dimensional photograph on a crystalline storage medium. Most current, experimental, holographic storage commonly displays data as adjacent images on a single large crystal. By creating the image inside a crystal, the image is not distorted by dust and other environmental contaminants in the air.

Holograms are formed when two related laser beams reflecting the same image (a reference beam and an object beam) intersect. Researchers at the University of Alabama, Huntsville, are experimenting with compact, high-density, page-oriented holographic memory (POHM). POHMs can store more than a gigabyte of data on a single page. It is hoped that these "pages" can be stored and accessed in parallel, supplying the type of storage critical to the massively parallel, optical computing systems of the future. Equally important, such holographic systems could provide the basis for true neural networks—optical computing systems that mimic the operation of the human brain.

A small Texas company called Microelectronics and Computer Technology Corporation has constructed a working prototype of holographic storage capable of storing up to a gigabyte of data. The company has patented a number of component devices, including one that uses an array of tiny crystals to store data rather than the traditional single large crystal. The advantage of this array technique is that it prevents interference between adjacent holographic images that exist within the same crystal. This multiple crystal design is also less expensive to produce. The storage capacity of this crystalline array is essentially the same as that of single crystal devices. With Microelectronics' patented process for regenerating holographic patterns, images are not destroyed after multiple "reads" of the data image.

Researchers believe that holographic storage can be inexpensively made for use with computers, high-definition TV, and video and audio recordings. As with other optical storage, holographic storage using lasers may be the light that records the future.

SUMMARY

Information is stored in the computer's memory in the form of **files.** Locating information in a sequentially organized file requires the user to search the entire file from the beginning until the information is found. Direct access file organization uniquely addresses information so that the user can locate it easily without having to examine other data. Indexed file organization uses features from both sequential and direct access organization. Files are sequentially stored, and information is addressed for easy access.

The oldest form of mass storage is the **computer card,** on which characters are stored in the form of holes punched in paper cards. **Paper tape** stores characters as holes punched in a continuous one-inch strip of paper.

Magnetic tape stores information as magnetized dots along the surface of the tape. Coded information forms **logical records** that are processed as a unit. To increase the storage capacity of the tape, logical records are combined into blocks, or **physical records.** Magnetic tape is highly portable, inexpensive, and reusable, but must be processed sequentially.

A **magnetic disk** is a flat platter with magnetized dots storing information on tracks. **Records** are individually addressed for easy access. Addresses can be defined using sectors or cylinders. **Floppy disks** are used predominantly on microcomputers. A **Winchester disk** is a device containing disks and access hardware sealed in a container to protect the contents from damage by airborne contaminants.

Optical storage comes in three formats. **CD-ROM** is a highly compact, *read only* medium that uses the same technology as that found in audio compact disc players. High-powered lasers are used to burn pits in the disk that represent bits. **WORM** disks are *write once* and then *read only* optical computer disks employing the same technology as CD-ROM. With WORMs, the user determines what is stored on the disk. The third type of high-density, optical storage is the **magneto-optical disk,** which combines lasers with a magnetic recording medium. Lasers heat the disk's surface, while a magnet causes the surface of the heat-sensitive disk to be charged in one of two directions representing a bit.

Backup is a safety technique whereby stored data are usually duplicated either on magnetic tapes or floppy disks.

Current research on memory devices is focusing on increasing storage capacity. **Perpendicular recording** realigns the magnetized dots of data stored on disks. **Holography** is a method of storing data by making a two- or three-dimensional photograph on a crystalline storage medium.

Key Words

As an extra review of the chapter, try defining the following terms. If you have trouble with any of them, refer to the page number listed.

access arm *(103)*	computer (punched) card *(98)*
addressable *(104)*	crash *(113)*
backup *(113)*	data item *(96)*
CD-ROM *(110)*	disk pack *(103)*

field *(96)*
file *(96)*
floppy disk (diskette) *(106)*
full backup *(113)*
holography *(115)*
interblock gap (IBG) *(103)*
interrecord gap (IRG) *(102)*
logical record *(102)*
magnetic (hard) disk *(103)*
magnetic tape *(99)*

magneto-optical disk *(112)*
partial backup *(113)*
perpendicular recording *(114)*
physical record (block) *(103)*
punched paper tape *(98)*
read/write head *(103)*
record *(96)*
seek time *(105)*
Winchester disk *(106)*
WORM *(111)*

Test Your Knowledge

1. What is a computer file?

2. Briefly describe the differences between sequential, direct access, and indexed file organization.

3. How was information stored on punched cards?

4. List the five types of magnetic tape.

5. What is the difference between logical and physical records on magnetic tape?

6. Briefly explain how data are stored on magnetic tape.

7. Why is it often necessary to block data on magnetic tape?

8. What is a disk pack?

9. Briefly explain how data are stored on magnetic disks.

10. Define *addressable*.

11. How is an address defined using the sector method of disk addressing?

12. How is an address defined using the cylinder method of disk addressing?

13. How does a floppy disk differ from a hard disk?

14. What are the advantages of Winchester disks over disk packs with retractable access arms?

15. How do CD-ROMs differ from WORMs?

16. Why is backup necessary on computer systems?

17. What is the difference between a full and a partial backup?

18. What are the advantages of magneto-optical disk technology over magnetic disks?

19. How does perpendicular storage of data on magnetic disks differ from the standard storage techniques?

20. Why are holograms of interest to computer memory designers?

Expand Your Knowledge

1. Identify 15 applications areas (excluding those listed in the text) where sequential, direct access, and indexed file organization would be appropriate (five for each). For example, direct access files are used for airline reservations.

2. Compare the capacities and capabilities of Winchester disks with magneto-optical disks. Why do you feel that NeXT has included optical disks with some of its machines? If price were no object, which would you buy? Why?

3. Write a brief paper on backing up a hard disk on a microcomputer. Include why such backups are necessary, how they are performed, and information about the different media that can be used for such backups.

4. Write a brief paper on one application of superconductivity to computing. Use at least two sources.

5. What is cellular mass storage? How does it differ from other forms of magnetic storage? What are its advantages and its disadvantages?

5

Input and Output

CHAPTER OUTLINE

119

Computers are all around us. We use them so often in our daily lives that we may take them for granted. The way we purchase our groceries and do our banking is heavily influenced by computers. However, we often confuse the computer with the devices we've created to communicate with it. These devices are designed to make working with computers more natural and comfortable. Input and output devices often are responsible for much of the computer's mystique.

The hardware devices attached to a computer are usually referred to as **peripherals** or **peripheral devices.** This connected but external equipment includes input, output, and mass storage devices. Mass storage devices were discussed in detail in Chapter 4, so we will focus here on the other devices we attach to computers. Many peripherals are dedicated to either input or output (see Figure 5.1).

However, modern peripherals are often combination devices that may contain input, output, and memory components.

After studying this chapter, you will be able to:

- Understand what peripherals are.

- Identify dedicated input or output devices.

- Discuss various keyboard alternatives.

- Understand the major types and uses of computer monitors.

- Distinguish impact printers from non-impact printers.

- Describe different types of terminals.

- Understand voice technology and print recognition devices.

- Appreciate the role of input and output devices in assisting the handicapped.

- Discuss common combination systems used by stores and banks.

DEDICATED INPUT DEVICES

In Chapter 1, we defined *input* as the data entered into the computer for processing. This can be either the initial, raw data gathered or it can be the result of previous processing. *Output* was defined as the information, or result of computer processing. An **input device** is computer hardware that transmits data to the computer. An **output device** is computer hardware that communicates the results of computer operations. A *dedicated* device (input or output) is one that can <u>only</u> be used to either enter input into the computer or to produce output. People use both input and output devices to communicate with computers.

Keyboards

Modern keyboards are designed to suit the changing needs of users. Despite an increasing array of alternative input devices, the **keyboard** continues to be the most commonly used means of entering data and instructions into a computer system.

While keyboard layouts differ somewhat from manufacturer to manufacturer, they all have the same basic features (see Figure 5.2). Most keyboards

Figure 5.1 Computer Peripherals: Modern peripherals often combine input, output, and memory components.

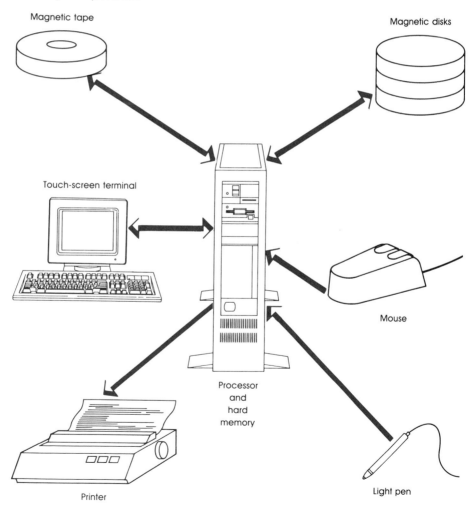

Figure 5.2   Modern Keyboards: Although differing somewhat from one manufacturer to another, modern keyboards such as the (a) IBM PC/enhanced keyboard, the (b) Macintosh extended keyboard, and the (c) Macintosh Classic standard keyboard all have the same basic features.

(a)

(b)

(c)

contain the following:

1. *The standard typewriter keys.* These keys include a number line at the top and the necessary shift keys for uppercase and lowercase letters.

2. *A numeric keypad.* This resembles the number layout on a hand calculator. Number pads make entering large amounts of numeric data fast and easy.

3. *Special keys.* These keys include CTRL, ESC, BREAK, and others, which are required to communicate with the computer. Keyboards on intelligent terminals, workstations, and most microcomputers have additional keys, called **function keys,** that can be programmed through the built-in microprocessor to perform specific tasks independent of the main computer.

4. *Arrow keys.* On a typewriter, the typehead moves across each line as we type. A marker indicates the position of the next character to be typed. A cursor on a computer screen functions in the same way. The **cursor** is usually a flashing light, most often in the shape of a rectangle, underscore, or an arrow, that indicates on the screen where the next character will appear. The arrow keys control the cursor.

The keyboard is a wonderfully flexible device for entering data, doing word processing, writing programs, and performing many other tasks. However, the use of a keyboard as an input device calls for several assumptions about the individual who will use the computer. First, a keyboard is used most effectively by a person who is a good typist. The "hunt and peck" system of typing ("I know the key is out there—I just have to find it!") is frustrating and tedious. In recognition of this, typing-tutor software is available for most microcomputers. Second, a keyboard can be used only by someone who is *willing* to type. Recent surveys have shown that many executives resist using a computer, in part because they lack typing skills. Unfortunately, lack of keyboard skills is only part of the problem. Many executives are uncomfortable typing information into a computer because they consider this a clerical task. As scheduling and decision-aiding programs have become available, this has been changing. Managers are becoming convinced by the considerable evidence available that efficiency and productivity will improve through their use of these machines. Another assumption is that the user is physically capable of using the keyboard. Keyboards can be used only by those capable of typing. Many physically impaired individuals cannot use a keyboard.

Input Alternatives

In an effort to make computers easier for everyone to use, including the physically impaired, a number of keyboard alternatives and enhancements have been developed. Some, such as the light pen and graphics tablet, have been available for specialized use for some time. Yet even these devices have found new uses. Let's turn to some common input alternatives.

Joystick   The most common keyboard alternative, the **joystick,** is used almost exclusively with microcomputers and is an integral part of many computer games. A joystick consists of a vertical rod set into a base. The rod, or stick, can easily be moved from side to side and up and down (see Figure 5.3).

The cursor (or some image replacing the cursor) duplicates the rod's motion on the screen. While the joystick is usually used to manipulate the cursor, it can be used to initiate simple requests by pressing the *fire* button.

Mouse   In some ways the **mouse** is a joystick's more sophisticated cousin. A mouse is a palm-sized pointing device joined to the computer by a thin cable (see Figure 5.4). Wireless versions are also available.

The mouse's underside typically contains a ball designed to roll easily over a smooth, flat surface. The movement of the mouse on a desktop is reflected in the movement of the cursor on the computer screen. The top of the mouse contains one or more buttons. By using the mouse to move the cursor to a specific position and then pressing a button, the user can issue simple commands or make selections among options displayed on the screen.

Figure 5.3   The Joystick: Used primarily with home computers, the joystick is the most common keyboard alternative.

Figure 5.4   The Mouse: (a) The Macintosh mouse and (b) Microsoft's mouse, which is used with the IBM PC and IBM Personal System/2, are used to issue simple commands and select options.

(a)   (b)

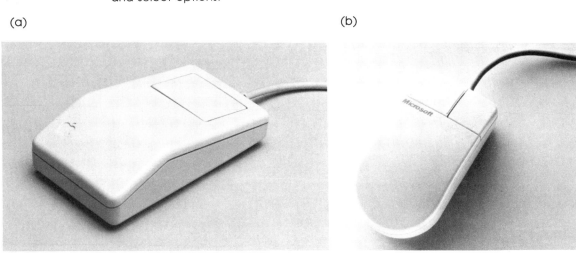

Looking at this small fast-moving object with a cable "tail," it's easy to see how this device got its name.

Trackball   A **trackball** is sometimes referred to as an upside-down stationary mouse. A trackball is usually rectanglar, measuring between 4 and 5 inches on each side. In the center is a ball about one inch in diameter that is moved by the fingers (see Figure 5.5).

As with the mouse, the movement of the ball is duplicated by the movement of the cursor on the screen. The trackball is especially useful when space is restricted since it leaves more of the desktop free. A mouse has to be moved around on a surface, whereas a trackball requires simply moving the ball.

Light Pen   Another convenient way to interact with a computer is to write or draw directly onto the monitor's screen. A **light pen** is a hand-held, penlike instrument with a light-sensitive point. Like the mouse, it is connected to the computer by a thin cable. Photoelectric cells create the connection between the light pen and the screen. Since the tip of the light pen is much smaller than a finger, it can be used to draw fine lines directly on specially designed monitors (see Figure 5.6).

Figure 5.5   Trackball: A trackball is a pointing device that acts like a stationary mouse.

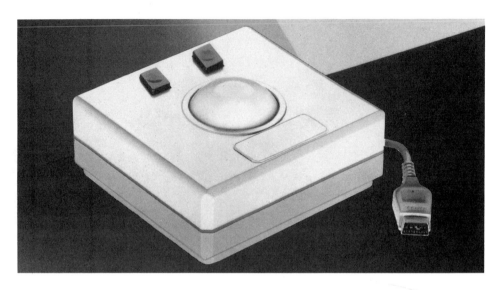

Figure 5.6   Light Pens: Hand-held drawing devices, light pens are commonly used in computer-aided design.

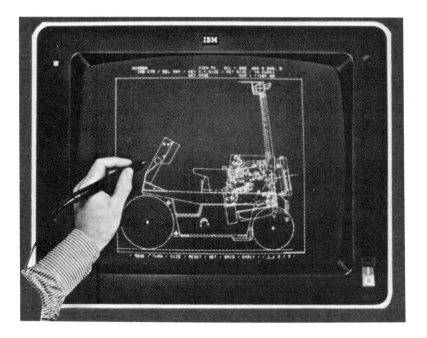

The image drawn with a light pen is stored digitally as a series of points. Light pens are used to enter drawings, correct or alter previously stored images displayed on the screen, change the color and thickness of sketched lines, reduce or enlarge a diagram's size, or simply to point to anything displayed on a monitor's screen.

Until the early 1980s, light pens and their associated technology were very expensive, a factor that restricted their use to industrial design. Now, however, light pens and the software to run them are available for many microcomputers for as little as $100.

Digitizer   Another type of input alternative designed for drawing makes use of a **digitizer.** Often called a **graphics tablet,** it is a flat padlike device. The tablet's surface contains very thin wires etched in a grid pattern. The tablet is connected to the computer by a cable, and a stylus or "pen" attached to the tablet is used for drawing (see Figure 5.7). Paper is placed on top of the tablet. The pen is moved across the paper. Where the pen touches a wire on the tablet a

---

Figure 5.7   Digitizer: An electronic drawing device such as this from Applicon, the digitizer transfers free-form drawings onto the computer screen.

circuit is completed. The sketch is immediately translated into electronic signals, and simultaneously appears on the monitor. Software is used to adjust and manipulate the sketch. Erasures and changes can be made quickly and precisely.

Touch Screen   If pointing with a mouse makes computers especially easy to use, what could be more natural than pointing with your finger? This idea has

---

Figure 5.8   The Touch Screen: Touch screens can be used in (a) business applications and (b) by children.

(a)

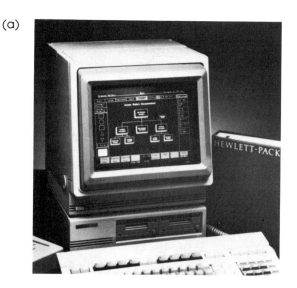

(b)

been incorporated directly into a computer screen in the form of a **touch screen.** A touch screen lets a person make choices or activate commands simply by putting a finger or stylus on an item displayed on the screen (see Figure 5.8).

Several technologies make touch screens possible. The most common is based on crisscrossing beams of infrared light. When the screen is touched, the infrared light beams are interrupted. The place on the screen where the interruption occurred is registered by light-sensitive receptors and transmitted to the CPU. This is the same principle as the photoelectric eye widely used in security systems and on automatic door-opening mechanisms in stores and airports.

Another common touch-screen design uses a grid of pressure-sensitive electrodes etched into a thin plastic sheet that coats the surface of a computer monitor. The electrodes register the position being touched and transmit the information to the CPU. This is similar to the buttons used in many elevators.

Touch screens are well adapted to industries where data are collected so quickly that there is no time to type in information (see Figure 5.9). Traders on the American Stock Exchange in New York can use touch-sensitive terminals to make transactions. Similarly, Chemical Bank's foreign currency traders use touch screens to trade the world's currencies.

Figure 5.9   Touch Screen Speed: Touch screens are used in business to enter data quickly.

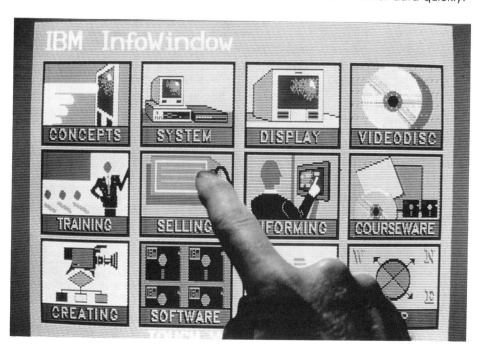

Touch screens have become a popular means of providing information to tourists. In Walt Disney's EPCOT Center in Florida, information directories use terminals with color-graphic touch screens. Visitors can find out about events, check restaurant menus, and even ask directions by touching entries on information screens found throughout the park. Similar touch screen directories of events and services are being used by large hotel chains and some office buildings.

DEDICATED OUTPUT DEVICES

Computer output comes in many forms. The results of computer processing can be stored in memory in machine-readable form. When needed, these results can be displayed as words, graphs, or pictures on a computer screen. They can be spoken with an increasingly human-sounding computer voice or they can be printed on paper. A copy of a letter on a video screen is temporary. You can read it but it can disappear in a flash. Output in temporary form is often called **soft copy.** Computer output that is printed on paper is often called **hard copy.**

Soft Copy: Monitors

Today's computers are equipped with a monitor for displaying information. Although graphics play an increasingly important role, most computer-generated information continues to be in the form of words and numbers. One-color, or **monochromatic,** monitors were originally designed to display crisp, clear text, but not graphic images. The reverse was also true: graphics monitors were not designed to display clear text. In either case, text and graphics are displayed as a series of closely placed dots of light. These lighted dots are called **pixels,** short for picture elements. **Resolution** is a measure of pixel density on a screen. The more pixels per square inch, the higher the resolution of a screen image, and the clearer and crisper it appears. With the introduction of high-resolution graphics monitors, it became possible to display both clear, readable text and graphics on a single monitor (see Figure 5.10).

One cannot simply replace a monochromatic monitor with a color graphics monitor. The picture elements (pixels) on a monochromatic monitor and on a graphics monitor are controlled differently by the computer. Each type of monitor requires a different set of computer chips to operate. For a graphics monitor to run on a computer, a special internal **graphics board** is required.

We will examine the five most popular types of monitors. More specialized monitors exist, but they are very expensive and not widely available.

Monochrome Monitors   Most monochrome monitors use lighted pixels of a single color to produce images on a dark background. Monitors with green,

Figure 5.10   Computer Graphics: High-resolution color graphics monitors are now standard on many microcomputers such as this IBM model.

amber, or white images are popular. Amber characters on a dark gray background have been found to cause less eye strain than other combinations. Noncolor Macintosh computers and colorless workstations display black characters on a white background. Monochrome monitors are designed to produce high-resolution characters, having as many as 720 by 350 possible pixels on the screen.

In response to the demand for graphics and high-resolution text, Hercules Computer Technology developed an inexpensive monochrome graphics board in the early 1980s that could produce high-resolution characters and graphics on a monochromatic monitor. Through the use of shading, images could take on texture and depth. The **Hercules board** became the standard for monochromatic graphics.

Color Monitors Most color monitors use a **red-green-blue (RGB)** format. When these three colors of light are mixed, white light is produced. Just as with a color television, a wide range of colors can be obtained by mixing these three colors. Monitors using color combinations other than RGB are popular with computer artists because of the unusual effects they can produce. Color monitors are somewhat more expensive than monochromatic monitors, requiring more complex hardware. Each color requires independent yet integrated hardware to light the different-colored pixels in the desired combinations. In addition, keeping track of and controlling the more complex hardware that manages the pixels requires more memory. As the price of memory has dropped, high-quality color monitors with increased resolution have become more affordable.

Color graphics adaptor (CGA) monitors are considered low-resolution systems, having a pixel density of only 640 by 200 pixels. With the rapid decline in the cost of color monitors, most users are opting for higher-resolution versions.

Enhanced graphics adaptor (EGA) monitors are similar to CGA systems except that they produce more clearly defined images. Their higher resolution is produced by having a density of 640 by 350 pixels. Character resolution close to that offered by monochromatic monitors makes such systems useful for both text processing and graphics.

Video graphics adaptor (VGA) monitors are higher-resolution systems than either CGA or EGA (at least 640 by 480 pixels) and produce very clear images. Such systems can display hundreds of colors easily. This higher resolution requires additional memory and support hardware. However, the newest microcomputers come with more than sufficient memory to support VGA monitors.

SuperVGA monitors have been developed by several different companies. All are super-high resolution systems. "Low-end" models boast 800 by 600 pixels, while medium-resolution superVGA models display 1024 by 768 pixels. The most complex models have the photographic quality resulting from a pixel density of 1280 by 1024. Such systems can display 256 colors, and require graphic boards that contain dedicated microprocessors and large amounts of memory to control the pixels and their associated colors.

Hard Copy: Printers and Plotters

You can read printed information as it comes out of the computer system the next day and several weeks, months, or years later without being connected to a computer. The printed word holds a unique place in our world. It enables us to keep a permanent record of our thoughts, ideas, and history. It is not transient: it has staying power. Printers are important output devices in most computer systems. There are two basic types of printers: impact and non-impact.

Impact Printers   All **impact printers** work the same way. Characters are formed on paper by tiny hammers striking against an inked ribbon to create an inked impression on the paper. Impact-printer technology is molded on the familiar print methods of the typewriter.

A **letter-quality printer** is modeled directly after a typewriter. Each strike of a hammer prints a completely formed character on paper. Letter-quality characters are indistinguishable from those formed by an electric typewriter. Just as with typewriters, a variety of striking mechanisms exist in letter-quality printers,

On Line

ARE VDTs A HEALTH THREAT?

Over the last several years, computers have caused tremendous change in our offices. This change has come with a human cost, however.

Office workers regularly complain that video display terminals (VDTs), including microcomputer screens, cause problems ranging from eyestrain, to finger, arm, and shoulder pain, to chronic backaches. Some insist that VDTs cause cataracts and miscarriages. Over the last few years, researchers have been investigating the health effects of VDTs. Eyestrain, general body aches, and back strain have been documented, but research indicates that poorly designed physical work environments, including incorrect desk height, poor chair design, poor lighting, and glare are the culprits, not VDTs.

Diana Roose of 9 to 5 reported in *USA Today* that "we're seeing an epidemic of reports from women all over the country with repetitive strain injuries." Repetitive strain injuries include carpal tunnel syndrome (where nerve damage occurs in the hands), tendonitis, and pain in the hands or elbows with repetitive motion.

In an effort to reduce repetitive strain injuries, California-based IOcomm International Technology has developed a keyboard called the Wave. The Wave has a curved or wavy design that supports the palms of the hand while positioning the fingers properly on the keyboard. Users have found it appreciably more comfortable than traditional keyboards during extended use.

Many workers spend large portions of the day sitting in front of a VDT in the same hunched position. Electronic mail and data bases have eliminated the need to move around. This and the lack of social interaction contributes to stress. To make matters worse, some VDT workers are electronically monitored. Every keystroke entered can be counted by the computer and used as a measure of productivity. One study discovered that some VDT operators experienced higher stress levels than air traffic controllers because of this.

Properly designed offices and humane managers can eliminate these short-term effects. The long-term health effects of VDTs continue to be studied. In response to reports that surfaced in the early 1980s of "cluster-miscarriages" among groups of women who are heavy VDT users, the National Institute for Occupational Safety and Health (NIOSH) has been doing extensive research. A report released by NIOSH and reported in the March 1991 issue of *The New England Journal of Medicine* found no increase in miscarriages among the VDT users studied. The four-year NIOSH study tested 2,340 telephone operators, half of whom worked at computer terminals and half of whom did not. Over the period of the study there was no significant difference in the rate of miscarriages between the two groups. Other recent studies support NIOSH's conclusions. These results differ however from those found in 1988 by the California-based Kaiser Medical Care Program. Kaiser found that pregnant *managers* who spend half their week using VDTs were 70 percent *less* likely to have a miscarriage than their peer control group. On the other hand, Kaiser also found that *clerical* workers who spend 20 hours or more per week using VDTs had a 140-percent *higher* risk of miscarriage. NIOSH researchers believe that some unique additional factor was influencing the Kaiser study.

Sources: Mark A. Pinsky, "VDT Radiation," *The Nation,* January 9/16, 1989, p. 41. Chris Shipley, "The Wave Keyboard Eases Typing Pain," *PC Computing,* January 1991, p. 52. Marilyn Elias, "VDT study: No Link to Miscarriage," *USA Today,* March 14, 1991, pp. 1A, 1D, 2D.

133

among them print balls, thimbles, and daisy wheels. Daisy wheel printers are among the most common (see Figure 5.11).

A **daisy wheel** resembles closely spaced spokes on a bicycle wheel. On the outer edge of each spoke of a daisy wheel (sometimes called a petal; hence, daisy) is a single character. All the spokes taken together form a circle or wheel. As the hammer strikes each spoke against the inked ribbon, an entire character is transferred through the ribbon to the paper behind it.

A wide variety of character shapes or **fonts** is available, a number of which are shown in Figure 5.12. Fonts are not limited to the English alphabet. There are also Braille printers, which print the raised dots of Braille in place of the inked impact characters used on other impact printers. With this simple change, hard-copy output is readable by the visually handicapped.

Letter-quality printers, like the typewriters they mimic, print clearly but slowly. The fastest of these can produce no more than 60 characters per second.

Figure 5.11 Daisy Wheel Printers: Consisting of a rotating wheel with a set of spokes, daisy wheel printers such as this Panasonic KX-P3131 work by striking an inked ribbon.

Figure 5.12   Shown here are some of the different fonts (typefaces, or character styles) now available. Changing the font can dramatically change the appearance of a document.

Aa Bb Cc Dd Ee

Aa   Bb   Cc   Dd   Ee

𝕬𝖆 𝕭𝖇 𝕮𝖈 𝕯𝖉 𝕰𝖊

Aa Bb Cc Dd Ee

Aa Bb Cc Dd Ee

Aa Bb Cc Dd Ee

Although this is slower than other printers, it is faster than what all but the most exceptional typists can produce.

The most popular impact printers are **dot matrix printers.** Their popularity over letter-quality printers stems from their lower cost, faster speed, and versatility. Dot matrix printers are used to produce not only characters, but graphs, charts, and even pictures. Each character typed consists of a pattern of dots. Characters are stored in the computer's memory as a pattern of dots.

The printhead (similar to the hammer in letter-quality printers) contains several rows of tiny pins. As instructions for each character pattern are sent from memory to the printer, the appropriate pins strike an inked ribbon. The pins push the ribbon against the paper to form the dots that make up the character, as Figure 5.13 indicates.

Since there are few moving parts, dot matrix printers can type very quickly. The fastest printer approaches 1000 characters per second. Since each character is formed in memory, a wide range of print sizes, shapes, and fonts can easily be created by programming the computer. Letter-quality printers, on the other hand, are restricted to the characters that can fit on one daisy wheel, print ball, or thimble (a print element). To change type sizes and fonts, it is usually necessary to change to a different print element.

Dot matrix printers are used to print computer graphics as well as standard characters (see Figure 5.14). Essentially, a pattern formed on a video screen is

Figure 5.13   Producing a Dot Matrix Character: A series of pins in the printhead strike the paper from left to right to form a character.

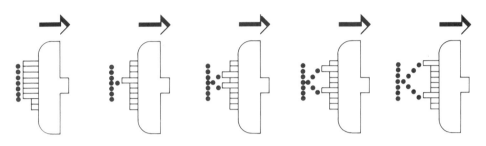

converted into a pattern of dots that is transferred piece by piece to the printer. With the use of multicolored ribbons, graphics can be printed in color by some dot matrix printers.

Given the speed and versatility of dot matrix printers, letter-quality printers might seem unnecessary. However, dot matrix type is not as clear as letter-quality type and does not present as professional an image. Dot matrix printers are often used for preliminary drafts of reports and papers, while letter-quality printers are used for final copies or whenever a "finished" look is required.

Figure 5.14   Dot Matrix Printers: Versatile and fast, dot matrix printers such as this Panasonic KX-P2624 are popular, inexpensive impact printers.

Unlike other impact printers, **line printers** type an entire line of output at once (see Figure 5.15). Duplicate character sets and multiple hammers are used to strike the paper and ribbon. Although fast, line printers are very noisy, often requiring sound-proofing. In addition, the print may lack clarity. High-speed impact line printers are still a fixture in many organizations, but they are likely to be replaced by high-speed non-impact printers.

Non-Impact Printers A number of alternative printer technologies have been developed that print with a minimum of noise. All **non-impact printers** use a dot-matrix technology whereby the characters are sent from memory as a set of dots. No hammers strike the paper, however. For this reason, non-impact printers are quiet.

Thermal printers transfer their character dot patterns to special heat-sensitive paper. When character patterns are sent from memory to the printhead, tiny wires are heated. These wires react chemically with special paper, causing the dot pattern for the character to appear. Chemically based **electrostatic printers** work essentially the same way. An electric charge rather than heat activates chemically treated paper. Thermal and electrostatic printers are slow,

---

Figure 5.15   Line Printers: Line printers such as this IBM 4245 type an entire line at a time, but they are noisy and may lack clarity.

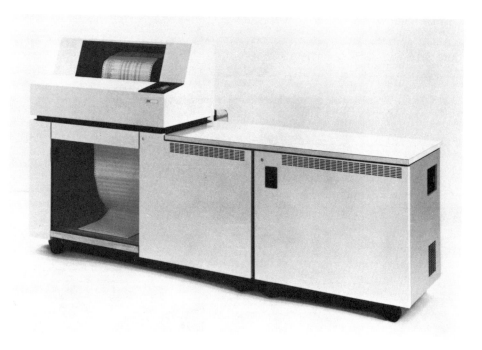

and often the characters lack clarity. Such printers are inexpensive to purchase, but the special paper they require is expensive. In their defense, they are very light, often portable, and very quiet. Color thermal printers that produce full-size, high-resolution, photographic quality output use a thermal-wax transfer method that produces brilliantly colored hard copy. The price of these printers can be as much as $10,000.

Like thermal printers, **inkjet printers** are quiet. However, their print is clearer than that of most noncolor thermal printers, and they are much faster (see Figure 5.16). In these printers, character patterns are sent from memory, and tiny dots of ink are squirted on the surface of the paper to form each character. Inkjet characters contain more dots than those produced by dot matrix impact printers, making them clearer and easier to read. Inkjet technology is most useful for reproducing color graphics. Printheads containing multiple jets with different color inks produce clear, colorful pages.

Laser printers are the fastest printers currently available. They combine lasers with the ink-transfer technology used in many photocopy machines. As with other printers that use dot matrix technology, the characters are transferred from memory. However, the dot density of a laser printer is more than 300 dots per inch, which produces a print indistinguishable from letter quality to the naked eye (see Figure 5.17).

In the laser printer, the character pattern sent from memory controls the laser, which is a special type of light beam. The pulsing laser, reflecting the character pattern, passes over an electrically charged drum. The laser neutralizes

---

Figure 5.16   Inkjet Printers: Clear and quiet, inkjet printers such as this Hewlett-Packard DeskJet form characters by squirting tiny dots of ink onto paper.

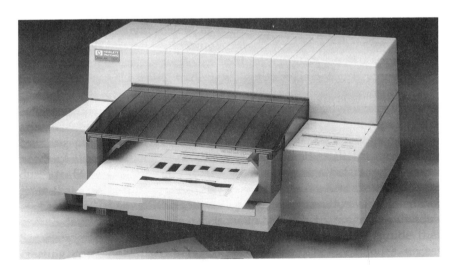

Figure 5.17   The Dot Matrix Versus the Laser Printer.

```
                    INTRODUCTION TO VAX/VMS


1. OVERVIEW


The VAXcluster computers provide an interactive, user-friendly
environment for creating and editing files, executing programs,
and managing data.  An extensive help facility is available to
users; this facility can be accessed by typing the word HELP.
```

                    INTRODUCTION TO VAX/VMS

          1. OVERVIEW

          The   VAXcluster   computers   provide   an   interactive,   user-friendly
          environment   for   creating   and   editing   files,   executing   programs   and
          managing data.   An extensive help facility is available to users: this facility
          can be accessed by typing the word **HELP**

the drum's charge wherever it touches. When an entire page of information has been transferred to the drum, the drum is coated with a special dry ink that sticks only to the charged spots. Then the drum rolls the full page image onto the paper. Laser printers are quiet and have the ability to print characters of varying sizes and shapes (see Figure 5.18).

Since they print entire pages at once, laser printers are very fast. As recently as five years ago, laser printers were very expensive—a factor that restricted their use. However, with the advent of the replaceable plastic drum (containing the printer's equivalent of ink), now common on most photocopiers, prices have dropped dramatically.

Although laser printers are still more costly than impact printers, their use in industry is increasing rapidly where high-quality graphics and speed are considerations. A number of laser printer manufacturers have developed color models.

Plotters   Hard-copy output is not limited to words and characters. A **plotter** is an output device specifically designed to reproduce computer graphics. Plotters have produced high-quality graphs, charts, maps, and blueprints for almost 25 years. Using shading, three-dimensional drawing techniques, and color, they can duplicate the most detailed drawings.

Figure 5.18   Laser Printers: High-quality graphics can be produced by laser printers such as this HP LaserJet III, which makes use of lasers and electronically charged drums.

On a plotter, ink-filled pens move across paper to create a graph, a chart, or an illustration stored in the computer's memory. To produce multicolor drawings, plotters use multiple pens, each containing a different color ink. Most plotters are designed for use with paper of varying dimensions, allowing them to produce drawings of different sizes. The hard-copy output of many plotters is not limited to paper. Drawings can be made directly on transparencies and other materials (see Figure 5.19).

Although dot matrix impact printers can be used to reproduce such drawings, the results lack clarity. Laser-printed graphic output, while clear, is limited to standard letter- or legal-size paper and black-on-white output.

Two plotter styles are popular. The **flatbed plotter** holds the paper still while the pens move across the page. **Drum plotters** position the paper over movable drums that rotate as the pens move. Drum plotters can produce more complex designs because both the paper and the pens can move. In addition, they can handle very large pieces of paper. Drum plotters are more expensive and more versatile than flatbed plotters.

Figure 5.19   Plotters: Specifically designed to produce graphics, plotters such as the HP
DraftMaster move pens across paper or other materials to produce high-quality
graphs, charts, maps, and blueprints.

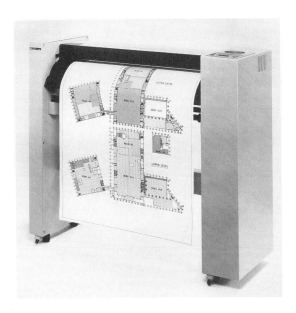

THE MONITOR: AN INPUT/OUTPUT DEVICE

Not too long ago, there seemed to be a clear distinction between input and output. Input consisted of stacks of computer cards, and output was reams of paper. But this distinction is no longer valid. With a few exceptions, both input and output can be accomplished through the same medium. Even the traditional punched cards could be produced as output if the results of one program were then to be used as raw data for another program. Magnetic tape and disks can contain raw data, programs, and results.

As another example, a keyboard and the screen associated with it can mistakenly be considered an input device. The monitor "echoes" what is entered at the keyboard. We use them to enter data or a program, or to start a game. However, when we run our game or program, the results are often directed back to the screen. As we work at a monitor, it reflects the entered input and acts as an output device at different stages of the process. In all stages however, the terminal serves as a medium of communication between people and the computer.

The most common means of communicating with a computer is with a

video display terminal, or **VDT.** In its most standard form, a video display terminal consists of a keyboard attached to a screen or monitor, as Figure 5.20 shows. A person using a terminal is in two-way communication with the computer. Data or a program are entered at the terminal keyboard, and some kind of information is returned on the terminal monitor.

Some terminals are classified as "dumb," while others are said to be "intelligent." A **dumb terminal** is not a terminal used by an inexperienced user. It is a terminal that can be used only for entering data or viewing output. It contains no memory of its own. A dumb terminal must always be connected to a large computer. For example, terminals used to make airline reservations at airports or in travel agencies are dumb terminals. If the computer to which a terminal is connected is not operating, the terminal cannot be used. If data are entered incorrectly at the dumb terminal, they will be transmitted as is, and be incorrect. The dumb terminal is a direct communication link with the computer.

An **intelligent terminal** contains its own built-in microprocessor. It is capable of performing limited processing tasks independent of the computer to which it is attached. Intelligent terminals often have expanded editing capabili-

---

Figure 5.20   The Video Display Terminal: Most commonly, a video display terminal consists of a keyboard and mouse attached to a screen or monitor. This is a Unisys model.

Figure 5.21   Desktop machines: This SPARC station can work independently and has expanded capabilities.

ties, so the user can manipulate and double check the data before they are sent to the computer.

Increasingly, desktop microcomputers and workstations, which were discussed in Chapter 1, are being used as intelligent terminals in offices. These desktop computers are connected or networked to larger computers. They can function as independent machines where data and programs can be edited, organized, and prepared directly. By using special communications software, they can also transfer and receive information, programs, and instructions from a central or larger computer (often called the *main computer*). Files that are transmitted as a unit to a main computer are **uploaded.** Files also can be **downloaded,** or transmitted from the main computer to the desktop machine. A microcomputer or workstation connected to a larger computer can act as a dumb terminal as well, allowing for simple two-way communication without any processing. Using desktop computers to replace terminals has a number of advantages (see Figure 5.21).

- Expanded editing and checking capabilities are available.

- Some processing can be done on the data before they are transmitted to the main computer.

- Data and programs can be entered into the desktop computer for later transmission to the central or main computer.

- Graphics and color become affordable and available, improving tools for analysis and reflecting the fact that people see the world in color.

Using desktop computers, large amounts of data can be assembled and organized over a period of time, and transmitted to the main computer all at once. Or data and programs can be entered into a microcomputer or workstation even when the main computer is unavailable.

Of course, there are disadvantages as well.

- Desktop computers are more expensive than most terminals.

- If the standalone processing properties of these machines are not required, then a traditional terminal is a more economical medium for human-to-computer communication.

SPECIALIZED TECHNOLOGIES

Most human communication is oral. We teach our language, our history, even our values and morals by talking to one another. Although the vast stores of printed information found in libraries and computer data bases are designed to help us to remember and record our world for the future, we communicate almost entirely through speech. The future will place at least as much value as the past on the spoken word, perhaps more.

All of the devices we have been discussing so far have been designed to make it easier for people to communicate with computers. We have gone from typing words, to pointing to printed words and symbols, to actually touching the computer screen. Increasingly, our communications with the computer have become more and more natural. The next step is to make these communications even more human.

The Voice as Input

For many years, researchers have sought ways for us to talk directly to our computers and for computers to talk back to us. A computer's ability to understand spoken information and instructions is known as **speech or voice recognition.** Speech recognition devices are of two kinds: (1) *speaker dependent* devices that understand only specific voices and (2) *speaker independent* devices that understand natural language as spoken by anyone (see Figure 5.22).

Research and development of speaker dependent devices have been fruitful. A human voice, like a fingerprint, is unique to each individual. A word or phrase spoken by one person cannot be exactly duplicated by anyone else. Our

Figure 5.22   Speech Recognition: Devices that recognize specific voices and spoken language in general enable people and computers to communicate.

individual speech and sound patterns are unique, as Figure 5.23 indicates. As a result, the electronic signals produced by a person speaking into a microphone are unique. Voice recognition systems based on the voices of specific individuals use this principle.

A limited dictionary of verbal commands consisting of words or phrases is spoken into a microphone and stored in the computer's memory (usually on disk) as electronic signals. In this way, the computer is "taught" a specific vocabulary as spoken by a particular individual. When this person then talks to the computer, issuing verbal commands from this limited vocabulary, the computer compares the spoken words with those in its vocabulary. If a match is found, the appropriate action is taken. Otherwise, nothing happens.

Systems such as DragonDictate are designed to understand approximately 30,000 words. After the dictionary is stored, a user can speak into a headset and the identified words appear on the computer screen. This system has become popular with disabled users who can now "type" by speaking. Tests indicate that with an experienced user, the system can understand, store, and display up to 40 words per minute.

Such systems have enormous potential. Large-scale versions of voice recognition systems are used on some Ford automobile loading docks and Lockheed

Figure 5.23   The Human Voice: Because each person's voice is unique, it produces unique signals that can be graphed. Shown is a spectrogram with three pronunciations of the word *baby*.

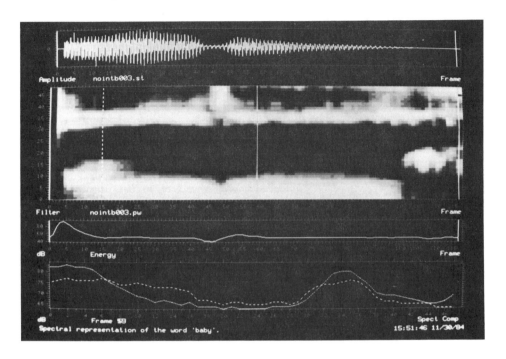

Aircraft assembly lines. They are frequently found in security and military systems. Doors, for example, will not be unlocked unless the speaker's voice is recognized.

Recent advances have made voice recognition systems available and affordable for microcomputers. A number of manufacturers have voice recognition systems that let a person give spoken commands to a number of existing software packages.

Such systems are being used to give computer power to severely disabled people who are unable to type or even point accurately at a touch screen. Word processing and spreadsheet software can be redesigned to accept spoken commands, but the use of voice input systems extends beyond traditional software. Such systems can be used to operate wheelchairs, elevators, and other mechanical devices, giving greater independence and mobility to handicapped people.

Research and development of speaker independent devices for *natural language recognition* has been slower. Work that may lead to computers and equipment that can understand anyone's speech continues at many universities and corporations. There is as yet no general voice-processing system. Natural language recognition is discussed more fully in Chapter 16.

Voice Synthesis as Output

There are also two types of systems for computerized voice output, or **voice synthesis.** In the simpler systems, frequently used words and phrases are prerecorded and stored in the computer's memory. These sentence components can then be retrieved in any desired order. The number of words that can be used in such systems is limited. Of course, fairly complex thoughts can be expressed even with a limited vocabulary.

The second type is based on the finite number of sounds that make up natural language. All our spoken words and phrases are combinations of these distinct sounds, or *phonemes*. In this type of voice output system, phonemes, not complete words, are recorded into the computer's memory. The computer is then programmed to synthesize words from these basic building blocks. This method should enable the computer to reproduce all words spoken in a particular language. Different languages have different sets of phonemes.

The most common use of computerized voice output is for the telephone, and is based on the first type of system. Computer-generated telephone messages such as "The number you have reached, 6-3-2 4-1-1-2, has been changed . . ." are composed of a prerecorded voice saying the first and last parts of the sentence combined with a computer crafted phone number built out of individually prerecorded numbers.

Like telephone messages, most of the other voice output devices now available form sentences from prerecorded words or phrases. Examples include children's toys such as Texas Instruments' "Touch & Tell," talking Coke machines, and even talking dashboards in cars, which remind you to "Buckle Up!" (see Figure 5.24)

Synthetic voice output can also be an outstanding aid for the disabled. One use is to give voices to people with extremely limited motor skills who are unable to speak intelligibly. Voice output systems can be combined with other devices such as special keyboards or joysticks. The disabled person manipulates the input device with any part of the body (head, foot, hand) that he or she can use to type out or point to words or phrases, and the speech synthesizer will voice the person's thoughts. (See *On Line: A Voice for Matt.*) Voice synthesis is also used to help handicapped children learn to speak by reinforcing the relationship between the spoken name of an object and its picture on a touch screen. Children with reading and writing difficulties can improve their skills by associating the spoken word with pictures or with the printed equivalent of spoken words.

Speech recognition and synthesis devices have not yet become commonplace, except in science fiction. Yet, this technology holds enormous potential for creating truly easy-to-use computer systems.

Figure 5.24   Voice Synthesis: Texas Instruments' Touch & Tell forms sentences from prerecorded words to teach children the names of objects.

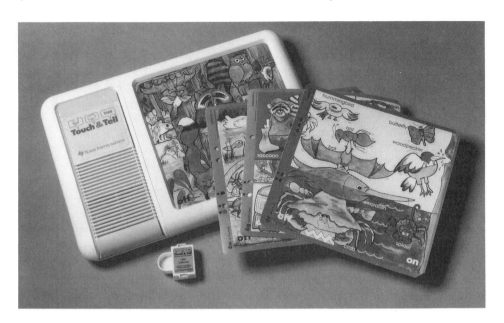

Print Recognition Technology

All of the devices we've looked at so far have involved the interaction of people with computers. Anything that eases this interaction is said to be **user-friendly.** Voice input and touch screens are considered more user-friendly than keyboards. However, the speed of entering information with any of these devices is limited by the abilities of their human users.

Although speech is the most common and comfortable form of human communication, many of our most important communications take place on the printed page. Our businesses, industries, and schools produce mountains of printed material daily. Computers can interpret characters and symbols only after they have been translated into machine-readable form, and considerable attention has been paid to designing equipment that can directly input printed information.

Techniques used for direct input of printed material fall into three categories: (1) optical mark reading (OMR), (2) magnetic ink character recognition (MICR), and (3) optical character recognition (OCR).

On Line

A *VOICE FOR MATT!*

Matt is 13 years old. He is attending public school at Mill Middle School and like most children his age he is studying social studies, science and foreign language (French). Matt is an excellent student, liked by his peers and teachers. Unlike the other students in his class, Matt has cerebral palsy and is a severely handicapped paraplegic. He is unable to speak, and has little if any control over his limbs. For many years Matthew totally relied on his parents for care and they had to guess at his needs. His wants were locked in his brain because he had no means of expressing them.

In 1985, through the creative imagination of SUNY at Buffalo's Dr. S. David Farr, and the ingenuity of Dr. Victor Demjanenko, Matt was given a "voice." Using specialized software and hardware, an Apple IIC, and Morse code, Matt was able to put together words and communicate. His first communication told his parents he loved them.

The current system, known as MorseWriter Mac, consists of a portable Macintosh computer mounted on Matt's wheelchair, and a specialized set of electrical switches mounted near Matt's head. By moving his head to one side a "dot" is sent, in the other direction, a dash is transmitted. *UB Today* reports that the current system "can display type on a computer screen, produce printouts and speak via a synthesized voice."

Fellow students find the voice synthesizer "neat." By using a letter code system Matt can combine built-in phrases. "z" stands for "thank you," and "o" produces "Hello. My name is Matthew, I use my computer to talk." One youngster remarked that the built-in exclamations have real personality.

Farr hopes eventually to enable handicapped users to create their own message codes, thereby making the system more individualized. The MorseWriter Mac and its easier-to-use Apple IIC cousin have already been put to use by handicapped youngsters and adults around the country.

Source: Sue Wuetcher, "Morse code with a new twist," *UB Today*, Summer 1990, p.4.

Optical Mark Reading   **Optical mark readers (OMR)** are designed to read pencil marks on specially designed forms. OMR devices are most commonly used for analyzing answers on multiple-choice tests and survey questions. Properly designed forms using this technology can be used for a variety of business applications as well. In an OMR device, a light beam passes over the marked form. The presence of a mark creates an electronic signal that is then entered into the computer and processed (see Figure 5.25).

Magnetic Ink Character Recognition   In the late 1950s, a system known as **magnetic ink character recognition (MICR)** was developed and adopted by

Figure 5.25   Optical Mark Readers: Light beams read handwritten pencil marks on special forms and then pass on the signals to the computer.

COURSE AND INSTRUCTOR ASSESSMENT (Indicate the degree to which you agree or disagree with STATEMENTS NO. 6–20: A = STRONGLY AGREE, B = AGREE, C = NEUTRAL, D = DISAGREE, E = STRONGLY DISAGREE.	
▬ 6. The instructor speaks audibly and clearly.	Ⓐ ● Ⓒ Ⓓ Ⓔ
▬ 7. The instructor is able to convey ideas and concepts in a manner I can understand.	Ⓐ ● Ⓒ Ⓓ Ⓔ
▬ 8. The instructor gives well-organized presentations.	Ⓐ ● Ⓒ Ⓓ Ⓔ
▬ 9. Course material is presented at a reasonable pace during each class.	Ⓐ Ⓑ ● Ⓓ Ⓔ
▬ 10. The instructor has stimulated my interest during the course.	● Ⓑ Ⓒ Ⓓ Ⓔ
▬ 11. The instructor has effectively challenged me to think.	● Ⓑ Ⓒ Ⓓ Ⓔ
▬ 12. The instructor appears sensitive to assisting individual students with questions and problems in the course.	Ⓐ ● Ⓒ Ⓓ Ⓔ
▬ 13. I understand what is expected of me in this course.	Ⓐ ● Ⓒ Ⓓ Ⓔ
▬ 14. Assignments in this course are of definite instructional value.	Ⓐ Ⓑ ● Ⓓ Ⓔ
▬ 15. I am generally pleased with the written materials (texts, readings, etc.) utilized in this course.	Ⓐ Ⓑ ● Ⓓ Ⓔ
▬ 16. Exams accurately assess the degree to which I have learned the content of this course.	Ⓐ Ⓑ ● Ⓓ Ⓔ
▬ 17. Exams are graded fairly and impartially.	Ⓐ ● Ⓒ Ⓓ Ⓔ
▬ 18. The content of this course is relevant to my needs.	● Ⓑ Ⓒ Ⓓ Ⓔ
▬ 19. The amount of material covered in this course has been reasonable.	Ⓐ Ⓑ Ⓒ ● Ⓔ
▬ 20. I would recommend to others a course taught by this instructor.	Ⓐ ● Ⓒ Ⓓ Ⓔ

the American Banking Association (ABA). The ABA sought to automate the processing of the millions of checks Americans issue daily. Automatic processing would speed up transactions at a time when the use of checks was increasing sharply. Under MICR, the numbers on the bottom of checks are printed in a shape designed for easy reading by both people and computers (see Figure 5.26). The ink in which the numbers are printed contains particles of iron oxide.

Figure 5.26   Magnetic Ink Characters: Magnetic ink characters at the bottom of checks are read by processing machines that sense the iron oxide in their ink.

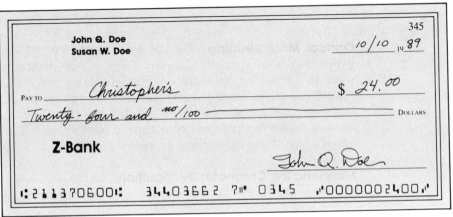

The checks are read as they pass through a machine that senses the magnetic iron oxide in the ink. The magnetic numbers are understood by the machine and entered so they can then be processed directly. The design of MICR devices is similar in principle to that of other magnetic devices of the second computer generation, such as magnetic tape. Its continued use reflects its ease and efficiency.

Optical Character Recognition Optical character recognition (OCR) works by comparing the shape of printed material with similar shapes stored in memory. A photoelectric light beam scans the printed material, transforming it into a pattern of light and dark spots. This pattern is then compared with patterns stored in memory. If a match is found, the printed material is entered and processed. In some optical scanners, including those found in supermarket checkout counters, the print information passes over a fixed light source such as a laser beam. Print-recognizable material can also be read by a light source

---

Figure 5.27   Optical Characters: Photoelectric light beams scan optical characters, match patterns in the computer's memory, and process the information. The OCR WAND reader is shown.

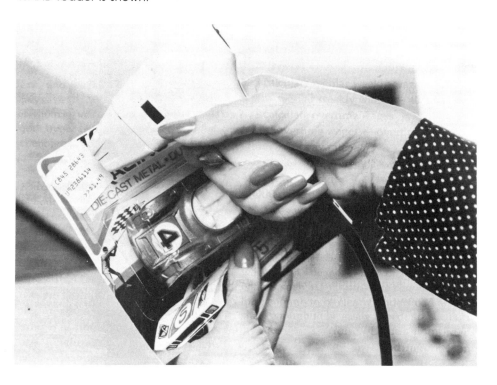

contained in a hand-held wand. As a person moves the wand directly over the printed material, the print information is read and entered into the computer for processing. These hand-held readers are increasingly popular in libraries, department stores, hospitals, and factories (see Figure 5.27).

Two forms of print material are suited to optical character recognition: bar codes and direct optical recognition of characters such as letters and numbers. **Bar codes** are the familiar groups of black bars of varying thickness, such as those found on supermarket products (see Figure 5.28).

The most common bar code is the **Universal Product Code (UPC),** adopted by the grocery industry in 1973 in anticipation of the widespread use of optical scanners. UPC bars contain information identifying each grocery item with a unique product description, including its manufacturer. For example, a half-gallon of Sealtest 2% milk will have a different code from that found on a quart of Sealtest 2% milk or on milk produced by another dairy. Recently, the U.S.

Figure 5.28   Bar Codes: Black bars of varying thickness found on supermarket products contain information that is read by optical recognition devices.

Postal Service began using character and bar code readers to assist in the routing of mail.

Direct optical character recognition (direct OCR) has potentially more far-reaching applications than either bar codes or MICR. With direct OCR, printed characters can be read directly by the computer without the need for special ink such as that used in MICR. Any printed character, including carefully handwritten characters, can conceivably be processed. Until recently, the computer was programmed (trained) to expect characters from particular typewritten fonts. Many current systems combine training with specific curves and shapes ("gestures") to improve scanning accuracy. Direct OCR devices are designed to suit the user's needs. Individual characters can be read using a hand-held wand, which is common in factories or department stores, or entire pages can be read directly.

In addition to the hand-held wands common in department stores, two other print and graphic OCR devices or scanners are popular.

Hand scanners are used to capture images and text for desktop systems. They produce images with near-photographic quality. The hand-held scanner, measuring 3 to 4 inches in width, is slowly moved over the image, storing it in memory and duplicating it on the screen. Accompanying software aligns images that have been scanned slightly off-center (see Figure 5.29).

Figure 5.29   With hand-held scanners, such as this Scanman by Logitek, users can capture images and text from a variety of sources quickly and easily.

Flatbed scanners are more appropriate for capturing and duplicating pages of text and images larger than a standard sheet of paper. The paper is placed in the "bed" or tray of the scanner and an optical sensor moves slowly across the page. In some systems more than one pass is required. If the captured image is text, it can be stored in a variety of word processor formats. It is hoped that software that can recognize entire pages will eliminate the need to transcribe text into computer readable form. This is especially important for libraries and companies that need to store massive amounts of noncomputer-generated printed material (see Figure 5.30).

OCR can be taken a step further. The Kurzweil reading machine was invented to scan typed or computer-generated text and, using voice synthesis, read material to visually handicapped people (see Figure 5.31). Until recently, the reader was a standalone system. It is now available as an add-on board for

---

Figure 5.30   With a flatbed scanner such as this from EPSON, a full page image can be read in at once.

the IBM PC family of computers. The new Kurzweil PC includes software and a desktop scanner. A speech synthesizer must be purchased separately. The PC version makes printed material available to the visually impaired at an attainable price.

Pen-based Systems   **Pen-based systems** involve a modified form of handwriting recognition. The pen or stylus-based systems let users print characters on a touch-sensitive screen. The hand-printed characters are then converted into computer readable form by complex handwriting recognition programs. A number of companies have developed pen-based portable microcomputer systems. Some users and developers believe that writing is more natural to use than using a keyboard or a mouse. Such systems are finding very specialized applications where the pen-based system can replace clipboards and paper forms. The GRiDPad, shown in Figure 5.32 for example, is used by Chrysler Corp. to replace paper questionnaires used in its design review process.

Figure 5.31   The Kurzweil Reading Machine: Invented to scan machine-printed text, the Kurzweil reading machine reads material to visually handicapped people.

Figure 5.32   Pen-based systems accept handwritten characters as input.

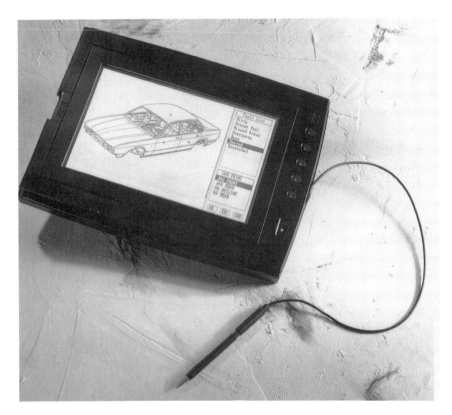

GRiDPad was designed principally for use in combination with electronic versions of printed forms used in exit polling, sales, and insurance claims adjusting. Other developers include IBM, the backer of GO Corp.'s PenPoint, Microsoft's PenWindows, and NCR. While all of the systems will recognize carefully hand-printed characters, all agree that it will be years before pen-based systems will be able to interpret cursive writing.

COMBINATION SYSTEMS

We do not need to look to the home or office of the future to see how complex computer systems are used. Such systems are in use today. Let us look at two common systems that incorporate a variety of input and output devices.

The Automated Cash Register

Automated cash registers are found in supermarkets, stores, and restaurants. They process business transactions at the location, or point, where the sale occurs. They are often called **point-of-sale (POS) systems.**

The automated cash register actually contains multiple input and output devices, all housed in a single package. Let us focus on a supermarket system. These cash registers usually have the following input devices:

> an optical bar code scanner
> a numeric keyboard
> an electronic scale (an analog device)

They also have at least one of the following output devices:

> a monitor screen listing item and price
> a printer

How do these cash registers work? As the clerk passes each item over a window in the countertop, the optical scanner reads the bar code on it. If the scanner cannot read the code or if there is none, as on fresh produce, the clerk types the code on the keyboard. The computer looks up the code on a list (stored in memory) of all the items stocked in the store. When it finds a match, the current price is returned and appears on the monitor, and the English name of the item as well as its price are printed on the sales receipt (see Figure 5.33). Taxes and any discounts are automatically calculated by the computer after the clerk presses appropriate keys, and the store's inventory records are automatically adjusted to reflect the sale. Some stores have experimented with voice synthesizers to announce prices and totals. Such systems have not been favorably received.

How does the customer benefit? Transactions are performed rapidly, so time spent in line at the register is reduced. Fewer errors are made by cashiers, and receipts with the items and their costs are printed so customers have a written record. Inventory figures are continually updated, providing appropriate sales analysis. This helps the store personnel provide better service by reordering promptly and stocking appropriate quantities of the items customers want. These advantages serve the supermarket as well. Rapid transactions enable fewer registers to serve more customers. Accurate transactions directly save money, and up-to-date inventories prevent stock outages on items that sell well.

Department store systems are similar to those found in supermarkets. Wand readers replace the fixed bar code scanners, reading price tags with distinctly shaped characters that can be understood by both computers and people. Inventory is automatically updated and itemized receipts are produced. In addition, charge cards can be immediately verified. An immediate credit check is run, and if the card is valid, the customer's account is automatically updated for

Figure 5.33   Automated cash registers scan bar codes to determine the price of an item. They print out sales receipts and display prices on a small monitor.

billing. If the card has been reported lost or stolen, or if the account requires attention, a message is sent to the cashier and the transaction is interrupted. This protects both the card holder and the store.

The automated gas station, a variation on the department store system, is being tested in a number of locations. The customer inserts a plastic card into a special gas pump. An identifying number is then typed into the computerized pump on a small keyboard. If the card is valid, the customer purchases the desired amount of gas and is automatically given a receipt. The customer's account is then automatically updated for later billing (see Figure 5.34).

Restaurant systems are simpler than either supermarket or department store systems. Information is entered at a keyboard that in many cases has the name

Figure 5.34   The Automated Gas Station: Completely automating gasoline purchases, this type of station saves time for both the customer and the company.

of the food or beverage item printed directly on the key. When the key is pressed, the item's price is looked up in the computer's memory. As with the other systems, cashier errors are reduced. In hotel and restaurant chains, inventory and ordering can be automatically maintained (see Figure 5.35).

Automated cash registers speed the checkout process, keep accurate records, reduce errors, and enable businesses to provide the products their customers want more consistently, whether they are menu items or the latest fashions. In part, supermarkets, department stores, and restaurants are in the business of service. The better they serve their customers, the better their business.

Automated Teller Machines

Just as supermarkets have automated their checkout operations, banks have increasingly automated their services. Whether the customer uses a human teller or an electronic one, most bank transactions include immediately updating the customer's account.

The banking industry is increasingly moving toward the use of **automated teller machines,** or **ATMs,** for basic banking transactions. ATMs are accessible

Figure 5.35   Restaurants: Automated cash registers speed the checkout process and keep accurate records in the restaurant industry.

24 hours a day and can be found outside banks, in supermarkets, airports, malls, on college campuses, and in many other locations. Banks find they reduce paperwork because all transactions are entered directly into the computer. They also reduce labor costs because ATMs can perform many of the basic transactions that previously required a human teller.

To use an ATM, the customer needs a plastic card that is associated with one or more of the customer's bank or credit card accounts. The customer chooses a unique personal identification number (PIN) that acts as a password. The PIN typically consists of a sequence of four numerals known only to the customer. When a customer inserts the card into the ATM, the magnetic strip on the back of the card is read by the machine and links the user with the bank's computer. Then the customer confirms his or her identity by pushing keys on a simple keyboard and following simple, straightforward instructions that appear on a monitor. These instructions guide the customer in common transactions such as cash withdrawals, deposits, and transfers of funds between accounts. The banking industry has found that automatic teller machines make operations more efficient (see Figure 5.36).

ATMs, however, are not without their failings. Customers are often frustrated by machines that are not operating (down), that run out of cash, or that don't respond as expected. Although we feel a bit childish, we all count the cash received at an ATM even though there is often no person to complain to if the transaction was incorrect. Many people feel that ATMs are removing a significant component of human interaction from our lives. One common com-

Figure 5.36
Automated Teller Machines: The banking industry has found that automatic teller machines make operations more efficient.

plaint is that banks are no longer in the business of serving customers, but are only interested in making money. Some banks encourage customers to use ATMs by charging for transactions performed by human tellers. Although this move may have economic justification, it also increases our reliance on machines while reducing our contacts with other people.

Banks also have negative ATM experiences. They lose hundreds of thousands of dollars annually due to lost, stolen, or misused cards. Despite the negative aspects of ATMs, they have radically changed the way most people use banks.

Computers and peripherals are changing our world, from supermarkets, to post offices, to our homes. Change often has both positive and negative effects. To enhance the positive effects, we must be aware of changes brought by computers. We must understand how these devices work and demand that businesses and manufacturers balance cost-cutting measures with the very real need of people to interact with one another.

SUMMARY

Peripheral devices have become so heavily used in the everyday world that we often do not recognize them as input and output devices for computers.

A computer is useless unless it can communicate with people. **Input** and **output devices** are designed to make communication between people and computers possible. Increasingly, **peripheral devices** are becoming more **user-friendly.**

While the **keyboard** is still the primary input device, devices such as the **mouse, joystick, trackball,** and **touch screen** are common. Such easy-to-use devices enable users to rapidly point to and select information displayed on a computer screen. These and other specialized input alternatives, such as touch tablets, **light pens,** and **digitizing tablets,** have brought computer graphics into our homes, schools, and businesses.

Output devices produce information in a variety of forms. Images can be produced on monitors or printed directly on paper. The availability of color is making computer use more natural. Printers and **plotters** provide hard copies of graphs as well as the printed word. **Impact printers** include both **dot matrix** and **daisy wheel printers. Non-impact printers** include **thermal, inkjet,** and **laser printers.**

Increasingly, peripherals serve as both input and output devices. **Terminals** provide visual confirmation of information going into our computers and also display the results of our work. Mice, touch tablets, and light pens enable us to interact directly with images on our monitors, making computer use easier. Touch screens find popular use on information terminals located in stores, malls, and amusement parks.

Specialized technologies are being developed that will enable us to talk to our computers and have them respond to us in the same way. Computerized voice output is called **voice synthesis,** while the ability of a computer to understand the spoken word is called **speech or voice recognition.**

Computers can read printed information. **Handheld** and **flatbed scanners** make it easier to transform printed text and graphics into computerized formats for processing and storage. **Pen-based systems** let users input hand-printed characters.

Grocery and retail purchases can be automatically processed by computers using **optical scanners.** Many restaurants and retail stores make use of computerized cash registers, called **point-of-sale (POS) systems,** that not only calculate change but check credit and keep track of inventory. **Automatic teller machines** have transformed the banking industry.

Key Words

As an extra review of the chapter, try defining the following terms. If you have trouble with any of them, refer to the page number listed.

automated teller machine
  (ATM) *(159)*
bar code *(152)*
color graphics adaptor (CGA) *(132)*
cursor *(123)*
daisy wheel *(134)*
digitizer (graphics tablet) *(127)*
direct optical character recognition
  (direct OCR) *(153)*
dot matrix printer *(135)*
download *(143)*
drum plotter *(140)*
dumb terminal *(142)*
electrostatic printer *(137)*
enhanced graphics adaptor
  (EGA) *(132)*
flatbed plotter *(140)*
flatbed scanner *(154)*
font *(134)*
function key *(123)*
graphics board *(130)*
hand scanner *(153)*
hard copy *(130)*
Hercules board *(131)*
impact printer *(132)*

inkjet printer *(138)*
input device *(120)*
intelligent terminal *(142)*
joystick *(124)*
keyboard *(121)*
laser printer *(138)*
letter-quality printer *(132)*
light pen *(126)*
line printer *(137)*
magnetic ink character recognition
  (MICR) *(149)*
monochrome display *(130)*
mouse *(124)*
non-impact printer *(137)*
optical character recognition
  (OCR) *(151)*
optical mark reader (OMR) *(149)*
output device *(120)*
pen-based system *(155)*
peripheral (peripheral device) *(120)*
pixel *(130)*
plotter *(139)*
point-of-sale (POS) system *(156)*
resolution *(130)*
RGB (red-green-blue) format *(131)*

soft copy *(130)*
speech recognition *(144)*
superVGA *(132)*
thermal printer *(137)*
touch screen *(129)*
trackball *(126)*

Universal Product Code (UPC) *(152)*
upload *(143)*
user-friendly *(148)*
video display terminal (VDT) *(142)*
video graphics adaptor (VGA) *(132)*
voice synthesis *(147)*

Test Your Knowledge

1. What is a peripheral device?

2. List four types of keys found on computer keyboards.

3. List and describe four keyboard alternatives.

4. What does VDT stand for?

5. Define hard copy.

6. Hard copy and soft copy both describe computer output. How are they different?

7. Describe how an impact printer creates characters.

8. Identify three types of non-impact printers. How are they alike? How do they differ?

9. How do impact and non-impact printers differ?

10. List three types of dot matrix printers.

11. Does a laser printer use dot matrix technology? Support your answer.

12. What is a plotter?

13. What is an intelligent terminal? How is it different from a dumb terminal? How is it different from a personal computer?

14. Peripherals are becoming more user-friendly. Explain why this statement is true or false.

15. OCR devices (which read typed characters) and MICR are similar because they both process data that humans can read directly. How are they different?

16. What are pen-based systems? What types of organizations have found them useful?

17. What is voice synthesis? Explain the two techniques used to create voice output.

18. List those peripherals that can be used to assist the handicapped.

19. What is a POS system? Why is it useful?

20. List the advantages of automated teller machines. What are the disadvantages?

Expand Your Knowledge

Write a brief paper on each of the following questions.

1. Line printers *appear* to type entire lines at once. However, they do not actually do so. How does a line printer work? Is there more than one kind? If so, explain how they differ.

2. Why have some supermarkets chosen to attach voice synthesis devices to their cash registers? What are the benefits to customers? Why are other supermarkets not using these devices?

3. What are the positive and negative consequences of the falling cost of peripheral devices?

4. Visit your local supermarket. Interview customers and store personnel, getting their reaction to using automated cash registers. Analyze your results, focusing on the following:
   (a) Do customers view the systems favorably?
   (b) Are customers comfortable using such systems? What problems have customers had with such systems?
   (c) Do store personnel find them as useful as they expected?
   (d) What in-store problems have these automated systems caused?
   (e) Did the stores experience any unexpected benefits?

5. Visit a local retail store such as Sears, J.C. Penney, or K-mart and analyze its POS system using the guidelines detailed in question 4.

6. Research the use of peripheral devices that assist the physically disabled. Describe one device or set of devices and explain the assistance provided.

6

Problem Solving

CHAPTER OUTLINE

Problem solving is a continuous human endeavor. Working and learning is problem solving. From struggling with our first steps, to learning to talk, to making our way in the world, our days consist of solving problems. This makes it sound as if our lives are a continuous struggle, an uphill battle against insurmountable odds. Clearly, for most of us that is not the case. The trouble with the phrase *problem solving* is that we instantly imagine major problems such as world hunger or the possibility of nuclear war. However, if we redefine *problem* as a task that needs to be completed, we easily see that we are solving problems—completing tasks—all day long. Most of us are not even conscious that the process is ongoing. We sometimes make decisions and choose among alternatives without even realizing we are doing so. This chapter explores the steps in problem solving, introduces you to computer programming, and explains how the two are related.

After studying this chapter, you will be able to:

- Understand how we naturally approach problem solving.
- Explain why learning to program is valuable.
- Illustrate how flowcharts and pseudocode are used.
- Understand top-down analysis.
- Trace the steps in problem solving.
- Identify and demonstrate the six steps in writing a program.

PROBLEM SOLVING

Let us look at a problem we solve essentially unconsciously every day. The problem is eating lunch. You may think that this is not a problem because it doesn't require making a decision. Let's examine the process involved in eating lunch.

Figure 6.1 indicates the step-by-step set of instructions, in pictorial form, for solving the problem of when, where, and what to eat for lunch. Notice that the diamond-shaped boxes indicate the decisions and alternatives used in solving this particular problem. If we are hungry at lunchtime, it does not necessarily follow that we will be eating lunch. We may have decided to diet today or we may have a class from noon to one requiring that we eat later. Where to eat requires decisions as well. Do we eat on campus or off? If we choose to eat on campus we need to find an appropriate eating place. Once we find an eating place, the decisions really begin. What to eat and how to pay for it must be considered.

Everyday solutions are seldom documented in such detail. If we did, practically nothing would ever get done. But what if we wanted to train our household robot to do a task for us? Would this detail be appropriate given that a

Figure 6.1 "Eating Lunch" Flowchart.

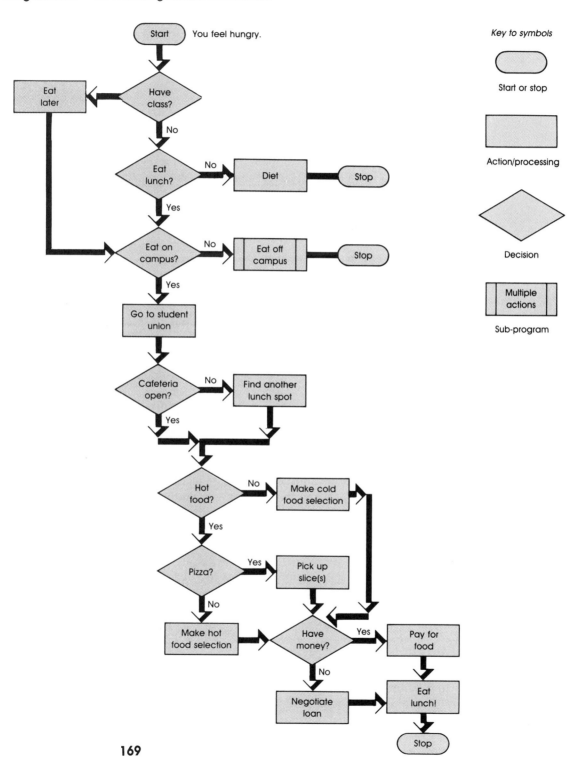

robot would be carrying out the task? The amount of directions needed to complete a task is related to the difficulty of the task and the intelligence level of the person or thing carrying out the task.

What Is an Algorithm?

A procedure for solving a problem is called an **algorithm.** It is a step-by-step set of instructions or directions that, if carried out exactly, solves the problem. The word "algorithm" may sound complex, yet algorithms need not be. A recipe is an algorithm. To solve the problem of baking a cake, you simply need to follow the recipe on the back of a cake mix box. If the directions are followed exactly, meaning that the cake mix is combined with the correct amount of water and eggs, and is baked for the specified amount of time, the solution to our problem, a cake, will be created.

A computer is a machine that follows specific instructions very rapidly; it does only and exactly what it is told. Algorithms are needed to design specific instructions. Computers will always follow your instructions, assuming, of course, that the instructions are given in a way the computer can understand. An algorithm written so that it can be carried out by a computer is called a **program.** To be understood by a computer, the program must be written in a programming language.

Why Program?

As we have seen in earlier chapters, thousands of computer programs are already available. Unless we plan on becoming a programmer, why should learning to design algorithms or write programs be necessary? In the first place, problem solving is not limited to working with computers. The process of carefully designing an algorithm for a computer is a critical thinking technique that can be applied to any problem in our lives—including eating lunch. We cannot solve the problems of world hunger, find a cure for cancer, or even plan for a successful career unless we learn to think critically and to approach problems in a rational way. Learning to design algorithms is not just a computer skill; it is a life skill.

Second, no matter how many programs are already written, situations will arise in which existing programs are inadequate. For example, while many accounting programs exist, they are often too general or too specific to meet the needs of a particular business. A business can either alter its accounting procedures to fit the available software (which rarely is satisfactory), or write a program that exactly suits its needs.

Last of all, many of the software packages currently available encourage the user to develop additional instructions to tailor the package to individual needs. Some programs, such as dBASE IV, Excel, and Lotus 1-2-3, guide the user in creating commonly used sets of instructions. The techniques necessary for creating these additional instructions are identical to those necessary for designing a program.

Problem-solving skills, whether used to write programs, use prewritten software, or find a cure for cancer, enable us to deal effectively with the world.

FLOWCHART VERSUS OUTLINE

Over the last few years, a considerable debate has occurred over what is the best way for programmers to design their algorithms before they begin to program. Two popular techniques exist, and both have their proponents. A pictorial method of depicting an algorithm in which the focus is on the program's logical flow, such as in Figure 6.1, is called a **flowchart.** Flowcharts are particularly useful as a diagram of the final algorithm. However, flowcharts are difficult to modify and reflect programming languages designed in the second and third generation of computers.

Flowcharts focus on the program's logical flow or the order in which statements will be acted upon by the computer. There is an alternative technique for displaying an algorithm that focuses on the development of detailed and easy-to-follow instructions. **Pseudocode** is a written method using English phrases in outline form to indicate the step-by-step instructions necessary for solving a problem. Each statement or formula represents a single task in pseudocode. It has the appearance of a computer program, yet all the statements are in English; hence the name *pseudocode.* It looks like computer code but it's still English. Although it is possible to write pseudocode in any spoken language, English most closely matches many programming languages. One advantage of pseudocode is that it is easy to modify or expand. For example, a complex statement can be broken down into a series of simpler statements. These simpler English statements can then be directly translated into program statements written in a computer language.

Both techniques have their place in programming. However, the use of pseudocode more closely matches the way people solve problems. We will use pseudocode outlines to display algorithms throughout this chapter.

CHOOSING A PLAN

Let us look at our natural, although often unconscious technique for solving problems. The same method is used whether we are writing a 20-page research paper or planning a party. When we are planning a party, what is the first step? As soon as the idea strikes us, we start making a list. Our list might look something like this:

Food
Possible location
Music
Guests

Notice what we have done. The problem of planning a party has been broken down into parts. Each of the four items listed is essential to the success of a party. The next planning step would be to take each of the topics listed and break them down into smaller and smaller steps until each small task is manageable. For example, *food* might become: beverages, junk food, hot snacks.

If we put all our scraps of paper together, our party's outline might take the following form:

Food
   Beverages
      Wine
      Soft drinks
   Junk food
   Hot snacks
Possible locations
   My house
   On campus
   Friend's house
Music
   Tapes
   CDs
   Video
   Live band
Guests
   Who to invite
      Self
      Penny A. Day
      Frank N. Stein
      Phil Errup

   How to invite
      Send invitations
      Call on phone

TOP-DOWN ANALYSIS

A large, complex task like planning a party is unmanageable if attacked as a whole. The problem must be broken down into its basic parts, into a series of subproblems. Each of these smaller problems in turn can be divided into separate, smaller tasks. The goal is to identify the subproblems that can be solved easily.

This method of making a problem manageable is called **top-down analysis.** Top-down analysis is not limited to use with computers. It is the standard problem-solving technique in all fields from business and medical research to life's daily problems.

PROBLEM-SOLVING STEPS

Before we can begin to program, we must break down the problem into manageable parts. The most difficult part of the process is defining the algorithm in sufficiently detailed steps so that the computer can follow its instructions. People naturally think at a level of abstraction far too complex for even the most advanced and futuristic computer. When people solve problems, they make all kinds of assumptions about how the world works. In a sense, when defining problems for computers, we need to think simply. The assumptions we make need to be identified and included in our instructions. For the present, the world of the computer is very detailed, requiring simple instructions. There are six steps in focusing attention on the details needed to successfully write programs. We need to:

(1) Define the Problem
(2) Define the Output
(3) Define the Input
(4) Define the Initial Algorithm
(5) Refine the Algorithm
(6) Define the Program

Define the Problem

Before attempting to solve any problem or design any program, it is necessary to have a clear understanding of the goal. While this may seem obvious, it is a critical step. When designing a program, the first step is to write a clear but general statement of the problem. In this way, the problem is looked at with a critical eye. A problem that seemed clear in our minds can be very difficult to write down on paper. The action of writing a problem statement focuses attention on the assumptions we make. For example:

Problem: Calculate the miles per gallon your car gets.

As the problem is defined, it cannot easily be solved by a computer. In fact, it could not be solved by a person who is not familiar with the method. Too many assumptions have been made. The following is a better problem definition:

> Problem: Using two consecutive odometer readings, calculate the miles per gallon your car obtained between gasoline fill-ups.

The key difference between these statements is that the second problem statement specifies many of the assumptions, such as using two odometer readings obtained between fill-ups, absent in the original definition.

Define the Output

It may seem a bit backward to define the results at the outset. However, we must know where we are going in order to figure out how to get there. To write a program or solve any problem, the expected results need to be identified. Decisions are made at this stage. For example, what elements would we want included in the output of a program to print out a list of a student's grades? Is the student's name alone sufficient? What would happen if there were two John Smiths in the class? Adding the social security number might help. What about using *only* the social security number? If that is done, will the instructor be able to locate student grades easily? By asking questions such as these about the end product, attention is focused on the specifics of the problem. Our field of view is narrowed and those items that are really important in the output are identified. In the miles-per-gallon problem just specified, the only output required is the miles per gallon.

> Output: miles per gallon

Define the Input

Once we know where we are going, we can look critically at the information needed to get there. Our attention can focus on the information (input) needed by the computer to produce the desired result. For example, to produce a student grade list, what information is needed? Should student addresses or year in school be part of the input? These questions should not be offhandedly dismissed. Will they be needed to produce the required output? An instructor might want to send notices to students doing poorly at the midterm, or to gather statistics on how well students in a given class perform.

Just as with output, the decisions made when identifying the necessary input will have a direct effect on the results of the program. It is often the case that much of the input appears as output without being changed. Let us look at the input required by our miles-per-gallon problem.

> Input: old odometer reading
> new odometer reading
> gallons used

To calculate miles per gallon, all three of these values must be known.

Define the Initial Algorithm

By this stage, our attention is clearly on the problem. A clear and concise statement of the problem has been written, and initial information (input) as well as the anticipated results (output) have been identified. To identify the steps needed to solve the problem, it is often helpful to work through the problem step by step using specific sample data. If the problem cannot be solved with pencil and paper using sample data, it will be impossible to write a program to solve it. As we work through the problem with sample data, we must clearly identify each of the steps used in solving the problem. More than one set of sample data may be needed before all the specific steps have been identified. By writing down the steps followed in solving the problem, we are developing an initial algorithm. The algorithm identified this way will be a sequence of instructions. These instructions should be so clear and straightforward that anyone or anything could follow them. The initial algorithm for our miles-per-gallon problem could look like this:

Initial algorithm: Record old odometer reading
Record current odometer reading
Record gallons used
Calculate miles per gallon
Write out miles per gallon

Refine the Algorithm

Our initial algorithm needs to be examined with a critical eye. Assumptions have been made and steps have been left out of our solution. Each step in our algorithm is not simple enough for our literal-minded computer. It is unlikely that an initial algorithm will work perfectly. We can expect to refine the steps many times before all the details are specified. Only then will the algorithm solve the problem.

Let us look at our miles-per-gallon algorithm. If we apply sample data, we immediately find that the algorithm cannot be used to solve the problem. The phrase "calculate miles per gallon" does not provide sufficient detail to solve the problem and must be further clarified.

Refined algorithm: Record old odometer reading
Record current odometer reading
Record gallons used
Calculate miles traveled
Calculate miles per gallon using miles traveled and
gallons
Write out miles per gallon

This algorithm can now be translated into pseudocode, which combines English-like phrases and mathematical symbols. The symbol ← represents the words *is defined by.*

Pseudocode: Record old odometer reading
Record current odometer reading
Record gallons used
Miles traveled ← current odometer − old odometer
Miles-per-gallon ← miles traveled / gallons used
Write out miles per gallon

At this stage, if we apply sample data to our algorithm we get the expected results.

Define the Program

In all of the five preceding steps, no mention was made of a specific programming language. The algorithm, written in the English-like sentences of pseudocode, does not depend on any particular computer language. The step-by-step set of instructions specified in the algorithm is a method for solving the problem. Translating these instructions into Greek, or programming languages such as Pascal or BASIC, has no bearing on the solution.

The algorithm must be prepared for a computer by translating it into a programming language. As an example, we will translate our algorithms into both BASIC and Pascal. Figure 6.2 is the translation of the miles-per-gallon algorithm.

Remember, computers do not "speak" English or any other natural language. They do not even speak pseudocode. If they did, step 6 (Define the Program) would not be necessary. The choice of computer language depends both on the problem and the availability of languages. We take a closer look at the various programming languages in Chapter 8.

SAMPLE PROBLEMS AND SOLUTIONS

Now let us look at a number of common problems. Most people, at some time or other, work for an hourly wage. We are all familiar with the method used for calculating such wages. Using this as an example, we can pay attention to the process of designing the algorithm rather than struggling with formulas. The first example calculates the wages of an hourly employee using the steps just discussed.

Example One

STEP 1: Define the Problem. In this example, the following statement explains what we want to know:

Calculate the gross wages (total, before taxes, and other deductions) of an hourly employee. We know the number of hours worked and the employee's pay rate.

Figure 6.2   Miles-per-Gallon Algorithm in BASIC/Pascal.

BASIC

```
100   REM   -- USING ODOMETER READINGS AND GALLONS, --
105   REM   --     CALCULATE MILES-PER-GALLON. --
110   PRINT "ENTER OLD ODOMETER READING: "
120   INPUT O
130   PRINT "ENTER CURRENT ODOMETER READING: "
140   INPUT C
150   PRINT "ENTER GALLONS USED: "
160   INPUT G
165   PRINT
170   LET   T = C - O
180   LET   M = T / G
190   PRINT " MILES-PER-GALLON =", USING "###.##";M
200   END
```

Algorithm

Get old odometer reading
Get current odometer reading
Get gallons used
Calculate miles traveled
  Miles traveled ← Current
  odometer – Old odometer
Calculate miles per gallon
  Miles per gallon ← miles
  traveled / gallons used
Write out miles per gallon

Note: While standard BASIC restricts variable names to a letter followed by a number, the BASIC found on most micros allows the use of longer names such as "GALLONS". However, only the first two characters (GA) are actually recognized by some systems.

Pascal

```
program travel(input, output);
   (*  Using odometer readings and gallons,   *)
   (*      Calculate miles-per-gallon.        *)
var
   oldodometer, currentodometer: real;
   gallons, milestraveled: real;
   mpg: real;
begin
   write('Enter old odometer reading:');
   readln(oldodometer);
   write('Enter current odometer reading:');
   readln(currentodometer);
   write('Enter gallons used:');
   readln(gallons);
   writeln;
   milestraveled := currentodometer - oldodometer;
   mpg := milestraveled/gallons;
   writeln;
   writeln('Miles-per-gallon = ',mpg:4:1)
end.
```

Algorithm

Get old odometer reading
Get current odometer reading
Get gallons used
Calculate miles traveled
  Miles traveled ← Current
  odometer – Old odometer
Calculate miles per gallon
  Miles per gallon ← miles
  traveled / gallons used
Write out miles per gallon

Note: The English-like words such as gallons, oldodometer, and mpg can be of any length. Names such as oldodometer and mpg were chosen to be long enough to be clearly understood and short enough to be easily typed.

This statement is clear and concise. We will see in step 5, though, that it will still be necessary to make sure we know what is being asked. There is nothing obvious about the statement "calculate the gross wages of an hourly employee" unless it is assumed that everyone either knows the appropriate formula or can easily find it out. When working with computers, it is "necessary" to make no assumptions and to specify everything in detail. In this way, the machine's need for specifics and literal statements will not be a surprise.

Designing a program requires careful thought. Our unconscious problem-solving technique must be made conscious. We must always remember that computers are *not thinking machines*.

STEPS 2 & 3: Define the Output and Input.

$$\text{OUTPUT} \quad \leftarrow \quad \text{INPUT}$$

$$\text{wages of employee} \leftarrow \begin{cases} \text{hours worked by employee} \\ \text{pay rate of employee} \end{cases}$$

STEP 4: Define the Initial Algorithm. List the step-by-step instructions for solving the problem:

> Record hours and pay rate
> Calculate wages
> Print wages

STEP 5: Refine the Algorithm. Look at each statement in the algorithm carefully. If a statement is clear it requires no further refinement. Remember, the algorithm must specify everything. For the computer to carry out the procedure, each step must specify exactly what is to be done. The statement "calculate wages" may seem clear to us, yet our computer will need more precise instructions to do this. This phrase requires further refinement:

> Record hours and pay rate
> Calculate wages
>   wages ← hours × pay rate
> Print wages

Our algorithm is composed of English phrases in outline form, or pseudocode. It has the appearance of a computer program, yet all the statements are in English.

STEP 6: Define the Program. If our algorithm has been properly designed, it should be easy to translate it into any computer language. For demonstration purposes, we will translate our algorithm into both BASIC and Pascal, as shown in Figure 6.3.

Even if we know neither BASIC nor Pascal, we can see that our algorithm can be translated directly into a computer language with only minor changes.

Figure 6.3   Gross Wages Algorithm in BASIC/Pascal.

BASIC

```
10    REM -- Using hours and payrate --
15    REM -- calculate wages.        --
20    PRINT "ENTER HOURS AND PAYRATE: "
30    INPUT H, R
40    LET  W = H * R
50    PRINT USING "WAGES = ##.## ";W
60    END
```

Refined Algorithm

Get hours and pay rate
Calculate wages
    wages ← hours × pay rate
Print wages

Note: While standard BASIC restricts variable names to a letter followed by a number, the BASIC found on most micros allows the use of longer names such as "WAGES". However, only the first two characters (WA) are actually recognized by some systems.

Pascal

```
Program PayrollA (input, output);
(*  Using hours and payrate      *)
(*  calculate wages.             *)
var
  hours, payrate, wages : real;
begin
  write('Enter hours and payrate: ');
  readln(hours, payrate);
  wages := hours * payrate;
  writeln('wages = ',wages:5:2)
end.
```

Refined Algorithm

Get hours and pay rate
Calculate wages
    wages ← hours × pay rate
Print wages

Let's examine a somewhat more complex problem. As with the first payroll problem, we will follow the same six steps for designing an algorithm. As we move through these steps, we must carefully examine all of our assumptions. Computers have no built-in understanding. We must specify every step if we expect the computer to complete the task.

Example Two

STEP 1. Define the Problem. The following statement defines the problem:

Calculate the gross wages (before taxes and deductions) of an hourly employee, including overtime. You know the hours worked and the employee's pay rate.

Although this problem statement is clear, we must bear in mind that phrases such as *gross wages* and *overtime* are meaningless to a computer. Our algorithm must define every term by expressing it as a formula. Only then will the computer be able to follow our instructions.

STEPS 2 & 3. Define the Output and Input. Note that the output and input for this problem are the same as those in the preceding problem.

$$\text{OUTPUT} \quad \leftarrow \quad \text{INPUT}$$

$$\text{wages of employee} \leftarrow \begin{cases} \text{hours worked by employee} \\ \text{pay rate of employee} \end{cases}$$

STEP 4. Define the Initial Algorithm. List the step-by-step instructions for solving the problem:

> Record hours and pay rate
> Calculate wages using formula
> Print hours, pay rate, and wages

Not surprisingly, this initial algorithm is nearly identical to the one devised in the previous problem. In the most general way, the same problem is being solved. In both examples we are trying to determine the wages of an employee given the total number of hours worked and the employee's rate of pay. The differences occur when the phrase "calculate wages using formula" is examined.

STEP 5. Refine the Algorithm. The phrase "calculate wages using formula" should bring to mind a number of questions. They include: What is the formula? What is meant by overtime? How is overtime determined? If questions arise, then our algorithm is incomplete. Our algorithm needs to be refined until our literal-minded computer can successfully follow the algorithm to its logical conclusion. The algorithm must be generalized enough to be able to calculate the wages of *any* employee. However, it is easier to recognize the steps needed by looking at a specific problem. Let us assume our employee worked for 46 hours at a regular rate of $5 per hour, and that overtime begins after 40 hours of work and is paid at time and a half.

Forty-six hours consist of 40 hours at the regular rate and 6 hours at time and a half. Therefore:

		overtime rate	pay rate		
weekly hours	40 ×	↓	↓ 5.00	= 200.00	weekly wages
overtime hours	6 × 1.5	= 9 ×	$5.00	= +45.00	overtime wages
				$245.00	total wages

With this example as a model, it is clear that first we determined the number of overtime hours the employee worked. Next, overtime wages were calculated.

Then overtime wages were added to regular weekly wages to find gross wages. The *refined algorithm* might look like this:

> Record hours and pay rate
> Calculate wages
>   calculate overtime hours worked
>   calculate regular weekly wages
>   calculate overtime wages
>   gross wages ← regular weekly wages + overtime wages
> Print hours, pay rate, gross wages

Using this technique, it was easy for us to write a refined algorithm. However, a critical look at the algorithm finds that it is still incomplete. This algorithm applies only when an employee has worked overtime. What happens if that's not the case? Since this algorithm will not work for all situations, it requires more revision.

Let us try to refine our algorithm further so it can be used to calculate the wages of various employees. Using another set of sample data, let's revise our algorithm again. If another employee worked 35 hours for $5 per hour, what would be the gross wages?

Now, 35 hours consists of 35 hours at the regular rate, and no hours at the overtime rate. Therefore:

weekly hours	pay rate	weekly wages
35 ×	$5.00 =	$175.00

This example shows that early in our calculation we must decide, based on the number of hours worked, whether the employee is entitled to overtime wages. The answer to that question will determine which wage formula to use. Now we can further refine our algorithm as follows:

> Record hours and pay rate
> If hours > 40
>   calculate overtime hours
>   calculate regular weekly wages
>   calculate overtime wages
>   gross wages ← regular weekly wages + overtime wages
> Otherwise
>   gross wages ← hours × pay rate
> Print hours, pay rate, gross wages

If we look closely at our sample solution, we realize we made some significant assumptions that are not necessarily true. We assumed, for example, that overtime is defined as any number of hours greater than 40, and that the overtime rate is time and a half. While these assumptions are based on practices that are often true, we do not know that they are true for this particular company, and should make no assumptions about companies in general. This company might not pay overtime unless more than 50 hours are worked, and the overtime rate might be double time. Assumptions are not necessarily wrong, but they must be verified before they are used in a program. In this example, overtime is granted for all hours that are more than 40, and the overtime pay rate is time and a half.

The final step in defining our algorithm is to provide all of the formulas that are needed. Here is the *refined algorithm:*

> Record hours and pay rate
> If hours > 40
>   calculate overtime hours
>   overtime hours $\leftarrow$ hours $- 40$
>   calculate regular weekly wages
>   regular weekly wages $\leftarrow 40 \times$ pay rate
>   calculate overtime wages
>   overtime wages $\leftarrow$ overtime hours $\times 1.5 \times$ pay rate
>   gross wages $\leftarrow$ regular weekly wages $+$ overtime wages
> Otherwise
>   gross wages $\leftarrow$ hours $\times$ pay rate
> Print hours, pay rate, gross wages

All of the phrases used in our algorithm are in English, although a bit mathematical in style. This again is pseudocode.

STEP 6. Translate the Algorithm into a Computer Language. Since this algorithm is more complex than that in the first example, the translations for the computer will also be more complex. However, the special relationship between the algorithm and the completed program still exists, as Figure 6.4 shows.

Our algorithm solves the stated problem, and the translation from pseudocode to a programming language is fairly straightforward. Some experts might argue correctly that our algorithm is not completely general. The algorithm is valid only for the special case where overtime is granted for all hours greater than 40, and where the overtime rate is time and a half.

We could further refine our algorithm, making it still more general:

> Record company's regular hours and overtime rate
> Record employee's hours and pay rate
> If hours worked $>$ regular hours
>   calculate overtime hours
>   overtime hours $\leftarrow$ hours worked $-$ regular hours
>   calculate regular weekly wages
>   regular weekly wages $\leftarrow$ regular hours $\times$ pay rate
>   calculate overtime wages
>   overtime wages $\leftarrow$ overtime hours $\times$ overtime rate $\times$ pay rate
>   gross wages $\leftarrow$ regular weekly wages $+$ overtime wages
> Otherwise
>   gross wages $\leftarrow$ hours $\times$ pay rate
> Print hours, pay rate, gross wages

Figure 6.4   Gross Wages Refined Algorithm in BASIC/Pascal.

BASIC

```
100     PRINT "ENTER HOURS AND PAYRATE:"
110     INPUT H, R
115     REM -- DEPENDING ON HOURS WORKED DOES --
116     REM -- EMPLOYEE GET OVERTIME PAY. --
120     IF H > 40 THEN 150 ELSE 200
150         O = H - 40
160         R = 40 * R
170         O1 = O * 1.5 * R
180         W = R + O1
190     GOTO 300
195     REM -- CALCULATE WAGES WITHOUT --
196     REM -- OVERTIME PAY. --
200         W = H * R
300     PRINT " HOURS   RATE    WAGES"
310     PRINT USING "   ##     #.##   ###.##";H,R,W
999     END
```

Algorithm

Get hours and pay rate
If hours > 40
   calculate overtime hours
     overtime hours ← hours − 40
   calculate regular weekly wages
     regular weekly wages ← 40 × pay rate
   calculate overtime wages
     overtime wages ← overtime hours ×
     1.5 × pay rate
   gross wages ← regular weekly wages +
   overtime wages
Otherwise
   gross wages ← hours × pay rate
Print hours, pay rate, wages

Pascal

```pascal
program payrollB (input, output);
var
   hours, payrate, othours, otwages: real;
   regwages, wages : real;
begin
   write('Enter hours and payrate: ');
   readln (hours, payrate);
   (*  Depending on hours worked does   *)
   (*    employee get overtime pay.     *)
   if hours > 40 then
     begin
       regwages := 40 * payrate;
       othours := hours - 40;
       otwages := othours * 1.5 * payrate;
       wages := regwages + otwages;
     end
   else
     (*  Calculate wages without   *)
     (*       overtime pay.        *)
     wages := hours * payrate
   writeln(' HOURS   RATE   WAGES');
   writeln(hours:5, payrate:8:2, wages:9:2)
end.
```

Algorithm

Get hours and pay rate
If hours > 40
   calculate overtime hours
     overtime hours ← hours − 40
   calculate regular weekly wages
     regular weekly wages ← 40 × pay rate
   calculate overtime wages
     overtime wages ← overtime hours ×
     1.5 × pay rate
   gross wages ← regular weekly wages +
   overtime wages
Otherwise
   gross wages ← hours × pay rate
Print hours, pay rate, wages

Note: The English-like words such as hours, wages, and otwages can be of any length. Names such as othours were chosen to be long enough to be clearly understood and short enough to be easily typed.

Figure 6.5 More General Gross Wages Algorithm in BASIC/Pascal.

BASIC

```
 95    PRINT "ENTER REGULAR HOURS AND OVERTIME RATE: "
100    INPUT T, P
105    PRINT "ENTER HOURS AND PAYRATE:"
110    INPUT H, R
115    REM -- DEPENDING ON HOURS WORKED DOES --
116    REM -- EMPLOYEE GET OVERTIME PAY. --
120    IF H > T THEN 150   ELSE 200
150       O = H - T
160       R1 = T * R
170       O1 = O * P * R
180       W = R + O1
190    GOTO 300
195    REM -- CALCULATE WAGES WITHOUT --
196    REM -- OVERTIME PAY. --
200       W = H * R
300    PRINT " HOURS   RATE    WAGES"
310    PRINT USING "   ##     #.##   ###.##";H,R,W
999    END
```

Pascal

```
program payroll2 (input, output);
var
   hours, payrate, othours, otwages: real;
   regwages, wages, reghours, otrate : real;
begin
   write('Enter regular hours and overtime rate: ');
   readln (reghours, otrate);
      (*   Depending on hours worked does   *)
      (*     employee get overtime pay.      *)
   write('Enter hours and payrate: ');
   readln (hours, payrate);
   if hours > reghours then
     begin
      regwages := reghours * payrate;
      othours := hours - reghours;
      otwages := othours * otrate * payrate;
      wages := regwages + otwages;
     end
   else
      (*   Calculate wages without   *)
      (*        overtime pay.         *)
      wages := hours * payrate;
   writeln(' HOURS   RATE   WAGES');
   writeln(hours:5, payrate:8:2, wages:9:2)
end.
```

Algorithm

Get regular hours and overtime rate
Get hours and pay rate
If hours > regular hours
   calculate overtime hours
      overtime hours ←
      hours – regular hours
   calculate regular weekly
   wages
      regular weekly wages
      ← regular hours × pay
      rate
   calculate overtime wages
      overtime wages ←
      overtime hours × over-
      time rate × pay rate
   gross wages ← regular
   weekly wages + overtime
   wages
Otherwise
   gross wages ← hours ×
   pay rate
Print hours, pay rate, wages

Note: The English-like
words such as hours,
wages, and otwages can be
of any length. Names such
as othours were chosen to
be long enough to be
clearly understood and
short enough to be easily
typed.

Figure 6.5 shows the algorithm as it translates into BASIC and Pascal.

Creating a program requires careful planning. Our unconscious problem-solving technique must be made conscious. Computers are not thinking machines. They require carefully thought out, literal instructions to solve problems.

Therefore, our algorithms must lead the computer step by step through the solution of the problem. Our algorithms will naturally reflect the way each of us deals with the world. However, they must be detailed enough so that our machines can follow them.

Research in the artificial intelligence area of natural language processing is attempting to teach computers to speak and understand human languages such as English. Should such natural-language processing become commonplace, we would have no need for computer languages. However, we would still need to develop algorithms. Regardless of what language computers speak, they will still be machines requiring very detailed instructions.

SUMMARY

We solve problems every day. For a computer to solve a problem, not only must the solution be very detailed, it must be written in a form the computer can understand. An **algorithm** is a procedure for solving a problem. It is a step-by-step set of instructions that, if carried out, exactly solves the problem. Although a computer follows instructions very rapidly, it does only and exactly what it is told. Algorithms are used to design these very specific instructions.

A **program** is an algorithm written in a programming language so that the algorithm can be carried out by a computer.

Learning to design algorithms and write programs is important for a number of reasons. First, the process of carefully designing an algorithm for a computer is a critical thinking technique that can be applied to any problem. Learning to design algorithms is not just a computer skill; it is a life skill. Second, no matter how many programs have been written, more are required to meet the needs of a changing world. Third, to make effective use of many of the most popular software packages, the user needs to develop a series of instructions to tailor the package to individual needs. Knowing how to design algorithms makes this process more straightforward.

Two different techniques are commonly used for designing algorithms. A **flowchart** is a pictorial method of depicting an algorithm in which the focus is on the program's logical flow. **Pseudocode,** on the other hand, is a written method using English phrases and formulas in outline form to indicate the step-by-step instructions necessary for solving a problem.

Large, complex tasks are unmanageable if attacked as a whole. **Top-down analysis** is a technique for breaking down problems into subtasks. These subtasks can be further divided, if necessary, until each subtask can be solved directly.

There are six steps needed to effectively design programs. They are: (1) Define the problem, (2) Define the output, (3) Define the input, (4) Define the initial algorithm, (5) Refine the algorithm, and (6) Define the program. The first five of these steps can be used to solve any problem in any field and are unrelated to computers.

Key Words

As an extra review of the chapter, try defining the following terms. If you have trouble with any of them, refer to the page number listed.

algorithm *(170)*   pseudocode *(171)*
flowchart *(171)*   top-down analysis *(173)*
program *(170)*

Test Your Knowledge

1. Explain the difference between an algorithm and a program.

2. Why is a detailed algorithm necessary prior to writing a program?

3. Is a recipe a program? Explain your answer.

4. Give two reasons why learning to program is a valuable skill.

5. Name the two common techniques used when describing algorithms.

6. What is a flowchart?

7. How is a flowchart different from pseudocode?

8. How does pseudocode differ from a program?

9. Explain top-down analysis.

10. List the six steps involved in writing programs.

11. How is using sample data helpful in designing an algorithm?

12. Why do algorithms need to be refined?

13. Algorithms are designed to be computer-language independent. What does this mean?

14. Could the miles-per-gallon program be used to calculate the average miles per gallon used on a long trip during which more than two gasoline fill-ups were required? Explain your answer.

15. Rewrite the gross wages algorithm given on the top of page 182 to reflect overtime given only after 50 hours with an overtime rate of twice the standard rate (2.0).

Expand Your Knowledge

1. Write an algorithm to find the total amount of change (coins) in your pocket.

2. Create an algorithm to make a slice of toast with a buttered or unbuttered option.

3. Write an algorithm to convert from Fahrenheit degrees to Centigrade.

4. Write an algorithm to calculate the grade-point average achieved by a student in your school in a given semester. *Hint:* A grade-point average is a "weighted" average of the grades received.

5. Write an algorithm to solve the following problem: An instructor in a pass/fail course wants to write a program to determine if students are passing the course. Two exams are given in the course, a midterm and a final. Each exam contains 100 points. The midterm is worth 40 percent of the final grade and the final is worth 60 percent of the final grade. A course average of 50 points is required to pass.

6. An instructor has given an exam to a class. Write an algorithm for calculating the mean (average), median (middle grade), and mode (most common grade) for the class.

7. Write an algorithm to solve the following problem: You plan to travel to Europe during Spring Break on the newest of the low-cost airlines. The price of a one-way ticket is $259. To keep ticket prices low, the airline charges a baggage fee for all checked baggage. The baggage charge for a one-way trip is $3.00 plus 12 cents per pound. If you know the weight of your luggage, how much will the one-way trip to Europe cost?

7

Processing a Program

CHAPTER OUTLINE

Translating Programs
On Line: The History of the Bug

Executing Programs

Debugging
Hand Simulation • Intermediate Results

Testing

Documentation

As we have seen, computers help people by solving problems. To solve problems, computers must use appropriate programs. A program is a step-by-step set of problem-solving instructions written in a programming language so that the instructions can be carried out by a computer. These step-by-step instructions (or algorithms) are often called the logic of the program. In the previous chapter, we examined the steps involved in developing an algorithm and converting it into a computer program. Designing the program does not solve the problem by itself, but it is an essential first step in that direction. The program is the blueprint the computer will follow when solving a problem.

Once an algorithm has been developed on paper, it must be written in a programming language so it can be understood by the computer. Then it is entered into the computer and, using the appropriate data, the program is processed in the CPU.

After studying this chapter, you will be able to:

- Understand the use of computer files.
- Explain the difference between an interpreter and a compiler.
- Distinguish between a source program and an object program.
- List and define the different types of program errors.
- Understand how to correct program errors (debugging).
- Explain the role of documentation.

Every program run on a computer requires the use of computer files. This is true whether the program is a prewritten application package (written by a software company in a programming language) such as a word processor, or a user-designed program written in a computer language such as Pascal or BASIC. In addition, all the data required by the software are stored in a computer in the form of files. We explained in Chapter 4 that a computer file, like paper files stored in a file cabinet, is a collection of related information. For example, a computer file can contain a letter entered into a word processor, lists of information such as student names and grades in a course, or the data required by a given program.

Paper files in a file cabinet are identified by a word or phrase written on the tab of the file folder. This label names and describes the contents of the folder. For example, paper folders might be labeled *Tax Info. 1992* or *CS 101 Class Notes*. In much the same way, all computer files have names. Each file name must be unique. Computers can distinguish one file from one another because they have different names. For example, the computer would have no difficulty distinguishing between these two files: *taxinfo.92* and *taxinfo.93*. The file names themselves mean nothing to the computer. To the machine, any unique set of random characters (letters and digits) would be as useful a file name as characters that form words. However, human beings as well as computers must be able to read computer file names. It is important, therefore, to choose file names that are meaningful to people. File names should suggest the contents of the file. Although names such as *apple, stuff,* or *xyz123* might be valid file names, they are not likely to identify the contents of the file. Useful file names are critical for finding information. Meaningful file names include *resume,* describing a file containing a resume; *gradeinfo,* containing grade information; or *taxcalc,* a program to calculate federal tax returns.

TRANSLATING PROGRAMS

Once a program is entered into a file, it must be processed in order to get results. Today, most user-designed programs are written in high-level, English-like computer languages such as Pascal, COBOL, BASIC, or C. High-level computer languages use words and phrases that are similar to the human languages we understand. However, computers *do not* understand these high-level computer languages. These languages are designed for human use, to make the task of programming easier. Computers understand only bits—the 1's and 0's of machine language. As a result, a program written in a high-level language must be translated into machine-readable form or it will be meaningless to the computer.

A **compiler** is a program that takes the program written in a high-level language as input and translates it, producing a machine-readable version of the program as output. The high-level language version of the program is called the **source program** or **source code** (the words *program* and *code* are interchangeable).

The translated machine-language version is called the **object program** or **object code.** The source program is the input, the object program is the output. A compiler translates the entire source program in a single operation. The translated program is incomplete. To be processed and to produce output, it must be combined with other programs that reside in memory. These programs, which control input, output, and critical processing tasks such as disk access, are called **utility programs.** In addition, the object program may require prewritten mathematical routines, such as square root, that are combined at this stage. This linking of programs is automatically performed by a **linkage editor** or **link/load program.** The resulting loader program is ready to be processed. An object program can be loaded and run, or *executed,* as often as the user wishes, skipping the translation phase.

For some computer languages, most notably BASIC, there is an alternative to translating an entire program before it is executed. An **interpreter** translates and executes a program one statement at a time. In other words, each program statement is translated and then executed before another statement is translated.

There are advantages and disadvantages to both procedures. Despite the careful efforts of the programmer, programs rarely translate perfectly the first time. Something in a statement or a series of statements may be inaccurate,

On Line

THE HISTORY OF THE BUG

In common English, a bug is an insect. The word *bug* in computer jargon means a programming error, but it has ties to these humble creatures.

During the development of the Harvard Mark I, the system abruptly stopped working one hot summer day. The Harvard Mark I's program was directly wired into its circuitry, so anything that interfered with the system's circuits would interrupt its processing. Researchers began a careful search of all the circuits and relays. Beneath an electromagnetic relay, they discovered a smashed moth. The moth was

carefully removed with tweezers so the relay would not be damaged. The Harvard Mark I returned to operation, and the smashed moth was taped to a log book as evidence.

Whenever Harvard Mark I researchers encountered errors after the incident, they jokingly said they were searching for "bugs" as they examined the circuitry. Over the years, system and programming errors became known as bugs.

Source: M. Zientara, "Capt. Grace M. Hopper and the Genesis of Programming Languages," *Computerworld,* November 16, 1981, p. 50.

---

missing, or typed incorrectly. Statements with such problems cannot be translated by the computer. Errors made in the use and structure of the programming language are called **syntax errors.** Syntax errors can occur in spoken languages, such as English, as well as computer languages. They are errors in grammar, spelling, and punctuation. Any error in a computer program is called a **bug.** Finding and correcting errors is called **debugging.**

Since an interpreter can translate and execute a statement as soon as it is typed in, errors are identified immediately. This makes it possible to correct mistakes immediately rather than waiting for the entire program to be keyed in and then translated by a compiler. Beginning programmers often find such immediate reinforcement supportive. On the other hand, every time such a program is used, each statement must be translated again. This is very time-consuming. Figure 7.1 shows how an interpreter works.

A compiler, on the other hand, translates an entire source program at once. Correcting errors is more difficult because a single error may affect many statements but may not be detected until the entire program has been entered. However, once the source program has been compiled properly, the resulting object program can be run repeatedly. Figure 7.2 shows how a compiler works.

When a program is translated by an interpreter or a compiler, two results are possible as each statement is converted into machine code. Either the statement translates and the process continues, or an error message is produced that attempts to diagnose the problem. Such **diagnostic messages** attempt to locate

Figure 7.1   How an Interpreter Works.

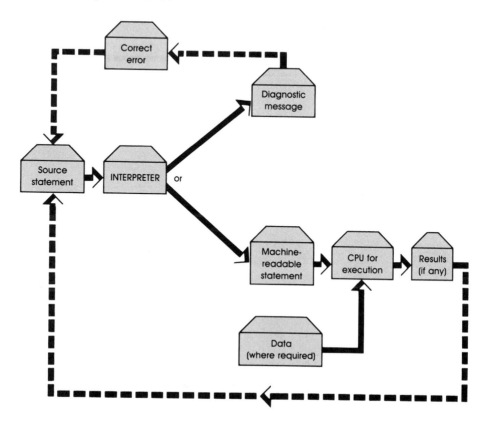

the syntax errors that made the statement impossible to translate. Corrections must be made to the source program. The corrected source program statement is then translated. This process is repeated until no syntax errors appear. Only when all syntax errors are corrected and a valid translation is made can a program produce the desired results.

Using the miles-per-gallon example in Chapter 6, the programs in Figure 7.3 have statements that contain syntax errors and cannot be translated.

Whenever a compiler or interpreter encounters such statements, the incorrect statement is identified and a diagnostic message is produced to assist the programmer in the statement's correction.

Figure 7.4a contains the BASIC program along with the associated diagnostic messages. Lines 130 and 170 contain errors. In line 130 the word PRINT is missing, and in line 170 the formula has been written backward:

170 LET C - O = T   should appear as
170 LET T = C - O

Figure 7.2   How a Compiler Works.

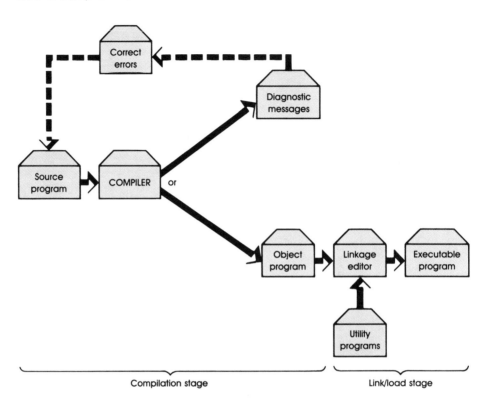

Compilation stage   Link/load stage

When these statements are corrected, the program translates and can be executed.

In a similar fashion, the Pascal program in Figure 7.3b contains three syntax errors. When compiled (Figure 7.4b) these errors are identified and suggestions are provided for their correction. Diagnostic messages indicate the location in a program where translation became impossible. The messages try to assist the programmer. However, the messages themselves sometimes require interpretation. For example, look at the first message produced by the program in Figure 7.4b:

`Error 41: Unknown identifier or syntax error`

This is trying to tell the programmer that the word *wrte* cannot be translated. It has been misspelled and should have been *write*. The remaining error messages more clearly identify and correct what is wrong with each statement.

Figure 7.3 Programs with Errors: Compilers and interpreters identify incorrect statements and issue diagnostic messages in (a) BASIC and (b) Pascal.

(a) **BASIC**

```
100 REM -- USING ODOMETER READING AND GALLONS, --
105 REM --        CALCULATE MILES-PER-GALLON. --
110 PRINT "ENTER OLD ODOMETER READING: "
120 INPUT O
130 "ENTER CURRENT ODOMETER READING: "
140 INPUT C
150 PRINT "ENTER GALLONS USED: "
160 INPUT G
165 PRINT
170 LET C - O = T
180 LET M = T / G
190 PRINT "MILES-PER-GALLON =", USING "###.##";M
200 END
```

(b) **Pascal**

```
program travel (input,output);
   (* Using odometer readings and gallons   *)
   (*        calculate miles-per-gallon.     *)
var
   oldodometer, currentodometer: real;
   gallons, milestraveled : real;
   mpg : real;
begin
   write('Enter old odometer reading: ');
   readln(oldodometer);
   wrte('Enter current ododmeter reading: ');
   readln(currentodometer)
   write('Enter gallons used: ');
   readln(gallons);
   milestraveled := currentodometer - oldodometer;
   mpg = milestraveled/gallons;
   writeln(' Miles-per-gallon = ',mpg:5:2)
end.
```

Figure 7.4 Miles-per-Gallon Program with Diagnostic Messages in (a) BASIC and (b) Pascal.

(a) **BASIC**

```
100 REM -- USING ODOMETER READING AND GALLONS, --
105 REM --        CALCULATE MILES-PER-GALLON. --
110 PRINT "ENTER OLD ODOMETER READING: "
120 INPUT O
130 "ENTER CURRENT ODOMETER READING: "
140 INPUT C
150 PRINT "ENTER GALLONS USED: "
160 INPUT G
165 PRINT
170 LET C - O = T
180 LET M = T / G
190 PRINT "MILES-PER-GALLON =", USING "###.##";M
200 END
Ok
RUN
ENTER OLD ODOMETER READING;
? 1234
Syntax error in 130
Ok
130 "ENTER CURRENT ODOMETER READING: "
130 PRINT "ENTER CURRENT ODOMETER READING: "         (correction)
RUN
ENTER OLD ODOMETER READING:
? 1234
ENTER CURRENT ODOMETER READING:
? 1900
ENTER GALLONS USED:
? 20
Syntax error in 170
Ok
170 LET C - O = T
170 LET T = C - O        (correction)
```

(b) **Pascal**

```
program travel (input,output);
  (* Using odometer readings and gallons  *)
  (*        calculate miles-per-gallon.    *)
var
  oldodometer, currentodometer: real;
  gallons, milestraveled : real;
  mpg : real;
begin
  write('Enter old odometer reading: ');
  readln(oldodometer);
  wrte('Enter current ododmeter reading: ');
       ^
Error 41: Unknown identifier or syntax error.
  readln(currentodometer)^

Error 1: ';' expected.
  write('Enter gallons used: ');
  readln(gallons);
  milestraveled := currentodometer - oldodometer;
  mpg = milestraveled/gallons;
      ^
Error 7: ':=' expected.
  writeln(' Miles-per-gallon = ',mpg:5:2)
end.
```

EXECUTING PROGRAMS

A program's complete translation implies nothing about the results produced by the program. Translation simply converts the program from a high-level language into machine-readable form. The machine-readable instructions, the logic of the program, may very well be faulty. If that is the case, the program results will not provide a useful solution to the problem. It is as though you received an invitation to a party, including directions, in the mail. Unfortunately, you find that the directions are written in a language that you cannot read. After finding someone to translate the directions, you leave for the party. If the translation is accurate, you will arrive at the party only if the directions are also correct. But if the directions are wrong—perhaps calling for a right turn where you should make a left—no matter how carefully you follow them you will never get to the

Figure 7.5   Executing a Program.

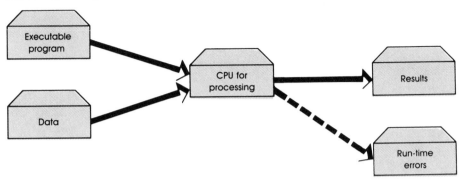

Figure 7.6   Properly Executed Programs in (a) BASIC and (b) Pascal.

(a) **BASIC**

```
100 REM -- USING ODOMETER READING AND GALLONS, --
105 REM --           CALCULATE MILES-PER-GALLON. --
110 PRINT "ENTER OLD ODOMETER READING: "
120 INPUT O
130 PRINT "ENTER CURRENT ODOMETER READING: "
140 INPUT C
150 PRINT "ENTER GALLONS USED: "
160 INPUT G
165 PRINT
170 LET T = C - O
180 LET M = T / G
190 PRINT "MILES-PER-GALLON =", USING "###.##";M
200 END
Ok

RUN
ENTER OLD ODOMETER READING:
? 1234
ENTER CURRENT ODOMETER READING:
? 1900
ENTER GALLONS USED:
? 20
MILES-PER-GALLON =                 33.30
```

party. The same is true with a computer program. An accurate translation of the program (compiler or interpreter) will produce the expected results only if the instructions, the logic of the program, are correct.

Translating the program only makes it possible for the computer to follow the instructions. For the computer to produce the desired results, the program has to be run, or executed. When executing a program, each translated statement must be sent to the CPU, where the instructions can be followed. If data are to be processed, the data are read into the machine during the execution phase and results are produced (see Figure 7.5).

When a program is executed, three things can happen: (1) The program can work perfectly, producing the expected results; (2) The program can produce incorrect results; or (3) The program can stop executing or running, with the computer printing an error message **(run-time error)**. A program that does not produce the desired results is said to have **aborted** or **bombed.**

(b) **Pascal**

```
program travel (input,output);
   (* Using odometer readings and gallons   *)
   (*       calculate miles-per-gallon.      *)
var
   oldodometer, currentodometer: real;
   gallons, milestraveled : real;
   mpg : real;
begin
   write('Enter old odometer reading: ');
   readln(oldodometer);
   write('Enter current ododmeter reading: ');
   readln(currentodometer);
   write('Enter gallons used: ');
   readln(gallons);
   milestraveled := currentodometer - oldodometer;
   mpg := milestraveled/gallons;
   writeln(' Miles-per-gallon = ',mpg:5:2)
end.
Running
Enter old odometer reading: 1234
Enter current odometer reading: 1900
Enter gallons used: 20
  Miles-per-gallon = 33.30
```

Obviously the first result is the most desirable, as shown in Figure 7.6. However, programmers usually expend considerable effort adjusting a program's statements or code before correct results appear.

Run-time errors are the easiest execution errors to correct. This is because the error message hints at what is wrong. Run-time errors occur when the computer finds it impossible to complete the instruction being executed. For example, a calculation could result in the machine being asked to divide by zero—which cannot be done (Figure 7.7), or to read more data than are available. If the correction requires a change in the program rather than the data, the source program must be adjusted. Then the translation process must be completed all over again before the revised program can be executed again.

Figure 7.7   Run-Time Errors in (a) BASIC and (b) Pascal.

(a) **BASIC**

```
100 REM -- USING ODOMETER READING AND GALLONS, --
105 REM --          CALCULATE MILES-PER-GALLON. --
110 PRINT "ENTER OLD ODOMETER READING: "
120 INPUT O
130 PRINT "ENTER CURRENT ODOMETER READING: "
140 INPUT C
150 PRINT "ENTER GALLONS USED: "
160 INPUT G
165 PRINT
170 LET T = C - O
180 LET M = T / G
190 PRINT "MILES-PER-GALLON =", USING "###.##";M
200 END
Ok
RUN
ENTER OLD ODOMETER READING:
? 1234
ENTER CURRENT ODOMETER READING:
? 1900
ENTER GALLONS USED:
? 0
Division by zero
```

If the program executes completely and there is no output or incorrect output results, there is a **logic error** in the program (Figure 7.8). A logic error occurs when the algorithm or logic of the program is incorrect. A computer will follow the instructions provided exactly. If these instructions are incorrect (garbage in) the expected results will not appear (garbage out). Logic errors are the most difficult to correct. No error messages have been produced to guide the programmer. Logic errors need to be located and corrected by the programmer who must go back and re-analyze the algorithm and adjust it so that it solves the problem.

(b) **Pascal**

```
program travel (input,output);
   (* Using odometer readings and gallons   *)
   (*         calculate miles-per-gallon.    *)
var
   oldodometer, currentodometer: real;
   gallons, milestraveled : real;
   mpg : real;
begin
   write('Enter old odometer reading: ');
   readln(oldodometer);
   write('Enter current ododmeter reading: ');
   readln(currentodometer);
   write('Enter gallons used: ');
   readln(gallons);
   milestraveled := currentodometer - oldodometer;
   mpg := milestraveled/gallons;
   writeln(' Miles-per-gallon = ',mpg:5:2)
end.
Running
Enter old odometer reading: 1234
Enter current odometer reading: 1900
Enter gallons used: 0
Run-time error 02, PC=2E32
Program Aborted
```

Figure 7.8   Programs with Logic Errors in (a) BASIC and (b) Pascal.

(a) **BASIC**

```
100 REM -- USING ODOMETER READING AND GALLONS, --
105 REM --          CALCULATE MILES-PER-GALLON. --
110 PRINT "ENTER OLD ODOMETER READING: "
120 INPUT O
130 PRINT "ENTER CURRENT ODOMETER READING: "
140 INPUT C
150 PRINT "ENTER GALLONS USED: "
160 INPUT G
165 PRINT
170 LET T = C - O
180 LET M = T - G
190 PRINT "MILES-PER-GALLON =", USING "###.##";M
200 END
Ok

RUN
ENTER OLD ODOMETER READING:
? 1234
ENTER CURRENT ODOMETER READING:
? 1900
ENTER GALLONS USED:
? 20
MILES-PER-GALLON =                    646.00
```

DEBUGGING

As we have seen, any error found in a program is called a bug, and the process of correcting errors is called debugging. There are three kinds of program bugs: (1) syntax errors, (2) run-time errors, and (3) logic errors. Generally, it is easy to locate and correct syntax and run-time errors, because the computer's error messages indicate the location and nature of the error.

Logic errors, on the other hand, indicate an error in the programmer's solution to the original problem. A logic error occurs when the algorithm is incorrect and does not solve the problem. Logic errors also occur when an algorithm has been incorrectly programmed; that is, when the program statements do not correctly state the steps to be taken by the computer.

(b) **Pascal**

```
program travel (input,output);
   (* Using odometer readings and gallons   *)
   (*        calculate miles-per-gallon.     *)
var
   oldodometer, currentodometer: real;
   gallons, milestraveled : real;
   mpg : real;
begin
   write('Enter old odometer reading: ');
   readln(oldodometer);
   write('Enter current ododmeter reading: ');
   readln(currentodometer);
   write('Enter gallons used: ');
   readln(gallons);
   milestraveled := currentodometer - oldodometer;
   mpg := milestraveled - gallons;
   writeln(' Miles-per-gallon = ',mpg:5:2)
end.
Running
Enter old odometer reading: 1234
Enter current odometer reading: 1900
Enter gallons used: 20
  Miles-per-gallon = 646.00
```

Correcting logic errors requires attention and persistence. The two most common methods for correcting logic errors are hand simulation, or desk checking, and the printing of intermediate results.

Hand Simulation

The objective of **hand simulation, desk checking,** or **tracing** the output is for the programmer to find logic and syntax errors. The programmer uses pencil and paper to act the part of the computer. Starting with the very first program statement, the programmer follows the instructions set down in the program just as the computer would. By stepping through each instruction and knowing what the expected result should be at each stage, the programmer should be able to identify the step or steps that are producing the error and correct them. This is a time-consuming procedure. The programmer must carefully follow the instructions exactly as they are written, not as they were intended to be.

Intermediate Results

Every program contains some statements that produce output. In addition, throughout the program, partial or **intermediate results** are calculated and stored in memory. These results are not usually printed as output because they are not needed to support the program's conclusions. When an executed program produces results that are incorrect, it is often useful to go back and examine these intermediate results. The programmer should go back to the source program and add output statements to enable all intermediate results to be printed as output. When this new version of the program is reviewed, not only will the original results (incorrect as they may be) be produced, but all the intermediate results will be visible as well. By examining these intermediate results and comparing them to the expected results at each stage, the programmer can locate the source of the problem and correct it.

The miles-per-gallon examples found in Figure 7.8 translate without syntax errors. However, as indicated, they do not produce the correct results. With an old odometer reading of 1234 miles, a current reading of 1900 miles, and 20 gallons of gasoline used, we can see that the miles per gallon calculated should be 33.3.

$$
\begin{array}{rl}
1,900 & \text{current odometer reading} \\
-1,234 & \text{old odometer reading} \\
\hline
666 & \text{total miles traveled}
\end{array}
$$

mpg = total miles traveled / gallons used
mpg = 666 / 20 = 33.3

Unfortunately, the programs in Figure 7.8 do not produce the expected results. In Figure 7.9 additional statements have been added to both the BASIC and Pascal programs to write out the values of total miles traveled and gallons used. An examination of these values and the programs reveals that the formula for calculating miles per gallon in each program is incorrect. A subtraction sign has been used instead of division. Correcting this error produces a program that executes properly. The now-extraneous output statements can be removed.

Programmers often use hand simulation and the printing of intermediate results to analyze and correct errors in an algorithm. Some systems include special software debugging tools to assist programmers in finding and correcting errors.

Figure 7.9

Incorrect Results: When program results are incorrect, obtaining intermediate
results may help the programmer find the error in (a) BASIC and (b) Pascal.

(a) **BASIC**

```
100 REM -- USING ODOMETER READING AND GALLONS, --
105 REM --          CALCULATE MILES-PER-GALLON. --
110 PRINT "ENTER OLD ODOMETER READING: "
120 INPUT O
130 PRINT "ENTER CURRENT ODOMETER READING: "
140 INPUT C
150 PRINT "ENTER GALLONS USED: "
160 INPUT G
165 PRINT
170 LET T = C - O
175    PRINT "T =",T
176    PRINT "G =",G
180 LET M = T - G
190 PRINT "MILES-PER-GALLON =", USING "###.##";M
200 END
Ok

RUN
ENTER OLD ODOMETER READING:
? 1234
ENTER CURRENT ODOMETER READING:
? 1900
ENTER GALLONS USED:
? 20
T =              666
G =               20
MILES-PER-GALLON =           646.00
180 LET M = T / G                                  (correction)
RUN
ENTER OLD ODOMETER READING:
? 1234
ENTER CURRENT ODOMETER READING:
? 1900
ENTER GALLONS USED:
? 20
T =              666
G =               20
MILES-PER-GALLON =            33.30
DELETE 175
Ok
DELETE 176
```

205

Figure 7.9   Continued

(b) **Pascal**

```
program travel (input,output);
   (* Using odometer readings and gallons   *)
   (*        calculate miles-per-gallon.      *)
var
   oldodometer, currentodometer: real;
   gallons, milestraveled : real;
   mpg : real;
begin
   write('Enter old odometer reading: ');
   readln(oldodometer);
   write('Enter current ododmeter reading: ');
   readln(currentodometer);
   write('Enter gallons used: ');
   readln(gallons);
   milestraveled := currentodometer - oldodometer;
   mpg := milestraveled - gallons;
   writeln(' Miles-per-gallon = ',mpg:5:2);
end.
```

```
Running
Enter old odometer reading: 1234
Enter current odometer reading: 1900
Enter gallons used: 20
 Miles-per-gallon = 646.00
```

```
program travel (input,output);
   (* Using odometer readings and gallons   *)
   (*        calculate miles-per-gallon.      *)
var
   oldodometer, currentodometer: real;
   gallons, milestraveled : real;
   mpg : real;
begin
   write('Enter old odometer reading: ');
   readln(oldodometer);
   write('Enter current ododmeter reading: ');
   readln(currentodometer);
   write('Enter gallons used: ');
   readln(gallons);
   milestraveled := currentodometer - oldodometer;
       writeln('milestraveled =', milestraveled:5:2);
       writeln('gallons =',gallons:5:2);
   mpg := milestraveled - gallons;
   writeln(' Miles-per-gallon = ',mpg:5:2);
end.
```

```
Running
Enter old odometer reading: 1234
Enter current odometer reading: 1900
Enter gallons used: 20
milestraveled =666.00
gallons =20.00
 Miles-per-gallon = 646.00

program travel (input,output);
   (* Using odometer readings and gallons   *)
   (*        calculate miles-per-gallon.     *)
var
   oldodometer, currentodometer: real;
   gallons, milestraveled : real;
   mpg : real;
begin
   write('Enter old odometer reading: ');
   readln(oldodometer);
   write('Enter current ododmeter reading: ');
   readln(currentodometer);
   write('Enter gallons used: ');
   readln(gallons);
   milestraveled := currentodometer - oldodometer;
      writeln('milestraveled =', milestraveled:5:2);
      writeln('gallons =',gallons:5:2);
   mpg := milestraveled / gallons;
   writeln(' Miles-per-gallon = ',mpg:5:2)
end.

Running
Enter old odometer reading: 1234
Enter current odometer reading: 1900
Enter gallons used: 20
milestraveled =666.00
gallons =20.00
 Miles-per-gallon = 33.30
```

TESTING

Once a program appears to work and produces the expected results for a given set of data, it should be tested for accuracy. It is possible that a program will work with one set of data and not with another. Every section of the program's code must be thoroughly tested. Test data should be chosen to resemble the real-life data that the program would normally deal with. For example, it is common for real-life programs to encounter incorrect or insufficient data. A well-written program should deal with common and even unexpected errors in some reasonable way. There are a number of different types of test data. Each type checks different aspects of the program. Testing a program with valid data verifies that the basic algorithm is correct. Using valid data that contains special exceptions assures that such exceptions are handled by the code. Finally, using invalid or incorrect data lets the programmer know what will happen when incorrect data are used. Programmers need to expect incorrect data.

DOCUMENTATION

No program is complete without documentation. **Documentation** is a report in which the programmer explains how the program works. The role of documentation is to provide information and instruction to a program's users. This information is critical for other programmers who will be called upon to modify, update, or correct the program as well as for anyone who will use the program. Even simple programs should be documented. The memory of the original programmer cannot be relied upon. What seems obvious today will not be obvious in a few months or next year when one returns to alter or reuse even an easy program.

Program documentation should include the following: (1) A clear, specific definition of the problem. (2) A description of the procedure used to solve the problem. Where possible this should include the formal algorithm in pseudocode or a flowchart. (3) A copy of the program's source code. (4) Detailed information on the testing process including samples of the test data and results. (5) A user's manual designed for a nonprogrammer explaining how the program operates. This should include input details, expected output, and a description of possible error messages and how to make sense of them. Sample data and output should be included. (6) If changes, modifications, addition, and deletions are made to the program, a log of these alterations should be maintained. Adjusting a program is clearly a dynamic process and documentation is the only way to retain a record of the changes.

The best documentation is written as the program is being developed, programmed and tested. Unfortunately most documentation is written after the programming process is completed, and it is usually written by the programmer. In one sense, the programmer is the most logical person to write the documentation, having the best knowledge of the code. Such intimate knowledge, however, makes it all too easy to leave out essential operating instructions that seem obvious to the programmer but are not obvious to the typical user. Good documentation shows that the programmer cares not only about solving the problem, but about making the solution available, useful, and adaptable to all those who will use the program.

Developing successful programs is 10 percent inspiration and 90 percent concentration. While it is possible to design and debug programs by randomly changing things to see what happens, this technique is very inefficient. It is time-consuming and produces programs that are difficult to adjust and impossible to follow. Careful planning, attention in designing algorithms, and patience in debugging programs ensures their accuracy and produces rewarding results. Good documentation makes the program easier to use.

SUMMARY

Computer programs, both prewritten applications packages and user-designed programs, use computer files. A computer file is a collection of related information. Unique file names distinguish one file from another. Well-chosen file names help to identify the contents of the file.

Programs written in high-level languages cannot be directly understood by computers. They must be translated into machine-readable form. The high-level language version of the program is the **source program;** the machine-language version is the **object program.**

A **compiler** translates an entire source program in a single operation. The translated object program is then executed. An **interpreter** translates and executes a program one statement at a time. During translation, a program's individual statements either translate or produce **syntax errors.**

Translating a program only makes it possible for the computer to follow the indicated instructions. For the computer to produce results, the program must be executed. An executed program can either (1) work perfectly, (2) produce incorrect results, or (3) stop executing as the result of **run-time errors.**

Debugging is the process of correcting program errors. Debugging includes **desk checking** and the listing of **intermediate results** to verify computations.

Test data should be used to verify that all sections of a program operate properly.

Documentation provides information and instruction to a program's users.

Key Words

As an extra review of the chapter, try defining the following terms. If you have trouble with any of them, refer to the page number listed.

aborted (bombed) *(199)*
bug *(192)*
compiler *(191)*
debugging *(192)*
diagnostic message *(192)*
documentation *(208)*
hand simulation (desk
   checking) *(203)*
intermediate results *(204)*

interpreter *(191)*
linkage editor (link/load
   program) *(191)*
logic error *(201)*
object program (object code) *(191)*
run-time error *(199)*
source program (source code) *(191)*
syntax error *(192)*
utility program *(191)*

Test Your Knowledge

1. How should file names be chosen?

2. Give two examples of well-chosen file names.

3. What is a compiler?

4. How is a source program different from an object program?

5. How does an interpreter differ from a compiler?

6. What role does a linkage editor play in processing a program?

7. What is a syntax error? What causes it?

8. What role do diagnostic messages play in error correction?

9. If a program translates correctly, does that imply that the correct answers will be produced when executed? Defend your position.

10. What occurs when a program is executed?

11. What are the three types of errors frequently encountered in programs?

12. Why are logic errors so difficult to find?

13. How is desk checking used to debug a program?

14. How are intermediate results used to debug a program?

15. List the six key items program documentation should contain.

Expand Your Knowledge

1. Go to your school's computing center and find out what language translators are available. What departments are heavy users of these translators? Are they compilers or interpreters?

2. Prewritten software can contain errors. Go to a local computer store and investigate what a user can do if such software contains errors and does not perform properly.

3. Using the hourly salary with overtime example analyzed in Chapter 6, develop a set of test data that could be used to check the program. What kinds of incorrect data might a user type into the program? Include these in your test data.

4. Using the computer system you have available at your school and either BASIC or Pascal, enter one of the programs found in Figure 7.8. Compile or interpret the program. Examine the errors messages and the output. Correct the syntax and logic errors you have entered.

5. For one of the programs in Figure 7.8, write a User Manual. Include all the information a nonprogrammer would need to make effective use of the program.

8

Programming Languages

CHAPTER OUTLINE

Computers are machines. They are tools for problem solving that require detailed, literal instructions to perform any task. These instructions, or programs, must be provided in languages that computers can understand. As we have seen, computers do not understand human language. Programming languages have been developed so that people and computers can communicate relatively easily.

It certainly would be easier to talk to a computer in English than it is to write a computer program. Yet English—or any human or natural language (the languages written or spoken by people) for that matter—can be ambiguous. The literal meanings of our words may not fully express our intentions. We often say one thing and mean another or give incomplete directions. Our facial expressions, tone of voice, and body language usually help us to communicate and often change the meaning of our words. Natural language is rich in slang and idiomatic expressions, and colorful speech may lead to misunderstandings. For example, a student rushes into class late and in a frustrated voice says to a friend who is not a native speaker of English, "My car broke down on me!" The friend responds, "Oh no! Were you badly hurt?" The friend interpreted the statement literally and understood that the car had actually broken on top of the speaker, causing possible physical injury. The idiom, of course, simply implied that the car was not operating properly.

Communicating with computers leaves no room for ambiguity. Computers require very specific instructions. We cannot simply tell the machine to perform addition; we must specify that A is added to B and C in a mathematical expression: $A + B + C$.

A **programming language** is a language that people use to communicate with computers. It has a specific and limited vocabulary and a set of syntax rules for structuring statements. Each word, phrase, and symbol has a very specific meaning and must appear in a particular order to be understood by the computer. These programming languages are the subject of this chapter.

After studying this chapter, you will be able to:

- Describe the categories of computer languages.
- Explain the differences between low-level and high-level languages.
- List the criteria for choosing a programming language.
- Identify the most commonly used programming languages.
- Describe the advantages and disadvantages of three of the most common computer languages.
- Describe the basic features of six popular programming languages.
- Examine object-oriented programming.

TYPES OF COMPUTER LANGUAGES

There are hundreds of different computer languages, but only a few, such as FORTRAN, BASIC, Pascal, and C, are widely used. A number of attempts have been made to develop a single language that does all things well. Such languages have not caught on, however. These languages are by necessity very complex, difficult to learn, and usually run only on large systems.

Computer languages relate to the computer in different ways. In a sense, not all computer languages are "created equal." Computer languages fall into a number of broad categories. The less complex the language's statements (the lower its sophistication level), the closer its relationship to the machine itself. The higher the sophistication, the easier it is to use the language to write programs. From lowest to highest, the classifications are:

- machine language
- assembly language
- high-level languages
- natural language processing

Early computers, built in the late 1940s and early 1950s, were programmed by adjusting the wires and switches that made up the machine. The resulting circuitry could be used to solve a particular problem. To solve another problem, the wires and switches had to be readjusted. This was a very slow and arduous task requiring an intimate knowledge of the machine. Putting a program into the machine often required an entire day.

As we saw in Chapter 2, von Neumann developed the concept of the *stored program*, in which a lengthy sequence of instructions could be stored in the computer's memory along with data. This became possible when instructions were expressed as a code that corresponded to the circuit path needed to solve a problem. Von Neumann's ideas led to the development of machine language.

Machine Language

Machine language is a code used to communicate with a particular computer. Instructions are coded as groups of ones and zeros (binary numbers), which represent the electronic pathways necessary for solving a problem. Machine language or machine code is the only language the computer directly understands. It is the computer's "native" language. Since computers manufactured by different companies have unique internal designs, each brand and model of computer has a unique, **machine-dependent** machine language. An IBM mainframe will have a different machine language or code from a Digital Equipment Corp. machine. Similarly, the machine code for the Macintosh is different from that used by the IBM Personal System/2 or Commodore Amiga.

Every statement in machine language contains an instruction and the data or the location of the data that the instruction will use. Compared to rewiring the machine for each problem, machine language was a giant step forward. However, writing long sequences of binary digits is as intricate as plugging in hundreds of wires. It is very easy to make mistakes. Machine language is very difficult to write, incredibly error-prone because it is entered by humans, and requires considerable knowledge of machine hardware because its statements represent circuit paths.

Assembly Language

Because writing programs in machine language is so tedious and prone to errors, **assembly languages,** or simply **assemblers,** were invented. Instead of statements consisting of long series of zeros and ones, assembly language instructions contain easily remembered abbreviations or mnemonics such as SUB for subtract, CLR for clear, or MOV for move. Data are specified directly as numeric quantities or represented by a name given to the location in computer memory where the required data can be found.

Compared to machine language programs, assembly language programs are much easier for people to write and fairly understandable to read. However, like machine languages before them, assembly languages are machine-dependent. That is, different computers require different assembly languages, and programs written for one machine will not run on another. Moreover, assembly-language programs cannot be executed (processed) directly by a computer. First they must be translated, or *assembled,* into machine-readable form (machine code) before they can be processed. Despite their considerable improvement over machine language programs, assembly language programs are still very detailed. They are usually quite long and, like machine language, are error-prone. Each assembly language statement translates directly into a single machine language instruction. A thorough knowledge of the computer hardware on the part of the programmer is often required for writing efficient code. Figure 8.1 illustrates the mathematical equivalent of $C = A + B$.

With the development of high-level languages, fewer problems are being solved with assembly languages. However, assembly languages continue to be valuable tools for solving the kinds of problems that call for direct communication with the computer's hardware. Much of the operating system software used to operate computer systems is written in assembly languages. In addition, program sections that "talk" to peripheral devices such as printers, disk drives, and monitors frequently use assembly language. Assembly language programs run very quickly and take up very little space in memory.

High-Level Languages

Although assembly languages are an improvement over machine language, using one still requires concentration on the machine rather than on the prob-

Figure 8.1

Assembly Language Example: This program segment is written in MACRO-11, the assembly language of the VAX-11 family of computers from Digital Equipment Corp. The program picks up two integers stored in memory, adds them, and puts the result back into memory. This is the mathematical equivalent of $C = A + B$.

```
A:   .WORD      123            ;reserve a word for A and initialize
B:   .WORD      307            ;reserve a word for B and initialize
C:   .BLKL      1              ;reserve a long word for C
     .ENTRY     EXAMPLE,0      ;define entry point into code
     CLRL       R7             ;set 32-bit registers R7 and
     CLRL       R8             ; R8 to zero
     MOVW       R7,A           ;bring A and B from memory into and
     MOVW       R8, B          ; R8 in the CPU, respectively
     ADDL2      R7,R8          ;add R7 and R8, result in R8
     MOVL       R8,C           ;move R8 to memory in C
     $EXIT-S                   ;exit program
     .END       EXAMPLE        ;end of code
```

lems being solved. The development of high-level programming languages allowed programmers to focus on finding procedures to solve problems. In contrast to both machine and assembly languages, they no longer had to concentrate on how the computer would process the program.

High-level languages have a structure more like that of natural languages such as English. Each high-level language is designed around a set of rules that define how words and mathematical expressions can be combined within the language. These rules are known as the *syntax* of the language.

High-level languages are easier for people to understand than assembly or machine languages because they use familiar English terms and follow a limited set of rules. Statements resemble a combination of English sentences and mathematical equations.

Unfortunately, while people find high-level languages somewhat readable, computers do not. High-level languages, like assembly language programs, must be translated into machine-readable form before they can be processed by any computer. One statement in a high-level language may translate into many machine-level instructions. A translator program is required to handle many of the hardware details that would have required the programmer's attention in a lower-level language. As discussed in Chapter 7, translator programs transform statements written in a particular high-level language into the machine language appropriate for the specific computer being used. Although high-level languages remain essentially the same from machine to machine, translator programs are keyed to specific computer hardware. As a result, most high-level languages are **machine-independent,** which means they will operate on any computer for which an appropriate translator program exists. High-level languages are **portable,** meaning that programs can be moved from machine to machine with only minor changes required. In this way, programs can solve problems on machines used by many different people.

Programming in a high-level language is easier, less time-consuming, less frustrating, and less error-prone than assembly language programming. For these reasons, high-level languages lend themselves to the solution of more complex problems than their lower-level counterparts.

Natural Language Processing

As we have seen, computer languages have become more and more "English-like" over the years. The next logical step in the development of computer languages would seem to be systems that understand natural languages, the languages spoken by people. A major research area today within the computer science field of artificial intelligence is natural language processing, or natural language understanding.

Scientists studying natural language and its implications for computers approach the topic from two different directions. Some computer scientists work with colleagues in linguistics and psychology to explain how people learn and understand language. They develop computer models of natural language to better understand how we use language. The more closely the computer model mimics natural language, the more clearly language and the human learning process is understood. The focus is on understanding language and the human mind.

The other approach, popularized by Japanese research and reflected in some applications software available in the United States, is the development of software that appears to understand natural language. However, such natural language systems may not process language the way people do. The focus here is on the computer and getting the machine to "speak" in human ways. In such systems, a person can give a computer an instruction or information in ordinary sentences and receive appropriate answers from the computer. Natural language is further discussed in Chapter 16.

CHOOSING A COMPUTER LANGUAGE

Today hundreds of computer languages exist. With such variety, how do programmers choose the languages they use? Ideally, programs should be written in the language that is most appropriate to the task. Of course, "most appropriate" will mean different things in different settings. The following criteria can prove helpful when choosing a language:

1. *Familiarity.* In many cases, programmers simply choose from among the languages they know best. Although most programmers can learn a new lan-

guage fairly quickly, a problem that requires an immediate solution allows little time for learning.

2. *Availability.* Not all languages are available on all machines. Availability is not limited exclusively by hardware; it is often limited by what an organization can afford. Translator programs can be very expensive, and organizations may choose to use what they already own rather than purchase additional software to solve a specific problem.

3. *Suitability.* Some languages are particularly well suited to solving specific types of problems. For example, FORTRAN is an excellent language for solving scientific and engineering problems. COBOL is very effective in generating the voluminous output required by many businesses, and MUMPS was developed for the medical community to assist doctors in diagnosing diseases. For consistency, many organizations require that all programs be written in a specific language or selected from a limited number of languages. In such cases, programmers have no choice but to use what is required. For example, the U.S. Department of Defense intends to require that all programs written for the military use Ada.

4. *Efficiency.* Assembly language programs run faster than those written in high-level languages, but they take longer to write and debug. As a result, most applications are written in high-level languages. However, not all translator programs are equally good. Even within a specific language, many translators are available and some execute programs faster than others. A program written in UCSD Pascal, for example, will run much slower than one written in the more recently released TURBO Pascal.

5. *Longevity.* Computer hardware changes constantly. Such changes need to be considered when choosing a programming language. Languages that are standardized and popular are more likely to survive rapidly changing hardware technology. Some older languages, such as COBOL, seem to live longer than expected simply because of the vast numbers of programs that exist in the language. In many cases, it is less time-consuming and therefore less expensive to update and modify an existing code than to rewrite it in a language that might be more efficient.

6. *Supportability.* All programs require regular updating and maintenance, and languages must be chosen with an eye to the future. A language that is no longer being revised and improved is a poor choice in the changing world of computers. A program will not be overly valuable if it is written in a language that is not available on the new machine an organization purchases. Within organizations, a language that can be used by more than one programmer can be very important. In this way, programmers can help each other debug programs, and modifications can be made by someone other than the original programmer.

COMMON LANGUAGES

To more clearly understand the differences between languages, we will examine in detail three of the most popular languages. Three programs will be presented that illustrate the algorithm developed in Chapter 6 for calculating the pay due to an individual who works for an hourly wage with overtime. However, one cannot get a true feel for the variety of programming languages with only three examples. As a result, we will briefly examine a number of other commonly used languages.

FORTRAN

FORTRAN is an acronym for FORmula TRANslation. It was created at IBM in 1954 and two years later became the first high-level language to be commercially available. It was designed to process the large amounts of numeric data common in mathematical, scientific, and engineering problems.

Uses and Limitations FORTRAN was the first widely used programming language. It is still in use after nearly 40 years, which makes it very, very old in terms of the life span of modern computers. FORTRAN is a concise, compact language whose statements closely resemble mathematical equations. This is its outstanding feature. FORTRAN remains, as its developers intended, one of the best languages for programs involving numeric information and complicated formulas. To ensure that a program written in FORTRAN will run on a variety of computers with little or no modification, there is a standard version. This makes FORTRAN programs highly portable. The FORTRAN standard has been regularly revised and updated.

FORTRAN has some shortcomings. Designed to handle numeric information, it is difficult to process character information (data expressed in letters) using FORTRAN. Despite changes reflected in the current standard (FORTRAN 77), input and output statements are very formal and inflexible, which makes them difficult to use. FORTRAN does not deal well with information stored in multiple files. These factors make it a poor language for most business applications. In addition, FORTRAN programs are often hard to follow by simply reading them. They require extensive documentation explaining how the program works.

Organization As we can see in Figure 8.2, a program written in FORTRAN consists of a sequence of statements.

Statements appear one to a line in the order in which they are executed. Branching statements, which alter the order in which statements are executed, are included where necessary. The IF-THEN/ELSE/ENDIF block is an example of a branching statement. All statements must start in specific locations on the line and may be no more than 72 characters long. This length reflects the for-

Figure 8.2   A FORTRAN Program.

```
C       FORTRAN 77 PROGRAM
C       CALCULATE HOURLY SALARY
C
C       INPUT DATA
        READ(5,10) REGHRS, OTRATE
        READ(5,10) HOURS, RATE
10      FORMAT(F4.1,2X,F5.2)
C
C       CALCULATE GROSS WAGES WITH OVER TIME FORMULA
        IF (HOURS .GT. REGHRS) THEN
            OTHRS = HOURS -REGHRS
            REGPAY = REGHRS * RATE
            OT = OTHRS * OTRATE * RATE
            GROSS = REGPAY + OT
        ELSE
C       CALCULATE GROSS WAGES WITH NO OVERTIME
            GROSS = HOURS * RATE
        ENDIF
C
C       OUTPUT RESULTS
        WRITE(6,40)
40      FORMAT(1X,'  HOURS   RATE   WAGES')
        WRITE(6,50) HOURS, RATE, GROSS
50      FORMAT(3X,F4.1,2X,F5.2,1X,F8.2)
C
        STOP
        END
```

A statement with a "C" in column 1 is a COMMENT. A comment serves as explanation of the code and is not executed.

This FORMAT statement describes the data for the above READ.

The next 5 statements calculate gross salary if overtime is worked.

This statement calculates gross salary if there is NO overtime.

This FORMAT statement describes output.

This FORMAT statement describes output.

mat of punched computer cards that were used as standard input when the language was initially developed. Statement numbers, such as 10, 40, and 50, appear at the left margin of those statements referenced within the program. Reserved words are used to indicate tasks the computer is to perform, such as READ, WRITE, and FORMAT. Large, complex programs are often divided into parts called **subprograms.** Each subprogram solves a specific part of the problem.

BASIC

BASIC, which stands for Beginner's All-Purpose Symbolic Instruction Code, was invented in the early 1960s by Thomas Kurtz and John Kemeny to teach programming at Dartmouth College. BASIC was derived in part from FORTRAN and in some ways is a simplified version. It became available for general use in 1965. BASIC was designed to let users communicate, or *interact*, with the computer as programs executed. In other words, data are supplied by the user as needed by the program. This produces an environment where programmers are actively involved in the processing of a program. BASIC programs are more user-friendly than those written in FORTRAN.

Uses and Limitations   Many people believe that BASIC is easy to learn and use. Beginners can write and run simple programs after only a few hours of study. There are relatively few commands to learn. BASIC handles many programming details for the user and can be used to solve a wide variety of problems. It can process both numbers and characters (letters and symbols) and can be used to solve fairly complex mathematical problems. It is usually an interpreted language, although a standardized compiler was approved in 1988. BASIC interpreters and compilers require little memory and run on even a minimally equipped microcomputer.

Having so few rules, BASIC programs are frequently hard to follow. BASIC does not foster good programming style. Many consider BASIC a "quick and dirty" language. Its very strength of simplicity for quick learning is its major weakness. It tempts novices to try to solve a problem without first working through the steps needed for the solution. Although BASIC was not designed to handle large amounts of data, its availability on microcomputers and ease of learning has led to its use by many small businesses. There is a standardized version of BASIC, but it is limited. Most translator manufacturers produce versions with many modifications and extensions. As a result, there are many different BASICs, and programs may require major changes for use on different machines. Long programs can be very difficult to follow and a person must rely on documentation to understand the program.

Organization   Figure 8.3 illustrates the BASIC solution to the salary problem whose algorithm was developed in Chapter 6.

BASIC statements are usually entered one per line with each line consecutively numbered. Programs terminate with the END statement. Although subprograms exist, they are not as flexible as subprograms in other high-level languages, and programs are frequently written as single units.

In BASIC, reserved words such as INPUT, PRINT, and GOTO are used to direct the computer to perform a specific task. Early versions of BASIC required that variable names be restricted to a single letter, possibly followed by a number for numeric quantities and a letter followed by a dollar sign ($) for characters. Such variable names made undocumented programs rather unreadable.

Despite its availability on microcomputers, the tendency by its users to design hard-to-follow programs has led the National College Board to choose Pascal rather than BASIC as the language of its Advanced Placement (AP)

Figure 8.3   The BASIC Solution: This is the BASIC solution to the salary problem whose algorithm was developed in Chapter 6.

```
 95     PRINT "ENTER REGULAR HOURS AND OVERTIME RATE: "
100     INPUT T, P
105     PRINT "ENTER HOURS AND PAYRATE: "
110     INPUT H, R
115     REM -- DEPENDING ON HOURS WORKED DOES --
116     REM -- EMPLOYEE GET OVERTIME PAY. --
120     IF H > T THEN 150   ELSE 200
150        LET O = H - T
160        LET R1 = T * R
170        LET O1 = O * P * R
180        LET W = R1 + O1
190     GOTO 300
195     REM -- CALCULATE WAGES WITHOUT --
196     REM -- OVERTIME PAY. --
200        LET W = H * R
300     PRINT "  HOURS    RATE    WAGES"
310     PRINT USING " ##     #.##   ###.##",H,R,W
999     END
```

Data is entered with an INPUT statement.

REM stands for REMARK and like the comment in FORTRAN explains the code.

All statements are numbered. Statements are executed in numeric order unless an alternative is specified.

ELSE 200 causes a branch to statement 200.

GOTO 300 causes a branch to statement 300.

PRINT statements produce output. # indicates the location of a number.

---

exam. The AP exam awards college credits for knowledge of computer science and programming learned in high school. In an effort to return BASIC to its intended purpose as an easy-to-learn teaching language, Kemeny and Kurtz have developed a structured version of BASIC called TRUE BASIC. TRUE BASIC provides for additional syntax rules and encourages longer, more meaningful variable names, making its programs easier to read.

Pascal

Pascal was written in 1968 by Niklaus Wirth of Switzerland. It was intended as a general-purpose teaching language emphasizing top-down design. As you recall from Chapter 6, top-down design breaks a problem down into smaller and smaller parts until each of these subproblems can be solved directly. Pascal's syntax structure supports well-designed algorithms. The language is named after the French mathematician Blaise Pascal, who invented an early mechanical calculator (see Chapter 2). The first compiler was made available in 1971. Pascal is a powerful language capable of dealing with numbers as well as characters. Because it is easy to learn and imposes good programming style, it is taught as a first programming language in many colleges and universities.

Uses and Limitations Pascal's strength lies in its structure. It can be used to solve a wide range of programming problems. Yet Pascal has relatively few commands, and a novice programmer can learn to write simple programs very quickly. At the same time, it is better suited than many other languages to the development of large, complex programs. Using Pascal's international standard, most Pascal programs are portable. With its limited number of commands, fast compilers requiring very little memory are available on most microcomputers. Pascal is rapidly becoming a real competitor to BASIC as the primary microcomputer language.

Pascal has weaknesses as well. Because it is so powerful, its commands are very brief and concise. Documentation containing full translations helps to clarify the code. Pascal was not intended as a language for business applications and is limited in its ability to handle multiple files. Despite this, many businesses use Pascal for such applications.

Figure 8.4   The Start of a Pascal Program.

```
program payroll2 (input, output);
var
   hours, payrate, othours, otwages: real;
   regwages, wages, reghours, otrate : real;
begin
   write('Enter regular hours and overtime rate: ');
   readln (reghours, otrate);
      (*  Depending on hours worked, does    *)
      (*    employee get overtime pay?        *)
   write('Enter hours and payrate: ');
   readln (hours, payrate);
   if hours > reghours then
      begin
        regwages := reghours * payrate;
        othours := hours - reghours;
        otwages := othours * otrate * payrate;
        wages := regwages + otwages;
      end
   else
      (*  Calculate wages without .*)
      (*     overtime pay.          *)
      wages := hours * payrate
   writeln(' HOURS   RATE   WAGES');
   writeln(hours:5, payrate:8:2, wages:9:2)
   end.
```

var stands for variable. This section lists all variables used in the program and their type. begin indicates where the code starts.

Calculates wages including overtime.

Calculates wages without overtime.
write contains a description of the output.

Organization   As we can see in Figure 8.4, each program starts by stating the program name and specifying the files required by the program.

If only (input, output) are listed, data are expected to be entered from the keyboard with output going to the screen. The statements immediately following the var identify whether the values used by or calculated within the program will be integers, real numbers, characters, or true or false. Pascal encourages the use of subprograms.

Statements need not be entered one to a line. Placing more than one statement on a line is possible. Each statement must end with a semicolon. Usually, statements are written in standard outline form indented from the left margin to indicate the relationships between statements. Use of outline style has proven so easy to follow that modifications of this technique are now used with older languages such as BASIC and FORTRAN.

OTHER POPULAR HIGH-LEVEL LANGUAGES

In addition to the languages described, hundreds of other computer languages exist. While programs have been written in all of them, only a few are commonly used, and several new languages are gaining acceptance for specific purposes. Let us examine some of these languages.

Ada

Ada was introduced in 1980 after considerable study and revision. It is named after Lady Ada Lovelace, the first programmer (see Chapter 2). It was commissioned by the U.S. Department of Defense, the largest purchaser of software in the world. The department's existing software, written in dozens of languages, was becoming increasingly difficult to maintain and update. Officials decided they needed a single language capable of doing every computer-related task. Ada was the result. Ada is an all-purpose computer language that can be used to program everything from business applications to **embedded computers.** Embedded computers are computers built into other devices. They are an integral part of large electromechanical weapons systems such as missiles, submarines, and airplanes, as well as nonmilitary devices such as microwave ovens, automobiles, hospital intensive care unit equipment, and air traffic control systems.

Like Pascal, Ada is a highly structured language. Unlike Pascal, it is capable of communicating directly with the computer hardware as if it were an assembly language. It is ideal for creating very large software systems in which subsystems are developed independently by different teams of programmers. With Ada, program changes and adaptations are easy to make and require only minimal changes to the larger system.

Ada requires a very large compiler and must be run on computer systems with considerable memory. The Defense Department intends to exert considerable pressure on software developers to encourage the use of Ada. Eventually the Defense Department plans to refuse any programs not written in Ada.

C

C is a programming language developed at Bell Labs in the early 1970s by Dennis Ritchie. Many computer experts consider C to represent the modern form of the assembly language. C has the syntax structures found in such high-level languages as Pascal along with the ability to communicate directly with the hardware. C is very portable. It is used not only to develop operating systems (for which it was originally designed), but for language compilers, editors, word processors, and many other popular software systems. C is used to develop operating systems on minis and micros, and many microcomputer and workstation compilers are available. Programs written in C require very little memory and are extremely efficient. Unfortunately, C is not user-friendly; it is difficult to learn. Considerable programming skill is needed to write or understand C programs.

COBOL

COBOL stands for COmmon Business Oriented Language. It was invented in the late 1950s at a conference organized by the U.S. Defense Department and attended by representatives of government and industry. The purpose of the conference was to develop a standard language for business applications in which programs could easily be moved from one machine to another. To spur the use of COBOL, in the 1960s the federal government required that all the computers it purchased run COBOL, and that all government software be written in COBOL. Use of any other language required convincing evidence that COBOL was not appropriate. Since the government was the largest consumer of computer products at the time, COBOL spread rapidly.

COBOL uses English verbs such as READ, WRITE, ADD, SUBTRACT, MOVE, and COMPUTE to indicate the operations to be performed. COBOL was designed as an English-like, self-documenting language that a nonprogrammer could follow. It deals well with large amounts of character data, such as names and addresses. Numeric data, including dollars and cents, and numeric codes such as social security numbers are easily processed. The language is not designed to perform complex calculations. In addition, COBOL programs are incredibly wordy, making it almost impossible to write a short COBOL program.

LISP

LISP, for LISt Processing, was developed in 1958 at The Massachusetts Institute of Technology (MIT) by John McCarthy as a language for developing artificial intelligence (AI) programs. It is an interactive language designed to manipulate non-numeric information such as characters, symbols, words, phrases, and even shapes. Objects are associated with lists of features. LISP is the most popular AI language, and it is used in applications areas such as natural language processing, robotics, developing mathematical proofs, and pattern recognition. Figure 8.5 illustrates the LISP version of the problem discussed in Chapter 6.

LOGO

Based on LISP, LOGO was developed by Seymour Papert in the early 1960s at MIT. It is an interactive language designed to teach programming to children. It makes use of on-screen graphics to develop and reinforce problem-solving skills. By using a limited set of commands, children can draw complex pictures by moving a cursor called a *turtle* around the screen. Originally this cursor was a triangle, but recent versions include a variety of shapes. Commands are grouped together, letting the user create larger and more complex pictures. In this way, new instructions, actually simple subprograms, are developed. LOGO is widely used in grade schools to introduce computers, programming, and problem-solving methods in an entertaining environment.

Modula-2

Modula-2 is an improved and updated version of Pascal. It was developed by Niklaus Wirth, who created Pascal, and was released in 1978. Designed to teach programming and computer concepts, Pascal unexpectedly gained wide use in

---

Figure 8.5   LISP: This illustrates the LISP version of the salary problem discussed in Chapter 6.

```
(defun compute-wages ()                                    Read in data.
 (princ "Enter hours worked > ")                           Read in hours worked.
 (setq hours (read))
 (princ "Enter pay-rate > ")                               Read in pay rate.
 (setq payrate (read))
 (princ "Enter number of regular hours > ")               Read in regular hours.
 (setq regular-hours (read))
 (princ "Enter overtime pay-rate > ")                      Read in overtime pay rate.
 (setq overtime-rate (read))
 (wages hours payrate regular-hours overtime-rate))

(defun wages (hours payrate regular-hours overtime-rate)   Calculate wages.
 (cond ((> hours regular-hours) (+ (* regular-hours payrate)
 (* (- hours regular-hours) overtime-rate)))
 (T (* hours payrate)))))
```

custom-designed software for business and industry. Modifications needed to make Pascal better-suited to these purposes led to the development of Modula-2. In Modula-2, the structured features of Pascal are combined with the ability to control system hardware. Modula-2 is designed to support the writing of large programs through the careful use of subprograms or modules. Additional features enable the programmer to directly manipulate peripheral devices and memory. Modula-2 is increasingly finding use as a teaching language in computer science departments at many universities.

OBJECT-ORIENTED PROGRAMMING

Computer users demand software that is easy to use, reliable, and efficient. Users crave software that can be adapted quickly to their individual needs. During the 1970s and 1980s, programming languages became easier to use as they became more structured. Despite this, programming continues to be time consuming, difficult, and expensive. The results are all too often error prone. A new development in software design, called **object-oriented programming,** has as its goal the development of software that can be easily understood and shared within the user community while being more efficient, more cost effective, and more reliable.

Object-oriented programming is built around the philosophy that programming components need to be reusable, interchangeable, adaptable, and easily maintainable. Rather than designing a program from scratch, as a new problem presents itself for solution, a programmer or sophisticated user could assemble the code from preconstructed parts. Software would build on the work of others by using generic components.

Object-oriented programming is a radical departure from traditional software design techniques. Current programming methods treat data as distinct from the program that uses the data. Object-oriented programming combines data with the operations that act on the data into a single unified structure called an **object.** Objects are self-contained units, independent of each other, and therefore easier to test, evaluate and maintain.

Objects communicate with each other by passing **messages.** These messages ask the object to carry out one of its operations. Since objects are distinct, the same message sent to different objects would produce different responses.

A critical component of object-oriented programming is **inheritance.** With biological inheritance, a child inherits basic genetic characteristics, such as hair, eye color, and overall height, from parents. In addition to these inherited characteristics, each child has its own unique qualities.

Inheritance within "families" or classes of *objects* works very much the same way. A "child" object inherits everything contained within its "parent" object's definition. The description of this new object needs to contain only those properties that make the child different from its parent. A child object has available to it all the data and operations of the parent object along with some of its own unique components. This sharing increases code reuse.

As an example, imagine that our *object* is a motor vehicle. Inheritance could be described as follows: A *car* is a subclass of motor vehicles. As such, a car inherits the following attributes: an internal combustion engine, four wheels, and passenger and cargo space. In addition, a car possesses additional unique attributes that distinguish it from other motor vehicles, such as its size, shape, the way it handles, the engine size, and the number of passengers it seats. When a

On Line

SELECTING A PROGRAMMING LANGUAGE THE EASY WAY

With such a large selection of programming languages, it can be difficult to choose one for a particular project. However, most people already have a fairly good idea of how various automobiles compare. So to assist those trying to choose a language, this list matches programming languages with automobiles.

Assembler: A Formula I race car. Very fast, but difficult to drive and expensive to maintain.

FORTRAN II: A Model T Ford. Once it was king of the road.

FORTRAN IV: A Model T Ford.

FORTRAN 77: A six-cylinder Ford Fairlane with standard transmission and no seat belts.

COBOL: A delivery van. It's bulky and ugly, but it does the work.

BASIC: A second-hand Rambler with a rebuilt engine and patched upholstery. Your dad bought it for you to learn to drive. You'll ditch the car as soon as you can afford a new one.

C: A black Firebird, an all-macho car. Comes with optional seat belts and an optional fuzz buster ("escape to assembler").

Pascal: A Volkswagen Beetle. It's small but sturdy. Was once popular with intellectuals.

Modula-2: A Volkswagen Rabbit with a trailer hitch added on.

LISP: An electric car. It's simple but slow. Seat belts are not available.

LOGO: A kiddie's replica of a Rolls Royce. Comes with a real engine and a working horn.

Ada: An army-green Mercedes-Benz staff car. Power steering, power brakes, and automatic transmission are all standard. No other colors or options are available. If it's good enough for the generals, it's good enough for you. Manufacturing delays due to difficulties in reading the design specifications are starting to clear up.

Source: D. Solomon and D. Rosenblueth, University of Waterloo, Waterloo, Ontario, BITNET, October 1986.

programmer constructs a new object, based in part upon an existing object (its parent), only its new features need to be described since those that the object inherits are already defined.

Object-oriented programming has taken the software development community by storm. The first of these languages, Simula and Smalltalk, were developed in the mid-1960s. Smalltalk has been repeatedly revised to reflect advances in hardware. Of the currently popular object-oriented languages, most are variations on popular traditional languages. These include: C ++, an object-oriented version of C; CLOS, an object-oriented version of LISP; TURBO Pascal Version 5.5; and Oberon, an object-oriented version of Modula-2.

The current interest in object-oriented techniques and languages is significant because object-oriented programming has the potential to revolutionize the programming process. Programs can be made more responsive to the user community while simultaneously being more effective and efficient. Software that is generic and that can be created from preconstructed parts has the potential of not only being quicker to produce, and at a lower cost, but more adaptable, maintainable, and error-free. If current interest persists, improvements in software development may be very close at hand.

As we have seen, programming requires careful planning and organization. Before writing the code for a given algorithm, the programmer must consider which language would be most appropriate. Few languages do all things equally well, and not all languages are available on all machines. Using a language suited to the application can ease the task of programming.

SUMMARY

There are four categories of computer languages. From the lowest to highest these are: machine language, assembly language, high-level languages, and natural language processing.

Machine language consists of instructions coded as a series of ones and zeros. It is the only language that the computer directly understands. Each type of computer has its own code. These languages are **machine-dependent**.

Assembly language instructions contain mnemonics specifying tasks to be performed by the computer. Like machine languages, assembly languages are machine-dependent. Assembly language programs cannot be executed directly by the computer. They must first be translated, or assembled, into machine-readable form.

High-level languages have a structure similar to natural languages. These languages are **machine-independent** and **portable.** High-level languages must be translated into machine-readable form to be understood by the computer.

Natural language processing, or natural language understanding, is a research area within artificial intelligence that is looking at the development of computer languages and systems that understand and use natural language.

Hundreds of computer languages exist today. When choosing the most appropriate language for a given task, the following criteria should be considered: familiarity, availability, suitability, efficiency, longevity, and supportability.

A wide variety of high-level languages is available, each with its own strengths and weaknesses.

Ada, named after Ada Lovelace (the first programmer), was commissioned by the Department of Defense to be an all-purpose computer language capable of doing all computer-related tasks. It is a highly structured language and is capable of communicating directly with computer hardware.

BASIC, which stands for Beginner's All-Purpose Symbolic Instruction Code, was invented as a tool to teach programming. It is an interactive language. BASIC interpreters and compilers require little memory and run on most microcomputers.

C is often considered a modern form of assembly language. It has syntax structures of a high-level language along with the ability to communicate directly and easily with computer hardware. C is very portable.

COBOL, which stands for COmmon Business Oriented Language, was invented in the late 1950s, with the support of the U.S. Department of Defense, as a standard language for business applications.

FORTRAN, which stands for FORmula TRANslation, supports mathematical, scientific, and engineering programming. It is a highly standardized language that has been regularly updated and revised.

LISP, which stands for LISt Processing, is the dominant language for artificial intelligence programming. It is designed to manipulate lists of non-numeric information.

LOGO was developed as an interactive language to teach programming to children. It makes use of on-screen graphics to develop and reinforce problem-solving skills.

Modula-2 is an improved version of Pascal and has the ability to control system hardware. Modula-2 is designed to support the development of large programs through the careful use of **subprograms.**

Pascal, named after the mathematician Blaise Pascal, is a general-purpose teaching language emphasizing top-down design.

Object-oriented programming is built around the philosophy that programming components need to be reusable, interchangeable, adaptable, and easily maintainable. An **object** is the combination of data with the operations that act on the data. Objects communicate with each other by passing **messages** that ask the object to carry out its operations. Objects **inherit** properties from other objects. When a programmer constructs a new object, based in part upon an existing object, only its new features need to be described because those that the object inherits are already defined.

Key Words

As an extra review of the chapter, try defining the following terms. If you have trouble with any of them, refer to the page number listed.

assembly language (assembler) *(216)*
embedded computer *(225)*
inheritance *(228)*
machine-dependent *(215)*
machine-independent *(217)*
machine language *(215)*

message *(228)*
object *(228)*
object-oriented programming *(228)*
portable *(218)*
programming language *(214)*
subprogram *(221)*

Test Your Knowledge

1. List the four levels of computer languages.

2. How does assembly language differ from machine language?

3. How do high-level languages differ from assembly languages?

4. Why do high-level languages require translators to be understood by computers?

5. When is a computer language machine-independent?

6. What is natural language processing? Describe the two different research approaches used in this field.

7. List the criteria programmers should use when selecting a computer language.

8. Briefly describe FORTRAN. What are its most important features? What are its limitations?

9. Briefly describe BASIC. What are its most important features? What are its limitations?

10. Briefly describe Pascal. What are its most important features? What are its limitations?

11. Define *portable* as it applies to computer languages.

12. Identify and briefly describe four other commonly used computer languages.

13. What do COBOL and Ada have in common?

14. What single feature is most likely to lead to an increase in the use of Ada?

15. What is object-oriented programming? What is meant by inheritance?

Expand Your Knowledge

1. Talk with people in your computing center. Write a short report indicating two of the more widely used computer languages on campus. Identify two departments that use them and what applications they are used for.

2. Talk to people in your computer science department. Write a short report examining the language used to teach programming to CS majors. Why was this language chosen? Has the department considered changing languages? If so, what languages have been considered and why?

3. Make a list of the languages provided by your computing center. Identify the machines they run on and the department or group that uses each language.

4. Some people feel that everyone should use the same computer language. Others feel such a move would be unrealistic. Choose one position and defend it.

5. Go to your local bookstore and examine the books available on computer languages. What languages are represented? Judging from the number of books available, which are the most popular languages? Has the store had requests for books on languages such as Ada and CLOS?

6. Research object-oriented programming and Apple's HyperCard. Write a short paper comparing object-oriented programming with the principle behind Apple's HyperCard. Is HyperCard a simplified version of an object-oriented programming environment? Support your point of view.

9

Ethics and Responsibilities

CHAPTER OUTLINE

Throughout the first half of this text, the tool called the computer has been examined and discussed. A *tool* sounds innocuous; it is merely an aid humans use that is incapable of influence or effect. Yet, tools do indeed make a difference. They do more than provide assistance. Their use can alter the very nature of the human experience. The harnessing of fire changed life for ancient man, as did the invention of the wheel, the steam engine, and other traditional tools. Written language, number systems, and mathematics helped make sense out of an increasingly complex world. Tools enabled us to travel across the seas and build magnificent structures, and empowered us to reach for the stars. The printing press put the world in our hands, and the invention of the steam engine and the harnessing of electricity not only altered the nature of work, they irreversibly changed our daily lives.

After studying this chapter, you will be able to:

- Identify common computer crimes.
- Describe destructive hacking.
- Discuss intellectual property.
- Understand copyright law as it applies to computer software.
- Discuss software plagiarism.
- Understand how computers can affect personal privacy.
- Describe computer matching.

COMPUTERS, AN AGENT OF CHANGE

It is perhaps too early to tell if the computer will have as powerful an effect on modern humanity as the taming of fire did on our ancient ancestors, or as profound an effect on our lifestyles, employment, and behavior as the steam engine. But by any account, the effects of the computer on humanity are not, and will not, be trivial.

Changes that alter the structure of society are never simple or easy. Growth and progress always cost something. "There is no free lunch," the saying goes. Or, as Clarence Darrow exclaimed: "Unless a fellow moves ahead, he's left behind." While progress and change may inevitably alter the course of humanity, the direction and effects of such change are under our control. Significant changes in how we live require, perhaps even demand, that we reexamine the ethical, moral, and human underpinnings of our society. The computer is affecting society and will not go away, any more than other inventions that caused societal disruptions. The computer is here to stay. As its use becomes more pervasive, it will affect us more, not less. Its potential to benefit humanity is incredible. Its potential to negatively affect each of us and society is equally real.

As were the tools of the Industrial Revolution before it, the computer is just a tool, a machine. The potential for positive or negative effects rests not with the computer but with humanity. We, the people, must decide how, where, in what ways, and for what purposes this machine will be used. The opportunity and the responsibility rest with each of us.

Earlier chapters in this text focused on the structure of these machines and programs and how they are used. This chapter examines the issues and conflicts the use of computers has caused. Included are threats to personal privacy, the value of intellectual property, plagiarism, computer crime, and civil rights, to name a few. The problems caused by the introduction of the computer into our lives are complex, the solutions elusive. The changes wrought by the computer require that we reexamine how we behave toward each other and society. We as individuals must take responsibility for the computer—now and in the future.

COMPUTERS AND CRIME

Computer crime has an aura of mystery. The criminal is cracking a complex safe filled with unusual, hard-to-describe, and valuable property (information). No blood is spilled, no fingerprints are left behind, and in most cases nothing is visibly broken, no one has been hurt. Or so it appears.

For the mass media, crimes involving computers have a certain magic. In reality, the computer is only the most modern tool in the criminal's arsenal. The crimes are as old as "civilized" man: theft, fraud, destruction of private property, breaking and entering, and vandalism. However, there is a difference between computer crime and its equally serious counterparts on the streets. Computer crimes are harder to trace, easier to get away with, and are infrequently prosecuted. Little evidence is left behind to point to the perpetrator. The crime can be carried out without physically coming into contact with the victim, his or her office, or home.

The following facts are frightening:

- The American Bar Association surveyed a wide cross-section of companies and public agencies and found that more than 25 percent of these organizations had experienced incidences of crime against their computer systems in a one-year period. The financial losses in one year approached $1 billion.

- Surveys have found that a considerable portion of computer crime goes unreported. Organizations fear that reporting such crimes will publicize the fact that their computer systems are vulnerable, their security lax, thus making the organization a target for further abuse and user distrust.

- Studies indicate that approximately 80 percent of all computer crime is committed by people with an insiders' knowledge of the computer systems. In other words, computer crime is committed by employees against their own employers.

- Possession of illegal copies of software—software piracy—is so widespread that one investigation revealed that 35 percent of all computer users had "bootleg" copies of games on their machines. It is estimated that as many as 75 percent of all microcomputer owners regularly use an illegal duplicate of some copyrighted software.

Although it is easy to claim that no one is hurt in such crimes because there is no blood, the reality is quite different. The direct cost in stolen revenue, compromised equipment, and lost files is quite high. The indirect costs, measured in repair and programmer time to correct debilitated machines and programs, are significant. These losses are directly passed on to consumers. What might these crimes look like?

- An employee is fired or laid off. Before leaving, the employee adds a few "innocuous" instructions to the company's payroll program. When the system attempts to delete the disgruntled employee, the program instructs the system to delete all other employees as well. While we may be sympathetic to the fired employee, is the damage to the company's records insignificant? What about the considerable inconvenience to the other employees whose paychecks may be delayed?

- A bank programmer adjusts the rounding portion of the program that calculates interest. Every time any account has its interest rounded down for posting, such as from 25.321 to 25.32, these fractions of pennies are placed in the programmer's account. Given the vast number of accounts processed and sufficient time, the programmer's account can accumulate to a tidy sum. Who is being hurt? Each customer loses only a tiny amount. Is a little theft from a lot of people a less significant crime?

- An insurance agent invents a client, has the accounts activated, makes regular changes and adjustments to the client's policies to give them a normal appearance, and eventually cashes in or makes claims against the policy. If your insurance rates are raised by the number of claims made, is no one hurt?

- A teenager breaks into a hospital's computer system to "look around," just to prove it could be done. Nothing is stolen and no one is hurt—or so the youngster claims. However, if the program entered contains the chemotherapy records of cancer patients, apparently insignificant, unanticipated changes that might have been caused by accidental erasures can be critical. If the system that is breached monitors intensive care patients, even a momentary interruption could be deadly. Is no one hurt when such risks are involved?

- The father of a teenager arrested for breaking into a number of computers across the country says he is proud of his son. The father claims the son is practicing skills that will prove useful in the future. Would he feel the same way if his son were found breaking into and entering his neighbor's house? Is there a difference?

- A Cornell graduate student plants a computer virus on the Internet network that connects thousands of university, corporate, research, and government computers. This virus replicates (reproduces itself) among the interconnected machines filling all available memory, until 6,000 machines, essentially the entire network, is slowed to a standstill. The cost of eradicating the virus is estimated at over $100 million. This figure does not reflect the cost to damaged research projects and lost records. Is this different from sabotage at an industrial plant?

All of these crimes involve computers. However, people committed them. The computer was merely a tool. People are responsible. The most frustrating and preventable of computer crimes are often committed by young people between the ages of 12 and 21.

HACKING

Breaking and entering, eavesdropping, harassment, vandalism, destruction of private property, possession of stolen goods, theft—in anybody's book these are crimes. However, when the property damaged, stolen, or lost is electronic information, the "place" broken into is a computer, and the perpetrators are often bright youngsters, the crimes appear to be taken less seriously by much of society, though not by the victims.

One dictionary's definition of a **hacker** is "someone who intentionally breaks into other computer systems, whether maliciously or not." Hackers are often computer-competent teens, many of whom have used their home computers to commit the crimes like those just described (see Figure 9.1).

Until recently hackers worked from the comfort of their bedrooms using the family phone. Recent government wiretaps and criminal investigations have created more mobile hackers. Modern hackers carry laptop computers, with specialized hardware that can attach to and use any phone including hotel extensions and pay phones.

Some hackers merely enter large computer systems, such as the NYNEX telephone system, unauthorized, just to prove it can be done. No harm is intended; they're merely looking around. They read electronic information and mail, and in some cases make copies of the information, leaving the original in-

On Line

COMPUTER VIRUSES CAN MAKE YOU SICK

Computer viruses are seemingly innocuous programs disguised as normal software. Their sole purpose, however, is to destroy programs and data on the computers of unsuspecting users.

Virus programs are commonly downloaded from computer bulletin boards where users can exchange public-domain software. Unsuspecting users select the virus program, advertised on the bulletin board as a useful program or utility. When the program is executed, it proceeds to destroy any available information.

Virus programs can ruin all of the programs and data stored on a microcomputer's hard disk in less time than it takes to bring up the system. All of the computers on a large network can be "infected" in less than a minute and a multiuser system can be crashed in less than five minutes. Operators of computer bulletin boards have become so outraged by virus programs that they are warning board users by circulating a list of the disk-killing programs that have been identified. Computing center officials on college campuses and large businesses and organizations are warning users of the potential threat from virus programs.

Viruses come in two varieties. The simplest variety is exemplified by Egabtr. Claiming to be an innocent program to enhance screen graphics, it contained disk-destroying code. Such programs are fast and deadly. They immediately destroy information stored on disks. Software viruses can be even more treacherous. Such programs can stay hidden for weeks or months, infecting hard disks and floppies alike. Then at a predetermined moment all contaminated software is disabled. Barry M. Simon, a professor at California Institute of Technology, told *The Chronicle of Higher Education* that "People who write viruses like to brag. They usually leave some clue that they've done something." Unfortunately, when their messages appear it is usually too late. Egabtr displays the words "Arf, Arf! Gotcha!" after it has destroyed disk information.

Computer pranksters have existed on college campuses for years. Unfortunately, the threat is no longer limited in scope. Viruses can affect computers everywhere. Any user that connects to a bulletin board, is part of a computer network, or shares disks with others is vulnerable. Some have suggested "computer celibacy" (never sharing disks) as a solution. However, such a solution eliminates one of the major advantages of modern computers: sharing ideas and information. A less radical approach seems best. Program disks should be write-protected and backups should always be made. All programs received from acquaintances, bulletin boards, or networks should be tried with hard drives turned off and backup copies of the operating system available. Be vigilant. Programs making incredible claims may turn out to be quite different; they might contain a virus.

Solutions other than celibacy exist. A number of programs, including Data Physician, CHK4Bomb, SAM (Symantec AntiVirus for Macintosh), and Vaccine have been designed to pretest software for viruses. However, no program can guarantee protection against all viruses. Vigilance, backup copies of software and critical data, and very careful use of bulletin boards are the only guarantees against computer viruses.

Sources: Judith A. Turner, "Worries Over Computer 'Viruses' Lead Campuses to Issue Guidelines," *The Chronicle of Higher Education,* March 2, 1988, p. A15. "15 Tips to Forestall Viruses," *Personal Computing,* March 20, 1990, p 24.

Figure 9.1 In his book *Cuckoo's Egg,* Clifford Stoll describes how he tracked down a hacker who turned out to be a Communist spy.

tact. They have no interest in the information they find, since the thrill is in breaching the electronic security of the system. Some claim to be simply "gaining knowledge" or using the entered systems to learn how to solve complex problems. To others, illegal electronic entry is essentially a never-ending, authentic, role-playing adventure game, a real-life version of *Dungeons & Dragons,* with federal, state, local, and corporate authorities as the "bad guys." However, all of these youthful hackers *are* committing the electronic equivalent of voyeurism. The privacy of individuals and organizations is being violated.

Most unsettling is the lack of support that victims and law enforcement officials get from society, not to mention the parents of these young hackers. Cries of "No one has been hurt" or "It's the company's fault for not having better security systems," or even a feeling that the invaded computer system somehow benefits because security weaknesses have been uncovered, are all common excuses.

The people who find such crimes insignificant would not feel the same if mail were being read, or if the break-ins occurred in nearby houses. Hackers usually see nothing wrong with snooping. Why should they, if so many around them see little wrong? Yet the organizations and individuals victimized feel the same as if the crimes had occurred on the streets. Certainly where sensitive information is involved, can we afford to believe that nothing has been changed or compromised even by accident? More to the point, we have the right to expect our property and privacy to be protected, regardless of its form. Someone must take responsibility. Hackers need to know that what they are doing is wrong.

Computer networks are based on a common trust. Along with this comes an expectation that the privacy of individual files and accounts will be maintained. Hackers destroy the trust that helps computer networks flourish.

What is even more frightening is that some hacking is even more serious and destructive. The highly publicized Milwaukee 414ers (named after their area code) broke into dozens of computer data bases on supposedly secure machines just to look around. These included the Sloan Kettering Cancer Institute and Los Alamos National Laboratories as well as computers at the Defense Department. Other hackers have broken into credit card and credit bureau data bases such as TRW, copied information, and made purchases or harassed people they didn't like with this stolen information. Others have broken into school computers and changed or deleted grades and other "offensive" information. Satellite communications have been interrupted, mailing lists and other electronic information have been erased. In May 1990, indictments were handed down to four members of a hacker confederation called the Legion of Doom. Legion members are alleged to have spread information that could disrupt 911 emergency service.

To make matters worse, hackers often feel compelled to provide others with evidence of their ill-gotten information. It is not enough to break into a system; a hacker needs to tell others about the exploit. Hacker bulletin boards often include telephone numbers one can use to charge long-distance phone calls without a trace. Such free phoning is called **phreaking,** and has long-distance phone companies alarmed. Bulletin boards also list credit card information, as well as passwords and computer phone numbers needed for breaking into unsuspecting systems. Until 1986, it was illegal to obtain and use such information, but not illegal to make it public. Would you like your credit card information posted?

Are hackers pranksters or criminals? It is as much a question of law as a question of morality. Even if no one is physically hurt, does that make computer eavesdropping right? When hackers violate society's codes should they be held less responsible than their street-wise counterparts? The crimes are basically the same and should be considered just as illegal.

Computer ethics must be as much a part of learning about computers as learning to program or use software. Respect for another's rights and computer property are important values, as important as proper treatment of equipment. We must actively learn responsibility along with computer usage, or hacking will continue to be a problem.

Law enforcement groups realize every computer system that is accessible to others by telephone and every computer bulletin board could be a target for the actions of vandals and thieves. University and corporate computer systems, and, increasingly, home systems are being purposely damaged or erased by unknown computer vandals.

Until the mid-1980s, most states and the federal government had no formal statutes focusing on computer crime. Most computer criminals were charged with illegal use of phone lines. In 1984, at least partially in response to the computer invasions caused by the Milwaukee 414ers, the **Federal Computer Fraud and Abuse Act** was passed, making it illegal to tamper in any way with the federal government's computer systems. The act was expanded in 1986 to include computer crimes against most private computers. In addition, the 1986 **Electronic Communications Privacy Act** was passed, making it illegal to intercept electronic information including bank transactions and electronic mail. This law also made it a federal crime to transfer information obtained through computer break-ins. Providing others with computer information such as phone numbers, passwords, and the like became the equivalent of trafficking in stolen goods.

Sometimes, law enforcement officials are unresponsive. In the now publicized attempt *(Cuckoo's Egg)* by Communist agents to steal sensitive military and security information, Lawrence Berkeley Lab's systems manager and scientist Clifford Stoll found it almost impossible to interest the FBI or CIA in his intruder discovery. Government authorities advised him to lock the intruder out of the Berkeley system by changing account names and passwords. They were not concerned with identifying and prosecuting the individual. Fortunately, Stoll was incensed. "I saw it [the electronic break-in] as electronic terrorism." Through Stoll's efforts the intruders were brought to justice.

THEFT, PIRACY, AND PLAGIARISM

Anything that is valuable has the potential for being stolen. Computer software and hardware are no exception to the rule. The legal rules that apply to computer hardware are identical to those on any other physical product. The physical machine is property and its removal without the owner's permission constitutes theft. Reproducing a computer's hardware without the permission of its inventor/owner carries legal consequences. Although lawsuits involving hardware may take considerable time to resolve, the laws that apply are easily understood.

Protecting Intellectual Property

Computer software is a different story. Copyright law has been extended, to some degree, to protect software in much the same way a book or musical score is protected. However, computer software differs dramatically from books and sheet music. Two books can discuss the same topic, using different words, without really being the same. However, two different programs can be written that produce identical or very similar output. Is the second program violating the copyright of the original program? Copyright law is unclear with respect to the protection of ideas or, as software is often called, **intellectual property.** In fact, there is no clear definition, legal or otherwise, for the term *intellectual property.* The issue in question is whether ideas can be copyrighted and, if so, to what degree?

Software authors and software companies contend that the *idea* upon which the program is based constitutes the intellectual property because any number of different programming paths can be used to produce the same results. Classroom programming assignments exemplify this. One assignment can result in multiple versions of the same program. Most have unique features, yet they all produce the same results. This is quite different from the papers that result from an assignment in a composition class. Just as with the programming assignment, each student in the writing class is given the same charge. However, the ideas presented and the results produced by students differ significantly. The programming assignment produces different paths to the same result, whereas the writing assignment produces different paths to different results.

Therein lies the problem. Software authors, just like authors of the printed word, justifiably feel that what they have written is their intellectual property. It is the work of their minds, requiring considerable time and effort. Both software and print authors hope and expect to get reimbursed for their work and to have their work protected (see Figure 9.2).

Such intellectual property issues are at the heart of a number of lawsuits currently in litigation. In 1987 Lotus Development Corp. brought legal action against Paperback Software (VP Planner) and Mosaic Software (TWIN) for copyright infringement. Lotus claimed that the "look and feel" of its product was an original idea and should be protected under copyright law. Opponents claimed that only the code itself has copyright protection, not the user interface (what the user sees). Further, they claimed that protecting the outward look of software would stifle creativity. Every programming advance, it was claimed, borrows from current ideas. In the summer of 1990, Lotus won the first stage in its legal battle. Lotus' user interface was deemed copyrightable. Although Paperback Software intends to appeal the decision, the suit more clearly defined intellectual property. Other similar cases are in the courts. Apple Corp. is suing both Microsoft and Hewlett-Packard for copyright violation. Microsoft and Hewlett-Packard have developed software that seems to duplicate the Macin-

Figure 9.2

A Software Licensing Agreement: Copyright agreements such as this one accompanying Microsoft's software protect software by restricting its use. The purchaser "agrees" to the contract by breaking the package seal. (Reproduced by permission of Microsoft.)

This License Agreement is your proof of license. Please treat it as valuable property.

Microsoft License Agreement

This is a legal agreement between you (either an individual or entity), the end user, and Microsoft Corporation. I. you do not agree to the terms of this Agreement, promptly return the disk package and the accompanying items (including written materials and binders or other containers) to the place you obtained them for a full refund.

MICROSOFT SOFTWARE LICENSE

I. GRANT OF LICENSE.
(a) Dedicated Use. Microsoft grants to you the right to use one copy of the Microsoft software program identified above (the "SOFTWARE") on a single computer ("Dedicated Computer"). You may transfer the SOFTWARE to another single computer PROVIDED you do so no more often than once every thirty (30) days and no copies of the SOFTWARE licensed herein are retained for use on any other computer. However, if one individual uses the Dedicated Computer more than 80% of the time it is in use, then that individual also may use the SOFTWARE on a portable or home computer.

(b) Transitory Use. Notwithstanding (a), you may transfer the right to use the SOFTWARE as often as you like if you require each user of the SOFTWARE to have physical possession of an original Microsoft SOFTWARE license (either this Microsoft License Agreement or an equivalent designated by Microsoft) at all times during the use of the SOFTWARE.

For the purposes of this section, "use" means loading the SOFTWARE into RAM, as well as installation on a hard disk or other storage device (other than a network server). You may access the SOFTWARE from a hard disk, over a network, or any other method you choose, so long as you otherwise comply with this Microsoft License Agreement.

2. COPYRIGHT. The SOFTWARE is owned by Microsoft or its suppliers and is protected by United States copyright laws and international treaty provisions. Therefore, you must treat the SOFTWARE like any other copyrighted material (e.g., a book or musical recording) except that you may either (a) make one copy of the SOFTWARE solely for backup or archival purposes, or (b) transfer the SOFTWARE to a single hard disk provided you keep the original solely for backup or archival purposes. You may not copy the written materials accompanying the software.

3. OTHER RESTRICTIONS. This Microsoft License Agreement is your proof of license to exercise the rights granted herein and must be retained by you. You may not rent or lease the SOFTWARE, but you may transfer your rights under this Microsoft License Agreement on a permanent basis provided you transfer this License Agreement, the SOFTWARE and all accompanying written materials, retain no copies and the recipient agrees to the terms of this Agreement. You may not reverse engineer, decompile, or disassemble the SOFTWARE. If the SOFTWARE is an update, any transfer must include the update and all prior versions.

4. DUAL MEDIA SOFTWARE. If the SOFTWARE package contains both 3.5" and 5.25" disks, then you may use only the disks appropriate for your single designated computer or network server. You may not use the other disks on another computer or computer network, or loan, rent, lease, or transfer them to another user except as part of a transfer or other use as expressly permitted by this Microsoft License Agreement.

LIMITED WARRANTY

LIMITED WARRANTY. Microsoft warrants that (a) the SOFTWARE will perform substantially in accordance with the accompanying written materials for a period of ninety (90) days from the date of receipt; and (b) any hardware accompanying the SOFTWARE will be free from defects in materials and workmanship under normal use and service for a period of one (1) year from the date of receipt. Any implied warranties on the SOFTWARE and hardware are limited to ninety (90) days and one (1) year, respectively. Some states do not allow limitations on duration of an implied warranty, so the above limitation may not apply to you.

CUSTOMER REMEDIES. Microsoft's entire liability and your exclusive remedy shall be, at Microsoft's option, either (a) return of the price paid or (b) repair or replacement of the SOFTWARE or hardware that does not meet Microsoft's Limited Warranty and that is returned to Microsoft with a copy of your receipt. This Limited Warranty is void if failure of the SOFTWARE or hardware has resulted from accident, abuse, or misapplication. Any replacement SOFTWARE will be warranted for the remainder of the original warranty period or thirty (30) days, whichever is longer. **These remedies are not available outside of the United States of America.**

NO OTHER WARRANTIES. **Microsoft disclaims all other warranties, either express or implied, including but not limited to implied warranties of merchantability and fitness for a particular purpose, with respect to the SOFTWARE, the accompanying written materials, and any accompanying hardware. This limited warranty gives you specific legal rights. You may have others, which vary from state to state.**

NO LIABILITY FOR CONSEQUENTIAL DAMAGES. **In no event shall Microsoft or its suppliers be liable for any damages whatsoever (including, without limitation, damages for loss of business profits, business interruption, loss of business information, or other pecuniary loss) arising out of the use of or inability to use this Microsoft product, even if Microsoft has been advised of the possibility of such damages. Because some states do not allow the exclusion or limitation of liability for consequential or incidental damages, the above limitation may not apply to you.**

U.S. GOVERNMENT RESTRICTED RIGHTS

The SOFTWARE and documentation are provided with RESTRICTED RIGHTS. Use, duplication, or disclosure by the Government is subject to restrictions as set forth in subparagraph (c)(1)(ii) of The Rights in Technical Data and Computer Software clause at DFARS 252.227-7013 or subparagraphs (c)(1) and (2) of the Commercial Computer Software—Restricted Rights at 48 CFR 52.227-19, as applicable. Contractor/manufacturer is Microsoft Corporation/One Microsoft Way/Redmond, WA 98052-6399.

This Agreement is governed by the laws of the State of Washington.

Should you have any questions concerning this Agreement, or if you desire to contact Microsoft for any reason, please write: Microsoft Customer Sales and Service/One Microsoft Way/Redmond, WA 98052-6399.

tosh's user-friendly operating environment on IBM-compatible machines. In 1988, Ashton-Tate (dBASE) brought suit against Fox Software for violating the "look and feel" of its data base software. Although this case technically has been settled, the newest release of Fox's data base has a different look and feel.

Unfortunately, the issue of copyright protection for intellectual property is more complex than it may first appear. It is in everybody's best interest to protect the efforts of software authors if we expect such people to continue writing the applications programs that are so useful on modern computers. However, when an idea becomes private property, it essentially becomes off limits unless permission is obtained for its use. Such limitations could stifle creativity since new ideas usually spring from the seeds of other ideas. If ideas are private property, they cannot be used as the building blocks for improvements on existing products or the development of new ones.

Some middle ground needs to be found so that the property of software authors is protected without dramatically restricting the creativity of others.

Plagiarism

No one would argue that it is ethical to copy someone else's book, article, or program and put your name on it as the author. But what about using another's work as a starting point for your own creation? With a few things changed, the revised version is presented as an original work. If the changes are merely cosmetic we would consider this *plagiarism*. However, how much has to change before the work can be considered original? In courses involving programming this is a major issue. A student would never consider handing in a photocopy of an English paper written by a friend (with the name changed of course), yet it is not uncommon to receive essentially identical programs containing perhaps a few changes in variable names and spacing. Individual assignments are not intended to become group projects. There is a clear difference between sharing ideas or helping others, and turning in identical programs. However, the time involved in writing and debugging programs, as well as the rigorous approach to problem solving that is required, sometimes causes students to collaborate rather than work alone. Individual programming assignments, as with any other written work, are expected to be done by the individual student. Anything else is plagiarism.

This problem is not limited to college campuses, and for this reason copyright protection for software is necessary. It is illegal to duplicate a book on a copy machine. It violates the author's copyright. To possess a copy of a printed work, we must pay for it. The author is entitled to just compensation for the work. Of course, it makes very little sense to duplicate a book on a copy machine because the cost of copying a book is often more than the purchase price. Furthermore, even the most sophisticated books are relatively affordable. Books rarely cost more than $50. With software, however, the reverse is true. Software is usually inexpensive to copy but has a purchase price of hundreds of dollars.

Is the violation different? Should our wallets affect our integrity? Unfortunately, software duplication is widespread, even though unethical and usually illegal.

PRIVACY

One of the cornerstones of our American Constitution is that as individuals we have a right to privacy. This means that no organization, person, or government agency has the right to invade the solitude of our minds or personal lives. The First Amendment protects freedom of religion, speech, press, and assembly, and the right to petition the government. The Fourth Amendment protects "the right of the people to (be) secure in their persons, houses, papers and effects against unreasonable search and seizure." The Constitution has granted us and all future generations the right of privacy. According to *Webster's Dictionary*, **privacy** is "the quality or state of being apart from company or observation." Things that are private are "not known or intended to be known publicly; unsuitable for public mention, use or display."

The computer is a powerful tool, and because it is invaluable for collecting, organizing, storing, and retrieving information, it has the potential to put our privacy at risk if misused. Businesses, organizations, and the government have always collected information about their constituencies and their adversaries. We pay taxes, take out insurance, purchase items on credit, use checking accounts, go to school, see our doctors, and license or register an incredible number of things every day. Computerized data bases have proven invaluable tools for making it easy to find and use this information, which in most cases has been freely given. For example, computerized medical records save lives, and computerized business records save time and money. However, it was not our intent that information freely given in one instance should be available to other organizations or individuals without our consent. Our right to be private individuals means that only those who have a "need to know" should have access to the intimate details of our lives, and that *we* determine who has a need to know.

Think about all the different kinds of information that has been collected about us. Every time we fill out a form, for any reason, we are supplying information to others about ourselves. We fill out job applications, tax returns, and credit card applications; we open bank accounts; give the post office and census bureau information about persons living in our homes, and have telephones connected in our homes and businesses (see Figure 9.3).

While this information may not be given totally voluntarily, especially in the case of tax returns, we are conscious that we are giving out personal information. Yet other information is collected about us of which we are often less aware. For example, every long-distance call we make is recorded, as is every check we write regardless of the amount. Every loan payment we make for such

Figure 9.3   Personal Data: Every time we fill out a job application, open bank accounts, or complete our tax forms, we are consciously supplying personal information that is entered into various data bases.

things as cars, homes, and educational loans is recorded. Every credit card purchase and payment we make, every school we ever attended, every class we ever took, every grade we ever got, every interaction we have ever had with the police, from traffic tickets to complaints, have been recorded someplace. The more we think about it the longer the list grows.

Without anyone intentionally watching, almost every action we take in our daily lives has been recorded. This realization can seem incredibly ominous. It would not be an impossible task for the government or any other organization that wished to do so to gather all of this information and place it in a single massive, centralized computer data base. If this occurred, "Big Brother" would indeed be watching. How would we feel? How would we act? What would have happened to our freedom? Even if the government did nothing more than collect the data, its very collection could affect they way we live our lives.

Before this picture gets too bleak, we need to recall that such a centralized data base does not exist and is unlikely to come into being. However, we should not lessen our vigilance. In the early 1970s, Congress passed legislation clarifying our rights and responsibilities regarding collected information. In 1970 the **Fair Credit Reporting Act** and the **Freedom of Information Act** guaranteed us access to, and the right to correct, the information government agencies and credit organizations collect about us. In 1973, the **Crime Control Act** was passed requiring that police agency records contain not only arrest information but the outcome of the case as well. An arrest does not imply guilt. The most important piece of legislation passed was the **Federal Privacy Act** of 1974. This act limits the kind and nature of the information the government can collect. Information must be "relevant and necessary." Gossip and secondhand information cannot be collected. This act further reinforced our rights to see and to correct information that is collected. It also prohibits the collection of information about our religious or political activities.

As long as the data collected about us are decentralized and we are conscious of our rights, computerized data bases are tools that benefit each of us. In most cases, information collected about us cannot be released without our consent, which is as it should be if our privacy is to be protected. Many people feel that the current controls are not strong enough. They feel that no information should be given out about us without our first reviewing that information and then giving our informed consent. While such an idea has merit in principle, in practice it would make transacting the nation's business almost impossible. In some cases such consent would make information inaccessible, even to those with a "need to know," and could threaten our lives. For example, if you were injured in an accident and doctors could not gain access to your medical records, critical information would not be available and your life could be at risk. On the other hand, we don't want our medical histories to become public knowledge. A delicate balance must be created between privacy and the need to know.

COMPUTER MATCHING

Ask even an experienced computer programmer what computer matching is and either a long dissertation on how to compare two lists using a computer will be given or the newest computer dating service will be described. Actually, **computer matching** uses a computer to compare two files or lists of information, seeking the same item on both lists. A computerized dating service is an excellent example of how computer matching works. Every person who purchases a membership answers a series of questions about himself or herself and specifies the qualities necessary in a prospective date. Then each client is compared with every other client. Those whose requirements match are given each others' names, addresses, phone numbers, and other important information so they can arrange to meet. While this may not seem romantic, such electronic matchmaking does take some of the trauma out of first dates. Such computer matching is done with the wishful consent of all the parties involved. Every client knows that he or she will be compared over and over again and willingly participates.

However, each of us unknowingly participates in electronic matching without our consent on a regular basis. Information we gave willingly for a particular purpose is being matched against other collected information without our knowledge or consent by federal, state, and local governments, and by businesses. The government uses matching for a number of seemingly altruistic purposes. For example, the state of New York and other states as well compare the names and social security numbers of all persons getting income tax refunds against a list of individuals convicted of failing to pay child support. If a match is found (and many are), the income tax check is withheld and the funds are used as partial payment for the unpaid child support. Another example is the comparison of motor vehicle registrations against tax records to find persons living in one state who register their cars in another state to avoid fees or taxes on their vehicles. Still another example is the comparison of federal tax records against military draft-registration records to locate young men who have not registered for the military draft.

At first glance, such matching may seem reasonable. However, it could be easily argued that matching violates our civil rights. Matching assumes guilt without due process of law. Our private records are compared without our permission. We may not have committed a crime and yet we are suspect as if we had criminal records. It would be all too easy to match for membership in questionable organizations where the individuals in power determined the definition of *questionable*.

Perhaps Big Brother is watching or at least matching. There is considerable risk to our civil rights in matching. It is arguable that matching, as it is currently called, is in the interest of both citizens and the government. However, where are the checks and balances? Who watches over the shoulders of the government agencies involved in matching to ensure that the rights of the individual are protected?

As we have seen, computer crime, hacking, software piracy, computer matching, and protecting our general privacy are complex issues brought on by our success at integrating computers into our society and our daily lives. Harnessing the power of computers carries problems with it. But these problems provide us with the opportunity to examine the way we live and let us choose the best path to our future.

To protect our privacy and reduce computer crime, each of us must assume responsibility for our actions. We must act ethically, whether there is a law to compel us or not. We must educate ourselves and future generations in both the pitfalls and the vast benefits that computers can bring. Computers are machines; tools for modern man. How we use them determines their effects. If they are harmful, it is because we employ them without caring for our fellow men and women. If they are beneficial, it is only because we strive to make them so. We can use these incredible tools wisely or foolishly. The future is up to each of us.

SUMMARY

The computer is the most modern tool used by the criminal. Crimes committed using computers include theft, fraud, destruction of private property, breaking and entering, and vandalism. Computer crimes are hard to trace and often go unreported.

A **hacker** is someone who intentionally breaks into other computer systems, whether maliciously or not. Hacking, the electronic equivalent of breaking and entering, is usually committed by youths aged 12 to 21. In many cases, hackers do not intend to do damage. Hacking using long-distance phone lines and charging the calls to unauthorized numbers is called **phreaking.** The 1986 Electronic Communications Privacy Act makes it illegal to intercept electronic information.

Copyright law has been extended to protect computer software. Software authors and companies consider **intellectual property** to be the ideas upon which software is based. However, the law is unclear with respect to the protection of ideas.

Americans believe in a right to **privacy,** which is the right to be left alone. Businesses, organizations, and the government collect vast amounts of information about people daily. The gathering of this information into a centralized data base could threaten our civil rights. A number of laws passed in the 1970s, including the Federal Privacy Act, address this issue.

Computer matching uses a computer to compare two files or lists of information, seeking the same items on both lists. Federal, state and local governments use computer matching to seek individuals violating the law. Matching may violate our civil rights because it assumes guilt without due process of law and uses collected information without a person's permission.

Key Words

As an extra review of the chapter, try defining the following terms. If you have trouble with any of them, refer to the page number listed.

computer matching *(249)*

Crime Control Act *(249)*

Electron Communications Privacy Act *(243)*

Fair Credit Reporting Act *(249)*

Federal Computer Fraud and Abuse Act *(243)*

Federal Privacy Act *(249)*

Freedom of Information Act *(249)*

hacker *(240)*

intellectual property *(244)*

phreaking *(242)*

privacy *(247)*

Test Your Knowledge

1. Why are computer crimes bloodless crimes?

2. Why are many computer crimes not reported to the police?

3. What is a hacker?

4. Define *phreaking*.

5. Who were the 414ers? How did they get their name?

6. What is the Electronic Communications Privacy Act? Why is it important?

7. How do software authors define intellectual property?

8. Is software copyrightable?

9. The American Constitution grants individuals a right to privacy. Why?

10. Define *privacy*.

11. How can computer data bases threaten this right to privacy?

12. Name three laws that protect privacy rights.

13. Define *computer matching*.

14. List two areas where computer matching benefits society.

15. List two areas where computer matching has had negative effects.

Expand Your Knowledge

1. In a three-page paper, defend the position: "No one is hurt by computer crime." Use at least three sources to support your conclusions.

2. If computer matching may violate our civil rights, why is it used? In a short (three to five page) paper examine computer matching. Compare the "greater good" theory with the risk to our civil rights. Use at least three information sources.

3. Research hacking. Write a short (three to five page) paper on hacking. Include the kinds of crimes that are committed by hackers, machines that have been compromised, and the outcome of legal prosecution or identification of hackers. Include at least four information sources.

4. Many people feel that there is nothing wrong with duplicating copyrighted computer diskettes. How do you feel? Using two information sources, write a three-page paper defending your viewpoint.

5. Lotus Corp. recently won a lawsuit against two of its competitors, VP-Planner and TWIN, for copyright infringement. Write a short (three to five page) paper on this lawsuit. What charges did Lotus make? How did VP-Planner and The Twin respond? In your paper, explain how this suit addressed the issue of intellectual property. Use at least four information sources.

6. Apple Corporation is suing both Microsoft and Hewlett-Packard for duplicating its Macintosh operating environment. Write a short (three to five page) paper on this lawsuit. Identify the positions of both parties to the suit. In your judgment, how will the conclusion of this suit influence future software developments?

10

Software

In the hands of different individuals, computers become different machines—tools actually—suiting the particular needs of each. For the artist the computer can be a drafting table and paintbrush. For the writer it is an organizer, reference library, and typewriter. For the business executive it is a record-keeper and bookkeeper, holding and organizing inventory, employee, and tax information. Software is what transforms the machine, making it a tool specific to hundreds of tasks. This chapter examines the different types of software and how they are used.

After studying this chapter, you will be able to:

- Identify the four categories of computer software.

- Describe the role of the operating system.

- Identify different operating systems.

- Discuss user interfaces.

- Describe the difference between specialized and general-purpose applications software.

- Describe some uses of specialized software in science, education, business, and the home.

- Discuss the uses of the five types of general-purpose applications software.

- Define software integration.

- Describe the differences and similarities between integrated packages, and families of software.

TYPES OF SOFTWARE

Software is the driving force of the computer. Programs, another word for software, make the system work, giving it the instructions and the ability to do all the jobs we call on it to perform. Computer software is divided into four major types: systems software, development software, user-interface software, and applications software.

Systems software controls the operation of the machine, the most basic functions the computer performs. The ways in which the computer receives input, produces output, manages and stores data, and carries out or executes the instructions of other programs are all determined and controlled by systems software.

Development software is used to write, update, and maintain other programs. Such software is used to create systems software as well as all applications packages. Programming languages, discussed in Chapter 8, are the prime examples of development software.

User-interface software are programs that make it easier for people to use the computer. They provide the mechanisms by which the user communicates with the system software on one hand, and applications packages on the other. User-interface software creates the environment, and determines the "look and feel" of the computer. These programs create the face the computer shows to the human world.

Applications software programs let the computer perform particular tasks or solve specific problems. Like the other types of software, applications software is required by computers of all sizes, from microcomputers to mainframes, and handles both large and small tasks. Airline reservation systems, spacecraft design, air traffic control systems, payroll operations, arithmetic and language drills, the printing of newsletters, and billing all require applications software. There are applications programs to help students select colleges and locate sources of financial aid, programs to entertain us, and programs to help fill in our family trees.

SYSTEMS SOFTWARE: THE OPERATING SYSTEM

Systems software makes it possible for people to interact with computers without having to concern themselves with controlling the system's operation. The most important component of systems software is the **operating system,** which coordinates or oversees the tasks performed by the computer.

Operating systems integrate the instructions of a specific program with the actual wiring of the computer's hardware. The operating system also provides communication between the user and the programs. It coordinates the transfer of data between mass storage and main memory, while organizing and maintaining the system's file structure. The operating system governs the execution of applications programs.

Operating systems also determine the number of individuals who can use the computer at a given time. Microcomputer operating systems are designed to coordinate the needs of a single user, while mainframe and minicomputer operating systems are designed as multiuser systems that process multiple tasks concurrently.

Proprietary Operating Systems

Mainframe and minicomputer operating systems are ordinarily **proprietary,** that is, they are written for and owned by the computer's manufacturer. Each manufacturer designs and maintains an operating system that is unique to its machines. These operating systems are machine dependent. When such a machine is purchased, the operating system designed for that machine is supplied by the manufacturer. While such operating systems are very efficient, because they directly communicate with specific hardware, they make the sharing of applications software and files difficult. Recent discussions between IBM and Apple may lead to the development of software that runs on both classes of machines. This would make the sharing of files between these machines easier.

UNIX

In the early 1970s a machine-independent minicomputer and mainframe operating system called UNIX was developed at AT&T's Bell Labs. **UNIX** contains a modest set of instructions and was originally intended for use by experienced programmers engaged in research and development. It was designed to make the sharing of files and ideas easy within and across a wide variety of machines. UNIX provides libraries of utility programs, called **tools,** that implement common tasks such as copying and listing files. The user-interface or shell is independent from the basic operating system and provides UNIX's working environment. A number of UNIX shells are popular though most are considered hard to learn. Some computer manufacturers, most notably NeXT, have introduced more user-friendly UNIX shells. Universities have found that UNIX provides an outstanding instructional and research environment. Following suit, many corporations find UNIX's flexibility valuable. The popularity of this operating system on mini and mainframe computers has led to the development of a number of microcomputer versions.

Operating systems are not limited to mainframes and minicomputers. Microcomputers require systems that are not only effective, but easy to learn. The most popular microcomputer operating systems include DOS, for Disk Operating System, designed by Microsoft for use on IBM computers and compatibles, the Apple Macintosh operating system, and OS/2 designed by IBM to run on the IBM PS/2 family of machines.

DOS

Originally called PC-DOS, this was the operating system shipped with all IBM PC computers. It was developed for IBM by Microsoft and became known as MS-DOS when used on compatibles. **DOS** is a character-based (also called **command-driven**) operating system where the user must remember and input a set of characters (commands) to get the system to perform the desired tasks. When the system is turned on, the operating system is read into memory, or booted (derived from being "pulled up by one's boot straps"). A prompt appears. With a floppy-drive system the **prompt A>** appears. On a hard drive system the prompt becomes **C>**. A prompt informs the user that the computer is waiting for a command. Commands include reading and writing information to and from disks, managing printers, and executing applications software. Since its original release, DOS has gone through a number of revisions, each reflecting hardware and software advances as well as a desire to make the system easier to use. Current versions, although command-driven, include the use of menus. DOS 4.0 through 5.0 support the use of mice. They also support the larger primary memory capacity available on the most current microcomputers and the large secondary storage capacity of hard drives. Microsoft's Windows, a user-friendly, icon- or picture-based interface, runs under DOS.

OS/2

In 1987 IBM released its PS/2 family of computers along with a new, more powerful operating system called **OS/2** (for Operating System 2). Initially character/command driven, a graphical interface called Presentation Manager soon followed. OS/2 was designed to overcome many of the limitations inherent in DOS, including its memory restriction of a 640K maximum. OS/2 provides for multitasking, or the running of more than one application package at once. Unfortunately, OS/2 was not designed with **backward compatibility,** the ability to run earlier versions of software. In other words, it would not run DOS applications programs. The user community was somewhat unwilling to switch to this new operating system when the programs they had learned to love, and heavily invested in, could not be used. More recent releases run applications software designed specifically for OS/2 as well as those written for DOS and DOS running Windows.

Macintosh Operating System

In 1984, Apple Corp. released its Macintosh computer and in so doing, introduced the first **graphical user-interface (GUI).** The Macintosh uses a mouse for pointing, and features an operating environment where pictures, or icons, indicate basic functions. Icons include file folders for creating files and a trash can for erasing files. By pointing to an icon and clicking on menus, the Macintosh lets the user execute programs and create files, as well as share and store information.

The Macintosh's interface was the first to combine a pointing device (mouse) and icons with a graphics monitor and window-oriented software. The Macintosh's operating system is designed so that multiple software applications can be activated or run at the same time. This is called **multitasking.** For the user to view these multiple operations, the screen can be divided into sections, or **windows.** Each window contains a different application. Windows appear to overlap, giving the impression of papers on top of one another with the most recently activated or opened application on the top (see Figure 10.1). Many software packages designed for the Macintosh allow information or graphics visible in one window to be copied or transferred to other open windows.

The newest release of the Macintosh operating system called System 7 has added more color, and created three-dimensional features and icons. System 7

Figure 10.1   Windows: The Apple Macintosh uses windows for multiple operations, with icons indicating basic functions.

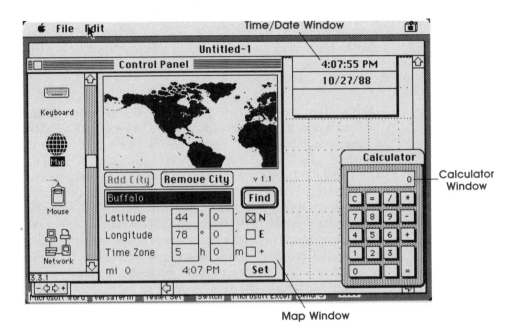

Map Window

Calculator Window

includes file sharing capabilities, making it easy to convert the Macintosh from a single-user environment to a small group system. It has expanded help features and tools to assist users in organizing their project.

USER-INTERFACE SOFTWARE

Until recently, the operating system exclusively controlled the computer by translating user's commands into instructions. Clicking on an icon that then opens a file is an example of the user-interface's role. It is often the case that users want to combine packages and share information between the packages. Using an operating system alone, files created by one package are often difficult to incorporate into files created by other packages. In some cases, transferring information between packages can resemble union/management negotiations; that is, although common ground exists, it is hard to find.

Creating this "common ground" has not been easy. In an effort to make communicating with the computer more natural, system software designers have created programs called **user-interfaces,** or **operating environments** that make interacting with the computer easier. On some systems, the user-interface

Applications Software in the Sciences

Science

The Deep Submergence Lab at Woods Hole Oceanographic Institute used a computer to produce this three-dimensional model of the USS *Monitor*, the sunken Civil War ironclad.

(© Vicom)

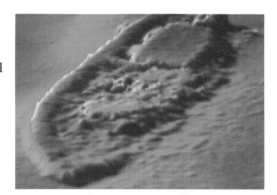

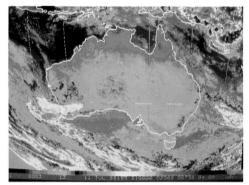

Scientists rely on computers to display weather information.

(© Bill Bachman/Science Source/Photo Researchers)

A false-color weather satellite photograph of a severe storm in the Bering Sea off the Kamchatka Peninsula. The picture was taken by the Nimbus 5 weather satellite.

(Photo Researchers, Inc.)

Computer simulation monitors takeoff performance in airplanes.

(NASA/Science Source/Photo Researchers)

Geology

Landsat photos are used to analyze collected data: (right) Indonesia and (below) the San Francisco Bay area in California.

(© Dan McCoy /Rainbow and Photo Researchers, Inc.)

A geological simulation on a PS/2 monitor. (IBM)

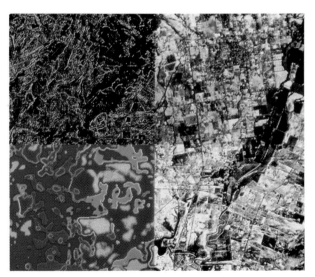

A single infra-red aerial photo with image processing functions performed on it. Clockwise from upper left: (1) the original data, (2) after applying a Laplacian filter to enhance edge information, (3) the result of a routine that classifies land use based on color, (4) after running both an adaptive contrast enhancer and a sharpening filter to bring out the detail in the image. (© Vicom)

Medicine

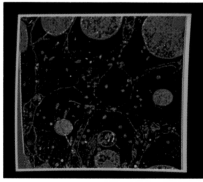

Computer graphics are used to represent DNA. This view is looking down the axis of a double helical DNA molecule.

(© Dan McCoy / Rainbow)

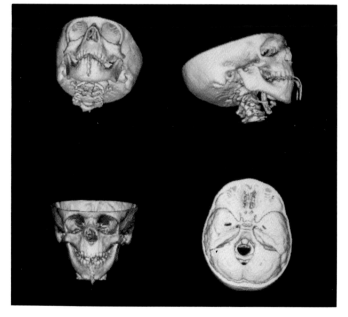

Computerized axial tomography (CAT) scans have become an invaluable tool in medicine.

(Dept. of Neurology, University of Wisconsin)

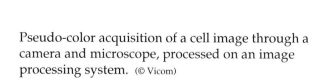

Pseudo-color acquisition of a cell image through a camera and microscope, processed on an image processing system. (© Vicom)

Space

Three images taken by the Voyager 2 satellite were combined by computer to create this dramatic photograph. (NASA)

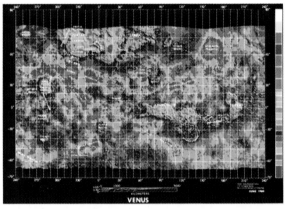

The data for this computer-generated, color-contour map of Venus was transmitted by the Pioneer-Venus orbiter. (NASA)

Computers make solar flares more visible.

(© Dan McCoy /Rainbow)

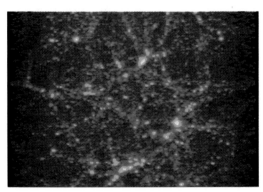

This image, showing galaxies and clusters of galaxies, represents a computer-simulated portion of the universe that is 150 million light years across.

(© Vicom, Data courtesy of Prof. Marc Davis, Univ. of California at Berkeley.)

On Line

AN OPERATING SYSTEM FOR ALL MACHINES?

The current world of operating systems is largely proprietary. Depending on the design of the CPU, a small number of operating systems are available for that system. DOS/Windows and OS/2 run on Intel microprocessors, the Macintosh operating system runs only on processors built by Motorola, and mini and mainframe manufacturers provide their unique systems. None of these operating systems will run on any other CPU design. None will run software developed for other systems.

The single exception to this rule is UNIX. Developed by AT&T's Bell Labs, it runs on all classes of machines from mainframes to micros. Unfortunately, UNIX is somewhat difficult to use and the popular microcomputer software does not run under this operating system.

The idea of portability, the ability for software to run on any computer, is currently only a hope and a dream. This dream, however, is moving toward a future reality. At least two organizations that have expressed interest in the idea have assembled research teams and begun work on turning their ideas into reality.

AT&T's Bell Labs (the inventors of UNIX) has begun developing what it is calling Plan 9. AT&T's group is working on building a system that incorporates the rapid improvements common in desktop machines, including easy network connections, bit-mapped, high-resolution graphics, and windowing, using high-performance microcomputers. Maintaining the integrity and security of individual files, as well as making file sharing easy, regardless of which machine runs the system, is also part of the research plan.

Apple Computer Corporation's plan is equally ambitious. Sources indicate that Apple has gathered 100 engineers and scientists to develop software that will run on all types of computers, from microcomputers and laptops to mainframes. Even parallel processing hardware is being taken into account. Apple has given the project the code-name "Pink."

Regardless of what happens along the research path in Plan 9 or Project Pink, major players in the software arena are taking seriously the desire by users to share not just information but applications software between computer systems.

Sources: "Operating Software Becomes More Versatile," *Wall Street Journal*, May 22, 1991, p. B1. Rob Pike, et al., "Plan 9 from Bell Labs," *Technical Report*, Murray Hill, NJ, AT&T Bell Laboratories, 1991.

is an integral part of the operating system. With others it is a distinct package resting "on top" of the operating system (see Figure 10.2). In either case, the user-interface determines the "personality" of the computer. It links the user and the computer together.

Two kinds of user-interfaces remain popular. With **character-based user-interfaces (CUI)**, words or symbols are typed in at a *prompt*. MS-DOS is the dominant microcomputer example of CUI, and there can be as many as 50 com-

Figure 10.2 The role of the *user-interface* is to make the computer easier for people to use.

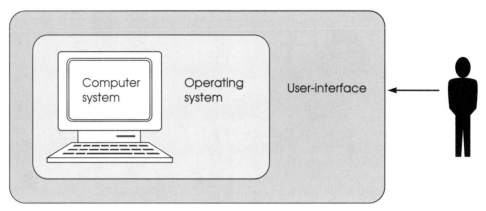

mands the user must remember to employ the system effectively. Although such interfaces are very powerful, they are somewhat difficult to use and make the sharing of information challenging.

The Macintosh computer exemplifies the **graphical user-interface (GUI)** by combining a pointing device (mouse), icons, and window-oriented software with multitasking. While dozens of GUIs exist, three dominate the field. The Macintosh operating environment provides the user-interface on all Macintosh machines. Microsoft Windows makes GUIs available to most DOS applications running on IBM and compatible systems. X-Windows is a complex windowing environment designed to run on all UNIX based workstations.

Regardless of the machine they run on, most GUIs include the following features:

- a pointing device, most commonly a mouse
- pull-down menus controlled by the pointing device
- windowing software that simultaneously displays multiple computer tasks by dividing up a single computer monitor
- multitasking
- graphical images that display what the computer is doing, and allow the user to tell the computer what to do
- icons to represent the different computer applications and tasks. Icons represent specific applications packages as well as files and system commands available to the user.

While individual users may debate the merits of different user-interfaces, researchers are examining how they influence productivity. Microsoft recently commissioned a study to determine which user-interface, character-based or graphical, enabled workers to be the most effective. The study found that workers who used GUIs improved productivity. GUI users got more work done in less time with 58 percent fewer errors. Workers also learned faster. It was found that once people had learned how to use the graphical interface on a particular application, the knowledge transferred to other situations. Learning another application became less time consuming.

The role of the user-interface is to make the computer and the operating system easier to use. Whether built into the operating system (Macintosh), or as an addition to it (Microsoft Windows, X-Windows), graphical user-interfaces transform the computer from a text-based system to a visually stimulating environment able to display multiple tasks at once.

APPLICATIONS SOFTWARE

From one point of view all software is applications software. Operating systems run computers, computer languages are used to write programs, checkbook programs keep track of checks, and other programs provide games to entertain us. Each program was created with a specific purpose or application in mind. But in general usage, applications software describes specifically those packages written to solve a human problem or satisfy a human need, and does not include those programs that make computers work.

Virtually all the applications programs written today are designed to be used by nonprogrammers. While a significant amount of software is written by business and research organizations to satisfy their unique needs, considerable software is written by software "houses" or companies to be marketed to the general public. These packages range from sophisticated three-dimensional graphics programs used to design aircraft to straightforward microcomputer spelling or arithmetic drills used by children. Applications software encompasses these and much, much more.

Applications software falls into two general groups. Programs that focus on a very specific task or group of tasks are called **specialized applications software.** These packages include software to teach typing, assist real estate agents and restaurant managers, calculate federal taxes, or perform the bookkeeping tasks of a major corporation. The other group is called **general-purpose applications software.** It includes programs that focus on particular areas but can also be adapted to individual needs. For example, a word processing program can be used to create any kind of document from a personal letter to a government report. A spreadsheet can contain the family budget or project the growth in domestic car sales. Although such software focuses on a specific task, the program has enough varied capabilities to perform a variety of subtasks.

Specialized Applications Software

Specialized applications software packages make it possible for us to use computers to solve specific problems or satisfy particular needs. So many of these programs have been developed that it would be impossible to examine them all. We will look at some software that has affected various areas of our lives.

Science, Engineering, and Mathematics Few areas have felt the impact of computers as dramatically as the sciences. Modern laboratories use computers to perform data analysis, such as tabulating the influence of marijuana in controlled-drug tests, analyzing the structure of the AIDS virus, and monitoring and running sophisticated experiments, such as stress-testing new cars. Scientists and engineers use computers to forecast the weather, to assist in predicting earthquakes and volcanic eruptions, and to search for scarce resources such as water, oil, and natural gas (see Figure 10.3). Statistical packages turn mountains of census data, for example, into meaningful information about the American family.

Computer photo enhancement and analysis has advanced our knowledge of space and our planet. Satellite pictures can locate polluting industries and make

Figure 10.3 Computers and the Sciences: Computers in the laboratory find use in drug experiments, the stress-testing of new cars, searching for oil and gas, and, here, in weather forecasting.

global weather projections. Analysis of satellite and spacecraft pictures enables us to venture to the stars to plan for the future and study the past. Software interprets data from the Magellan probe, giving us scenes from Venus. It has helped people land on the moon and locate the Titanic.

Computer-aided design (CAD) systems use three-dimensional graphics in the development of blueprints and architectural designs (see Chapter 14). Architects use CAD systems to design buildings and entire towns. Designers use them to plan aircraft, automobiles, spacecraft, and even computer chips (see Figure 10.4).

Not only can external structures be designed, but the internal parts can be positioned and displayed in color. For example, computer-generated building plans can include such items as air ducts and electrical wiring. CAD pictures can be rotated so the object can be viewed from all angles and directions.

The military is the largest consumer of computers and software. Software on laptops assists pilots in mission planning and accurate missile targeting. Micro-

Figure 10.4   Computer-Aided Design: Computers are used in the construction of aircraft and spacecraft.

computer software helps calculate helicopter fuel needs, and mainframes enable commanders to run battle simulations and coordinate radar defense systems. Software also keeps track of the location of military supplies from food and medicine to munitions and vehicles.

Medicine Running the office of a doctor, dentist, or other health-related professional is a sophisticated business. Specialized software maintains patient records, keeps track of appointments, generates patient bills, and processes insurance claim forms. Medical tests that used to take days to process in a lab now can be done in minutes in the doctor's office by specialized equipment. This equipment contains embedded microprocessors that are, in effect, specialized programs. Programs also exist to tailor diet and exercise routines to individual patients.

In hospitals, applications programs run on large mainframes to process patient bills, maintain records, keep track of inventory, assist in meal preparation, and handle the mammoth data-processing tasks associated with running any large organization. In addition, software is available that helps doctors diagnose illness, monitor patient progress, and analyze blood and urine samples. Specialized software systems monitor babies in neonatal intensive care units, alert pharmacists to possible drug interactions, and assist in the analysis of X-rays, CAT scans, and other medical procedures. Specialized software has been at the forefront of advances in modern medicine.

Education and Training Computer science is now an academic discipline, and computers are used as an educational aid from kindergarten through graduate school. They also help modern schools run more efficiently.

Since their first appearance, computers themselves have become a topic of study and the subject of an increasing number and variety of courses. Courses in computer literacy and programming are becoming basic educational requirements in many states. Students in elementary school learn computer logic through the programming language LOGO, and their older brothers and sisters study BASIC and Pascal (see Figure 10.5).

An increasing number of schools are making word processing software available to improve students' reading and writing skills. Course offerings in computer science and information systems are among the most popular in many colleges. Computer courses in continuing education programs are very popular as adults try to catch up with the micro-generation.

In the classroom, educational software uses graphics and sound to motivate students to learn. The most common educational packages reinforce the material taught in the classroom. Drill and practice routines, often in the form of games, support the math and reading curricula of many schools. Some learning games encourage slow learners to learn at their own rate through tutorials, while others provide enrichment for students exploring new areas. Self-paced instructional programs, called **computer-assisted instruction (CAI),** make use

Figure 10.5   Computers and Education: Learning to use a computer is now a requirement in many elementary schools.

of the ever-patient computer to give students immediate reinforcement when learning or reviewing material. Advanced programs can adjust to individual student needs, skipping unneeded sections and spending more time on areas where the student has difficulty. Some packages can even keep track of the student's progress and identify problem areas.

More exciting are programs that expand the horizons of students. There are programs to assist the handicapped in learning to their fullest potential, to help students choose a college, to study for standardized tests, or to teach colors and numbers to preschoolers. Computer simulations can depict the nervous system, the solar system, or an economic system. Students can reenact historic battles or analyze a rocket's lift-off and path in flight. In a computer simulation, students can see how a change can affect an entire system and they can test the effects of various solutions to a problem. The simulators used by most elementary and secondary schools run on microcomputers, but there are mainframe simulators as well. Medical schools and teaching hospitals use such systems to teach students correct diagnostic techniques. A simulated, unconscious patient with a set of symptoms is presented to the student-doctor, and the "game" is to make the patient well. It is as painless a learning technique for the student-doctor as it is for the patient, and mistakes are not fatal. Pilots train in flight simulators that combine mock aircraft with sophisticated computer-simulated visuals and equipment signals, enabling them to practice skills that would be too costly in terms of lives and equipment to test in real aircraft.

Computers are also used in a wide variety of other subjects ranging from math to psychology, English, and music. Laboratory sciences increasingly use computers to maintain, control, and evaluate experiments. Numerous colleges and universities encourage students to purchase their own machines by arranging for their purchase at considerable discounts. Many college bookstores and local computer stores, recognizing a new and growing market, offer computers and software for rent on a semester basis. Some schools, such as Clarkson, Carnegie Mellon, Dartmouth, Boston College, and the three U.S. military academies, require that students purchase machines at the start of their first year. These micros can be used as standalone computers or can be connected to the university's mainframe when appropriate. Computers are changing not only how we learn, but *what* we learn.

Management of schools is similar to management of businesses. Both generate reports, maintain records, purchase supplies, pay employees, and so on. Software for data processing is used for these tasks. Computers manage the office paperwork, maintain school budgets, perform accounting tasks, and control the inventory of everything from crayons to computers. Computers are used to create and generate lunch menus, and determine bus routes. Many small districts use microcomputers to calculate and prepare payroll checks. In addition, computers grade papers, keep and update class lists, manage student records, and maintain course information. Applications packages that provide up-to-date information on career guidance and college selection are available in the secondary schools.

Business Use   An incredible amount of applications software exists to help run our businesses. Indeed, businesses are among the largest consumers of applications software. The modern office makes significant use of general-purpose packages such as word processing programs and data base systems. But specialized software abounds as well. For both large and small systems, software is available to manage inventories, perform standard bookkeeping tasks, prepare payrolls, produce accounting reports, and analyze business finances. Not only can checkbooks be balanced, the actual checks themselves can be printed. Executives use computer simulations to analyze business trends. Software allows up-to-the-minute reporting, which assists in decision making. There are programs to control industrial robots that perform boring or dangerous tasks in factories (see Figure 10.6). Programs control such industrial processes as combining chemicals to produce mixtures, cleansers, or drugs and maintaining the critical temperatures necessary for processing food and medicines. Computer programs monitor the safety of our power plants, the performance of trains, and the sale of concert tickets.

Figure 10.6   Software in Manufacturing: An array of software is used in manufacturing, including controlling these industrial robots.

In the small business environment, the most popular packages are those that maintain business records and automate accounting procedures. Programs that keep track of the money expected from sales, the cost of equipment and supplies, and the payment of salaries and taxes are also in high demand.

Increasingly, many small business computer owners are subscribing to one or more computer information services such as CompuServe and Dow Jones. These services provide easy access to investment information, help identify market trends, and provide up-to-date national and world news. (See Chapter 15.)

Home Use Today, computers are found in many homes and are used there in a wide variety of ways. The most common uses include recreation, word processing, recordkeeping and money management, education, and, increasingly, home environment control. Home computer use reflects our work, our play, and our imagination.

Computers may seem like expensive toys because they are commonly used to relax, amuse, and entertain us. Computer games fascinate adults and children alike, whether they are arcade-style games that emphasize eye-hand coordination or interactive fiction games in which our strategy and problem-solving ability can affect the outcome. Popular board games such as chess, backgammon, and *Monopoly* have been redesigned for the computer. Computer simulation games that re-create real-life situations are rapidly gaining in popularity. *Flight Simulator* lets us try our hand at flying a light plane. *SIM City* transforms us into city managers, and we must decide where to place bridges, homes, and power plants. Other simulations let us pilot World War II submarines or play the stock market.

We can also become creative in the arts via our home machines. Painting programs let us express our creative nature without getting our hands dirty, and music software turns the home into a recording studio.

Other recreational uses aid hobbyists who need to process or store large amounts of information. For example, software is available to keep track of stamp or record collections, trace genealogies, maintain an exercise program, and provide shopping lists and recipes for cooking gourmet dinners.

The most common use of computers in the home is for word processing (see Figure 10.7). Word processing packages turn the computer, with an associated printer, into a text-manipulating typewriter that can be used for all types of family correspondence as well as for reports and papers needed at school, for volunteer activities, or for office work. With the addition of even simple graphics packages, greeting cards, newsletters, flyers, banners, and calendars can be easily created.

Computers can keep track of all kinds of household information, from recipes to tax data. There are programs to manage the family checkbook, keep track of all bank and investment accounts, maintain tax records, and organize any other kind of information that may accumulate. However, with the exception of software to assist with the preparation of federal tax returns, most software for home money management has not been overwhelmingly successful. Most people, including the majority of home computer owners, find it easier to continue to balance their checkbooks the old-fashioned way by using paper, pencil, and a hand calculator. Investment and financial software are popular with people for whom investing is a hobby or who personally manage large investments.

As our educational system puts increased importance on the use of computers in the schools, many families feel that their children need a microcomputer to keep up with their peers, or to have an advantage as they move into the changing work place. In the home, educational software entertains preschoolers

Figure 10.7   Word Processing at Home.

while teaching reading-readiness skills and provides drills related to what older children are learning in school.

Software is also becoming available to replace self-help and do-it-yourself books. It is now possible to learn how to type, speak a foreign language, reduce tension through biofeedback, play a guitar, or keep in shape with computer software.

Microcomputers are able to regulate the physical environment of the home as well. For example, if a thermostat has been installed in your home within the last few years it is likely to include an embedded microprocessor that will carefully control the temperature and humidity in the house. Such thermostats can have one setting for nighttime use, another for work hours and a third for evenings when everyone is likely to be home. We have lots of hidden computers in our homes. Microprocessors are routinely found in microwave ovens, televisions, VCRs, stereo systems, and many more electronic devices.

With the addition of special sensing devices, microcomputers can be used not only to regulate the temperature, but also to control the lights, and monitor the home's fire and security systems. Computers can answer the telephone and take messages when the family is away. If sensors are activated, advanced systems can even place telephone calls to the fire or police departments.

General-Purpose Applications Software

The most popular of the numerous types of applications software continues to be packages dedicated to word processing, spreadsheets, data base management, graphics, and communications. These five types are the critical building block programs with which almost any task can be accomplished. Indeed, every user will have at least one of these. We will look briefly at these five types of applications software and see how each of them is a unique tool. A more detailed look at each of these is found in Chapters 11 to 15.

Word Processing Writing and editing with a computer is known as **word processing.** Just about any printed text can be easily created using a word processor. Applications include reports, memos, term papers, letters, and even mailing labels (see Figure 10.8).

Figure 10.8   Word Processing Screen: Microcomputer word processing programs can be used to write letters.

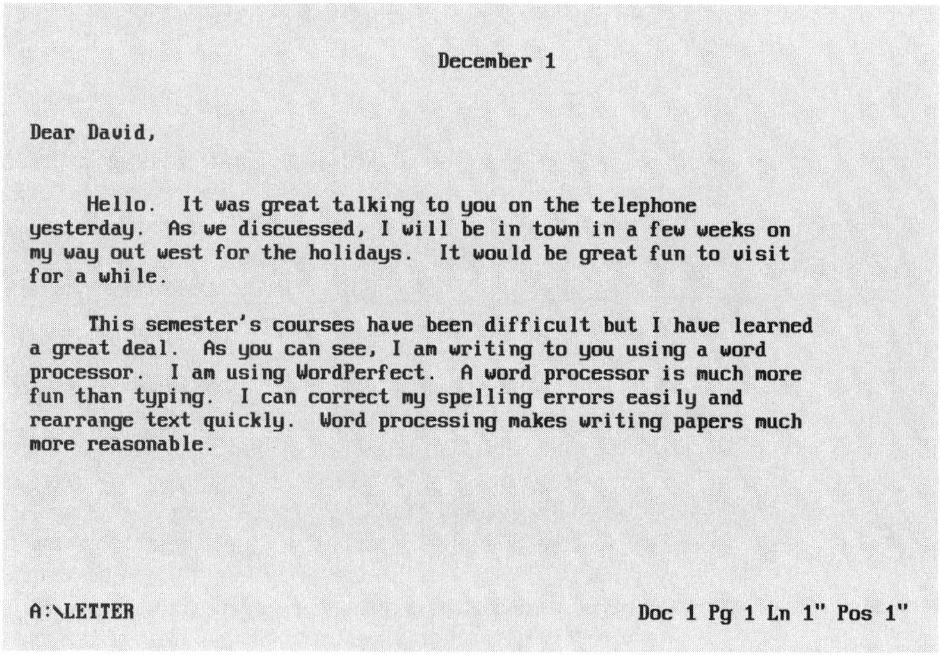

```
                                    December 1


Dear David,


     Hello.  It was great talking to you on the telephone
yesterday.  As we discuessed, I will be in town in a few weeks on
my way out west for the holidays.  It would be great fun to visit
for a while.

     This semester's courses have been difficult but I have learned
a great deal.  As you can see, I am writing to you using a word
processor.  I am using WordPerfect.  A word processor is much more
fun than typing.  I can correct my spelling errors easily and
rearrange text quickly.  Word processing makes writing papers much
more reasonable.




A:\LETTER                                        Doc 1 Pg 1 Ln 1" Pos 1"
```

Word processing software, whether it is an applications package used on a microcomputer or a dedicated system, is a tool for manipulating words, sentences, and paragraphs before they go on paper. Text can be entered, deleted, corrected, and reorganized quickly and easily. Equally important, text can be formatted or laid out for printing. An error-free document with underlining, boldfaced type, and straight righthand margins like those in this text, can easily be produced. Advanced word processing packages called desktop publishers, with sophisticated formatting abilities, can even produce printed matter that would otherwise require professional typesetting.

Word processing, which is discussed more fully in Chapter 11, is by far the most popular application available for microcomputers. Recent surveys by Consumers Union indicated that more than 90 percent of personal computer owners have at least one word processing package, and that 25 percent of home computing involves word processing. Even hunt-and-peck typists can produce perfect copy with this software. Revisions can easily be made and the revised document printed out without having to be completely retyped.

Many word processing systems include spelling checkers, which compare each word that is typed with an electronic dictionary. Errors are pointed out and systems frequently guess at the correct spelling or suggest words that are similarly spelled. A number of advanced systems include a computerized thesaurus that lists synonyms of specific words on request.

Word processors are being used to improve the writing skills of students from grade school through college. Students appear to be much more willing to revise and reorganize their papers when retyping is not required.

Electronic Spreadsheets When numbers, formulas, and mathematical calculations are involved, a spreadsheet is the software required. An **electronic spreadsheet** manipulates rows and columns of numbers in much the same way a word processor manipulates words. Spreadsheets are most frequently used to solve business and financial problems, but they can be used to balance checkbooks, maintain the family budget, or calculate student grades.

Each spreadsheet location is identified by a specific row (going across) and column (going down). The intersection of a row and column is called a cell.

	A	B
1	January	23.21
2	February	75.16	←— Cell

The highlighted box containing 75.16 is the intersection of row 2 and column B. Some cells may contain a word (January) or a formula that describes the properties or qualities of the number that will go there. As with a word processor, the entered information can easily be changed, deleted, or manipulated. New data can quickly be added.

A spreadsheet's most important feature is its ability to use formulas to perform calculations on the data stored within its cells. Formulas can be as simple as the sum of a given column or they can specify a complex relationship between cells. Some cells contain formulas. A cell's formula can call for simple arithmetic operations, such as addition and subtraction, or more complex sequences of operations, such as averaging, determining the maximum/minimum, and the solution of trigonometric functions. To calculate the value according to a formula, the software uses the numeric values found in specific cells. The result of the calculation is placed in the cell where the formula resides. For example, if we kept track of how much we spent on telephone and car expenses for a four-month period, we could use a spreadsheet formula to calculate the totals (see Figure 10.9).

The highlighted cell contains the formula: SUM(B3:B6), which means to sum the contents of cells B3 through B6. The effect is to sum the numbers 23.21, 75.16, 55.11, and 52.21.

Values calculated by formulas are readjusted every time the values of the appropriate cells change. So, if we realize we'd forgotten a car repair bill in our January totals, resulting in a true figure of $123.45, we would simply change the contents of the affected cell (C3) to that amount. In response to this change, the column sum would change to $268.11. The spreadsheet performs the recalculation automatically.

Figure 10.9   The Electronic Spreadsheet: This Excel spreadsheet keeps track of telephone and car expenses for the period from January to April.

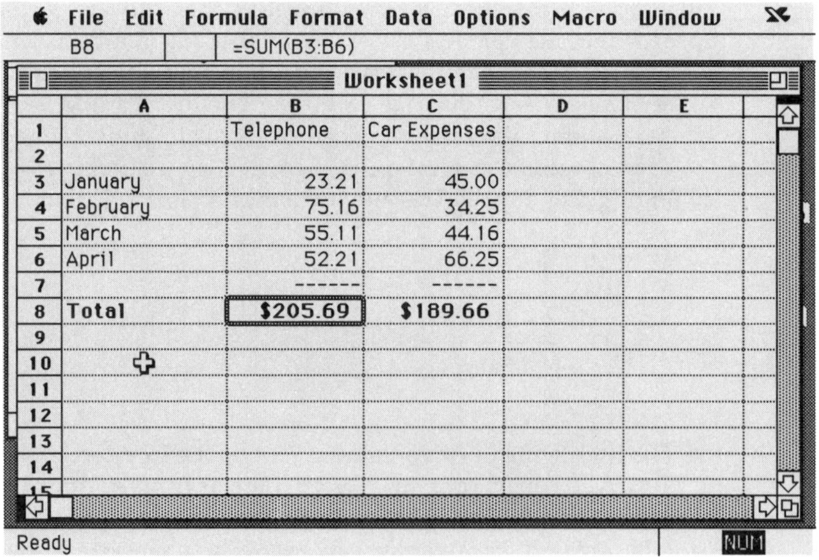

This ability to have formulas reflect changes in the sheet makes the electronic spreadsheet a valuable tool for testing or predicting change. For example, a spreadsheet can examine the effect on the cost of textbooks if all publishers raise prices by 10 percent next year. By adjusting formulas and data we can ask what would happen if prices were raised by 15 percent. How much more would students have to pay? In this way, we are using spreadsheet software to help predict something that has not happened yet. Such prediction is called a *what-if.* Such what-ifs assist the spreadsheet user in making sound decisions. Spreadsheets are discussed in greater detail in Chapter 12.

Data Base Software   We think of computers as incredibly fast calculating devices. Computers are also incredibly competent devices for storing large quantities of data and for locating information for us when we want it. We often call on computers to locate particular pieces of stored information and organize them in some way that is useful to us. A computerized collection of information is known as a **data base.** A data base is organized into files so that information can easily be stored, changed, searched, sorted, and retrieved. Such systems are useful whenever large amounts of information are involved, as you will see in Chapter 13.

Two types of data base software are available. The simpler variety organizes information into a single file and is called a **file management system.** These systems are useful for storing information such as mailing lists or an organization's membership data, which will frequently be changed. File managers are used to search through the file for particular data, sort it, and print the results.

When the information to be stored is more complex, a **data base management system (DBMS)** is used. Large businesses or institutions need this system when the information stored has many uses and is frequently changed. Data base management systems can contain many files. These files may hold different but related items of information. A university system would have files for student billing, grades, and registration information, in addition to employee payroll and benefit records. Such systems contain all the features of file management systems and are also able to combine information from the different files. For example, after searching the billing file for the names of all students with overdue accounts, registration information could be withheld from them until their bills are paid.

Data base software makes information easily available to users, enabling them to make more informed decisions.

Graphics Software   With the addition of special graphics monitors, software has been developed that can duplicate photographs, design and rotate three-dimensional objects, or create charts and diagrams that make statistical information easier to understand. Affordable, high-quality computer graphics packages are a fairly recent arrival on the software scene.

The most popular of the computer graphics packages design graphs and charts for business use. Graphics software also has statistical and scientific applications, such as graphs that summarize the results of an opinion poll or a laboratory experiment. Graphics software is designed to transform information stored in computer files and present it in diagram form. Graphics let us summarize and understand vast amounts of information very quickly. Many spreadsheet and statistical packages include the ability to create some graphs and charts. Figure 10.10 shows a graph created by Excel.

In addition to packages that produce specific types of graphs and charts, *object-oriented graphics* packages can be used to create almost any imaginable image by placing symbols such as circles, lines, and rectangles or entire pictures wherever the user wishes on the screen. Figure 10.11 shows one such image. These packages are used for everything from do-it-yourself greeting cards to professional newsletters. A number of packages can create color slides from screen displays. Computer graphics are discussed in greater detail in Chapter 14.

Communication Software   In our increasingly fast-paced society, rapid, reliable access to people and information is critical. The significance of communication software is that it provides access to shared ideas and information. Tele-

---

Figure 10.10   Graphics Software: This Excel graph is an example of how software can help summarize information. This uses the data from the spreadsheet found in Figure 10.9.

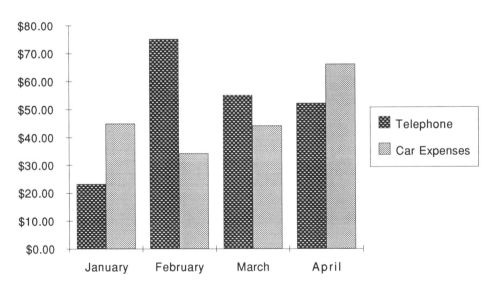

Figure 10.11   The Computer as Artist: Object-oriented graphics packages can be used to create a vast array of images on the computer screen.

phone lines and surface mail can connect us with offices, businesses, homes, and people almost anywhere. But it is not always possible to reach people by phone when we want to, and the mail is slow and sometimes unreliable. Computers are able to act as bridges between people and the information and ideas they require.

With communication software and specialized hardware, users can connect their machines with other computer systems regardless of location, assuming they have permission to do so. Students can use communication packages to dial into their university's mainframe to do course work at home, and researchers can connect to supercomputers in distant cities. Similarly, a company's employees can connect to the organization's mainframe from home or other remote locations to get or receive messages (electronic mail) or to transmit documents.

Researchers, scientists, and administrators have organized long-distance networks of telephone-connected computers through which information can be exchanged and resources can be shared. Papers, reports, and ideas can be transmitted between machines very quickly, and programs and equipment can be shared among participants who live and work in distant locations.

Microcomputer as well as mainframe users can connect to computer information services and gain access to everything from recent publications on medical research to airline flight schedules and up-to-the-minute stock quotes. Using electronic bulletin boards, users shop electronically, leave messages for friends, and share user-written software. Chapter 15 goes into more detail about computer communication.

We have just examined the range of software available on today's computers. The possible applications are limited only by our imagination.

SOFTWARE INTEGRATION

As we've indicated, a considerable amount of applications software is available. It is often the case that users want to combine packages and share information between them. Unfortunately, in most cases files created by one package are often difficult to incorporate into files created by other packages. Two different paths have been taken to create an environment where software is easy to use, and data, including graphics, are relatively easy to share. One approach has been to integrate or tie together software products. The other, discussed earlier in this chapter, has been the development of sophisticated operating systems and user-interfaces where standalone software packages can more easily share information. In both cases the purpose is to make computers and software easier to use.

The first integrated software application was exemplified by the release in 1982 of Lotus 1-2-3 by Lotus Development Corp. Lotus 1-2-3 was one of the first software packages to tie business graphics and data base concepts to a powerful spreadsheet. Its easy-to-use format enables users to share information between these three tools.

The opposite path, exemplified by the Macintosh, uses a complex graphical operating system involving a mouse and icons to make sharing information relatively painless.

Even with sophisticated graphical user-interfaces, sharing information between microcomputer applications can be an intimidating task. To solve this problem, two different integration approaches have been taken. **Integrated packages** combine powerful software tools such as word processing, spreadsheets, data base managers, and graphics into a single package. **Families of software** create integration by designing groups of standalone programs that store information in a common format and use a common set of operating commands.

Integrated Packages

The most difficult part of using an applications package is the considerable time and effort involved in learning the functions and commands. If multiple packages are used, the same learning curve is required for each package. Even when switching between packages we are familiar with, some time is spent getting up to speed and recalling how each package works. Integrated packages combine a number of different software applications into a single program. The most popular integrated packages (Lotus 1-2-3, Framework, ENABLE, First Choice, and most recently, Microsoft Works and Excel for IBMs and compatible machines; Excel and Microsoft Works for the Macintosh) combine a word processor with a data base manager, spreadsheet, and business graphics program. Many packages include communications components, and some have added desktop aids such as note pads, calendars, and calculators. All the components of an integrated package use a common set of operating commands. For example, in ENABLE, F10 always returns the user to the menu, as does the slash in Lotus 1-2-3.

In addition to having a common command structure, integrated packages, being a single complex program, are designed to share data between component programs. Information gleaned from a data base can be transferred directly to the word processor, and graphics can easily be generated by spreadsheet data. In many packages, the connections between the components are so clearly defined that updates in the spreadsheet will be reflected in data that have been copied to a word processing report.

For convenience, most integrated packages have incorporated windows so that different components can be used simultaneously. Some packages include overlapping windows similar to those used in the Macintosh environment (see Figure 10.12). Others split the screen into two or three nonoverlapping parts so that more than one operation is visible at a time. Others use function keys to switch between components that are active but not visible on the screen.

Integrated all-in-one packages are not perfect. They have a number of disadvantages. The individual components of such integrated packages are rarely as powerful or as comprehensive as their stand-alone relatives. For example, EN-ABLE's data base component is not nearly as versatile as the standalone package dBASE IV. Also, a combined package can easily contain more components than a user requires. If only one or two components are required, why pay for more? However, the total package usually costs less than all of the components purchased independently. Last of all, integrated packages require more memory than standalone packages because the program is larger and more complex.

Families of Software

Integrated packages are designed to combine different software components into a single unit, a super-package. A number of companies, most notably Software Publishing (the developers of the PFS Professional Family of Software), have taken a different approach. Each package in the series can stand alone and run independently of all other packages. However, each package uses the same set of commands and has the same organizational structure. In the PFS series, each package uses pull-down menus, and the function keys perform the same

Figure 10.12   Package integrators use overlapping windows to make more than one application or process visible at the same time.

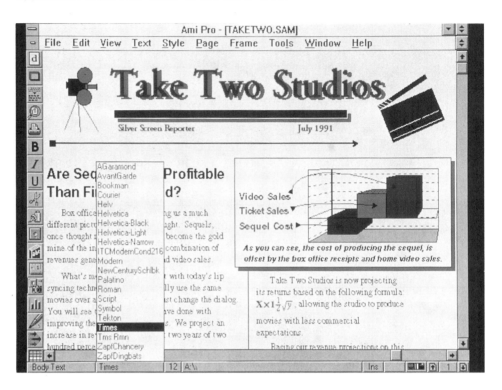

tasks. The output produced by one package in the family is organized so that it can be transferred to other packages. Since all packages use the same set of commands, after one package is learned, learning additional packages is easy. In addition, users need to purchase only the components they require, keeping costs down.

However, because each package in a family is independent, most families of software do not allow more than one program to be active at a time. Without a powerful user-interface (and often with one), transferring information from one application to another can be time-consuming.

Most software families consist of a spreadsheet, data base manager, and a word processor. Software families can focus on more specific needs. For example, a business application family can include accounting, bookkeeping, and payroll programs. Software families are usually designed to be easy to learn and very user-friendly.

Applications software turns the computer into an individualized tool, enabling us to solve problems, educate, and enjoy ourselves. As we have seen in this chapter, software brings the computer to life, transforming our world.

SUMMARY

Computer software is divided into four categories: systems software, development software, user-interface software, and applications software. **Systems software** controls the operation of the machine. **Development software** consists of programs used to create, update, and maintain other programs. **User-interface software** makes it easier for people to deal with the operating system. **Applications software** programs solve human problems or satisfy a human need, but commonly exclude programs that make computers work.

Operating systems coordinate the tasks performed by the computer. They provide communication between the user and software, direct the flow of information among the components of the computer system, such as the processor, memory, and peripheral devices, and govern the execution of applications programs.

User-interfaces are designed to make communicating with the computer and the operating system easier. **Character-based user-interfaces (CUI)** have words, or symbols are typed in at a **prompt. Graphical user-interfaces (GUI)** commonly include a pointing device, pull-down menus, windowing software, and complex graphical images and icons.

Specialized applications software packages focus on very specific tasks, while **general-purpose applications** software includes programs that focus on particular areas but can be adapted to individual needs.

In science, engineering, and mathematics, applications packages are used for data analysis and to monitor and run sophisticated experiments. Statistical packages are used to analyze all types of data. Computer-aided design is used in the development of blueprints and architectural drawings. In medicine, software assists in recordkeeping, disease diagnosis, medical testing, and patient care.

Computers are used as an educational aid in our schools and businesses. Administratively they maintain records, process payrolls, and control inventory. They reinforce the classroom by helping all students learn at their own rate. Simulations let students manipulate a model of a real-world event and study how changes affect the system. Computers themselves have become a topic of study.

The largest consumer of applications software is business. Companies make use of general-purpose software such as word processors and data base systems as well as more specialized software to manage records, prepare payroll, produce accounting reports, and analyze business finances. Software also controls industrial robots and factory machinery.

In the home, computers are used for recreation and entertainment, word processing, personal recordkeeping and money management, educational support, and maintaining a safe, comfortable environment.

The five building block programs currently used on computers are: word processing, electronic spreadsheets, data base management systems, computer graphics, and communication packages.

Word processing software is a tool for manipulating words, sentences, and paragraphs before they go on paper.

Electronic spreadsheets manipulate numbers and formulas that are presented in the form of rows and columns. Spreadsheets are most frequently used to solve business and financial problems, but can be used for any task that involves computation.

A computerized collection of information is called a **data base.** Data base software is used to organize data so that they can be stored, searched, sorted, and retrieved easily.

The most popular form of computer graphics is the design of graphs and charts for analysis of data. Alternatively, *object-oriented graphics* packages create images by placing symbols, shapes, and textures on the screen.

Communication software and specialized hardware connect computers and computer hardware over distances ranging from across the room to around the world. Such networks use telephone lines to share equipment and information.

Software integration works toward the development of computer applications that share information easily, and that are user-friendly.

Key Words

As an extra review of the chapter, try defining the following terms. If you have trouble with any of them, refer to the page number listed.

applications software *(257)*
backward compatibility *(259)*
character-based user-interface (CUI) *(261)*
command-driven *(258)*
computer-assisted instruction (CAI) *(266)*
data base *(275)*
data base management system (DBMS) *(275)*
development software *(256)*
DOS *(258)*
electronic spreadsheet *(273)*
families of software *(278)*
file management system *(275)*
general-purpose applications software *(263)*

graphical user-interface (GUI) *(259)*
integrated package *(278)*
multitasking *(259)*
operating system *(257)*
operating environment *(260)*
OS/2 *(259)*
prompt *(258)*
proprietary software *(257)*
specialized applications software *(263)*
systems software *(256)*
tool *(258)*
window *(259)*
word processing *(272)*
UNIX *(258)*
user-interface software *(257)*

Test Your Knowledge

1. Define *systems software.*

2. What is the purpose of an operating system?

3. What is the role of a user-interface?

4. What computer popularized the graphical user-interface?

5. How does a character-based user-interface work?

6. List three popular graphical user-interfaces?

7. What is the difference between specialized applications software and general-purpose applications software?

8. List two medical uses of applications software.

9. List three educational uses of applications software.

10. What is CAI?

11. List four kinds of software used in business.

12. What is recreational software?

13. List five uses of computer software in the home.

14. What is a word processor? How is it used?

15. What is an electronic spreadsheet? How is it used?

16. What is data base software? How is it used?

17. Describe two common uses for graphics software.

18. What is integrated software?

19. How does an integrated environment differ from other forms of software integration?

20. List the two software integration approaches and briefly describe each.

Expand Your Knowledge

1. Interview someone you know who works with computers. Have this person describe the tasks he or she performs on the computer and the kind of software used to help with these tasks. Write a short report on this interview.

2. Go to your local computer store and compare Microsoft Windows with the

Macintosh's user-interface. Write a short paper comparing them. How are they different? How are they similar? Which one do you prefer and why?

3. Go to your local computer store. Discuss with a salesperson the kinds of software the store sells and what packages are the most popular. List the 10 most popular packages. Include the name, manufacturer, and retail price (if available).

4. Contact your computing center and identify the 10 most popular microcomputer packages used on campus. List these packages. For each package, indicate its name and manufacturer, and whether it is used primarily for instruction, research, or administration.

5. Select a software application of interest to you. Using three periodicals, none more than one year old, write a three-page paper on your chosen topic. Be sure to explain how the software has made a difference to users.

11

Word Processing

CHAPTER OUTLINE

Computers have changed the way many people write and think about writing. When we speak, we often break some of the structural rules of our language, yet we are still understood. In fact, we often say very little but communicate a great deal through our facial expressions and gestures. Written communication, by comparison, must be very specific. We must write exactly what we mean and we must use correct sentence structure if we are to be understood.

Some people become so concerned with spelling and sentence structure when they write that they have difficulty putting their ideas down on paper. Most of us have experienced the frustration of correcting written errors, making changes, and then having to retype our letters and reports. However, if adding, deleting, and generally changing words and paragraphs could be made easier, then writing might become almost as easy as speaking. This is the power of word processing.

After studying this chapter, you will be able to:

- Describe what a word processor does.
- Distinguish between the two types of word processing programs.
- Describe how text is entered, changed, and deleted using a word processor.
- Explain the functions of text editing and formatting.
- Trace the development of desktop publishing.

CHANGING THE WAY WE WRITE

Writing with a computer is known as **word processing.** Programs for word processing make it possible for individual characters, words, and paragraphs to be added, removed, and switched around anywhere within any piece of written work. Entire paragraphs can be moved freely. Changes can be made, and a clean and neat copy can be produced without the entire document having to be re-typed.

When words can be changed so easily, writers are freer to experiment with ideas. For some, this may lead to a brainstorming or free-writing approach to composing text. The flow of ideas is simply entered into the computer as it occurs. After the ideas are on paper they can be reorganized, expanded, or de-leted. Many people feel that this freedom expands their creativity, and this is the main advantage of word processing for them. Others simply find that the main benefit is the removal of the drudgery of revising and correcting their work.

WHAT CAN A WORD PROCESSOR DO?

A word processor can do everything a typewriter can do and more. Everyone has to write. Anything we put in writing—letters, reports, tables, and lists—can easily be developed and printed using word processing software. Whenever written work must be changed or corrected, word processing is appropriate. Word processing is especially useful for individualizing form letters or making multiple original documents. Now with the aid of the computer, even poor typists and spellers can produce professional-quality work. Word processing software makes this possible.

All word processing programs require a computer with a keyboard and a display screen, a printer, and software. Some programs require additional hardware, such as a mouse, touch screen, or joystick. This makes them easier to operate for people who are not experienced typists.

TYPES OF WORD PROCESSING PROGRAMS

Regardless of the design of the system, all word processing software packages have two parts. The front end is concerned with entering and editing the text itself. This part controls the actual inputting and writing, as well as changing of the text. Paragraphs can be indented by setting tabs. Lines can be skipped or left blank.

The back end of a word processor is concerned with the layout, or **format,** of the text. This part controls the way the text will appear when it is printed. Formatting includes spacing, margin requirements, centering, underlining, boldfacing, and any other visual adjustments. Formatting may affect the entire document, as in line spacing, or only a single word, as in underlining.

Software manufacturers have taken two different approaches in designing word processing packages. With **text editor/text formatter** packages, the document seen on the screen contains the same text as the final document, but the layout on the screen is not what the printed version will look like. **What you see is what you get (WYSIWYG)** packages display the text on the screen as it will appear when printed.

Text Editor/Text Formatter

Using text editor/text formatter software, text is entered without paying attention to how it will appear on the page. When the text is being entered and edited, it is not necessary to be concerned with line length or spacing requirements. The user can add to and change the text until the words and content are completely as desired.

As text is being entered (or afterward), special formatting commands are also entered. These commands will appear throughout the text and can be seen as letters, numbers, or other symbols on the screen. When you are ready to print your document, these commands will be read by the formatting portion of the word processor. They are instructions to the formatter and will affect the final layout of the document.

In most text editor/text formatter systems, format commands sit on a line by themselves at the lefthand margin. They usually begin with a backward slash or dot, and are sometimes called **back-slash** or **dot commands.** They precede the text they are to affect. The back-slash indicates when paragraphs should begin, where underlining is to appear, what spacing is used between lines, and all other information necessary to produce the final document. In Figure 11.1, back-slash commands precede the document, and two others indicate the beginning of paragraphs.

After the text and the formatting commands have been entered and edited as necessary, the second stage of the processing begins (see Figure 11.2).

The formatter is a program that takes the typed text as input, follows the embedded instructions indicated by the back-slashes, and produces the document in ready-to-print format. The document in this form can either be stored in memory or sent directly to a printer.

Text editor/text formatter systems are popular on mainframes and are available for microcomputers. They contain more complex formatting commands and make it easier to customize text than many "what you see" word processors. However, the variety of commands makes them difficult to learn, and many people find that seeing back-slash commands followed by instructions on the screen interferes with their train of thought. Furthermore, to see what a document looks like, the user must leave the editor portion of the program and run the formatter portion. Once in the formatter, further changes to the document cannot be made directly. Later in this chapter we examine how to correct errors in the text.

Figure 11.1   Slash Commands: Portion of the Gettysburg Address (with errors) using the text editor/text formatter TeX on a minicomputer. (Phrases in parentheses are not part of the text but explain the backslash commands.)

\length = 7in   (line length is 7 inches)
\paraindent = 6   (indent paragraphs by 6 spaces)
\par   (begin paragraph)
Four score and eight years ago our fathers
brought forth a new nation.
Conceived in liberty, and dedicated to the proposition
that all are created equal.
\par   (begin paragraph)
Now we are engaged in a great war, testing whether
tha5t new nation, or any nation so conceived and so dedicated
can long indure. We are met on the bttlefield of that
great war. We have come to dedicate a portion of that field as
a final resting place of that great war.
\par   (begin paragraph)
It is although fitting and
proper that we should do this. . . .

Figure 11.2   This text was produced by a text editor/text formatter word processor. The embedded commands do not appear in the final version.

Four score and eight years ago our fathers brought forth a new nation. Conceived in liberty, and dedicated to the proposition that all are created equal.

Now we are engaged in a great war, testing whether tha5t new nation, or any nation so conceived and so dedicated can long indure. We are met on the bttlefield of that great war. We have come to dedicate a portion of that field asa final resting place of that great war.

It is although fitting and proper that we should do this. . . .

What You See Is What You Get (WYSIWYG)

As the name indicates, a WYSIWYG (pronounced *wizzy-wig*) word processor merges editing and formatting. As with the text editor/text formatter systems, text entered into a system can be immediately corrected and adjusted. However, when a formatting command is issued, it doesn't just appear as a code on the screen. Instead, it is immediately acted upon and the text on the screen is moved around to reflect the command. If a sentence or phrase is to be underlined or centered, the operation is done right then and there. As Figure 11.3 indicates, the end result is a document that appears on the screen almost exactly as it will appear in print.

HOW DOES WORD PROCESSING WORK?

A word processor electronically processes words or, more accurately, characters. The first step involves getting the words into the computer. With a typewriter, characters appear directly on paper as they are typed. With a word processor, the characters appear on a screen as the keyboard keys are pressed. At the same time, they are stored as electronic patterns in the computer's memory. Remember, however, that when the computer is turned off or the flow of electric current is halted, information stored in main memory is lost. For this reason, it is essential to copy the information into computer files on long-term storage devices such as floppy or hard disks. Computer files, like their paper counterparts, are given names that, to some degree, describe the contents of the file.

Figure 11.3   The Gettysburg Address as it looks in WordPerfect, a WYSIWYG word processor.

```
        Four score and seven years ago our fathers brought forth on
this continent a new nation, conceived in liberty, and dedicated to
the proposition that all men are created equal.

        Now we are engaged in a great civil war, testing whether that
nation, or any nation so conceived and so dedicated, can long
endure.  We are met on a great battlefield of that war.  We have
come to dedicate a portion of that field as a final resting place
for those who here gave their lives that that nation might live.

        It is altogether fitting and proper that we should do this.
But, in a larger sense, we can not dedicate - we can not consecrate
- we can not hallow - this ground.  The brave men, living and dead,
who struggled here, have consecrated it, for about our power to add
or detract.  The world will little not, nor long remember what we
pay here.  It is for us the living, rather, to be dedicated here to
the unfinished work which they who fought here have thus far so
nobly advanced.

        It is rather for us to be here dedicated to the great task
remaining before us - that from these honored dead we take
increased devotion to that cause for which they gave the last full
measure of devotion - that we here highly resolve that these dead
A:\GETTYS                                      Doc 1 Pg 1 Ln 1" Pos 1"
```

Some word processing programs require that you give your computer file a name before you begin entering text, while others have you name your file after it has been entered. The names you give to your files are used to call up, or **access,** documents any time you want to work on them. Many computer file names are limited to eight characters in length with a three-character extension. The initial eight characters represent the file's name, and the three-character extension identifies the nature of the file. For example, extensions of .TXT or .WPF often represent files created with a word processor, while files ending in .DBF often represent files created with a data base system. However, even names made up of eight characters can be meaningful. Although the computer will have no trouble distinguishing between files named junk1 and junk2, we will almost immediately forget what each file contains. File names such as budget92 or housing.let for housing letter help us remember their meaning over time.

Entering Text

Most word processors display important information as you enter text. This includes the position of the cursor on a given line, the current line number, the name of the file being used, and any special features in use such as insertion or caps lock (for typing capital letters). The line where this information appears on the screen is called the **status line**. It reflects the current status of the word processor. Some systems call this the **ruler line** and use a ruler image to reflect the position of the tabs. Many systems show the cursor position as well. Figure 11.4 shows the status line from *Microsoft Word* on the Macintosh. The word processor is set for inserting text, and the position of the cursor and margins are clearly indicated.

In most systems, text is entered into the word processor in much the same way a typewriter is used to put it on paper. First, a blank screen appears. Then text appears on the screen as it is typed. If the text is satisfactory when entered it can be saved on a disk and later printed. It is more likely that some changes are necessary, however. Words may have been misspelled, and other revisions may be required. The text can be revised immediately or stored on disk and revised later.

When text is entered at a typewriter, the carriage, containing the paper, moves to the left as characters are typed. When the last character on a line has been typed, the typist strikes the Carriage Return key or pushes a lever to move to the next line on the paper. Word processors do not require that the Return key be struck at the end of every line. The system sets up margins marking the maximum length of every line. When a word crosses this invisible bound-

---

Figure 11.4   The status or ruler line as it looks in *Microsoft Word* for the Macintosh.

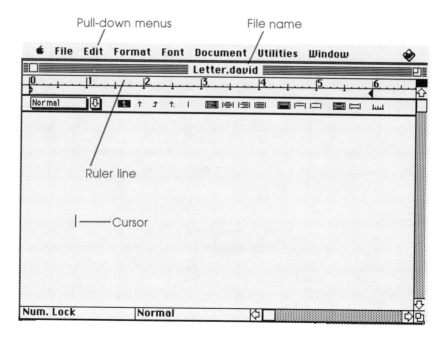

ary, it automatically moves to the next line. This is called **word wrap** because the words move, or wrap around, from one line to the next. Some systems, such as *Microsoft Word,* have an automatic hyphenation feature. When a word crosses the invisible boundary, if it can be hyphenated, the word processor does so and moves the rest of the word to the next line. If hyphenation is not appropriate, the entire word is moved to the next line. When we use a word processor, then, we can continuously type without paying attention to where lines begin and where they end. We simply type, and the software breaks lines at the appropriate places. Word wrap and automatic hyphenation improve efficiency, letting ideas flow faster and typing speeds increase.

Editing Text

Changing or manipulating text is called **editing.** All word processors include the most important text editing features. These are inserting, replacing, and deleting words or characters within existing text. Prior to word processing, a draft of a document produced on a typewriter was corrected or adjusted as needed and the entire report or letter had to be retyped.

For example, at the top in Figure 11.5 the document clearly requires changes, which have been entered by hand.

Making such changes on a typewriter would require retyping the entire document. Important documents were often corrected and retyped many times. This process is very time-consuming, so it is easy to see why documents may not always have been revised as often as necessary. Using a word processor to edit text enables us to make text adjustments without having to retype the unchanged portion of the document.

Inserting Text   Using a word processor, characters or words can be easily **inserted** into existing text. A command informs the word processor that until further notice all characters typed are to be inserted into the existing text at the present location of the cursor. With many systems, this command is activated by pressing the Ins (Insert) key on the keyboard. Repeating the command, for example (pressing the Insert key twice), cancels the command. (Pressing a key more than once to turn it on and then off is called **toggling.**) As the additional text is entered and the cursor moves to the right, the existing text appears to be pushed to the right, making room for the additional characters. For example, in Figure 11.5 the phrase

```
"all are created equal"
```

omits the word *men* between the words *all* and *are.* To make the adjustment, the cursor is moved to the space between the two words. The Insert command is then issued and the word *men* is typed. (Notice that a space also must be typed to separate the words properly.) As this happens, the remainder of the text, "are created equal" is pushed to the right to make room for the entered word.

```
"all men are created equal"
```

Figure 11.5 Editing and Formatting: The upper document is a hand-edited version of the Gettysburg Address. The lower document is the corrected and formatted version.

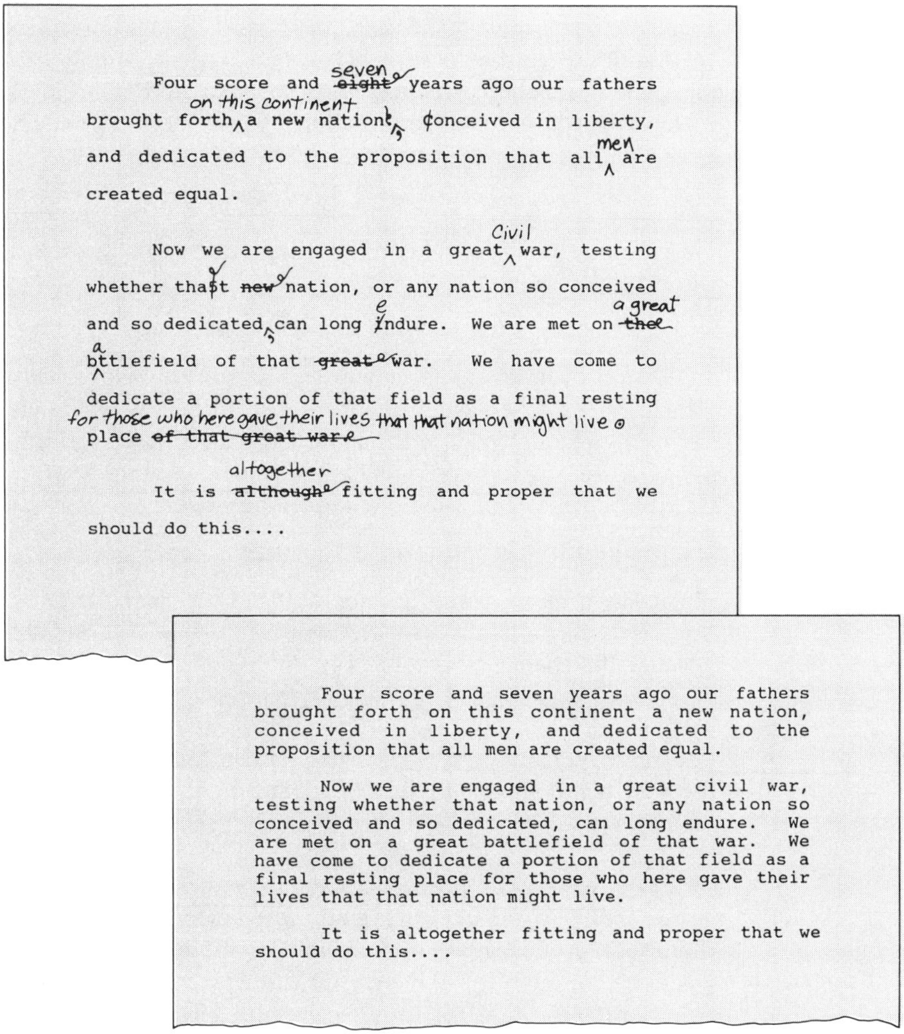

Four score and seven ~~eight~~ years ago our fathers brought forth on this continent a new nationt, ¢onceived in liberty, and dedicated to the proposition that all men are created equal.

Now we are engaged in a great Civil war, testing whether thast ~~new~~ nation, or any nation so conceived and so dedicated, can long endure. We are met on a great ~~thee~~ battlefield of that ~~great~~ war. We have come to dedicate a portion of that field as a final resting place for those who here gave their lives that that nation might live. ~~of that great war~~

It is altogether ~~although~~ fitting and proper that we should do this....

Four score and seven years ago our fathers brought forth on this continent a new nation, conceived in liberty, and dedicated to the proposition that all men are created equal.

Now we are engaged in a great civil war, testing whether that nation, or any nation so conceived and so dedicated, can long endure. We are met on a great battlefield of that war. We have come to dedicate a portion of that field as a final resting place for those who here gave their lives that that nation might live.

It is altogether fitting and proper that we should do this....

Replacing Text Occasions arise where we want to **replace** existing text instead of inserting additional text. For example, while entering text we might have typed the word *the* as *teh*. The easiest and fastest correction technique is simply to move the cursor to the *e* (in *teh*) and type the correct letters right over the incorrect ones. Although this could be done by deleting the existing characters and inserting new information, it is easier and simpler to enter the correct characters directly over the existing ones. Looking at our document again, in the first phrase the word *eight* should be replaced by the word *seven*.

```
"Four score and eight years ago"
```

As with a simple spelling correction, it is easy to replace a word or phrase with another word or phrase of the same length. Simply move the cursor to the location where the correction is to be made and type the new information directly over the existing information. As the new characters are typed, the old ones simply disappear from the screen.

```
"Four score and sevht years ago"
```

We continue to type over the existing text until the new text totally replaces the old.

```
"Four score and seven years ago"
```

Typing over letters is generally referred to as **overwriting** or **overtyping**. Care must be taken when using this replacement technique, since text usually cannot be recovered once it has been replaced. Overwriting works well as long as the corrected text contains *exactly* the same number of characters as the text it is replacing. If, however, our phrase had been:

```
"Four score and six years ago"
```

replacement alone would not be sufficient to make the correction. If we type the word *seven* directly over the word *six*, we will immediately run into trouble because the change (*seven*) has two more characters than the original word (*six*).

```
"Four score and sevenears ago"
```

The *seven* not only overwrites the *six*, but also the space between words and the *y* in *years*. A combination of replacement and insertion, or deletion and insertion, would be required here.

Deleting Text The third component in editing with word processing software is the ability to remove, or **delete,** unwanted characters. Deleting characters is the opposite of inserting characters. To delete, the cursor is moved so that it is positioned directly at the first unwanted character. A command informs the word processor that the user wishes to delete a character, and the character disappears from the screen. Many word processing programs make use of the Del (Delete) key for this purpose. Whenever the key is pressed, the character under the cursor disappears. As each character is deleted, the text moves one space to the left.

When a character or group of characters is deleted, the word processor automatically closes up the line where the character was, joining words together if necessary. For example, in our document the following line appears.

```
"testing whether tha5t new nation"
```

The word *new* should be removed, and obviously the 5 does not belong in the word *that*. First, the cursor is positioned at the 5, which is then deleted. Then the cursor is moved to the word *new* and, character by character, the word and the space that follows it are removed. The result is an adjusted phrase looking like this:

```
"testing whether that nation"
```

Recognizing that words, sentences, and groups of sentences are often removed from documents, most word processors include commands not only to delete individual characters but to delete whole words, sentences, and larger sections or blocks of text as well.

Correcting Text   Correcting text involves combinations of inserting, deleting, and replacing. There is no recommended technique. The commands are used in whatever order seems most appropriate. Using a word processor, our hand-edited version of the Gettysburg Address would now look like the document at the bottom of Figure 11.5. In all cases, remember that, once a document has been entered and corrected it must be saved on disk.

TEXT FORMATTING

The purpose of all word processors is to create clear, error-free printed documents with ease. With a what-you-see-is-what-you-get system, the printed version is essentially what was seen on the screen, even though you usually see only part of the document on the screen. With a text editor/text formatter, the printed form will reflect the embedded commands. Many word processors, especially text editor/text formatter systems, do have commands that will let you examine the document on the screen as it will appear on paper. This is called **previewing.**

Word processing systems make some assumptions about the kinds of documents we are most likely to print. Most systems assume that standard 8½- by 11-inch paper will be used in the printer. They preset the side margins and the amount of white paper to be left at the top and bottom of the page. These and other preset features are called **default parameters** or **default settings.** The system will automatically use these defaults unless told otherwise. These settings can easily be changed. As you can see in Figure 11.6, *Microsoft Word* indicates how much space is to be left at the top and bottom, and right and left side of the page. *Word* also indicates the default tab setting (every 0.5 inches).

Changing system defaults is an easy process. When you are ready to print, a screen showing the default settings can be displayed. You are asked to review the settings and make whatever changes are appropriate.

Most word processing systems let the user choose options from a list, or **menu.** The menu may be viewed by pressing a particular key or by pulling

Figure 11.6   The Document menu from *Microsoft Word*.

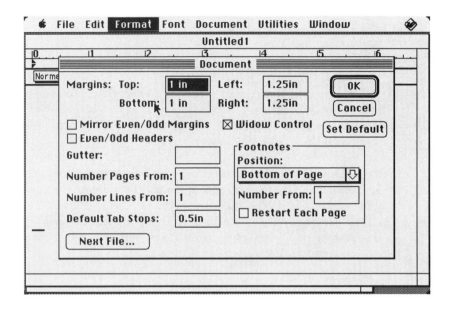

down the list with a mouse. Selections are then made by pointing to an item with the mouse or arrow keys, or typing in the number or letter that corresponds to the selection. Figure 11.7 shows a menu used in *Microsoft Word*.

On some systems, commands are issued directly, avoiding the need for a menu. Of course, such systems assume that the user will know the required command. Usually, menus are available just in case they are needed.

Regardless of the type of word processor being used, the way the document looks is completely under our control. We control the page layout as well as the characters in the text.

Page Layout

The formatting portion of word processing programs lets us adjust the number of lines on a page and paragraph indentation. It also lets us make right margins that are even, or right-**justified,** as they are in this textbook, or uneven, or ragged, as they are in this paragraph. All printed documents are left-justified, meaning that the left margin is even. Professionally typeset matter is often right-justified as well. Traditional typewriters cannot produce right-justified copy. Now any document typed with a word processor can be right-justified.

Figure 11.7   The Format menu from *Microsoft Word.*

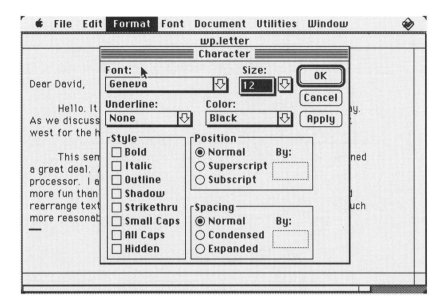

Margins can be adjusted to suit the document. For example, when a letter is typed, sometimes the last few lines or words and the signature may have to go on a second sheet of paper. By narrowing the side margins and reducing the top and bottom margins, the entire letter may fit on a single page. Using a word processor, the settings can simply be adjusted and the letter reprinted. Not a single word need be retyped.

Word processors also let us place information, separate from the main text, at the top and bottom of each page. Information at the top is known as a **header,** and at the bottom, a **footer.** Chapter titles, such as the words: *CHAPTER 11 / Word Processing* are headers, and page numbers printed at the bottom of a page are called footers. The word processor adjusts the page so this information fits. Some systems can also make adjustments for footnotes. The footnote information is entered and the word processor places it on the appropriate page and adjusts the amount of text on that page so it fits properly.

Character Adjustment

Word processors let the user adjust not only the way text fits on a page, but the way the text appears as well. Information can be centered on a line, and entire

Character Adjustment

It is often difficult to explain, in writing, word processing features that are visual. Therefore, rather than trying to explain what text looks like when **boldfaced,** or put in *italics*, or underlined, it seems easier to demonstrate.

Word processors, such as *Microsoft Word*, enable users to not only highlight characters as indicated above, but also to change the shape and style of the characters (their **font**).

For example:

This line, and the paragraphs above, are typed in a font style called Palatino.

This line is typed in a font style called Venice.

This line is typed in a font style called Chicago.

This line is typed in a font style called Monaco.

In addition, the size of characters can also be adjusted. All of the words thus far have been printed in a size commonly referred to as 12-point. The following lines will demonstrate different point-sized text while retaining the Palatino font.

This line is 24-point.

This line is 18-point.

This line is 10-point.

This line is 8-point.

sections of text can be indented. Individual characters, whole words, phrases, or sentences can be made to stand out through underlining, overprinting, or boldfacing. Some software packages can change the shape of individual letters. Such changes are used to highlight individual words or phrases. Not only can words be italicized, but the letters in headings and titles can be printed in a different type style, or **font** (see Figure 11.8).

Most word processing programs allow the use of subscripts (characters, usually numbers, below the line) and superscripts (characters, usually numbers, above the line). This feature is very important in mathematical and scientific documents and simplifies the use of standard footnotes. Figure 11.9 illustrates the use of subscripts and superscripts.

Any feature entered with a word processor can be easily removed or changed without retyping the document. If underlining is no longer necessary, it can be removed. A word can be italicized or a superscript can be added at any time. If an entire paragraph needs to be indented, the margin for that paragraph can be adjusted after the paragraph has been created. When margins or other space changes are made, the word processor adjusts the rest of the text automatically. Word processors take the drudgery out of writing, rewriting, and printing.

ADVANCED FEATURES

We have seen that word processing software makes it easy to create, edit, and print a document. In addition to the editing features we've discussed, most software includes two advanced features that make revisions even easier.

Search and Replace

Documents stored in memory can vary in size from short notes to very long reports. While it may be possible to display the entire contents of a short note

Figure 11.9   Subscripts and Superscripts.

subscript

Water is H_2O

superscript

Footnotes use superscripts.[5]

on the computer screen, most larger documents cannot be viewed in their entirety. In many cases, corrections are made on a printout or hard copy of the document. These corrections must then be entered at the keyboard. Locating the place in a document where a correction is to be made by looking through the document can be tedious and time-consuming.

Most word processing systems include a **Search** command. Using this command, you type the word or phrase you are looking for, and the computer will do the looking for you. Computers can search a document, even a long one, in moments. For example, in our original version of the Gettysburg Address in Figure 11.5, we might want to locate the word *dedicated.* We can use the search command to send the cursor directly to this word.

How does a search work? The first step is to move the cursor to the beginning of the document. This ensures that the system will look through every word. The search command is then issued. In many systems, one of the special function keys (F1 through F10) is pressed, or a command is highlighted in a pulled-down menu. The system then asks the user what to search for. Using our example, we would type *dedicated* in response to the question. After a brief wait, the system will place the cursor on the word or phrase sought.

Many systems take this process one step further. After being told what to search for, the system will ask for a replacement before it searches the document. Then when it finds the requested word, it immediately replaces it with the indicated word or phrase. This process is called **Search and Replace.** This time-saving technique can be very valuable when working with a large document.

The Search and Replace procedure just described works for a single substitution. It often happens that a given substitution must be made in more than one place. For example, a word or a name may have been consistently misspelled. Using a **Global Search and Replace,** every occurrence of the word or phrase will be replaced by the specified correction. The computer quickly performs this otherwise tedious task.

Global Search and Replace has other very useful capabilities. For example, when writing a document, it is easier to use abbreviations for such things as long corporate names, book titles, names of legal cases, and complex scientific or medical terms than it is to enter the entire phrase repeatedly. For example, TNC might be used throughout a report to represent the The Nature Conservancy. When the document is complete, a Global Search and Replace can be used to replace these abbreviations (TNC) with the full name. The full name (The Nature Conservancy) has to be typed only once, and it will appear wherever TNC formerly appeared in the document.

Moving Blocks of Text

Using editing commands, we can add or delete entire sections of text as easily as we can change a single word. Often, however, we want to change the location of an entire sentence or paragraph within our document. We could delete the words where they occur and retype them in the new location. But it is much easier to simply move or rearrange the existing text.

Word processing systems call the portions of the text to be moved a **block.** The first step in moving a block from one place to another is to mark or identify the block. To do this, the cursor is placed at the beginning of the block to be moved. A command is issued informing the system that a block is to be marked for moving. Then we move the cursor through the text until we reach the end of the block to be moved. In most systems, this highlights the appropriate text and identifies the block. When a mouse is available, we use the mouse to move the cursor through the text to identify and highlight the block (see Figure 11.10). On other machines, the cursor control keys are used.

The next step is to move the cursor to the block's new location. Another command is issued, and the system automatically moves the block of text. The space created when the block is removed is automatically filled in as the rest of the text moves up, just as space is automatically made for the block in its new location.

Many systems have two different types of "move" operations. Using **cut and paste,** a block of text is removed from one location and placed (pasted) into an-

Figure 11.10   Moving a Block of Text: A Macintosh screen with text to be moved.

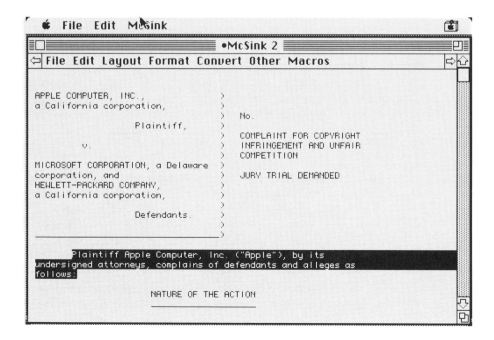

other location in the text. Using **copy and paste,** a copy of the highlighted block is made. The highlighted version remains in its original location, and a duplicate or copy of the block is placed (pasted) into its new location.

Additional Capabilities

As word processing software has been used for an increasing variety of writing tasks, systems have added a number of additional advanced features.

Mail-merge The **mail-merge** feature enables the word processing system to combine a list of names and addresses, such as a mailing list, with a form letter. This can produce a series of individualized letters, each of which looks specially typed. As the form letter is entered, it is marked in each location where an item from the mailing list will be placed. The mailing list and the form letter are entered into two separate files. Then both lists are processed together using special merge commands.

Spelling Checker and Thesaurus Many word processors include an additional program that compares the words in a document with words in an electronic dictionary. Such dictionaries contain as many as 100,000 words, and additional words usually can be added by the user. The spelling checker runs through the document, comparing each word to the words in the dictionary. If a match is found, it moves on to check the next word. If it does not find a match, the spelling checker either marks the word for later correction or asks the user to correct the error immediately. Some programs even offer suggested corrections, guessing at what the word is supposed to be. Spelling checkers have limitations. If *are* was typed instead of *art*, the spelling checker will not catch the error because both are legitimate words.

Some systems include a thesaurus. Having used a word often in a document, we may want to replace it in some places with another word of the same meaning. By issuing a command and identifying the word, a list of synonyms will appear on the screen. The user then selects alternative words with the same meaning to be placed in the document.

File merging Word processors increasingly contain features that make it possible to combine information in files from other applications software. Charts and tables created with spreadsheets and other packages can be combined with text created with a word processor. The result is a complete document that may incorporate work done with a number of different software packages.

Increasingly, word processors are including a variety of additional special features. They may contain calculator programs for simple on-line arithmetic and telecommunications software to transmit documents or mail messages over telephone lines (see Chapter 15). In addition, word processing software is the basis for the production of high-quality printed material used in a relatively new phenomenon called desktop publishing.

PROBLEMS AND PITFALLS

Up to this point, word processors have been helpful friends who have made the work of writing easier. But there are hidden pitfalls. We can avoid them, however, if we know where they are hiding. The following are some common word processing problems and some suggested solutions.

Editing Problems

There is a danger of losing data due to *overwriting*. Care should be applied when correcting text using the overwrite feature. Although typing over a character or word may appear easier than inserting and deleting, text that has been overtyped cannot be recovered. When correcting more than a word or simple phrase, it is often better to insert the new text and carefully examine the old text before it is deleted. A phrase or sentence that you replace may be useful elsewhere in the document, and you can easily move it to another position. Once it has been overtyped, it is lost.

Text also may be lost because of *hasty deletes*. Think carefully before deleting any block of text. Deleted text cannot be retrieved easily. Instead of deleting blocks of text that seem unnecessary at the moment, move them to the end of the file. Then you will be able to review them later and decide whether they contain valuable information. At the very least, hard copies of all deleted blocks should be made just in case they prove valuable later. Once text is deleted it is gone.

Search and Replace

Users must beware of *ambiguous word use* when searching. Care must be used when asking the computer to search for a particular word, portion of a word, or a phrase. The word or phrase being searched for should be unique enough to identify the specific item being sought. This is particularly critical if the automatic replacement feature is being used. For example, if you wish to change the word *auto* to *car*, the computer will search the file for the first occurrence of the set of characters *auto* and replace it with the characters *car*. Unfortunately, the first occurrence of auto may be in the word *automatically*, which will then get changed to *carmatically*—not exactly what you intended. There are two ways to prevent this from happening. You can use the Search without the Replace and enter the correction directly when the cursor finds the word. Or you can be very explicit in specifying the word being sought. In our example, if the set of characters the computer was searching for was *auto* (including the space before and after the letters), the computer would not confuse it with the same letters that were part of a word.

There is also a danger of *unwanted changes* using Replace. If you use Global Search and Replace for example, occurrences of the word or phrase will be replaced. It is possible that changes will be made where one is not wanted. A

Global Search and Replace is fast, but it may save time in the long run to make changes one at a time.

Spelling Checkers

Spelling checkers compare words in a document with words in an electronic dictionary. As a result, they cannot identify a word that is used incorrectly, such as *there* instead of *their.* They also will not locate typing errors that happen to form real words. If *then* rather than *them* is typed, a spelling checker will not read this as an error. Furthermore, a spelling checker is only as good as its dictionary. A correctly spelled word may be flagged as incorrect if it is not included in the dictionary. This is particularly likely to happen with people's names or technical terms.

Loss of Text

Any file created by any software package that makes use of a computer's main memory can be lost if there is an interruption of power. This is especially true of word processors, most of which store the text being processed in main memory until told to copy it onto a disk. It is wise to save text at regular intervals, either every 15 minutes or whenever anything significant has been entered. In this way, if the power fails or something goes wrong with either the hardware or software, most of your work is protected. Another good working procedure is to make a printout of everything you write with a word processing system, even if it is only a very rough draft. Hardware failures do occur, and disk files can be destroyed. Work that exists as a hard copy can be retyped if necessary. Retyping is easier than recreating ideas.

Special Effects

Special printing effects such as different fonts, boldfacing, overprinting, and underlining should be used sparingly. They are intended to enhance a document by making words or phrases stand out for emphasis. Overused, these effects can make a document hard to read or confusing.

DESKTOP PUBLISHING

Word processing has changed the way we think about writing as well as the way we write. It has also brought us to the doorstep of a another revolution. With new software and the advanced technology of today's microcomputers, low-cost laser printers, and color ink-jet printers, text can be combined with graphics and photographs to create documents at our desks that in the past

On Line

*H*YPERMEDIA — A NEW WAY OF READING AND WRITING

Ever since the invention of written language, text has been read from beginning to end.

Computers have made possible a new way of reading and processing information. With **hypermedia,** readers can move back and forth from one related idea to another at will. Equally important, hypermedia is not limited to textual material. Its connections can include text, graphics, video, and audio. *Media & Methods* describes hypermedia as "more a web of thoughts than a list of thoughts. The order of branching is not predictable because it will depend on the interests and experiences" of the user.

To understand hypermedia's connections, imagine you are browsing in the library. You are attracted to a book on Mozart. After reading a few pages, you learn that Mozart was an 18th-century composer. Curious about who else composed music in the late 18th century, you go to the card catalog, locate a book on famous composers, and find it in the stacks. Then you read about Mozart's contemporaries. This book also discusses piano concertos, so you go to the library's record collection and listen to a Mozart piano concerto. While listening, you are struck by the quality of the background orchestra and look up the instruments that made up an 18th-century orchestra. Somewhere along the line, you recall that the movie *Amadeus* was about Mozart and you borrow the library's copy and view parts of it. Your browsing could go on until your interest is satisfied or until the library closes.

You could perform all the same tasks with a hypermedia system. While reading about Mozart at your terminal, you become curious about other 18th-century composers. You mark the text and request more information. A list of articles about other 18th-century composers appears in a window on your screen and you select one. The process continues just as before, only this time you remain seated and the computer brings the material to you.

Hypermedia lets users browse through linked information in any order. Although still in its infancy, it is gaining in popularity. Hypermedia authoring programs are available for both IBM and compatibles and Macintosh computers. Minicomputer systems are also available. In all cases, the author must plan the links carefully. The component pieces must be organized so that the user gains access to the necessary information as required.

HyperCard on the Macintosh was the first commonly available system and has often been given away free by Apple Inc. The system (really **hypertext,** because the system is limited to text) is based on the idea of note cards similar to what you would use to take research notes in the library. Each card can hold text, graphics, electronic mail messages, or any other unit of electronic information. A group of cards forms a "stack." Cards within a stack are linked together, and links can be created between cards in other stacks. The system has proved so easy to use that people have used it to develop personalized party planners and flight planning books, and to author hypertext "books."

All hypermedia systems require large amounts of memory. Microcomputer users have complained that even with careful use it is easy to fill a hard disk with linked information. Nonetheless, hypermedia has the potential for becoming an important information-management and research tool.

Sources: Carol Schwab and James Murray, "Hypermedia: Enabling Instant Access to Information," *Media & Methods*, March/April 1991, pp. 8, 9, 52. Jane M. Tazelaar, "Hypertext," *Byte*, vol. 13, number 10, October 1988, p. 234.

would have required the services of artists and typesetting equipment. Packages like PageMaker and Ventura Publisher can combine word processing and graphics applications in ways that allow production of publishable pages. Such software enables users to access and adjust any image stored in the computer's memory. Laser printers print entire pages of text at once.

Small businesses, university departments, and organizations of all kinds can now produce documents, including newsletters and reports, that are camera-ready and can be directly duplicated either on a copier or phototypesetting machine. This is **desktop publishing.**

The concept of page processing using microcomputers is a natural outgrowth of the software and hardware capabilities of the Apple Macintosh. Page processing requires a high-resolution graphics monitor, an easy to use pointing device such as a mouse, and sophisticated software. The graphics monitor and mouse have always been standard on the Macintosh. Using advanced formatting software programs such as PageMaker and Ventura Publisher, pictures,

Figure 11.11   This document is being produced using Aldus PageMaker on a microcomputer. Until recently, this required professional typesetting. Now it is produced on the author's desktop.

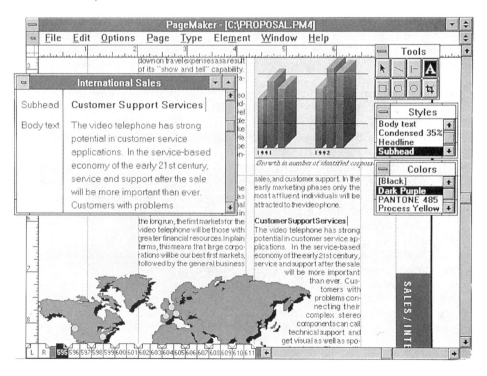

diagrams, and text can be combined into cohesive documents that can be printed using low-cost laser printers (see Figure 11.11).

Desktop publishing software includes features not commonly available from word processing software. These include special fonts, font sizes, character placement, and multiple columns of text, as well as indexing, advanced footnoting features and the ability to leave a specific amount of space for photographs and graphics.

Many of the desktop publishing features now available on microcomputers have been available for some time on mainframe computer systems. These large systems with their larger memory have more fonts, specialized symbols, and many other features that microcomputers cannot support. However, the cost of such systems can be quite high. Furthermore, these systems cannot realistically be called desktop because they are too large to sit on a desk.

Many computer professionals believe that page processing will have as revolutionary an effect on society as the microcomputer itself has had. Any individual or organization can now produce high-quality newsletters and documents at a reasonable cost. The ability to gather, assemble, and distribute information is no longer limited to large organizations. It is back in the hands and on the desktops of all of us.

Word processing can be a help to professional writers and to all of us who even occasionally need to put words on paper. Studies involving the use of word processors in writing classes find that students are more likely to adjust and revise their work when a word processor is available than when work is handwritten or typed. Presumably, the editing and block-move features of word processors make document adjustments easy. Students who learn word processing in computer classes report that they regularly use their word processing skills once the class is over.

Just as students benefit when word processing is available, office productivity studies find that word processors considerably decrease the time needed to prepare printed documents. Furthermore, organizations of all sizes are using desktop publishing techniques to improve the appearance and timeliness of documents, while saving money that was previously spent in typesetting and printing.

SUMMARY

Word processing makes it possible to add, remove, and change characters, words, and phrases within a document. All word processing programs require specialized software, a computer with a keyboard, a display screen, and a printer.

Word processing packages have two parts. The front end is concerned with entering and **editing** the text. The back end controls the way text will appear when it is printed, that is, its **format.**

With text editor/text formatter software, text is entered without regard to how it will look on the printed page. Along with the text, **back-slash commands** are entered. These back-slash commands are read by the formatter portion of the word processor and affect the final layout of the document.

The **what you see is what you get (WYSIWYG)** type of word processor merges the editing and formatting features of the software. When a formatting command is issued, it is immediately acted upon and the text on the screen is moved to reflect the command.

When entering text into a word processor, the **status line** reflects the current status of the system, indicating the line number and position of the cursor. Special features are also indicated. Word processors do not require that the Return key be pressed at the end of every line. Using **word wrap** and preset margins, the software breaks lines at the correct place.

All word processors include editing features that allow **inserting, replacing,** and **deleting** words or characters within existing text.

The way a document produced by a word processor looks is completely under the user's control. The formatter portion of word processing programs controls the number of lines per page, paragraph indentation, **justification,** and the use of headers and footers. Characters can be underlined, boldfaced, and overprinted. Many systems can change the font and size of individual characters. Sections of text can be indented, margins can be adjusted.

Using **search and replace** commands, information embedded within a document can be located by the software and adjusted as needed. Portions of text, or **blocks,** can be moved from one place to another within a document.

Most current systems include **mail-merge, spelling checkers,** and **file-merging** capabilities.

Word processing requires care. Text can be lost due to **overwriting** or hasty deletes, and electronic search and replace procedures can produce unexpected results.

Desktop publishing combines sophisticated software, microcomputers, and laser printers to produce camera-ready documents. Advanced formatting software combines pictures, diagrams, and text into cohesive documents that can be printed at relatively low cost.

Key Words

As an extra review of the chapter, try defining the following terms. If you have trouble with any of them, refer to the page number listed.

access *(290)*   block *(301)*
back-slash command *(288)*   cut and paste *(301)*

copy and paste *(302)*
default parameters (default
    settings) *(295)*
delete *(294)*
desktop publishing *(306)*
dot command *(288)*
editing *(292)*
font *(299)*
footer *(297)*
format *(287)*
Global Search and Replace *(300)*
header *(297)*
hypermedia *(305)*
hypertext *(305)*
insert *(292)*

justified *(296)*
mail-merge *(302)*
menu *(295)*
overwriting *(294)*
previewing *(295)*
replace *(293)*
Search *(300)*
Search and Replace *(300)*
status line (ruler line) *(291)*
text editor/text formatter *(287)*
toggling *(292)*
what you see is what you get
    (WYSIWYG) *(287)*
word processing *(286)*
word wrap *(292)*

Test Your Knowledge

1. List the three pieces of hardware, in addition to a computer, necessary for a word processing system.

2. What is editing?

3. What is formatting?

4. Explain the differences between *what you see is what you get* word processing systems and *text editor/text formatter* systems.

5. What are dot commands? When are they used?

6. What is word wrap? Why is it useful?

7. What information usually appears on the status line?

8. Using a word processor, how would you correct the word *cna* so that it is spelled *can?* Be specific. What commands would you use?

9. Using a word processor, how would you correct the word *tha5t* so that it is spelled *that?* Be specific. What commands would you use?

10. How does *insert* differ from *replace?*

11. When formatting a document, what are default parameters?

12. Define *justification* as applied to the appearance of a document.

13. Most word processors let you make adjustments to individual characters. What kinds of adjustments can be made?

14. Explain how the Search and Replace command works. Why is this useful?

15. What is a Global Search and Replace command?

16. What is a block move? Why is it useful?

17. What is mail-merge?

18. How does a spelling checker work?

19. Why should the Search and Replace command be used carefully?

20. What is page processing? How has page processing contributed to the rise of desktop publishing?

Expand Your Knowledge

1. Go to a local computer store and make a list of the word processing programs in stock. What system(s) do each of these packages run on? What do they cost? Check out integrated packages as well as standalone software. What is the most popular package for the IBM Personal System/2? What is the most popular package for the Macintosh? What other computer systems do they carry? What is the most popular word processing package on each of them?

2. Using the word processor available to you, enter the following passage from the Declaration of Independence. Use margins of your choice.

   When in the course of human events, it becomes necessary for one people to dissolve the political bonds which have connected them with another, and to assume, among the powers of the earth, the separate and equal station to which the laws of nature and of nature's God entitle them, a decent respect to the opinions of mankind requires that they should declare the causes which impel them to the separation.

   We hold these truths to be self-evident, that all men are created equal; that they are endowed by their Creator with certain unalienable rights; that among these, are life, liberty, and the pursuit of happiness. That, to secure these rights, governments are instituted among men, deriving their just powers from the consent of the governed; that, whenever any form of government becomes destructive of these ends, it is the right of the people to alter or to abolish it, and to institute a new government, laying its foundation on such principles, and organizing its powers in such form, as to them shall seem most likely to affect their safety and happiness.

   (a) Right-justify your passage.
   (b) Print out the passage single-spaced.
   (c) Adjust your passage and print it out double-spaced.

3. Write a short (three- to five-page) research paper discussing the advantages

and disadvantages of desktop publishing. Examine the use of Macintosh, IBM, and IBM-compatible equipment. Include at least three references.

4. Write a short (three- to five-page) research paper discussing the use of electronic thesauruses. What software packages contain them? How popular are they? How do they work? Who uses them? Resources can include magazine articles or interviews with computing-center or local computer-store staff.

5. The following paragraphs have *italicized* errors. Identify what is wrong with each highlighted error and indicate how it should be corrected. Using the word processor available to you, enter and print the paragraph, double-spaced, as you have corrected it.

> Until recently, desktop publishing programs could indicate only spot color — *four* example, a red border around the page. Four-color or continuous color images are now possible *woth produces* like Adobe PhotoShop and Letraset ColorStudio, Macintosh programs that *letyou* retouch scanned *photograpohs* and turn them into *teh* four overlay components needed for commercial printing.
>
> Previously, to *include for-color* photos in a publication, you had to use a specialized color house. At the *hghend,* these companies charge up to $500 per hour and work on machines that cost from one to two *milllion* dollars each; mid-range systems that cost about $300,000 reduce the cost somewhat. . . .

Source: "Publishing In Color," *Personal Computing,* July 27, 1990, p. 96.

12

Spreadsheets

CHAPTER OUTLINE

Spreadsheet software is the electronic equivalent of the accountant's green pad or ledger, with its long columns and rows filled with numbers. Spreadsheets, in pencil-on-paper form, have long been used in business by accountants, financial analysts, bankers, and bookkeepers. Spreadsheet software has brought new power to the numbers games of these professionals. It has also given the rest of us control over the numbers in our lives. Spreadsheets, especially the electronic variety, are not just for accountants any more. Just as word processing has revolutionized writing, electronic spreadsheets have revolutionized computation. Spreadsheets are for everybody. This chapter examines spreadsheet basics.

After studying this chapter, you will be able to:

- Describe an electronic spreadsheet.

- Discuss planning and designing a spreadsheet.

- Explain the use of formulas in spreadsheets.

- Discuss the use of *what-if* statements with spreadsheets.

- Identify spreadsheet programming tools.

- Understand common spreadsheet problem areas.

WHAT IS AN ELECTRONIC SPREADSHEET?

During the spring of 1978, Dan Bricklin, a graduate student at the Harvard Business School, was confronted with a homework assignment that required the use of business worksheets, or spreadsheets. In such problems, a single numeric change typically could affect many values on the spreadsheet, requiring significant, tedious recalculations. Bricklin realized that there had to be a better way. Sophisticated in the use of computers from his undergraduate days at the Massachusetts Institute of Technology (MIT) and prior work experience, he wanted to find a way to have a computer do the repetitive, predictable work. It occurred to him that he needed something like a word processor specifically designed to work with numbers in tables—an **electronic spreadsheet.**

Despite the skepticism of his Harvard professors, Bricklin collaborated with Robert Frankston, a computer-programmer friend from MIT, to develop and release the first electronic spreadsheet in 1979. It ran on an early Apple II computer and was called VisiCalc (for VISIble CALCulator). This program was designed to automate the calculations and recalculations customarily required on paper spreadsheets.

VisiCalc and its more recent and powerful cousins, such as Lotus 1-2-3, Excel, Quattro Pro, and WingZ have revolutionized the way we can deal with numbers. Any problem that can be solved with pencil, paper, and a calculator can be solved more quickly and accurately with spreadsheet software and a computer. Information, formerly hidden under mountains of unorganized numeric data, can be at the fingertips of anyone using an electronic spreadsheet.

With this software, data are organized into tables. Relationships among the data are established, and calculations such as sums and averages can be performed. As input data changes, new sets of answers can easily be computed.

Although spreadsheets are most often used to solve business and financial problems, they can easily be applied to other problems that involve mathematical calculations. Spreadsheets have become popular tools for engineers, for example. Balancing a checkbook, calculating student grades, and computing the values on a tax return are easily accomplished using spreadsheet software.

COMMON SPREADSHEET FEATURES

An electronic spreadsheet is a table consisting of vertical columns and horizontal rows. The columns and rows intersect to form a complex grid or matrix. Each of the boxes created by the intersection of a given column and a specific row is called a **cell.** Each cell is uniquely identified, in much the same way as an individual seat in a large theater. Each cell is identified by the letter or number labels for the column and row that define it (see Figure 12.1).

In packages such as Lotus 1-2-3, Excel, and Quattro Pro, each column is named with a letter, and each row is identified with a number. When the

Figure 12.1   Spreadsheet cells are formed by the intersection of rows and columns. Two naming systems exist. Cells can be labeled with a letter identifying the row and a number identifying the column, as in D5, or Row x and Column y, such as R5C4.

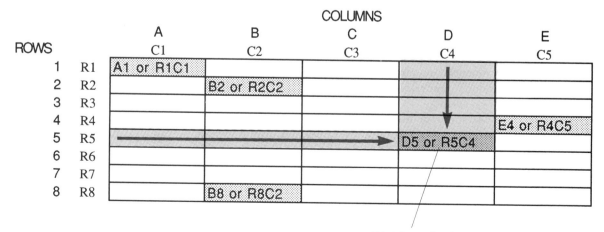

This intersection is a *cell.*

spreadsheet requires more than 26 columns, double letters such as AA and BD are used. Just as with theater seats, cells are then named by a letter or letters followed by a number representing the column and row whose intersection creates the cell. A cell formed by the intersection of column A and row 1 would be labeled A1.

Other software packages use other schemes for identifying cells. For example, in *Multiplan* and *PFS: First Choice*, cells have names such as RxCy for Row x and Column y. Cell D5 in a Lotus spreadsheet would be named R5C4 (for row 5, column 4) in *Multiplan*. Regardless of the naming scheme, each cell has a unique name or address that clearly identifies its location in the spreadsheet.

Each cell has a name, such as A3, S17, or R45C17, but the name tells us no more about the contents of the cell than the names on our mailboxes tell us about their contents (see Chapter 3). Spreadsheet cells can contain three types of data: values, formulas, and labels.

The numbers placed directly in a spreadsheet's cells are frequently known as **values.** Most spreadsheets allow values to be displayed in many different forms. Values can be whole numbers or integers (123), real numbers (0.456 or 1245.68), and dollars and cents ($1234.56). Some software packages also allow the use of scientific notation (1.23E-08).

Formulas are mathematical statements or sets of instructions. A formula can be stated in a simple way, such as A1+A2+D4. This means add the contents of cell A1 and cell A2 and cell D4. A formula can be more complex, such as @SUM(D3..D23). This means calculate the sum of all the values in the cells D3 through D23. In each case, the value resulting from the calculation is placed in the cell where the formula appeared (see Figure 12.2).

Formulas contain the names of specific cells, such as A1, C23, or D16. The cell names used in spreadsheet formulas refer to the contents of the indicated cells. These contents are used in calculations. All spreadsheets have a number of built in formulas, mini-mathematical subprograms, called **functions,** that can be called upon to perform calculations. These are used just as formulas are to calculate the contents of specific cells.

Labels are words, titles, or text that are used to form row and column headings. They usually describe what is displayed within the spreadsheet. For example, Employee Name, Gross Income, Dollar Amount, and Tax Amount could be used as column or row headings. Labels are also used to provide textual data. The names found under the heading Employee Name are text, but the spreadsheet considers them to be labels. Labels cannot be used in calculations. A label that begins with a number must be entered in a specific way to distinguish it from a value or formula. A very common example includes social security numbers or phone numbers. Even though they are numbers, social security numbers, phone numbers, check numbers, or student ID numbers are not used in calculations. As a result, they are stored in spreadsheet cells as labels.

A spreadsheet is a tool that can be used to solve problems. Using a spreadsheet requires no knowledge of programming. Nor is a high level of skill in

Figure 12.2   Spreadsheet Formulas: This spreadsheet contains checking account data. Some cell formulas are identified.

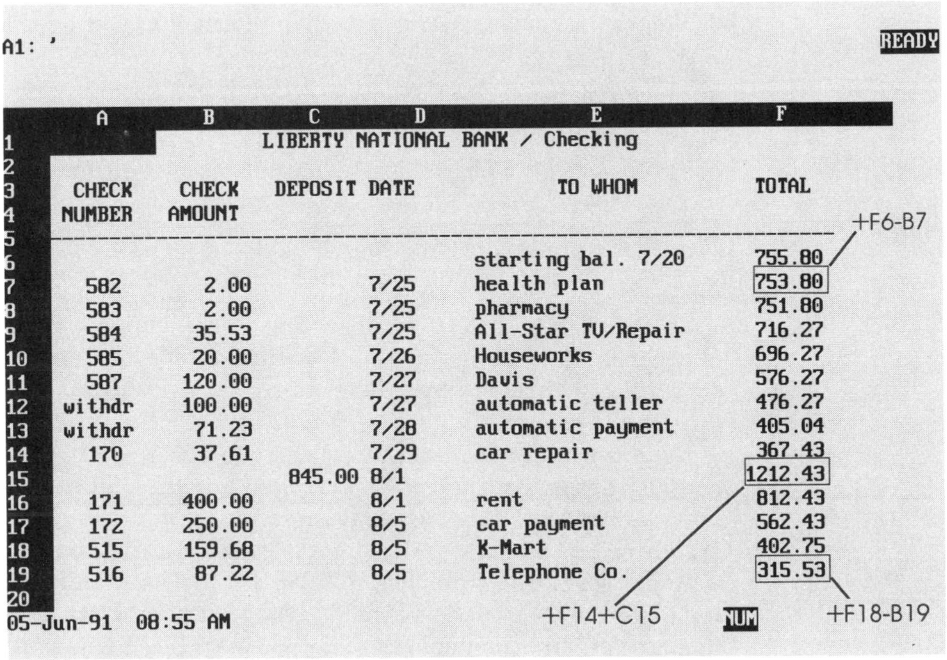

```
A1: '                                                                    READY

         A        B       C        D              E                F
 1                          LIBERTY NATIONAL BANK / Checking
 2
 3     CHECK    CHECK   DEPOSIT DATE              TO WHOM          TOTAL
 4    NUMBER   AMOUNT                                                        +F6-B7
 5    ─────────────────────────────────────────────────────────────────
 6                                      starting bal. 7/20       755.80
 7      582      2.00              7/25 health plan              753.80
 8      583      2.00              7/25 pharmacy                 751.80
 9      584     35.53              7/25 All-Star TV/Repair       716.27
10      585     20.00              7/26 Houseworks               696.27
11      587    120.00              7/27 Davis                    576.27
12    withdr   100.00              7/27 automatic teller         476.27
13    withdr    71.23              7/28 automatic payment        405.04
14      170     37.61              7/29 car repair               367.43
15                       845.00 8/1                             1212.43
16      171    400.00              8/1  rent                     812.43
17      172    250.00              8/5  car payment              562.43
18      515    159.68              8/5  K-Mart                   402.75
19      516     87.22              8/5  Telephone Co.            315.53
20
05-Jun-91   08:55 AM                             +F14+C15   NUM      +F18-B19
```

mathematics necessary. A spreadsheet presents solutions to problems. The more care and attention paid to planning the spreadsheet, the faster problems will be solved and the more direct the solutions will be.

PLANNING A SPREADSHEET

Planning saves time; it also helps to avoid mathematical errors. As with any computer application, spreadsheet results are only as accurate and reliable as the information given to the machine. Formulas that reference incorrect cell positions or have mistyped values will result in wrong answers. A common phrase used in computer science is, *Garbage in* produces *garbage out (GIGO).*

When designing a spreadsheet, it is often useful to lay it out on paper first. Your spreadsheet design should reflect the problem you need to solve. Identify the column headings and row headings needed. There is no standard spreadsheet format. Put the information in whatever order seems to best solve the problem. The following five steps will prove very useful.

1. *Understand the problem.*

2. *Specify the results.* Determine what information you need to compute. (OUTPUT)

3. *Specify the input.* Gather and organize the initial data if they are available. If not, locate the necessary data. (INPUT)

4. *Determine the formulas.* These formulas will transform the INPUT into the OUTPUT.

5. *Design the spreadsheet on the computer.* Label the columns and rows. Insert the values and formulas into their appropriate cells.

This list has a very familiar ring. We identified a similar procedure in Chapter 6 when designing an algorithm. In the next section, we apply these steps to a concrete example. Remember, a spreadsheet is merely a tool to assist in problem solving.

If you use a spreadsheet frequently to solve similar problems, you should consider designing a template. A **template** is the outline of a spreadsheet with only the key labels and formulas set in the appropriate places. This spreadsheet outline can be stored on a disk and used as a starting point whenever you have a similar spreadsheet problem to solve. For example, an instructor who is teaching three classes can use a spreadsheet to keep track of student grades, calculate final grades, and compute test and class averages. Each class requires a separate spreadsheet to contain students' names and grades. Yet all three will have the same major labels and formulas. It would be a considerable waste of time to retype this essential information when a single template can be used as a starting point for each class and reused next semester as well (see Figure 12.3).

BUILDING A SPREADSHEET

Learning to use a spreadsheet does not happen in a flash of light. It is more like learning to ride a bike; it takes time, careful attention to details, and a sense of balance. In the beginning, the sheet may fall flat, giving incorrect results. However, if you pick up the sheet, check the formulas, and head out again you're sure to get the hang of it.

Design the Spreadsheet

Let us build a simple spreadsheet, using as our model the data generated by a small but attentive class taking a computer course. At the beginning of each semester, the instructor receives a class list containing the names and social secu-

Figure 12.3

The Template: A spreadsheet outline, a template contains only key labels and formulas. This template was created for a class/grade-average spreadsheet. Too large to run across the page, the template is divided into two overlapping sections, (a) and (b). (Columns D, E, and F are duplicated in both (a) and (b).)

(a)

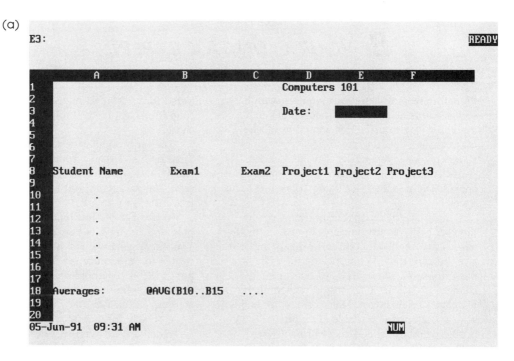

(b)

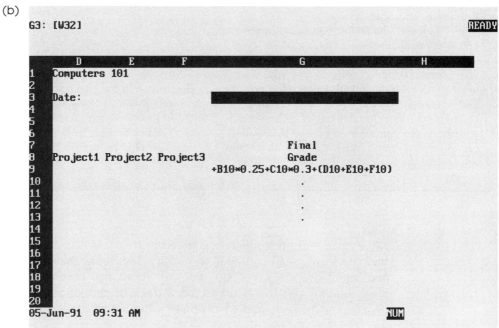

On Line

*B*E YOUR OWN TAX EXPERT

Preparing federal tax returns requires seemingly endless numeric entries and calculations. But there is a way to make this annual headache much easier—with a spreadsheet template or a standalone or independent package. Tax templates are available for many of the popular spreadsheet packages, including Lotus 1-2-3 and Excel.

Unlike standalone packages, templates let the user easily adjust formulas to meet individual needs. Templates are also relatively inexpensive, because they do not include the price of a powerful spreadsheet. Updates that reflect changes in the tax codes cost a fraction of the template's original cost. Many companies make state tax templates available at a nominal fee to people who buy federal tax return software.

Standalone packages include look-alike tax forms, pop-up screens with expert advice, tax definitions, and often translations of tax terms into common English. Most cost between $50 and $100.

Each year, more than 500,000 copies of standalone tax-support software are sold. Users agree that with some initial patience the programs are easy to use. All lead you line-by-line through the forms. In addition, as in the spreadsheet-style programs they are based upon, adjusted numbers result in automatic recalculations not only in the basic 1040 form but in all asso-ciated forms. Many standalone packages make state forms available at a nominal additional charge.

The most popular packages are TurboTax, TaxCut, J. K. Lasser's Your Income Tax and Personal Tax Preparer for IBM and compatible systems. TurboTax and MacInTax are also available in Macintosh formats.

In this age of electronic media, automatic tax programs have some unexpected advantages. You never need worry whether you have the correct form, because the programs produce output in IRS-acceptable format. In addition, all programs support the IRS's new electronic filing method. IRS insists that refunds will be paid more quickly for individuals filing electronically.

Whether you use a spreadsheet template or a standalone package, using your computer to assist in preparing your returns is easy and straightforward.

Sources: Kevin McCormally, "Taxes: Software to the Rescue," *Changing Times,* February 1991, pp. 56–58. "An expert of your desk," *U.S. News & World Report,* March 18, 1991, p. 90. Tom Badgett, "Taxes as Easy as 1-2-3," *Personal Computing,* Vol. 11, Number 12, December, 1987, pp. 70–74.

rity numbers of all students registered in the class. During the first class meeting, the instructor hands out an outline describing the grading policy, project and report deadlines, and the dates of the exams. A spreadsheet would be an ideal way for the instructor to keep track of the students' scores on exams, papers, and projects and to calculate a numerical grade for each student. The following steps apply the spreadsheet plan listed earlier in this chapter to produce a grade book:

1. *Understand the problem.* The problem is to design a spreadsheet to record student scores and calculate appropriate grades and averages.

2. *Specify the results.* The results that are needed are the average grade for each of the exams and projects, the final grade for each student, and the average final grade for the entire class.

3. *Specify the input.* The input will be the student names, two exam scores, and three project scores.

4. *Determine the formulas.* Exam 1 is worth 25 percent of the grade, Exam 2 is worth 30 percent of the grade, and each project is worth 15 percent of the grade. The formulas are:

   FINAL GRADE = (exam1 * 0.25) + (exam2 * 0.30)
   + (proj1 + proj2 + proj3) * 0.15

   EXAM AVERAGE = sum of all scores on a given exam / number of scores

   PROJECT AVERAGE = sum of all scores on a given project / number of scores

   CLASS AVERAGE GRADE = sum of all numeric grades / number of grades

5. *Design the spreadsheet.* First, gather all the available data and determine the type of desired results. Next, sketch a quick layout, including appropriate labels for columns and rows. Now you can review the entire sheet for overall usability. Identify the cells in which formulas and results will be located (see Figure 12.4).

Now that the spreadsheet has been designed, either on paper or directly on the computer, you are ready to key in critical information.

Enter the Data

Enter the data into the initial spreadsheet. Include all available data (student names) and the labels to indicate where formulas will eventually appear (average) (see Figure 12.5).

Now enter the formulas. Notice that the formulas that appear for each student under the heading Final Grade are similar. Additionally, the formulas to compute the averages for exam grades, project grades, and the final grade are also similar (see Figure 12.6). In each case, formulas are adjusted to reflect the appropriate cells.

Now that the spreadsheet has been initialized, it is ready to receive data as they become available. In this example, student grades will be gathered and entered over the course of a semester. As each grade is entered, the final grade will automatically be recalculated. Final grades have little meaning until all of the grades have been entered. Therefore, the interim final grades that a

Figure 12.4   Sketch of a Spreadsheet Layout.

Student Name	Exam 1	Exam 2	Project 1	Project 2	Project 3	Final Grade
Penny A. Day						
Bjorn Tolouse						
.						
.						
.						
S. Lee Zee						
AVERAGES						

These cells contain formulas for averages

These cells contain formulas for each student's final grade

Figure 12.5   Spreadsheet with Initial Data.

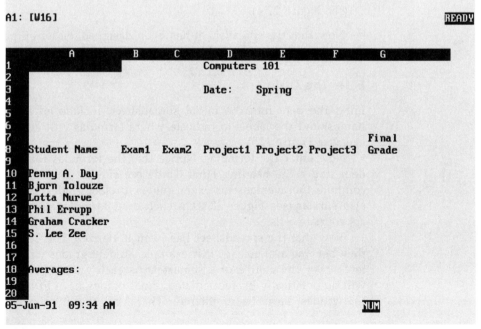

```
A1: [W16]                                                        READY

              A          B      C        D       E        F        G
1                                     Computers 101
2
3                                     Date:    Spring
4
5
6
7                                                              Final
8    Student Name     Exam1  Exam2  Project1 Project2 Project3  Grade
9
10   Penny A. Day
11   Bjorn Tolouze
12   Lotta Nurve
13   Phil Errupp
14   Graham Cracker
15   S. Lee Zee
16
17
18   Averages:
19
20
05-Jun-91  09:34 AM                                          NUM
```

Figure 12.6   Spreadsheet with Initial Data and Formulas. The spreadsheet is divided into two
sections, (a) and (b).

(a)

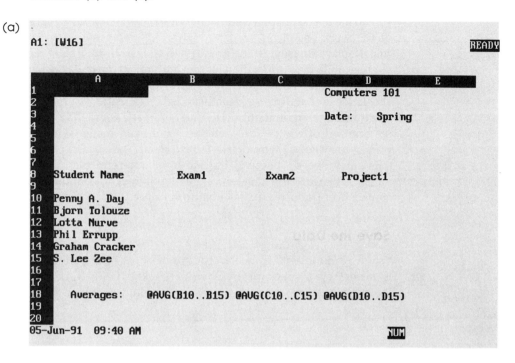

(b)

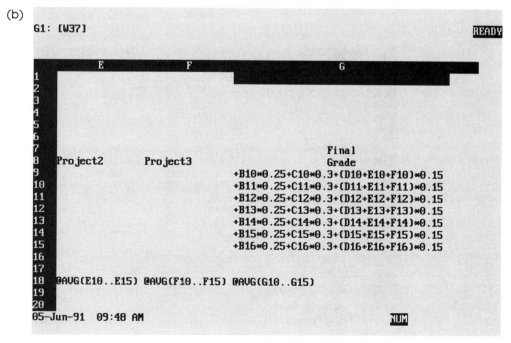

spreadsheet will display should be viewed as temporary, representing the result of the work completed to date. Figure 12.7 represents a completed spreadsheet that displays the semester's grades and the resulting final grade.

The ability to immediately **recalculate** all formulas when a data value is changed is one of the benefits of spreadsheet software. Most electronic spreadsheets let you activate or deactivate this automatic recalculation to facilitate the entry of large amounts of data. The automatic recalculate feature can be turned off until all of the required entries have been made. When dealing with complex spreadsheets, temporarily turning off the recalculation feature increases data-entry speeds because the sheet is not recalculating formulas after each entry. When all the data have been entered, a command is issued and the spreadsheet performs all calculations at once.

Save the Data

When working with an electronic spreadsheet or any other software package, it is necessary to periodically save or backup your work on disk. Information stored in primary memory can be lost through software problems or a momen-

---

Figure 12.7   Final Spreadsheet with Averages and Final Grades.

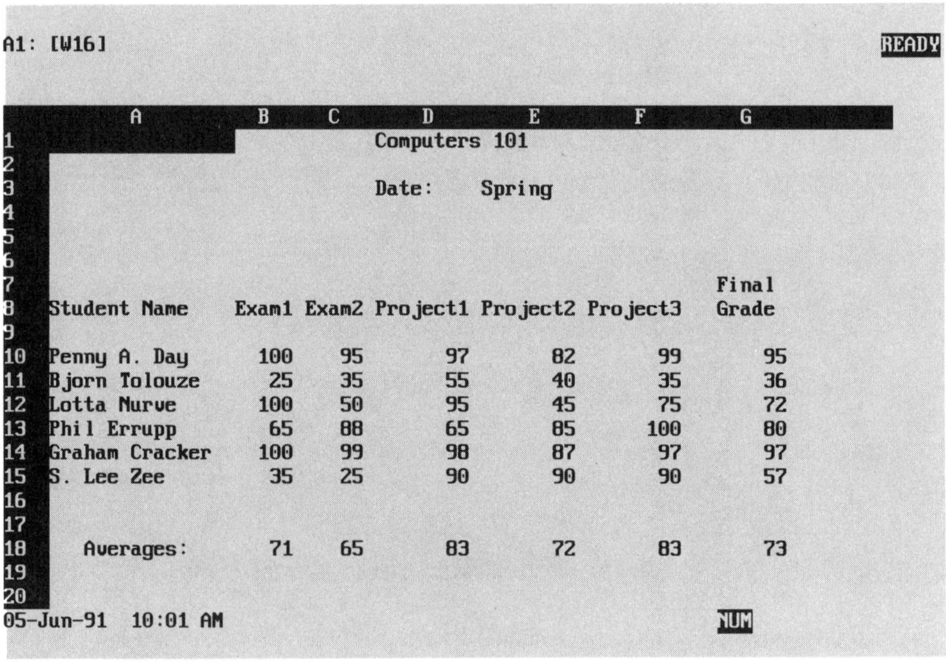

```
A1: [W16]                                                                    READY

            A          B     C      D         E         F       G
1                             Computers 101
2
3                            Date:     Spring
4
5
6
7                                                          Final
8  Student Name     Exam1 Exam2 Project1 Project2 Project3 Grade
9
10 Penny A. Day      100    95     97        82        99      95
11 Bjorn Tolouze      25    35     55        40        35      36
12 Lotta Nurve       100    50     95        45        75      72
13 Phil Errupp        65    88     65        85       100      80
14 Graham Cracker    100    99     98        87        97      97
15 S. Lee Zee         35    25     90        90        90      57
16
17
18     Averages:      71    65     83        72        83      73
19
20
05-Jun-91  10:01 AM                                            NUM
```

tary loss of power. After entering data into a spreadsheet, the few moments required to save the data protects it from possible loss. This is especially important prior to making major changes in the spreadsheet. Such backups ensure that if changes or adjustments to the spreadsheet do not produce the desired results, it is easy to return to the original spreadsheet by retrieving it from mass storage.

WHAT IF

Students often ask faculty members, usually just before the final examination, *"What* will my grade in this course be *if* I get an 85 (or 65 or 95) on the final exam?" This is known as a *what-if* question. Using a spreadsheet, the instructor can easily answer such questions. Simply enter the value (85 or whatever) and watch what appears in the appropriate cell. By entering student scores and watching the effect such scores have on a student's final grade, instructors are able to forecast an event that has not yet occurred. In general, spreadsheets make it possible for us to forecast or predict events in many different situations. Different scenarios for future events can be tested by typing in different values and noting their effects.

Let us see what the final grade of Penny A. Day might be by varying her final examination (Exam2) scores. We can ask the spreadsheet, *"What* will happen *if* final exam grades (Exam2) are 85, or 65, or 95?" By changing only the final score (Exam2) we can forecast the future. Care must be taken to distinguish the what-if data from the real data. The results are shown in Figure 12.8.

Spreadsheets have proven invaluable as forecasting tools in the business world. Companies now can test, based on correct initial assumptions, the effect of price cuts or increases, salary increases or decreases, the hiring or laying off of employees, changes made in purchasing procedures, cuts made in overhead costs, and hundreds of other factors that constitute costs of doing business or sources of income.

PROGRAMMING TOOLS

Most spreadsheets use essentially the same techniques for entering labels, numbers, and formulas. Each time a new spreadsheet is started, a blank ledger appears on the screen. Information is entered cell by cell, using either arrow keys or some other cursor control technique to move around the sheet.

Inserting and Deleting

Within a spreadsheet, changes can be made almost anywhere. In actual use, rows and columns often need to be added or deleted within a spreadsheet.

Figure 12.8   What If: This illustrates the result of asking the spreadsheet what would happen if Penny A. Day's final exam grade were (b) 85, (c) 65, or (d) 95. Her final grade prior to Exam 2 is represented in (a).

(a)

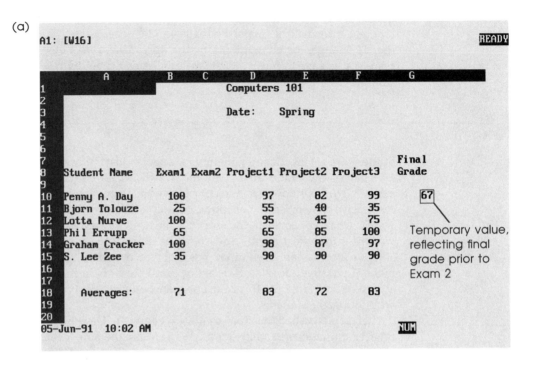

(b)

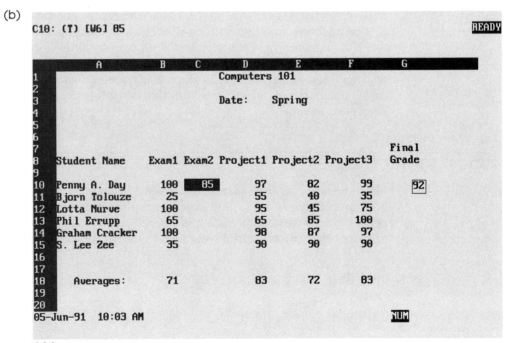

(c)

`C10: (T) [W6] 65`   `READY`

	A	B	C	D	E	F	G
1				Computers 101			
2							
3				Date:	Spring		
4							
5							
6							
7							Final
8	Student Name	Exam1	Exam2	Project1	Project2	Project3	Grade
9							
10	Penny A. Day	100	65	97	82	99	86
11	Bjorn Tolouze	25		55	40	35	
12	Lotta Nurve	100		95	45	75	
13	Phil Errupp	65		65	85	100	
14	Graham Cracker	100		98	87	97	
15	S. Lee Zee	35		90	90	90	
16							
17							
18	Averages:	71		83	72	83	
19							
20							

`05-Jun-91  10:03 AM`   `NUM`

(d)

`C10: (T) [W6] 95`   `READY`

	A	B	C	D	E	F	G
1				Computers 101			
2							
3				Date:	Spring		
4							
5							
6							
7							Final
8	Student Name	Exam1	Exam2	Project1	Project2	Project3	Grade
9							
10	Penny A. Day	100	95	97	82	99	95
11	Bjorn Tolouze	25		55	40	35	
12	Lotta Nurve	100		95	45	75	
13	Phil Errupp	65		65	85	100	
14	Graham Cracker	100		98	87	97	
15	S. Lee Zee	35		90	90	90	
16							
17							
18	Averages:	71		83	72	83	
19							
20							

`05-Jun-91  10:04 AM`   `NUM`

Continuing with our grade-book example, let us say the instructor decides to give three exams rather than two. To adjust the spreadsheet to allow for the extra exam scores, space must be created between column C (Exam2) and column D (Project1) for the new column, which will be headed Exam3. Using an **insertion command,** we can place new columns or rows wherever they may be needed (see Figure 12.9).

Similarly, as needs change, spreadsheet columns or rows may need to be deleted. If Bjorn Tolouze decides to drop the course, it will be easy to delete his name and information. **Deletion commands** make it possible to remove columns and rows that are no longer necessary (see Figure 12.10).

Copying Cells

Copy (replicate) commands make it possible to duplicate the contents of a cell or group of cells elsewhere on the spreadsheet. Values, formulas, and labels all can be copied with equal ease. Sophisticated spreadsheet software automatically adjusts formulas to appropriately reflect new locations. In our grade-book

---

Figure 12.9   Inserting a New Column: A new column is being added to this spreadsheet for extra scores. It is positioned between Exam2 and Project1.

(a)

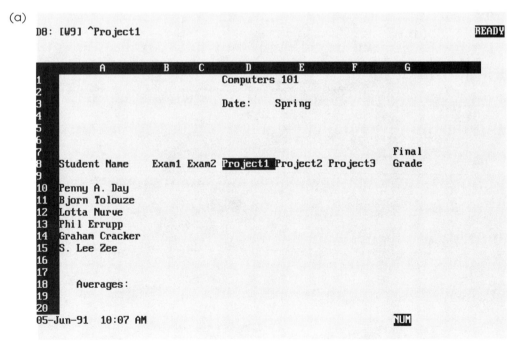

(b)

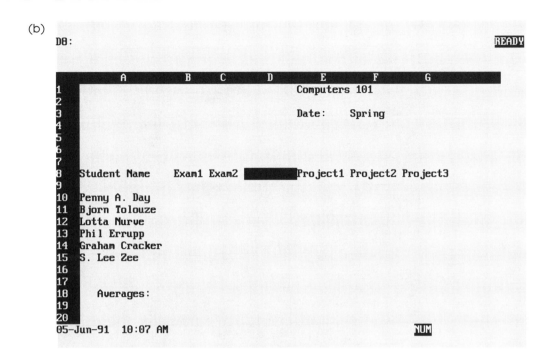

(c)

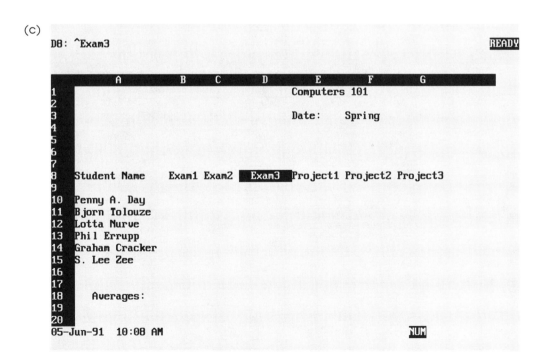

Figure 12.10 Deleting a Row: Rows and columns that are no longer needed can be deleted from spreadsheets. In this case, the name of Bjorn Tolouze is being deleted.

(a)

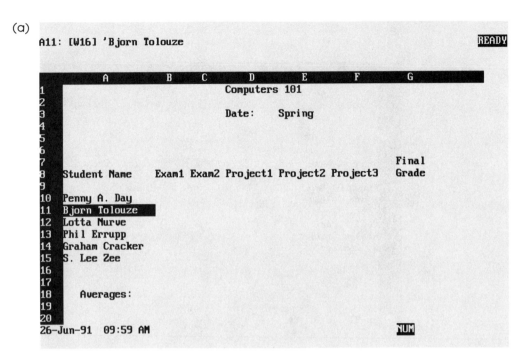

(b)

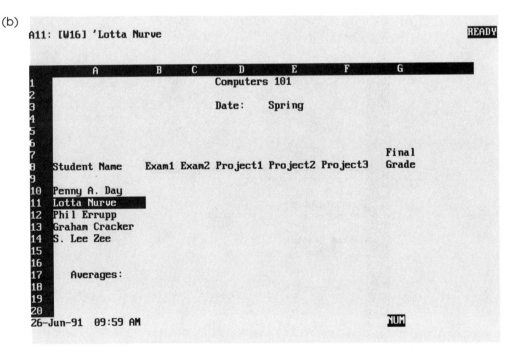

example, all the averages (exam, project, grade) are calculated in the identical fashion: All the values in a given column are added and their sum is then divided by the number of values. However, each formula must be slightly different because each reflects different columns. It is possible to enter the formula once and copy it to the other cells that require the formula. For example, when we copy the formula @AVG(B10..B15) from column B to column C, the software adjusts the formula so it reads @AVG(C10..C15) (see Figure 12.11).

Formatting Data

The way data are displayed on a spreadsheet is very important. The designers of spreadsheet packages recognized that to be clearly understood, a cell's contents need to be expressed in real-world terms. For example, labels such as names (alphabetic information) should be lined up at the leftmost character, or left-justified, when they appear in columns. Sometimes it is nice to center headings over a column. When information is lined up at the rightmost character it is said to be right-justified. For numeric quantities it may also be desirable

---

Figure 12.11   Copying Cells: The formula to calculate averages is copied from cell B18 into cell C18 and D18 by Lotus 1-2-3.

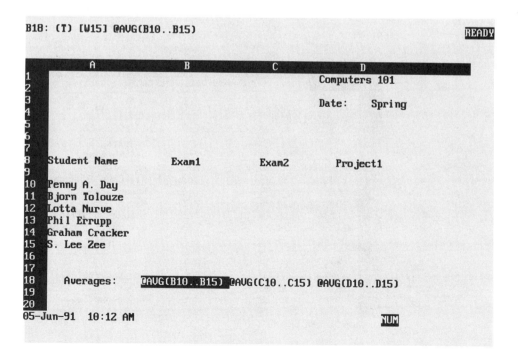

to line up, or align, numbers on their decimal points. Numeric values representing dollars and cents are more meaningful if they include a dollar sign and commas. Scientific notation can be used for very large or very small numbers. **Format commands** let the user display data as necessary within a cell (see Figure 12.12).

Mathematical Functions

Since formulas play such an important role in spreadsheets, all spreadsheets include built-in functions. **Functions** are special routines that perform specific tasks. These include routines such as sum (@SUM), average (@AVG), standard deviation (@STD), and square root (@SQRT). Some functions are used to help in decision making, such as @IF for what-if. The more complex a spreadsheet program, the more functions it provides. (The @ symbol before the function name is common to many spreadsheets, including Lotus and ENABLE; Excel uses an = sign.)

Figure 12.12   Formatting Data: This spreadsheet uses a number of different display formats.

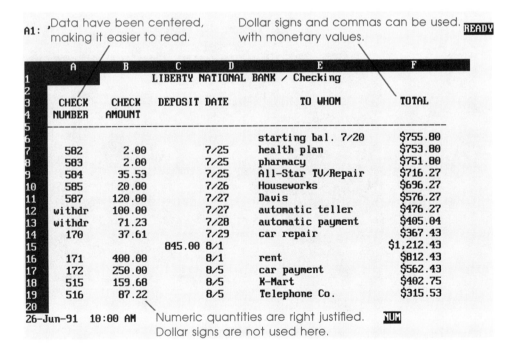

Many spreadsheet packages also include complex software routines that let the user sort columns or rows. Spreadsheet data can be displayed in graphic form (see Chapter 14).

PITFALLS, PROBLEMS, AND SOLUTIONS

Electronic spreadsheets have put more information at our fingertips. Those of us who never considered using an accountant's paper spreadsheet have found many uses for the electronic variety. Yet, electronic spreadsheets, like all software, have their pitfalls and problems. It seems that the more sophisticated a program is, the more problems it can present.

Most spreadsheet errors are caused by carelessness. But even a careful person can run into trouble. Here are some common problems:

1. *Formula specification.* Formulas indicate how the contents of cells and data are to be combined. Incorrect formulas will produce flawed results, even if the data have been accurately entered.

2. *Rounding errors.* Spreadsheets display a cell's contents in a format that has been selected by the user. However, the value that is actually in the computer's memory and used in calculations may vary somewhat from the value displayed in the cell. For example, in a dollar-and-cents format, a value may appear as $16.54 while the value actually stored in memory might be $16.5384. The computer "rounds off" the number to a display of $16.54. This difference between the actual number and the displayed number may be unimportant in working with one number or a single calculation. However, an accumulation of these discrepancies can be significant when complex calculations are performed.

3. *Division by zero.* Division by zero is mathematically impossible. However, it is possible to create a situation in a spreadsheet where a formula seems to require division by zero. This can happen when a cell's contents unexpectedly become zero and a formula that references that cell expects to divide by its value. For example, consider the formula: @SUM(A1..A5)/B2. This formula is perfectly sound mathematically except in the situation where B2 is zero. If B2 becomes zero, the formula is meaningless. Since such formulas are common and the contents of cells do change, division by zero may be encountered. Some spreadsheets automatically check for this occurrence. However, other spreadsheets simply attempt to carry out the required calculations, producing meaningless results.

4. *Formulas that don't adjust for insertions and deletions.* This is the most common of all spreadsheet problems. As data change and rows and columns are added or deleted, care must be taken to ensure that formulas continue to reflect the spreadsheet's data. In some spreadsheet software, formulas do not

automatically adjust to reflect these changes. As a result, incorrect formulas produce incorrect results.

5. *Writing over cells.* A spreadsheet is only as accurate as its data and formulas. However, a cell's contents are easily changed. When a cell's contents are altered, there may be a ripple effect throughout the entire spreadsheet. Equally troublesome is the situation where a value may be typed over a formula, thereby changing the meaning and content of that cell.

How can we protect the accuracy of our spreadsheet against these problems? An important concept in any computer environment is **documentation.** Spreadsheets should contain documentation, a clear written description of how the sheet is to be used. In some instances, a portion of the spreadsheet itself can be used. This is particularly useful for descriptions of formulas and their derivation, functions, and "what-ifs." The documentation explains the spreadsheet in terms that can be understood by anyone who has to make use of it, including *you* at a later date. For example, how well will you recall all the considerations you made in designing your spreadsheet one year from now?

It is useful to keep a record of when and where changes are made in the spreadsheet. In this way, if an error is later detected, it can easily be corrected.

Another way to reduce spreadsheet errors is to recognize the possibility of their existence. When you look at the results of key formulas, ask yourself: "Does this answer make sense?" Check some of the results by hand, using a calculator to validate the formula. When using complex formulas, have someone else check them for accuracy. At the very least, print out all formulas and check them over yourself, looking for possible errors.

Remember, spreadsheets can only be as accurate as the values, formulas, and labels placed in the cells. Paying attention to details, taking care in designing the sheet and entering the data, and checking to see whether calculated results are reasonable will ensure an accurate spreadsheet.

SUMMARY

In 1979, Dan Bricklin and Robert Frankston released VisiCalc, the first **electronic spreadsheet.** Any problem that can be solved with pencil, paper, and a calculator can be solved more quickly and accurately with an electronic spreadsheet.

An electronic spreadsheet is designed as a table consisting of vertical columns and horizontal rows. The boxes formed by the intersection of these rows and columns are **cells.** Some packages name their cells with a column letter followed by a row number (D6). Others use names such as RxCy for Row x and Column y.

Spreadsheet cells can contain three types of data: **values** (numbers), **formulas,** and **labels.** The numbers placed directly in a spreadsheet's cells are known as values. Formulas are mathematical expressions associated with a specific cell and are used to calculate the value of that cell. All spreadsheets have a number of built-in formulas, mini-mathematical subprograms, called **functions.** Labels are words, titles, or text that are used to form row and column headings or to provide textual information.

Five steps are useful in planning a spreadsheet: (1) Understand the problem, (2) Specify the results, (3) Specify the input, (4) Determine the formulas, (5) Design the spreadsheet.

What-if statements enable spreadsheet users to forecast events or test scenarios by adjusting values within a given spreadsheet and studying the changes produced.

Spreadsheet information is not static. It can be adjusted as needed. Rows and columns can be **inserted** or **deleted** to reflect changes in data. Data from cells can be **copied** into other cells easily. **Format commands** let the user justify (right, left, center) data as necessary within a cell, to display numbers in their most meaningful form, and to adjust the width of columns to allow for data of varying length.

Formulas play such an important role in spreadsheets that the most common mathematical and financial formulas come as built-in **functions** provided by the developer of the spreadsheet.

Most spreadsheet errors are caused by poor planning or carelessness. Common errors include incorrect use of formulas, roundoff errors, division by zero, and overwriting of information stored in cells. Attention to detail, careful entering of data, and the use of documentation can reduce these errors.

Key Words

As an extra review of the chapter, try defining the following terms. If you have trouble with any of them, refer to the page number listed.

cell *(315)*	function *(316)*
copy (replicate) command *(328)*	insertion command *(328)*
deletion command *(328)*	label *(316)*
documentation *(334)*	recalculate *(324)*
electronic spreadsheet *(314)*	template *(318)*
format command *(332)*	value *(316)*
formula *(316)*	

Test Your Knowledge

1. Who invented VisiCalc? What computer did it first run on? How long ago was it invented?

2. Define *cell.*

3. Describe two cell-naming conventions.

4. List the three types of data that can be stored in spreadsheet cells.

5. What is a formula?

6. What does GIGO stand for?

7. List the five steps in planning a spreadsheet.

8. When is it useful to design a spreadsheet template?

9. How are what-if statements used with spreadsheets?

10. Using the data found in Figure 12.7, what would Bjorn Tolouze's final grade be if he had gotten a grade of 90 on his last exam rather than a 35? Use the formula shown in Figure 12.6 to assist you.

11. Explain why the ability to insert a row into an existing spreadsheet is important.

12. Why is it sometimes necessary to delete rows and columns from existing spreadsheets?

13. How does a Copy or Replicate command work?

14. List the three ways data can be aligned in a cell.

15. What is a spreadsheet function?

16. In the spreadsheet shown in Figure 12.13, the formula used to total (sum) September's bills is @SUM(B5..B9). This formula is copied from cell B11 to cell C11. What will the formula in cell C11 read?

17. List three common problems associated with electronic spreadsheets.

18. For the three problems identified in question 17, describe how each problem can either be avoided or corrected.

19. Desribe spreadsheet documentation.

20. Fill in the missing blank in this sentence. A spreadsheet is to _____ what a word processor is to text.

Figure 12.13

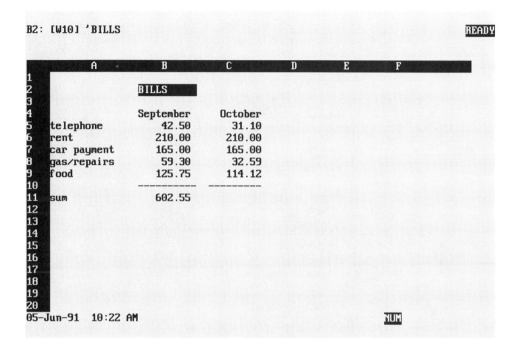

```
B2: [W10] 'BILLS                                              READY

            A    .       B           C          D      E       F
   1
   2               BILLS
   3
   4               September     October
   5  telephone         42.50       31.10
   6  rent             210.00      210.00
   7  car payment      165.00      165.00
   8  gas/repairs       59.30       32.59
   9  food             125.75      114.12
  10               ----------   ----------
  11  sum              602.55
  12
  13
  14
  15
  16
  17
  18
  19
  20
  05-Jun-91   10:22 AM                                    NUM
```

Expand Your Knowledge

1. Using a spreadsheet available to you, calculate your grade point average (GPA) using last semester's grades. Be sure to include your name and a heading for your spreadsheet. Check your formulas. A GPA is a weighted average with a three-credit course worth more than a one-credit course. Use labels that make your spreadsheet's contents easily understood and readable.

2. Many electronic spreadsheets include analysis graphics (see Chapter 14). Research one spreadsheet package that contains analysis graphics. Write a short paper that includes the following:

   (a) List the kinds of graphics the package provides.
   (b) Describe each type of graph and the nature of the data required to produce it.
   (c) Is special hardware required to view the graphs on a monitor?
   (d) Is special hardware required to print these graphs?

3. Electronic spreadsheets are very popular in business. Write a short (three- to five-page) paper explaining the use of spreadsheets in business. Include a discussion of financial forecasting. Use at least three sources of information.

4. A student organization kept the following financial information on paper for a three-month period (see figure below).

	September	October	November
Starting balance	83.00	———	———
Dues	110.00	25.00	50.00
Fund Raising	———	112.63	53.97
Paper & Supplies	127.62		
Photocopying	12.00	5.00	15.00
Advertising	6.00	6.00	6.00
Postage	20.00		20.00
Food	37.00	37.00	12.20
Plates, Cups, etc	11.50	2.25	9.75
Ending balance			

Enter this information into an electronic spreadsheet. You may want to adjust the layout. Using appropriate formulas, answer the following questions:

(a) Over the three-month period, how much was spent for each of the following: paper and supplies, photocopying, advertising, postage, food, and paper goods?

(b) Over the three-month period, how much was taken in through dues and fund raising?

(c) Calculate the ending balance for each month. (This is the starting balance for the following month.)

(d) Calculate the group's average monthly expenditure.

(e) Calculate the group's average monthly income.

5. Design a spreadsheet template you and your fellow students can use to calculate federal tax returns. The template should reflect the short form. Include all formulas and labels. These tax "formulas" are available in the IRS pamphlets available with the tax forms.

Use a spreadsheet to display and make the estimates required in questions 6 through 10.

6. A town has four middle schools. Casey Middle School had 967 students in 1992 and was expecting enrollment increases of 8 percent for each of the next three years. Heim Middle had 755 students in 1992 and was expecting a more modest growth rate of 5 percent in each of the next three years. The fastest growing school is Mill Middle. It had 875 students in 1992. It anticipates a growth of 5 percent in 1993, but with new housing construction it anticipates a growth of 10 percent in 1994 and 12 percent in 1995. On the other hand, Dodge Middle with a 1992 enrollment of 1003 is expecting a decline in enrollment of 3 percent in each of the next three years.

   Prepare and print out a worksheet that displays the expected enrollment for each of the schools for all four years, and a yearly total for the combined schools.

7. In the town mentioned in question 6, the high schools have had a fairly stable enrollment over the past few years. East High had 1201 students in 1992, South High's enrollment was 1352 and North High's enrollment was 1512. All of the high schools anticipate a decrease in enrollment of 2 percent in 1993. In both 1994 and 1995, East High expects to increase its enrollment by 5 percent. During the same period, South expects a decline of 4 percent in 1994 and then a 5-percent increase in 1995, and North expects a modest increase of 3 percent in each of the years.

   Prepare and print out a worksheet that displays the expected enrollment for each of the schools over the period in question, and a yearly total for the combined schools.

8. Using the data identified in question 7, make the following adjustments to your worksheet and print out the results.

   What would happen **IF**, due to the completion of a new housing project, East High's enrollment increased by 11 percent rather that the projected 5 percent in 1993? In addition, if South High experienced an increase in enrollment of 2 percent rather that the expected decline, what effect would this have? How would the school district's overall enrollment be affected? Print out a second worksheet reflecting these changes.

9. In the first quarter of this year, Peripherals Unlimited, a manufacturer of computer peripheral devices, sold 312 printers, 89 tape drives, 275 disk drives, and 156 CD-ROM drives. Sales of printers are expected to increase by 5 percent, and disk drives are expected to increase by 3 percent in each of the following quarters. Tape drive sales are expected to decrease by 7 percent, and sales in CD-ROM drives are expected to increase by 13 percent in each of the next three quarters.

   Prepare a worksheet that projects the sales for each device each quarter, and that displays the total sales for each device over the one-year period.

10. Using the data identified in question 9, make the following adjustments to your worksheet and print out the results.

   What would happen **IF** the manufacturer realizes that sales in CD-ROM drives were incorrectly recorded during the first quarter because an order of 34 devices was not reported? How does this affect the year's projections? In addition, if sales of the tape drives drop by an unexpected 22 percent in the fourth quarter of the year, how does this affect projections? Print out a second worksheet reflecting these changes.

13

Data Bases

CHAPTER OUTLINE

A data base is an organized collection of raw facts. We use data bases, although not computerized ones, all the time. Whenever we file material in a file cabinet, use a telephone directory, a dictionary, an encyclopedia, or *any* book, we are using data bases.

All data bases, whether they are manual systems, systems designed for large mainframes, or those available on the smallest personal computer, use the concept of files. As a starting point, think of a file cabinet (a data base) filled with file folders, each labeled with some key word (student name, ID number, course number) and ordered in some appropriate way (alphabetic, numeric, by date). Each folder is filled with information related to the key on the outside. So, our manual data base (file cabinet) is composed of folders. These folders each contain related information. In general, computerized data bases function in much the same way. File cabinets are replaced by electronic files, paper folders are replaced by records.

In this chapter we look at modern data base systems and their functions. We concentrate on software that lets us manage and manipulate data in order to process information. Until recently, access to data bases was limited to those few mainframe specialists who knew how to manipulate them. Today, access to data bases is readily available through modern data base tools. Data base software is often easier to learn than a word processor or the use of a spreadsheet. Although a word processor can be viewed as a glorified typewriter and an electronic spreadsheet as a computerized accountant's ledger, modern data base tools are further removed from their noncomputer counterparts.

After studying this chapter, you will be able to:

- Define *data base.*
- Distinguish between file managers and data base managers.
- Discuss the steps involved in planning data base files.
- Describe how a data base is created.
- Understand searching and sorting.
- Identify how changes are made in data base files.
- Explain how data bases can make use of more than one file.

WHAT IS A DATA BASE?

Some people think of a data base as "the stuff stored in computers." Some might be aware of *data banks,* such as those used by insurance companies to store statistical and financial records that go back for many years. Others may think of ominous Orwellian "Big Brother" data banks containing all sorts of personal facts about entire populations. Whether we use the words *data base,* or the somewhat older term *data bank,* all of these impressions reflect an understanding of the functions served by storing huge amounts of records or facts.

A **data base** is a set of facts, records, or data organized so that specific items are easy to find. Data bases are usually organized around a topic, an account number, or a **key,** which is an identifier such as a last name or social security number. This key, used primarily with direct-access storage methods such as magnetic disks and CD-ROM, makes individual data items and records easy to locate.

Paper Data Bases

Keeping careful records is essential in our world. A business's profits are directly linked to its ability to keep track of its clients. Schools keep records on every student, and accuracy is vital. For many decades, file rooms were the hub of every complex organization. However, as organizations grew and their work became more complex, the time needed to locate information stored in the file room increased. This made paper storage inefficient in large and complex organizations such as retail chains, universities, and banks. Paper storage became a limiting factor on the size of the organization itself. When the paperwork became too much to handle, some organizations had to restrict their growth.

The advent of computers brought an end to these limitations. Large organizations such as airlines, insurance companies, telephone companies, utilities, the Internal Revenue Service, and universities who could afford to purchase large mainframes did so. While mainframes could perform a number of tasks, their basic purpose for these organizations was electronic record keeping. In most cases, these electronic filing systems varied little from their manual counterparts, except that more data could be stored, and they could be located more rapidly and less expensively.

In manual filing systems, key records such as a student's name and address were often duplicated in many files to make the processing of information easier. For example, a student's name and address might appear in the university's grade file, student billing file, and again in the general information file. Such duplication of data is clearly a waste of resources. In addition, it increases the risk of having a data base filled with unreliable data. Imagine that a student moves during a given semester. The student diligently fills out all the appropriate forms indicating the change of address. The student's address is correctly changed on the grade file and the general information file, but is unchanged on the billing file. The student receives an accurate end-of-semester grade report, but never receives a tuition bill and never pays the tuition for the next semester. As a result, the student is unable to register for the next semester. After considerable frustration, the registration office "has no record" that the student ever filed a change-of-address form, although the student correctly claims that he did. You can clearly see the problem.

Data integrity or reliability is directly related to the ability of the data base to remain current. *A data base is only as reliable as its data.* If information is updated incorrectly or inconsistently—if data are corrected in one file and not in another—then the integrity of the entire data base is in doubt. Maintaining the integrity of the data within a data base is not a trivial matter.

Modern Data Base Systems

To make the most efficient use of a data base, it is necessary to plan the way in which the data will be organized. Data need to be organized so they can be retrieved, or located and viewed, easily. Historical organization patterns must be carefully examined. Data should not be organized in a particular way simply because it has always been done this way. Whenever possible, duplicated data need to be eliminated and retrieval time minimized. The goal of a data base system is to make all data quickly and easily available to all who need access to them, while maintaining data integrity.

Mainframe and minicomputer data bases are designed to ensure high retrieval speeds. As a result, the structure of these data bases makes updating and changing complicated. Data base specialists are often required when working with such systems.

In modern microcomputer data bases, data are stored and their files are structured differently from their mainframe counterparts. Software must make it easy to create, update, and change a data base. Of course, there are some trade-offs: Microcomputer data bases are easier to use than their larger cousins, but they take more time to search and sort. However, these data bases do not have to process the huge amounts of data stored on larger systems. So, retrieval speeds are reasonable.

A data base is an ideal aid for decision making. When you use a data base, you can ask the computer to find individual items or sets of items that meet specific criteria. An individual query might be to find the grade report for Frank N. Stein. A search for a set of items might be a list of all juniors or seniors who have gotten an A in Computer Science 101, or an alphabetical list of all graduate students who have high school teaching experience. The data retrieved from the data base are then used to make decisions. For example, graduate students with high school teaching experience can then be assigned to teach small sections of introductory computer science classes.

A hand search through paper files in a large university's filing cabinets seeking all the grade reports for a single individual (Frank N. Stein) could take a considerable amount of time. It would take even longer to locate and list the set of graduate students who have high school teaching experience. Computerizing a data base is appropriate whenever the amount of data to be searched or sorted is too large to reasonably process by hand.

Microcomputer Data Base Systems

Microcomputer data base systems make use of one or more *files* designed as tables to store information. A file is the most complex level of the data base. Each file or table consists of rows and columns. Each row or *record* contains related information, such as a student's name and address. Records correspond loosely to file folders in a manual system. Each column or *field* contains a specific type of information such as last name, first name, or zip code. At the most specific level is the *data item*, which resides at the intersection of a specific record with a particular field. In Figure 13.1, Penny Lofers' information forms a record, and the street column is a field. Cemetery Row is a data item.

The simplest kind of data base packages are **file managers,** or file management systems. These are patterned after an index-card file. The records, reflecting individual index cards, can be searched and sorted on any of the fields in the record. File managers are commonly menu-driven, because the user selects the required task from a list. Reports organizing data from many records can easily be created. Many file managers can perform simple calculations on gathered information. File managers deal with data contained in one file at a time. As a result, records (rows) in a file may contain fields (columns) that are only

| **Figure 13.1** | Fields and Records. |

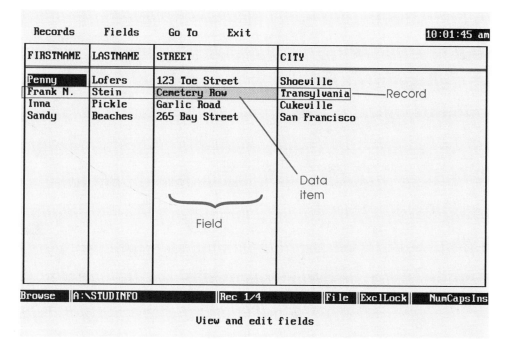

Figure 13.2   (a) In dBASE IV, a command file can be used to customize a screen.
(b) Customized dBASE screen produced by using the command file shown in (a).

(a)

```
                                                    NumCaps



  . TYPE SCREEN.FMT
  SCREEN.FMT 06/20/91                                              1

  @ 8,25 SAY "STUDENT INFORMATION INPUT SCREEN"
  @ 12,12 SAY "LAST NAME:"
  @ 12, 24 GET LASTNAME
  @ 12, 45 SAY "FIRST NAME:"
  @ 12, 58 GET FIRSTNAME
  @ 14, 12 SAY "STREET NAME:"
  @ 14, 27 GET STREET
  @ 16, 12 SAY "CITY:"
  @ 16, 19 GET CITY
  @ 16, 36 SAY "STATE:"
  @ 16, 43 GET STATE
  @ 16, 49 SAY "ZIP CODE:"
  @ 16, 60 GET ZIP
  @ 18, 12 SAY "STUDENT STATUS:"
  @ 18, 29 GET YR
```

(b)

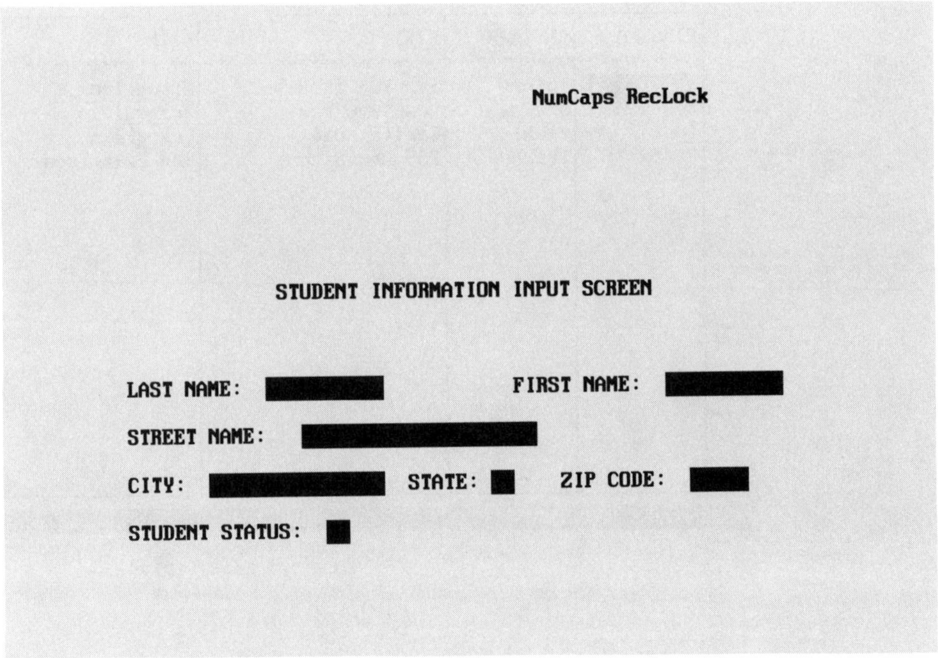

```
                                        NumCaps RecLock




                  STUDENT INFORMATION INPUT SCREEN


       LAST NAME: ▮▮▮▮▮▮         FIRST NAME: ▮▮▮▮▮▮

       STREET NAME: ▮▮▮▮▮▮▮▮▮▮▮

       CITY: ▮▮▮▮▮▮▮     STATE: ▮    ZIP CODE: ▮▮▮▮

       STUDENT STATUS: ▮
```

slightly related. File managers are excellent for manipulating simple data files such as mailing addresses, appointments, and lists of phone numbers. However, besides dealing with only one file at a time, they usually do not reorganize data to produce new data files, to produce involved reports, or to perform complex searches and sorts.

The more complex **data base managers** or data base management systems can do what file managers do and more. The best known of these packages are dBASE IV, Paradox, and FoxPro.

Sophisticated data base managers have two modes. Like simpler file management software, they can be menu-driven or they can be command-driven. The menu-driven mode helps new users learn the software and start entering data. As the user becomes more familiar with the package, the menus can be turned off and the software becomes **command-driven.** In this mode, commands can be directly given to the machine. Files can be created containing groups or lists of commands that are frequently used together. Such files are called **command files.** By calling on this file, a single command can set a whole series of commands in motion. Command files let data base managers incorporate many of the essentials of a programming language into their structure. Some systems such as FoxPro contain a built-in compiler so that command files can be more efficiently used. The advanced user can create screens that request data in a specific order (see Figure 13.2), display output in a useful format, and customize reports tailored to specific needs. Data base managers have more flexibility and can organize data in a greater variety of ways than can file managers. However, their complexity makes them harder to learn, harder to use, and much more expensive.

STEPS IN GETTING STARTED

Whatever type of data base is used, the data must be entered into the system before anything can be done with it. Certainly, it is possible to enter data into a microcomputer data base without thinking about how it will be used. But such a haphazard approach would result in more time being needed to retrieve the data later on. Planning before the data are entered will save hours of frustration later, while waiting for the system to gather the data items we request. The following six steps will help us to plan now to save time later. These steps are very similar to those used to design an algorithm (Chapter 6).

1. *Understand the problem.* Identify the kind of queries we expect to make of the data base. If a paper system is currently used, what questions are asked and what information is regularly requested?

2. *Identify the output.* Determine the kind of output reports the data base will generate. What kind of reports are created by the manual system currently in use? Are there any other types of reports that should be produced? Specify exactly the information to be contained in these reports. Allow for flexibility.

3. *Identify the input.* The input to a data base is directly determined by the output. We cannot get something out of the data base if we haven't put it in. What data do we need to produce the desired reports? What data are currently being used?

4. *Organize the data.* Plan your files. Does it make sense to place all the data in a single file? Or does the information logically break down into a series of files? Determine what information is needed and decide its order in the records.

5. *Test and revise your data base.* Enter sample data and use it to test the data base. Can the required reports be created? Expect to find that revision is necessary. Recognize assumptions and reorganize the data base to reflect needs.

6. *Enter the data.* Caution and care are needed when entering data. Remember, a data base is only as reliable as its data. Once the data have been entered, reports that previously took weeks to gather are almost instantly available.

THE DATA BASE IN USE

Planning, however, is only the beginning stage in using your data base as a problem-solving tool. Somehow all the required information must get into the machine. These data will then be searched, sorted, and extracted to suit particular needs and generate reports. To be effective, data base software must help the user to do all of the following:

1. Create the data base.
2. Search the data base for specific items.
3. Sort the data by key.
4. Add, delete, and update the data base.
5. Report the results.

Data base software for microcomputers is designed to be quickly and easily understood by users. For this reason, the basic procedures are fairly similar in all major packages. Most packages use words or phrases from common speech as commands. Create, List/Display, Browse, Show, Edit, Sort, and Delete are common data base commands. These commands and all the data base examples used in this chapter are from dBASE IV.

Creating a Data Base

Creating the data base itself is a fairly straightforward task. Every data base from the simplest to the most complex has a structure. Microcomputer data bases put few restrictions on how data are to be entered.

Let us create a data base containing general data about students in a computer science class. First we must determine the data that we want in our file. What data items will we need to search for? For this example, we want each student's name, address, and year in school. Each student's name consists of letters, but the student's address is a more complicated matter. If an entire address—1210 Main Street, Downhome, Texas, 12345—were stored as a single data item, it would be impossible to use any parts of the address in a search. Suppose we wanted to gather data about all Texans in the class. We would not be able to search for Texas because the student's home state is combined with other information. The software needs to know the nature or *type* of the data to be entered.

Data entered into a data base must be divided into as many different *fields* as is appropriate. The number of fields will be determined by the categories for which we will need to search. We might want to search addresses in as many as four categories. Therefore, we set up four fields: street, city, state, and zip code. Using the address just mentioned, 1210 Main Street would be stored in the street field, Downhome would go into the city field, Texas into the state field, and 12345 into the zip code field. How many fields do we need for the student's name? It is likely that we would want the last name separated from the first name, so each of these would go in different fields. We would then need two fields: lastname and firstname. If we had a reason, we might even want the middle name to have a third, separate name field.

When creating a data base, the software will ask for a file name. As with all software, the file name should reflect the contents of the file. Our student data base could be called *studinfo*. The software will also ask questions that help to define the data base's structure. Before any data can be entered into the system, we need to specify the order and type of information we expect to enter. In response to queries from the software, we tell the system what specific fields will be needed, the names of the fields, what kind of data to expect (letters, numbers, or both), and how wide (how many characters) the field should be. No data have been entered into the data base yet. But we have reserved specific places for the data that will be entered.

The data base file structure for our student list could look like this:

Field	Field Name	Type	Width	Dec	Index
1	LASTNAME	Char/text	10		N
2	FIRSTNAME	Char/text	10		N
3	STREET	Char/text	20		N
4	CITY	Char/text	15		N
5	ST	Char/text	2		N
6	ZIP	Char/text	5		N
7	YR	Char/text	2		N

Field names should be chosen so that their contents are obvious. An individual field's contents can be of various types. The type can be made up of characters, such as a student's last name, numbers intended for use in calculations, dates, or logicals (true or false).

In addition to type, we need to tell the machine the size of each field. For example, we need to specify that *LASTNAME* will occupy 10 spaces. Similarly the zip code *(ZIP)* will be exactly five spaces. The zip code can be stored as either a group of characters or as a numeric field because it is made up of digits. A numeric field can be used in calculations. However, calculations are not performed on zip codes. They are not mathematically manipulated in any way. As a result, it makes more sense to store the zip code as a character field. If a field is numeric, the software asks for the number of necessary decimal places. (dBASE IV also asks if the field will be used as an Index. Use of indexes will be discussed later.) All these specifications merely set up the environment in which our data base will live. No one has moved in yet. No data have been entered or stored.

A data base is only as effective as the data in it. Once the structure has been defined, the data items within *records* are entered one at a time, until all the required information has been entered. In Figure 13.3, the data for our general student file would be entered one student (record) at a time.

Figure 13.3   Student Information File: Data for this general student file are entered one student at a time.

```
                                                    Num




. use studinfo
. list
Record#  LASTNAME   FIRSTNAME  STREET               CITY            ST ZIP   YR
      1  Lofers     Penny      123 Toe Street       Shoeville       WI 53777 FR
      2  Stein      Frank N.   Cemetery Row         Transylvania    PA 34567 JR
      3  Pickle     Inna       Garlic Road          Cukeville       NY 12345 FR
      4  Beaches    Sandy      265 Bay Street       San Francisco   CA 67890 SO
      5  Errupp     Phil       1020 Station Road    Gasville        NJ 23890 SR
      6  Nomial     Polly      456 Equation Circle  Triangle Park   NC 23421 SO
      7  Mint       Said A.    Dirt Road            Diggersville    CO 97531 FR
      8  Itis       Senior     College Circle       Madison         WI 53706 SR
      9  Long       Harry A.   Main Street          Slowtowne       KA 55667 JR
     10  Ferma      Terry      789 Earth Avenue     Boston          MA 44668 SO
     11  Grahm      Telly      5325 Western Union   New York City   NY 11101 JR
     12  Maykitt    Willie     56 Main Street       Tryhard         FL 65432 SR
```

Just as we created a general file for our computer class, we can create another file in our data base containing other information about our class. Figure 13.4 contains the semester's grades in a file called *crsgrade*, for course grade. The file also contains each student's social security number. Our data base now consists of two files containing information about our students, the student information file—*studinfo*, and the grade file—*crsgrade*.

Searching and Sorting

We will want to be able to search or sort our files so that they provide the information we require. **Searching** means that the software will look through the stored data to find those items that satisfy particular criteria, much like the search function on a word processor. In Figure 13.5a, the student file *(studinfo)* was used to list the names and home towns of all students from Wisconsin and to list the names and addresses of all freshmen. Similarly, in Figure 13.5b we searched the grade file *(crsgrade)* to get a list of the names of all the students who received A's on their paper, and again searched the file for the names and grades of all those with scores of 70 or less on the midterm.

Figure 13.4   Semester Grade File: This file contains the semester grade and social security number of each student.

```
                                              NumCaps




   . USE CRSGRADE
   . LIST
   Record#  LASTNAME  FIRSTNAME  SSNUM        MIDTERM FINAL PAPER LGRADE
         1  Lofers    Penny      123-45-6789     100    95 A     A
         2  Stein     Frank N.   998-87-7654      25    45 C     G
         3  Pickle    Inna       555-55-5555     100    25 D     D
         4  Beaches   Sandy      098-76-5432      85    75 B     B
         5  Errupp    Phil       192-83-8475      85    69 B     B
         6  Nomial    Polly      999-88-7777      95    99 A     A
         7  Mint      Said A.    445-67-5678      75    80 C     C
         8  Itis      Senior     987-98-9876      85    65 D     D
         9  Long      Harry A.   234-56-7890      99    98 B     A
        10  Ferma     Terry      678-78-5678      95    80 B     B
        11  Grahm     Telly      666-11-1515      45    80 A     B
        12  Maykitt   Willie     777-80-8733      65    59 D     D
```

Figure 13.5   Searching a File: The software has sorted the file to find (a) all students from Wisconsin and all freshman, and (b) all students who received A's on their papers and those who scored 70 or less on the midterm.

(a)

```
                                                              NumCaps




. USE STUDINFO
. LIST FOR ST = 'WI' FIRSTNAME, LASTNAME, CITY, ST
Record#  FIRSTNAME  LASTNAME   CITY           ST
      1  Penny      Lofers     Shoeville      WI
      8  Senior     Itis       Madison        WI

. LIST FOR YR = 'FR' FIRSTNAME, LASTNAME, CITY, ST, ZIP
Record#  FIRSTNAME  LASTNAME   CITY           ST ZIP
      1  Penny      Lofers     Shoeville      WI 53777
      3  Inna       Pickle     Cukeville      NY 12345
      7  Said A.    Mint       Diggersville   CO 97531
```

(b)

```
                                      Ins     NumCaps




. USE CRSGRADE
. LIST FOR PAPER = 'A' FIRSTNAME, LASTNAME
Record#  FIRSTNAME  LASTNAME
      1  Penny      Lofers
      6  Polly      Nomial
     11  Telly      Grahm

. LIST FOR MIDTERM < 70
Record#  LASTNAME   FIRSTNAME  SSNUM         MIDTERM FINAL PAPER LGRADE
      2  Stein      Frank N.   998-87-7654        25    45 C     G
     11  Grahm      Telly      666-11-1515        45    80 A     B
     12  Maykitt    Willie     777-80-8733        65    59 D     D
.
```

Figure 13.6

Sorting a File: The student information file has been sorted by social security number. The original file is shown in (a), the sorted file in (b). The students' names have been left out to protect their privacy.

(a)

```
                                                    NumCaps



. USE CRSGRADE
. SORT ON SSNUM TO SORTSSN
  100% Sorted              12 Records sorted
. USE SORTSSN
. LIST
Record#   LASTNAME   FIRSTNAME   SSNUM          MIDTERM FINAL PAPER LGRADE
      1   Beaches    Sandy       098-76-5432        85    75 B      B
      2   Lofers     Penny       123-45-6789       100    95 A      A
      3   Errupp     Phil        192-83-8475        85    69 B      B
      4   Long       Harry A.    234-56-7890        99    98 B      A
      5   Mint       Said A.     445-67-5678        75    80 C      C
      6   Pickle     Inna        555-55-5555       100    25 D      D
      7   Grahm      Telly       666-11-1515        45    80 A      B
      8   Ferma      Terry       678-78-5678        95    80 B      B
      9   Maykitt    Willie      777-80-8733        65    59 D      D
     10   Itis       Senior      987-98-9876        85    65 D      D
     11   Stein      Frank N.    998-87-7654        25    45 C      G
     12   Nomial     Polly       999-88-7777        95    99 A      A
```

(b)

```
                                                    NumCaps





. LIST SSNUM, MIDTERM, FINAL, PAPER, LGRADE
Record#   SSNUM          MIDTERM FINAL PAPER LGRADE
      1   098-76-5432        85    75 B      B
      2   123-45-6789       100    95 A      A
      3   192-83-8475        85    69 B      B
      4   234-56-7890        99    98 B      A
      5   445-67-5678        75    80 C      C
      6   555-55-5555       100    25 D      D
      7   666-11-1515        45    80 A      B
      8   678-78-5678        95    80 B      B
      9   777-80-8733        65    59 D      D
     10   987-98-9876        85    65 D      D
     11   998-87-7654        25    45 C      G
     12   999-88-7777        95    99 A      A
```

Sorting rearranges the records in a data base file alphabetically, numerically, or by date. To sort, one or more fields in the data base are used. For example, we might want to sort the grade file (Figure 13.6a) into social security number order and then list the grade report without student names. This would let the professor post the grade report and protect the identity of the students. In Figure 13.6b, *crsgrade* is sorted by social security number. The resulting file is first listed with all fields showing, including each student's name. The file is then listed without student names.

Sorting a data base file is not done in quite the same way we would sort a stack of index cards. If we sorted a stack of index cards, the card file itself would change. Only in the simplest systems, such as the data base component of *Microsoft Works,* is the file directly sorted. With most microcomputer data base systems, when a data base file is sorted, the original file is not affected. A copy of the file is created in the specified order. In Figure 13.6b, the *crsgrade* file is sorted by social security number, and the reordered version is stored in a new file called *sortssn.*

Changing a Data Base

The information stored in most data bases needs to be changed or added to regularly as changes take place in the real world. As people move to new addresses, new employees join a company, and students take another examination, the appropriate files must be adjusted.

Adjustments to an existing file can be made in a number of ways. An entire record can be deleted when it is no longer needed, and new records can be added. When we delete a record by using the Delete or Remove command, the software removes it from the data base file. All the records that follow it will automatically be renumbered. Adding information to a data base file is just as easy as deleting. Most systems have commands such as Add or Append that ask the user to enter the data into the data base according to the specifications made when the data base was created. This ensures that the new data will conform to the style used when the original data were entered.

Stored data also may need to be corrected. For example, if a student has moved, the new address must replace the old one in the data base. Data can be corrected by using editing features built into the data base software. Editing features in a data base are similar to those in simple word processing software. Using the editor, entire data items can be changed, or simple typing errors can be corrected.

One of the most important adjustment features common in data bases for microcomputers is the ability to add fields to existing records. It often happens that after a data base has been designed and entered, new uses for the data become apparent. For example, after using our general student file, we might want to search the data base so that we could send special announcements to all students over 30, or to all students turning 18 as a reminder to register to vote. To do this, we need to add a date of birth field to each record. Without a date of

On Line

PUTTING THE BYTE ON CRIME

Police detectives are handing over more and more of their investigative duties to computers.

New crime detection software is allowing computers to take over a number of tedious and often time-consuming tasks such as ruling out suspects and keeping records. As a result, detectives have more time to plan investigations, locate and interview witnesses, question suspects, and search for evidence.

While specific software applications were originally designed to meet the needs of individual police departments, some are being purchased, licensed, and exchanged. A police user group has even been formed.

Applications include software to compile lists of wanted criminals, stolen cars, and credit cards; to put together data on crime incidences and the modus operandi of criminals; to compile lists of aliases, fingerprints, and criminal histories; and to analyze the movements and telephone calls of criminals.

The FBI, in association with local police departments, has developed an "intelligent" data base system to assist in solving burglaries. Burglars usually have predictable behaviors. They use the same break-in methods and often steal the same type of goods. Typically, they are repeat offenders. Using the "intelligent" data base, detectives can enter the burglar's modus operandi and the data base will come up with a list of possible suspects.

Across the United States, police departments are compiling data bases of fingerprints called AFIS, for Automatic Fingerprint Identification Systems. Each fingerprint is specially coded to identify its unique characteristics. Using such a system, more than 400 fingerprints per second can be compared with a suspect's prints. Fingerprints of known criminals are entered into the system, and the data base is expanded regularly to include new prints. By matching prints found at the scene of a crime with those on file, investigators are armed with added evidence. Jim Cox, an investigator with San Bernadino County, told *Redbook* magazine that computerized fingerprint analysis is "probably the greatest crime-fighting tool since the two-way radio."

Although police departments are generally enthusiastic about the computer's potential to assist in crime solving, some people are concerned that such data bases endanger the individual's right to privacy. Opponents fear that innocent people may be categorized as associates of criminals. Law enforcement officials say that they are aware of such potential problems and that they are taking care to restrict access to the systems and the data bases.

Sources: Richard and Katherine Green, "The New Crimebusters," *Redbook,* February 1991, pp. 40–46. Jack Bologna, "Software Applications Put the 'Byte' on Crime," *Computerworld,* December 14, 1987, p. 85.

---

birth field, such searches would be impossible. Most sophisticated data base systems let the user modify or change the structure of the data base itself. By adding a date field called *BIRTHDATE* we have essentially altered the nature of the data base. Every record in the file is altered by the addition of a new field. Of course, as when we created the data base, no information has been entered into the file. We have reserved a place for each person's birth date. Now we have to enter the data using the editing features available.

Generating Reports

All of the features discussed so far call for interactive communication between the user and the data base. The user and the computer talk directly to each other. The user gives a command, and the response appears on the screen. The user enters data, which appear on the screen and are stored in the computer's memory. However, the most effective use of a data base is to reproduce the results of searches, sorts, and changes in a more permanent form.

Data base **reports** can simply be paper or disk copies of summaries sent to the screen. Examples include a list of all students living in New York or of students with a course grade of B or better. But most systems also have various report-generating features. These make it possible to print reports with titles and column headings. They specify how many columns are to be printed and their order, and they indicate column spacing and margins. Many systems provide totals and subtotals of numeric fields where appropriate.

Although most systems send these reports to a printer, some systems store them as disk files. Many systems can do both. These disk files are stored on disk in a form readable by other software packages. They also can be read and adjusted by the data base itself.

As data base software becomes more sophisticated, solving even more complex tasks is possible. Several fields acting together can be used for searching and sorting. Specified numeric data can be subjected to statistical analysis. More than one file can be searched, and programs can be written using command files. These are just some of the advanced features available on current data base software.

COMPLEX SEARCHES AND SORTS

Suppose we want to identify those students whose grades on the final exam were between 65 and 75. If we used the comparisons of less than ($<$), greater than ($>$), equal to ($=$), and combinations of all three, we would still not get the necessary information. People often need to search a file to locate records that share several criteria at the same time. For this reason, most data base packages include the logical operations of AND, OR, and NOT. These provide additional ways to make use of data bases. Figure 13.7 shows a search of the course grade file for the students with final grades between 65 and 75.

We can also sort by multiple fields. For example, if we sort a large file alphabetically by last name, we will find that all the Smiths are together, but that they are not listed in alphabetical order by first name. Figure 13.8a shows what

Figure 13.7   Complex Searches: The course grade file has been searched for students with grades between 65 and 75.

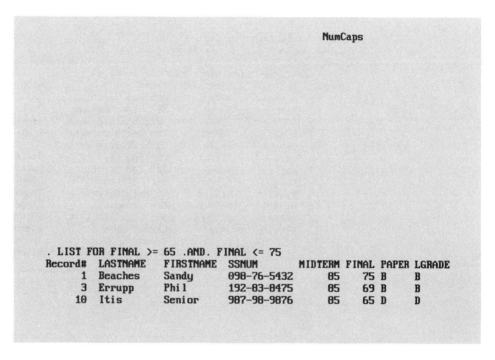

```
                                                              NumCaps




 . LIST FOR FINAL >= 65 .AND. FINAL <= 75
 Record#  LASTNAME   FIRSTNAME  SSNUM        MIDTERM FINAL PAPER LGRADE
       1  Beaches    Sandy      098-76-5432      85     75 B        B
       3  Errupp     Phil       192-83-0475      85     69 B        B
      10  Itis       Senior     987-98-9876      85     65 D        D
```

happens to our student data file when we sort alphabetically by last name only. The file is alphabetized correctly by last name, but Rocky Beaches follows Sandy Beaches and Frank N. Stein appears before Bere Stein. Two independent sorts will not do the trick; if we were now to sort by first name the results would not be in last name order. We must do a sort within a sort to get what we want. Figure 13.8b demonstrates such a complex sort—by two fields, first name *and* last name at the same time—producing the correct result.

USING MULTIPLE FILES

The main value of an electronic data base is to give fast and easy access to information. The more logical the organization of the data, the faster it can be retrieved. Data that naturally seem to go together should be contained in the same file, such as name, address, and phone number. However, the same records should not appear in more than one file. Address information should not ap-

Figure 13.8

Sorting by Multiple Fields: (a) A file sorted by last name and (b) a complex sort of two fields at the same time.

(a)

```
                                                              Num


. sort on lastname to last
  100% Sorted             14 Records sorted
. use last
. list lastname, firstname, street, city, st
Record#  lastname   firstname  street                city            st
      1  Beaches    Sandy      265 Bay Street        San Francisco   CA
      2  Beaches    Rocky      262 Stone Avenue      Rockville       MD
      3  Errupp     Phil       1020 Station Road     Gasville        NJ
      4  Ferma      Terry      789 Earth Avenue      Boston          MA
      5  Grahm      Telly      5325 Western Union    New York City   NY
      6  Itis       Senior     College Circle        Madison         WI
      7  Lofers     Penny      123 Toe Street        Shoeville       WI
      8  Long       Harry A.   Main Street           Slowtowne       KA
      9  Maykitt    Willie     56 Main Street        Tryhard         FL
     10  Mint       Said A.    Dirt Road             Diggersville    CO
     11  Nomial     Polly      456 Equation Circle   Triangle Park   NC
     12  Pickle     Inna       Garlic Road           Cukeville       NY
     13  Stein      Frank N.   Cemetary Raod         Transylvania    PA
     14  Stein      Bere       Happy Road            Milwaukee       WI
```

(b)

```
. sort on lastname, firstname to both
  100% Sorted             14 Records sorted
. use both
. list lastname, firstname, street, city, st
Record#  lastname   firstname  street                city            st
      1  Beaches    Rocky      262 Stone Avenue      Rockville       MD
      2  Beaches    Sandy      265 Bay Street        San Francisco   CA
      3  Errupp     Phil       1020 Station Road     Gasville        NJ
      4  Ferma      Terry      789 Earth Avenue      Boston          MA
      5  Grahm      Telly      5325 Western Union    New York City   NY
      6  Itis       Senior     College Circle        Madison         WI
      7  Lofers     Penny      123 Toe Street        Shoeville       WI
      8  Long       Harry A.   Main Street           Slowtowne       KA
      9  Maykitt    Willie     56 Main Street        Tryhard         FL
     10  Mint       Said A.    Dirt Road             Diggersville    CO
     11  Nomial     Polly      456 Equation Circle   Triangle Park   NC
     12  Pickle     Inna       Garlic Road           Cukeville       NY
     13  Stein      Bere       Happy Road            Milwaukee       WI
     14  Stein      Frank N.   Cemetery Row          Transylvania    PA
```

pear in a student grade file. Advanced data base systems allow different but related files within a data base to be linked together. In this way, information stored in one file is accessible to other files. This helps to avoid unnecessary duplication. It also greatly improves the integrity of the data, because changes need to be made to fewer fields. Files that can be linked together provide tremendous flexibility in gathering information.

Recall that our student data base consists of two files. One contains general student records and the other contains course grades. For most purposes these files will be processed independently, because they contain different kinds of information. For example, letters about tuition changes will go to all students listed in the general file. On the other hand, a search for students doing poorly on the midterm in our computer class would use only the grade file. However, if letters are to be sent to all students doing poorly on the midterm, then mailing-address data from the general file would be needed as well.

The major difference between file managers and data base systems is that data base systems are able to deal with more than one file simultaneously. Advanced systems such as dBASE IV, Paradox, and FoxPro allow the use of as many as 10 files or more. In systems that work with multiple files, the different files are linked together by matching fields that contain common information.

Fields that are shared by different files are called **key fields** or **keys.** Typical keys are social security, student, and employee numbers. However, any field that the files hold in common can be used. In our example data base, both the grade file and the general file have *LASTNAME* and *FIRSTNAME* in common. Although either of these could be used as a key, it seems more logical to use *LASTNAME* to relate the files together. However, common last names, such as Smith, Brown, and Stein, that belong to two or more students could cause confusion when files are linked together. For this reason, it is better to choose a field that is unique for all records, such as social security numbers.

By using the appropriate features of our data base, we could search the grade file for the names of all students receiving grades lower than 75 on the midterm. This would be the result:

Frank N.	Stein
Telly	Grahm
Willie	Maykitt

By linking together our files using *LASTNAME,* we could search the grade file for the required student names and extract their addresses from the general file.

Frank N.	Stein	Cemetery Row	Transylvania	PA	34567
Telly	Grahm	5325 Western Union	New York City	NY	11101
Wille	Maykitt	56 Main Street	Tryhard	FL	65432

ADVANCED FEATURES

People who make extensive use of data bases require software packages that are simultaneously fast, easy to use, and able to perform even more complex tasks than those we've already discussed. A wide range of advanced features is now available, although not all of them are in all systems.

- *Command flexibility.* The software can be run by selecting items from an on-screen menu or by issuing commands. Software that is both menu-driven and command-driven gives the novice an easy introduction to data base operations and still offers the advanced user greater flexibility.

- *Programming language features.* Many features of programming languages are built into the software. Statements for decision making, such as IF/THEN/ELSE, and looping statements such as WHILE, CASE, and GOTO are included. These, too, give advanced users greater flexibility.

- *Individualized command files.* Users can develop individualized command files, which are really programs. These can include the passing of data (parameters) between different command files.

- *Debugging aids.* Debugging aids designed to simplify the use of programming tools have been added to a number of systems (Chapter 7).

- *Information transfer.* The ability to transfer data base information to a word processor has become fairly common. Now, data bases may also transfer data to and from other standard packages, such as Lotus 1-2-3. Data also can be filed, transferred, and stored in binary format (*PFS: Professional File*) or in the more standard ASCII format.

- *Artificial intelligence.* The techniques of artificial intelligence using natural language tools are gaining in popularity, making data bases easier to use and understand.

- *Calculators and statistical functions.* In addition to being able to calculate totals and subtotals on numeric fields, advanced systems contain the mathematical capabilities of a calculator. Many have statistical functions including square root, natural log, and exponentiation as well.

- *"Sound-alike" searches and sorts.* Sophisticated systems include "sound-alike" searches and sorts. For example, when searching for a specific individual, it is useful to have the data base system retrieve all names that sound alike such as Schmidt, Schmitt, Schmit, etc. Using such systems, users do not have to know the exact spelling of the name in question.

PITFALLS, PROBLEMS, AND SOLUTIONS

Despite all that modern data bases can do, or perhaps *because* of their increased capabilities, they are often mastered more by trial and error than by formal instruction. Even experienced people, including programmers, may find problems in getting data base software to do what they want when they want it. Some typical problems can be solved by careful advance planning and attention to detail. Other problem areas may be avoided if they can be anticipated. Let's turn to several common problems and pitfalls, and their solutions.

Improving Sorting Speed

Microcomputer data bases were designed primarily to be easy to use. As a result, their structure may be efficient for entering data but not so efficient in retrieving records. Sorting through data base files can be time-consuming even for a computer. To improve sorting speed, most data base management packages include a feature called **indexing.** As each record is entered, it is given a number indicating the order of its entry into the data base. This is the record number. When sorting, an **index file** containing the fields being used in the sort and the corresponding record number is created.

When we do an indexed sort, the index file and not the original file is sorted. The records remain in the data base in the order in which they were entered. Since the index file contains much less information, it can be sorted through more quickly. The actual records can then be pulled from the original file in the specified order. This technique significantly improves the time involved in sorting. In addition, a given file can be indexed on any number of fields with a considerable saving of space.

Maintaining Data Integrity

A data base is only as reliable as the information it contains. All fields containing the same data must be updated at the same time. Data bases in which files are linked together should be designed so that as few fields as possible are duplicated. The less duplication there is in a data base, the easier it will be to update and keep accurate. In addition, when files contain data that logically belong together, it is easier to keep track of the data.

Avoiding Deletion Errors

To keep data up-to-date, it is obviously necessary to remove unwanted or outdated items. But once a record has been removed or a field overwritten, the previous data are gone. They cannot be retrieved. Some systems do not remove records as soon as the Delete command is used. Such records are marked for deletion but not removed altogether. They are unavailable for searching and sorting purposes, but they remain in the data base until a second command is given to complete the deletion. This gives the user a chance to make sure records are no longer needed before they are eliminated. In Figure 13.9, records 4 and 9 are marked with an asterisk (*) for deletion.

Avoiding Data Loss

Commands that change the structure of files or reports must be used with considerable care. Even simple changes in the spelling of a field name can lead to loss of data. In some data base systems, when the name of a field is changed from *LNAME* to *LASTNAME,* for example, all data in that field are removed. When the data base is recopied using the new structure, only those fields whose field names have remained constant are copied. The system assumes that a new name implies new data. Data base field names should not be changed unless new data accompany the change.

Changes in field width can cause similar problems. For example, if we wanted to have the information in our general student file printed out one

---

Figure 13.9   Records Marked for Deletion.

Num

```
. list
Record#   LASTNAME   FIRSTNAME   SSNUM          MIDTERM FINAL PAPER LGRADE
       1  Lofers     Penny       123-45-6789       100    95 A      A
       2  Stein      Frank N.    998-87-7654        25    45 C      G
       3  Pickle     Inna        555-55-5555       100    25 D      D
       4 *Beaches    Sandy       098-76-5432        85    75 B      B
       5  Errupp     Phil        192-83-8475        85    69 B      B
       6  Nomial     Polly       999-88-7777        95    99 A      A
       7  Mint       Said A.     445-67-5678        75    80 C      C
       8  Itis       Senior      987-98-9876        85    65 D      D
       9 *Long       Harry A.    234-56-7890        99    98 B      A
      10  Ferma      Terry       678-78-5678        95    80 B      B
      11  Grahm      Telly       666-11-1515        45    80 A      B
      12  Maykitt    Willie      777-80-8733        65    59 D      D
```

record per line, the length of a number of fields (including *LASTNAME*) would require shortening. Such changes do not become a problem until the general student file and course grade file need to be linked together using *LASTNAME* as a key. When the system is asked to display the names and addresses for all students with poor midterm grades, there is no problem in displaying the names. However, when the system tries to find the addresses in the general file, blanks are displayed. The reason for this is not obvious. The *LASTNAME* field in the general student file has been reduced in width for printing. The effect was that the computer was asked to compare an 8-character *LASTNAME* with a 10-character *LASTNAME* in the linked file. When linking two fields together, the system looks for *exact* matches. Eight characters do not match exactly with 10 characters. To avoid this problem, key fields must be defined in identical ways.

OUR CHANGING LIBRARIES

We think of libraries as repositories of the printed word. As such they are the keepers of the culture, writings, and experiences of humanity. Traditionally, libraries have been filled with books, but now they are changing. Although books remain predominant in our libraries, information is available on other media as well. Records, audio and video tapes, games, and, increasingly, software and computers can be consulted and borrowed in libraries. In the Peterborough, New Hampshire town library, for instance, patrons borrow personal computers in much the same way they borrow books. In many places across the country, card holders can come to the library, use a microcomputer there or borrow software to take home and try out on their own computer.

Libraries, however, are more than book or media exchanges. Libraries are information resources. Card catalogs, reader's guides, and the like are data bases of information organizing the printed word. Increasingly these data bases are being computerized (see Figure 13.10). Computerized catalogs are now found in most of our nation's largest libraries, such as the Library of Congress and the New York Public Library, university libraries such as Carnegie Mellon and Columbia, and a majority of the nation's medical libraries. An increasing number of smaller libraries are also implementing such systems. Special-purpose software makes this possible.

Card catalogs are being replaced for a number of reasons. The cards themselves, especially in libraries with old and heavily used card catalogs, get worn out and need to be replaced. Space in the card drawers is not infinitely expandable as collections grow in size. Searching and following cross-references to subject matter are time-consuming. Electronic catalogs using modern computer data base software are easy to use and take up almost no space compared to the rooms required for traditional card catalogs. Cross-referencing is available with a keystroke or two.

Figure 13.10   Many libraries have computerized their card catalogs.

Using computers, library records of borrowing and returns are easy to keep, and overdue notices can be sent out automatically. Such automation improves the control of a library's inventory and frees librarians to provide additional services. A patron can find out which branch holds a particular book as well as whether the item is currently on loan and when it is due to return. Card holders have increased access to books, periodicals, and other items, including items in other locations.

Researchers increasingly need access to electronic data base services. LEXIS and NEXIS, provided by Mead Data Central, contain 60 years of legal documentation. MEDLINE, the data base of the National Library of Medicine, contains the most up-to-date collection of medical and other health-related articles published in the world's professional journals. These are constantly being updated, with LEXIS adding new legal decisions and MEDLINE adding new journal articles. Libraries may eventually make access to such systems possible to individuals nationwide. At present such access is available only in the specialized collections of law and medical school libraries and some law offices and hospitals.

In addition to computerized catalogs, books, articles, and other kinds of information are increasingly available in electronic form. This electronic material is easier to store, more compact, inexpensive to move from place to place, and easier to organize and retrieve than printed material. However, it is not feasible to retype everything ever printed. Improved scanners are helping in this regard, but even they require careful proofreading.

More and more data bases are being created on and for computers, including new dictionaries and encyclopedias. In fact, almost everything being published today is in computerized form at some if not all stages of writing and production. However, most library users are neither interested nor willing to read books or magazines through computer terminals. There is something to be said for the comfortable feeling of holding a book. Only in jest do we talk about "curling up with a good computer program."

SUMMARY

A **data base** is a collection of facts organized around a **key**. Data need to be organized so that they can be retrieved, or located.

A data base is only as reliable as its data. Data integrity or reliability is directly related to the ability of the data base to remain current.

Microcomputer data base systems use files designed as tables composed of rows and columns to store information. Each row or record contains related data, and each column or field contains a specific type of data.

There are two kinds of data base packages. **File managers** are patterned after an index-card file, with records reflecting individual cards. They are menu-driven and commonly use one file. Searches, sorts, reports, and simple calculations can be performed on that file. **Data base managers** are more sophisticated. They are both menu- and **command-driven.** They can organize data in a greater variety of ways than file managers.

Planning a data base will improve the retrieval of data. Six planning steps should be followed: (1) Understand the problem, (2) Identify the output, (3) Identify the input, (4) Organize the data, (5) Test and revise the data base, and (6) Enter the data.

Data base software must help the user to do all of the following: (1) Create the data base, (2) **Search** the data base for a specific item, (3) **Sort** the data by key, (4) Adjust the data base, and (5) **Report** the results.

Current data base systems allow for complex searches using AND, OR, and NOT, and complex sorts using more than one field. Data base managers can manipulate multiple files and contain decision-making statements such as IF/THEN/ELSE.

Sorting through use of an **index file,** containing the fields being used in the sort and record numbers, greatly improves the speed of microcomputer data base sorts.

Electronic data bases are revolutionizing our libraries. Computerized card catalogs make searching and cross-referencing easy, and systems such as LEXIS and MEDLINE enable researchers to access the most up-to-date information.

Key Words

As an extra review of the chapter, try defining the following terms. If you have trouble with any of them, refer to the page number listed.

command-driven *(347)*   index file *(361)*
command file *(347)*   indexing *(361)*
data base *(343)*   key field (key) *(359)*
data base manager *(347)*   report *(356)*
data integrity *(344)*   search *(351)*
file manager *(345)*   sort *(354)*

Test Your Knowledge

1. What is a data base?

2. Define *data integrity.*

3. Define *file, record,* and *field.*

4. How do file managers and data base managers differ?

5. How is a menu-driven data base system different from a command-driven system?

6. How do numeric and character data differ? Give examples of each.

7. If a social security number is made up entirely of digits, why is it most often stored in a character field?

8. What is a data type? List the four different field data types.

9. How are data types used when defining the structure of a file?

10. When entering student addresses in a data base, why should each part of the address be entered in a separate field?

11. What kind of adjustments can be made to existing data base files?

12. Define *searching.*

13. Define *sorting.*

14. What is a data base report?

15. Define *key field.*

16. What is a "sound-alike" search?

17. What data are used to index a file?

18. Explain the difference between an indexed sort and a standard sort.

19. What are the advantages of using an advanced data base system, which allows multiple files, over the simpler file-management system?

20. How are data bases being used in modern libraries?

Expand Your Knowledge

1. Many people fear that the rapid expansion of large data base systems is a threat to personal freedom. Do you believe that this a valid concern? If so, what would you do to minimize the effects? Research and write a five-page paper on this question.

2. Read George Orwell's *1984.* In a short (three- to five-page) paper, discuss the role of computers and data bases in the book.

3. Medical researchers urge the development of a nationwide medical data base beyond the capacity of the current MEDLINE. Research and write a short (three- to five-page) paper on how such a system could facilitate organ transplants and general medical research.

4. Using a data base system available to you, create a file of your record/tape collection. Include at least 15 records and tapes. Fields should include artist, title, type (CD, tape, record), condition, and cost.
   (a) Perform one search on your data base, such as a list of all CDs in your collection by a particular artist. Print out the results.
   (b) Perform one complex sort of your data base on two fields. For example, create an alphabetical list of your collection by artist and title. Print out the result.

5. Using a data base system available to you, create a special-occasion file of your family members. Include name, birthday data, anniversary data, and address for each family member. Plan your fields carefully so you can gather the information you need from your data base.
   (a) Perform one search on your data base, such as a list of all family members with birthdays in September. Print out your results.
   (b) Perform one complex sort of your data base on two fields. For example, create an ordered list by birth-month and birth-day of all family members. Print out your results.

6. Using the data base system available to you, create a bibliography file for a paper in any subject. Include author, periodical or book (source), title, page numbers, volume number, etc. Plan your fields carefully so you can produce a bibliography, footnotes, or endnotes with equal ease.

   (a) Search the data base for all sources written in the years between 1980 and 1990. List your results.

   (b) Search the data base for all sources written in the last 12 months.

   (c) Using the report generator, produce a bibliography sorted in the proper order.

7. Using the data base system available to you, create a file containing information on your favorite sport. If your sport were baseball, fields might include names of the players on your favorite team, RBIs, earned run average, hits, runs, errors, etc.

   (a) Perform one search on your data base, such as a list of all players with a specific earned run average. Print out your results.

   (b) Perform one complex sort of your data base on two fields. For example, create an ordered list by RBI and alphabetical by last name. Print out your results.

8. Using the data base system available to you, create a file containing information on local restaurants. Include fields for name of restaurant, food type (Mexican, Italian, Indian), cost (inexpensive, moderate, expensive), telephone, and its location. Location should be broken down into street and city or town.

   (a) Perform one search on your data base, such as a search for all Italian restaurants. Print out your results.

   (b) Perform one complex sort of your data base on two fields. For example, create an ordered list of all moderately priced Italian restaurants. Print out your results.

   (c) Using the report generator, produce a restaurant directory sorted by type.

14

Computer Graphics

Computer graphics create visual images using computers. If we think about computer graphics, what do we see? The images that frequently come to mind are the fast-moving creatures encountered in computer games or the dramatic special effects found in movies. Through computer graphics, we can display the molecules of life, view the frontiers of space, and experience the dog-fighting spacecraft of the future. While these creations are the most dramatic of the computer-generated images, they represent only a tiny segment of the computer graphics in use today.

Despite the incredible graphics displays used in the entertainment industry, the most common forms of human communication are spoken and written words. While we use pictures and other visual images to assist us, language remains the most fundamental and pervasive form of communication. Still, researchers studying memory have rediscovered that "a picture *is* worth a thousand words." Studies indicate that information presented graphically is remembered longer and with greater accuracy than equivalent information presented in written form. Using computers to create clear, easy-to-understand visual images that convey meaningful information is within our reach.

After studying this chapter, you will be able to:

- Identify how computer graphic images are created.
- Understand the use of computer graphics to analyze information.
- Identify the features of presentation graphics.
- Identify the important features in computer-aided design (CAD).
- Explain how computers are used to produce creative images.
- Identify the techniques used in computer animation.
- Discuss computer art.

CREATING IMAGES

Most artists do not use computers. Their creative images are composed of solid lines, shapes, and shaded areas. The artist places the pen, paintbrush, or chalk on a medium and, with a series of strokes or dots of color, creates an image. Computer images are not composed of strokes. Most are created out of thousands of points of light called **pixels** (for picture elements); a smaller number of images are created from tiny straight-line segments **(vectors)** placed close together. In both cases the human eye sees the image as continuous even though it is not. Newspaper photographs, television, and some modern motion pictures are all generated using pixel-like technologies.

For the creation of pixel-generated images, the computer screen is composed of thousands of light-sensitive locations, each of which can be lit independently. The more pixels that make up the screen, the higher the resolution of the image and the clearer the picture. **Resolution** is a measure of pixel density on a screen. Using graphics software to link each pixel to a specific memory bit or set of bits is called **bit-mapping** (each pixel "maps" onto a bit). Controlling the simultaneous lighting of thousands of pixels to create meaningful images requires complex software. Multiple colors complicate the process. Modern computer workstation-based graphics systems use special memory and processor chips to control the display screen.

IMAGES THAT ENHANCE UNDERSTANDING

Although specialized hardware is required to generate computer graphics (see Chapter 5), it is the graphics software that allows a computer to transform data into information and art.

We have already learned that computers play a significant role by assisting us in examining and analyzing data. Computer graphics provide an additional way for us to communicate what we have discovered. Currently, computer graphics used in this way fall into four categories:

- analysis graphics
- presentation graphics
- computer-aided design
- creative graphics

Analysis Graphics

As the name implies, **analysis graphics** are visuals used to analyze large amounts of data. A graph, chart, or picture can condense lists of numeric data and reveal relationships and trends. Analysis graphics software is widely available for all types of computers. Mainframe packages are used to analyze weather data, producing not only the traditional weather maps used on the evening news, but detailed maps of hurricanes and other storms in motion. In addition, graphics software is used to analyze data transmitted from exploratory space vehicles such as Voyager and the Hubble Space Telescope (see Figure 14.1).

Analysis graphics assist in the study of earthquakes, volcanoes, and the atomic structure of life. Scientists at IBM's Thomas J. Watson Research Center are developing graphic software to assist scientists in displaying their visions of the physical universe as well as images stemming from theoretical ideas. Such software can portray the structure of simple or complex molecules, or graphically represent mathematical formulas.

The sciences, business, and the arts are all heavy users of analysis graphics. Microcomputer analysis graphics take the form of line and bar graphs, scattergrams, and pie charts. Such graphics identify trends, reveal relationships, and

Figure 14.1   Analysis Graphics: Graphics software is used to analyze photographs such as this shot taken from the Hubble Space Telescope.

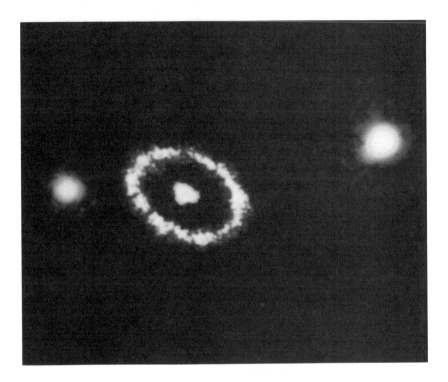

assist in locating patterns. When analysis software is used to decipher business data, it is often called **business graphics.**

Line graphs are used to look for trends. The upward or downward direction of the lines reflect the trend. For example, if we plotted gasoline prices over the last ten years, we would notice that despite some decreases, the overall trend is toward an increase in pump prices. In Figure 14.2, the number of students enrolling in programming courses over the last five years has been plotted. The graph indicates an increase, then a decrease, followed by a leveling off of total enrollment.

Scattergrams show the distribution among a set of values. To show the distribution of student grades, exam scores could be plotted. Scores may cluster around specific points or scatter throughout the entire range. Looking at a scattergram of raw data often provides valuable insights to relationships that may not be apparent in lists of numbers.

Bar graphs are used to show the differences within a single set of data and to compare the relationships between different sets of data. In Figure 14.3a, a bar graph is used to compare one class's average grades on three different

Computer Graphics

Graphics for Analysis and Presentation

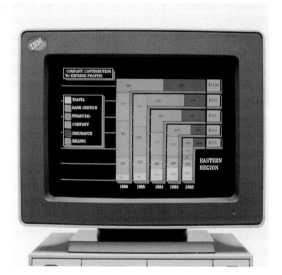

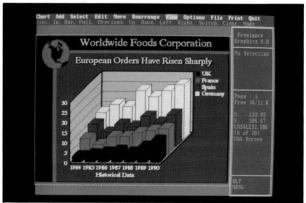

Computer graphics can enhance the appearance of left, annual reports and right, sales figures.

(Worldwide Foods Corporation and IBM)

New software such as NewWave with Windows allows users to combine word processing, spreadsheet, and graphics functions to create documents with greater impact than ever before.

(Hewlett Packard)

With Image Editors, photos can be incorporated into graphic presentations.

(Apple Computer, Inc.)

Computer-Aided Design and Manufacturing

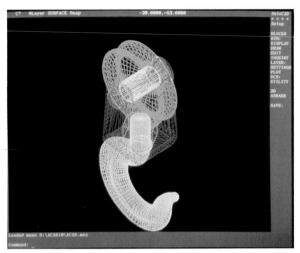

The first step in computer-aided design is often the creation of "wireframe" diagrams.
(IBM)

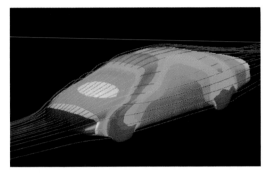

Computer simulation of air flow around a car being designed by computer.
(© Hank Morgan/Rainbow)

CAD is used to design electronic circuits and computer chips as well as buildings and machine parts.
(IBM)

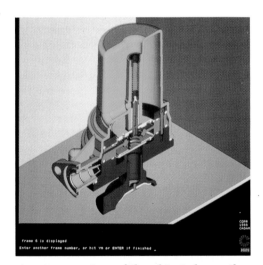

A cutaway view of the object shows the internal structure.
(IBM)

Computer Animation

The movie industry has made use of computer-generated special effects, as in this scene from *Return of the Jedi*.
(© Lucasfilm Ltd. (LFL) 1983.)

Computers can create cartoonlike images.

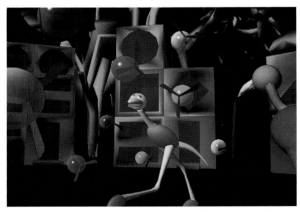

(© Ohio State University Computer Graphics/Dan McCoy/Rainbow)

(Ellis Herwig/The Picture Cube, both)

Computer Art

A still-life generated by computer.
(© Lucasfilm Ltd. (LFL) 1982.)

A three-dimensional computer graphics image of the Pike's Peak region of Colorado.
(Precision Visuals International/Science Photo Library/Photo Researchers, Inc.)

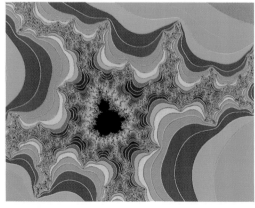

Three-dimensional art by computer artist Melvin Prueitt.
(© Melvin L. Prueitt/Photo Researchers, Inc.)

A computer graphics image entitled Candy Pillars, created through fractal geometry.
(Gregory Sams/Science Photo Library/Photo Researchers, Inc.)

Figure 14.2   Line Graphs: This line graph of student enrollment in programming courses compares Fall and Spring enrollments with total annual enrollments for a period of four years.

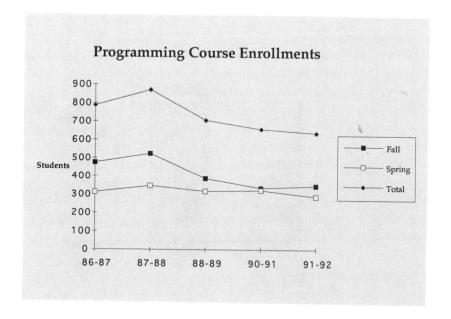

exams. By using multiple bars on a single graph, different classes can be compared on the same three exams (see Figure 14.3b).

Pie charts are used to show proportional relationships in a given set of data. For example, within a given class they can demonstrate the relationship between A's, B's, C's, D's, and F's (see Figure 14.4). This type of graph is most commonly used in portraying budgets. For example, it can display the proportion of the federal budget that goes to military spending as opposed to social programs.

Spreadsheets such as Lotus 1-2-3, Excel, and Quattro Pro, and a number of data base packages such as WingZ include analysis graphics. Increasingly, these packages can place graphs, charts, and text blocks on the same screen as worksheets. This provides users with access to a variety of information and analysis formats at once (see Figure 14.5). Analysis graphics software is relatively inexpensive and easy to use. Its popularity as a decision-making tool is growing rapidly.

Presentation Graphics

Analysis graphics and presentation graphics are very similar. Although analysis graphics provide insight into collected data, **presentation graphics** are designed

Figure 14.3   Bar Graphs: Printers can also create bar graphs, such as these (a) indicating one class's average exam grades and (b) the grades of three different classes on the same exam.

(a)

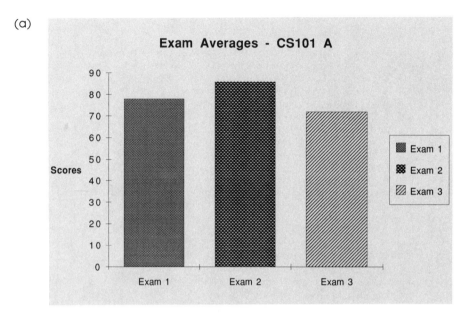

(b)

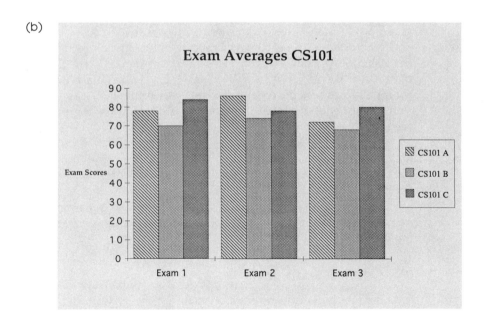

Figure 14.4   Pie Charts: Pie charts show proportional relationships, such as this one of the grade distribution within a class.

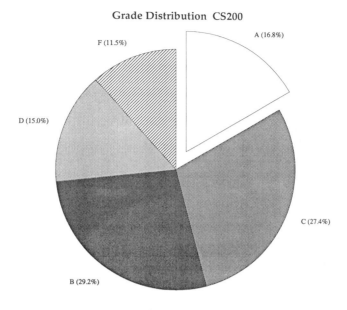

Grade Distribution CS200

Figure 14.5   Analysis graphics turn large amounts of numeric data into visual images that are easier to understand.

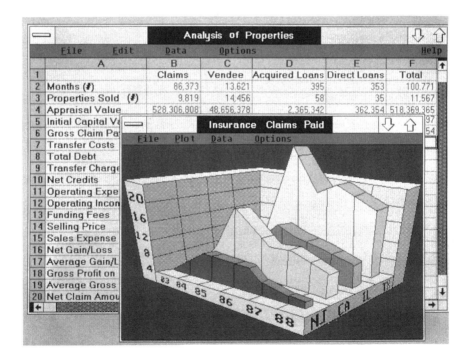

to assist in presenting these insights to others (see Figure 14.6). Both types of software produce similar graphics, such as line and bar graphs and pie charts, and both are heavily used in business. As with analysis graphics, most presentation packages such as PowerPoint, Freelance, Harvard Graphics, and Hollywood accept data from existing spreadsheets and data bases, and both are used to study and visualize data. Presentation graphics are designed for "pizazz."

The graphics produced by analysis packages are more than adequate for identifying trends and analyzing data. When giving presentations, however, audiences usually have limited time and quickly waning interest. The attention-getting features of presentation packages are often as critical to getting the information across as the content itself. Presentation graphics packages create dramatic effects by adding brilliant colors, three-dimensional diagrams, and a variety of letter fonts to analysis graphics. A number of packages include presentation **outliners** that provide fill-in-the-blanks outline formats to help users plan and organize their talks. In addition, they provide disk files of pictures, symbols, and drawings, called **clip art,** that can be inserted into graphic displays. Increasingly, the graphics produced by software packages such as Lotus 1-2-3, Excel, Quattro Pro, and WingZ incorporate many presentation features (see Figure 14.7).

Figure 14.6   Presentation Graphics: Used heavily in business, presentation graphics present data that attract attention.

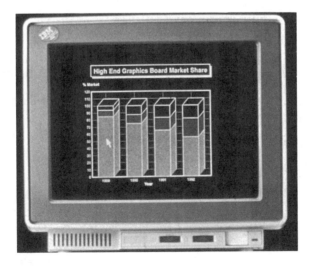

Figure 14.7   Many software packages such as Excel are now incorporating presentation features.

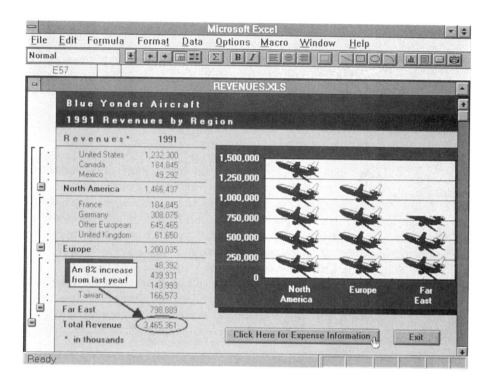

Most current presentation packages are designed to:

- Enhance the graphics produced by spreadsheets and data base software. In addition to making these graphics more visually appealing, such graphics can be reduced or enlarged as needed for inclusion in reports. Additional explanatory information also can be added to clarify the graph.

- Create graphs, diagrams, pictures, and charts from data entered at the screen.

- Create charts and diagrams from stored graphic symbols such as pictures, lines, curves, circles, and rectangles. The user, assisted by the software, acts as an artist combining pictures, lines, and words to create a powerful image.

- Include clip art graphics to enhance presentation.

- Create color transparencies, slides, and hard-copy visuals from on-screen displays. Specialized hardware attachments, such as a camera with color slide film, are required.

Through the use of presentation software, the people developing a presentation now have closer control over the graphics they will use. Graphics that previously took days or weeks to produce by professional artists can be created in minutes with presentation software. Time is no longer a factor; software-generated graphics can be tailored to specific audiences, and can reflect up-to-the-minute information.

Multimedia Presentations

Presentations are no longer limited to static slides or transparencies. **Multimedia presentations** add drama as well as pizazz. Through the use of video, on-screen animation, projections of interactive computer displays, as well as traditional transparencies, slides, and handouts, audiences can enter the world of the presenter. Faculty in computer-based courses nationwide are finding that video projection of interactive computer displays vastly improves instruction. Studies at the University of Southern California's Annenberg School of Communication found that although most presenters use transparencies and the chalkboards, those that included video, slides, and computer-based displays were far more effective in getting the message to the audience. With devices such as the Kodak Data Show, displaying computer images to small groups is fairly economical.

COMPUTER-AIDED DESIGN

The application of computer graphics to the design, drafting, or modeling of devices or structures is called **computer-aided design (CAD).** Computer-aided designs have traditionally been used to create tools and machine parts, buildings, aircraft, and cars (see Figure 14.8). More recently, computer chips have been designed using CAD. Perhaps the most intriguing use of CAD software has been in the development of special effects for the motion picture industry.

Historically, CAD has been a mainframe or minicomputer application. Such systems were predominantly used by engineers, architects, and draftsmen. Today, state-of-the-art CAD work environments are powerful, single-user workstations. These workstations include a desktop *mini*computer, a high-resolution, large screen, color graphics monitor equipped with a pointing device such as a digitizer, light pen, or mouse, and a keyboard. Specialized software that supports two-dimensional and three-dimensional graphics is required. Such workstations are often connected, or networked, to larger systems, where data bases of existing drawings are stored.

Figure 14.8   Computer-Aided Design: Computer-aided design is used in the development of many products.

There are two stages in using the computer as a design tool in industry. In the first stage, a geometric model of the machine part, aircraft, or building is designed on the graphics monitor. The designer creates all the lines, curves, and shapes that the diagram requires. With the assistance of CAD software, shading, perspective, and color are added, converting the design from a flat, two-dimensional diagram into a seemingly three-dimensional image called a **solid model.** This solid model can be rotated and viewed from any angle. It can be examined as a unit, enlarged, or reduced. It can be broken into its component parts, each of which can be further examined. Designs can be examined from the outside as well as from the inside. In a building model, for example, the outside walls can be stripped away, leaving the supporting structure visible (see Figure 14.9).

In the second stage, the model can be tested and analyzed as if it had already been constructed. In addition to the structural design, the physical constraints and limitations inherent in construction materials are also entered into the computer. Simulated stress tests then can be performed on the model. These stress tests evaluate the model's performance under specific conditions. The de-

Figure 14.9   Computer-Aided Design: Computer-aided design is also used in the design of buildings.

sign is studied for structural flaws. Using the results of these tests, the engineer can adjust or redesign the model to eliminate indicated problems. This type of pretesting is far less expensive than building a physical model and testing it for flaws, while netting the same results. Furthermore, revisions can be made more quickly and more accurately to CAD designs than to physical models.

Once CAD designs are complete, two-dimensional versions can be produced on paper in the form of extremely detailed blueprints. Alternatively, the design can be used directly in the development of the structures. The use of advanced technology to manage and control the manufacture of products is called **computer-aided manufacturing** or **CAM. CAD/CAM,** the combining of the computerized design with the manufacturing process, makes the production of complex commodities more economical. In some cases, such as the design and manufacture of rockets, spacecraft components, and supercomputer components, production would have been impossible without the computer's assistance.

In most cases, CAD designs are stored in memory as **digitized models** (binary versions of the design) and can be retrieved and used whole or in part as the foundation of future drawings. Such CAD data bases reduce the cost and time involved in the development of new products.

Although most CAD software operates on workstations or on larger systems, the increase in processing power and storage capacity of today's microcomputers has made high-quality CAD software available on these machines. Microcomputer CAD products are relatively inexpensive and they contain large libraries of drawings that are easy to modify. Microcomputer CAD has found its way into the design of clothing, jewelry, and thousands of other products.

CREATIVE GRAPHICS

As we have seen, computer graphics are finding use in business and education where drawings, pictures, diagrams, and charts are important. In many cases, software-generated graphics are replacing paper-and-pencil drawings with clearer, more colorful results.

Graphics Editors

Just as word processors and spreadsheets manipulate text and numbers, **graphics editors** create and manipulate images by lighting and unlighting thousands of pixels or points of light on the screen. Graphics editors, often called paint packages or computer easels, can create freehand sketches using a mouse, digitizer, light pen, or other pointing device. In addition, graphics editor software includes preprogrammed basic geometric forms such as circles, squares, points, curves, and lines, which can be entered on the screen and manipulated along with freehand drawings. Colors and shadings selected from a menu are applied to computer images in much the same way an artist selects colors from a paint palette and applies them to a canvas. Using software similar to CAD, two-dimensional sketches can be made to appear three-dimensional and the impression of texture can be added (see Figure 14.10).

Graphics editors can edit or adjust screen images. Sections of drawings can be erased or moved to other locations on the screen (similar to block moves with a word processor), enlarged, and reduced in size. Software can simulate the thin lines drawn with a pencil point, or the thicker lines and shading made with a paintbrush. The computer artist can even duplicate the effect produced by paint from a spray can.

At present, most graphics editors run on microcomputers and workstations. On single-user systems, both the processor and large amounts of memory can be dedicated to the tasks of drawing pictures. Manipulating individual pixels requires a large amount of dedicated memory. In the single-user environment, the computer can instantly respond to the artist's actions on the screen. In multiuser environments, graphics editor users must contend with noticeable delays between the time an image is drawn on the screen and its actual appearance.

High-end, advanced graphics editors, called **image editors** or **graphic illustrators,** such as PixelPaint, Image-In-Color, and Designer support a large number of color scanners (see Figure 14.11). They allow scanned images to be entered

Figure 14.10 Paint Packages: These computer easels can create freehand sketches or use preprogrammed graphics primitives such as rectangles and lines.

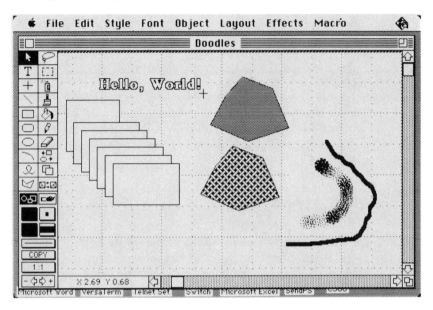

On Line

COMPUTER ANIMATION: REALITY OR ILLUSION?

When we think of animation, Saturday morning cartoons spring to mind. While **computer animation** may be used to create cartoonlike images, and some of the advanced presentation graphics packages include this capability, it is increasingly used to simulate or imitate reality. Animators can be used to invent lifelike illusions that include unexplored worlds, outrageous creatures, detailed futuristic spacecraft, and people so realistic that they are almost indistinguishable from the real thing. Companies such as Digital

Vision Entertainment (DVE) have produced three-dimensional, computer-generated actors used in PBS productions and public service announcements. The cost of computer animation remains quite high. The more lifelike the animation, the higher the cost, because complex movements require not just artistic quality but an understanding of human anatomy. To construct lifelike animation, the computer is used to sculpture the forms using lines, curves, and shading in much the way a sculptor might use

Figure 14.11   Image Editors: Photographs can be edited, changed, and manipulated using image editors.

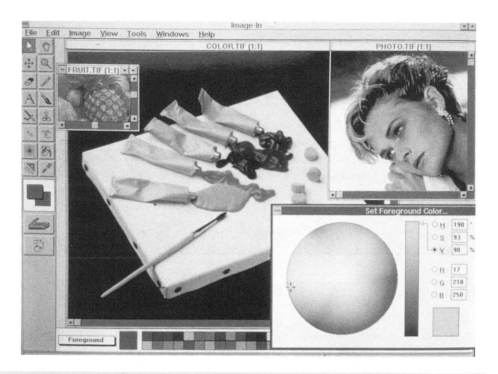

wires to create the basic structural frame of a person. Just as the sculptor would add a material to simulate the skin, so the computer creates a pseudoskin to cover the lines and curves (see Figure 14.11).

Computers have an advantage over the sculptor, however. Using image editing and still photography, images need not be constructed totally from scratch. Image editing has the potential for creating incredibly lifelike creations. Unfortunately, the same technology that is used in animation can be used to alter photographs of any kind, leaving little or no proof of alteration. The authenticity of photographic evidence is jeopardized.

As with computers in art, the use of computer animation is not limited to the motion picture and television industry. Packages such as

Autodesk's 3D Studio, a microcomputer-based animation package, can be used to produce animations and three-dimensional drawings at a fraction of the cost of minicomputer packages. Such packages are often used to construct still images as part of architectural plans as well as three-dimensional, animated tours of yet to be constructed buildings. 3D Studio has found applications in the production of presentations for trade shows and as part of medical demonstrations.

Sources: Robert Killheffer, "Live Illusions," *Omni,* January 1991, pp. 50–53. Eamonn Sullivan, "Autodesks 3D Studio Package Reduces the Cost of Animation," *PC Week,* April 1, 1991, p. 34.

directly into the package where their colors, shapes, and sizes can be easily adjusted. Text can be added almost anywhere on the screen. Photos can be retouched, and images can be made to look three-dimensional.

THE COMPUTER AS AN ARTISTIC MEDIUM

As we have already seen, the dominant use of computer graphics is to analyze and present information visually. We have also seen that computer graphics are also being used as tools for creative expression beyond that required for animation. Computer artists use the computer as a tool to create art (see Figure 14.12).

The motion picture industry is the most obvious place where computer graphics have affected our perceptions. Computers generate most of the dra-

Figure 14.12   Computer Art: Often dramatic, colorful, and detailed, computer art may not appeal to everyone.

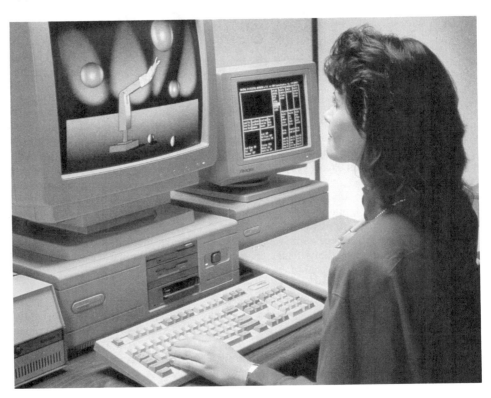

On Line

VIRTUAL REALITY

Art, Theater, Music, Movies, Television—all of these media provide us with an escape from reality to a different world, an alternative reality. They are, however, all passive. We watch or listen to what is going on without actively participating. All this is changing. Researchers are developing the newest "media," called **virtual reality.** Using a virtual reality system, we might choose to "walk" on the surface of Mars, "fly" like Superman, or "help build" an orbiting space station without leaving Earth.

Using a specially designed mask and glove connected to a computer running complex software, the user, like Alice in Wonderland, enters into an artificial 3-D drama as an active participant. The glove, called Data Glove, is a highly specialized input device that uses fiber-optic cable to sense finger and hand motions. The 3-D mask, called EyePhone, places tiny liquid-crystal screens inches in front of the user's face and is designed to display images directly into the eyes. The software produces images that appear to surround the viewer. Sensors in the glove provide feedback to the computer, indicating the user's location and hand motions. The computer coordinates the sensory information with the 3-D images, creating simulated interactions between the viewer and his surroundings.

Much of the current research into virtual reality is going on at NASA's Ames Research Center in California. NASA scientists have very practical goals in mind. In the long term, combining devices like the Data Glove and Eye-Phone with the vast amount of data collected from space probes, NASA hopes to accurately reproduce locations on the moon, Mars, and more distant planets. Using detailed, 3-D, simulated, artificial realities, scientists could "land" at potential sites, survey the landscape, and plan for further exploration. Such simulated missions could dramatically reduce costs and possibly save lives.

NASA's more immediate plans for virtual reality seem even more fantastic. Using virtual reality, NASA hopes to re-create space and to simulate weightlessness. Earthbound participants would be linked to "telerobots" that could imitate hand and body movements. Within the simulation, engineers would "appear" to build a space station. Robots located thousands of miles above the earth would duplicate their actions. Creation of such a space station is considered essential to NASA's plans for future space exploration, and virtual reality seems an ideal way to make this concept a reality.

The entertainment industry sees profitable opportunities through virtual reality technology. Mattel Toys is the manufacturer of the Power Glove and Power Glove II, inexpensive and simplified versions of the Data Glove. These plastic gloves translate hand and finger positions into the electronic signals used by Nintendo. Action games such as handball and tennis can be played without leaving the living room, and new games are being developed that will make even more dramatic use of the glove system. The Power Gloves have proved so successful that Mattel saw millions of dollars in sales in the first year. Other manufacturers have combined microcomputers and video cameras with additional hardware to allow the user to become a digitized "player," entering into the action appearing on the television screen. Still others, such as Synetic Systems in Seattle, Washington, are creating relaxing, meditative realities where users can "go" to reduce stress.

If virtual reality can simulate action games, why not simulate other "realities"? Educators and scientists see virtual reality as creating an entirely new dimension in computer simulations. For example, programs designed to teach surgery to medical students are being examined. Combining current virtual reality concepts with special feedback sensors that simulate the sense of touch, students could perform simulated operations in which the patient could not die and mistakes would be truly educational opportunities. Other researchers see virtual reality as a way to turn the sign language used by a deaf person into speech and to teach driving students how to deal with the unexpected. A California-based firm has developed an "architectural walk-through" program where architects and clients can walk around a possible building and examine it from the inside, before it is built.

With enough information, a computer, and the necessary hardware and software, it may someday soon be possible to turn dreams into reality through virtual reality.

Sources: Steve Ditlea, "Grand Illusion," *New York,* August 6, 1990, pp. 27–34. "A Vivid Experience—And You Are There," *Personal Computing,* August 1990, p. 34. "Exploring Inner Space," *Personal Computing,* July 27, 1990, p. 34.

---

matic special effects currently used on television and in the movies. A graphics system called Pixar produces computer-generated visual effects that cannot be distinguished from natural photography. Pixar was developed by Lucasfilms. Unlike photography, however, Pixar graphics need not reflect the real world. They reflect the artist's imagination.

Although graphics editors are the most popular means of producing artistic images on a computer screen, two additional techniques are available. Using one of these techniques, some computer artists write programs that mathematically describe the images they wish to create. Equations describe the shapes, sizes, and colors of objects on the screen. Such programs are extremely complex and require considerable programming expertise. The second technique uses a digitizing camera to convert a drawing or photograph into a computerized copy in binary form (digitized). The copy is then stored in memory. This binary information is next converted into lit or unlit pixels on a computer monitor. This digital image can then be manipulated using graphics software.

Computer generated special effects create alternative realities. Movies such as Star Wars, Indiana Jones, Back to the Future, and Star Trek trace much of their success to computer graphics. Motion picture industry computer graphics firms, such as Industrial Light and Magic, combine mathematical modeling, digitizing photography, and creativity to make the imaginary appear real.

Computer art is not limited to special effects in the motion picture and television industry. Some artists are turning from paints and pencils to high-resolution, color computer screens. Computer art is often dramatic, colorful, and incredibly detailed. Its images range from the real to the surreal. As with any form of art, it may not appeal to everyone.

As the cost of graphics hardware decreases and computer users become more aware of the benefits of computer-generated graphics, the demand for high-quality computer graphics will continue to increase. Just as computers have altered the way we approach writing, calculating, and storing information, so too will computer graphics change our image of information.

SUMMARY

Computer graphics is the creation of visual images using computers. Computer images are created out of points of light called **pixels** or segments of straight lines called **vectors.**

The greater the density of pixels that make up screen images, the higher the **resolution** of the image. Using graphics software to link each pixel to a specific memory bit or set of bits is called **bit-mapping.**

Graphics software can be used to examine and analyze data or create art. **Analysis graphics** use visuals to analyze large amounts of data. **Presentation graphics** add dramatic effects to analysis graphics for use in presenting information.

Computer-aided design (CAD) applies computer graphics to the design, drafting, or modeling of devices or structures. Most CAD software operates on powerful single-user workstations that combine a minicomputer, color graphics monitor, and a pointing device with sophisticated modeling software. **Computer-aided manufacturing (CAM)** is the use of advanced technology to manage and control manufacturing. **CAD/CAM** is the combination of computerized design with the manufacturing process.

Graphics editors manipulate images by lighting and unlighting pixels. They combine preprogrammed graphics primitives with freehand drawing. Images can be enlarged, reduced, and adjusted at the screen.

Computer animation combines **image editing,** CAD, and creativity to create lifelike, three-dimensional images.

Computer art's most popular application is in the motion-picture industry. Pixar generates computer visuals that look like photographs.

Key Words

As an extra review of the chapter, try defining the following terms. If you have trouble with any of them, refer to the page number listed.

analysis graphics *(371)*
bar graph *(372)*
bit-mapping *(371)*
business graphics *(372)*
CAD/CAM *(380)*

clip art *(376)*
computer-aided design (CAD) *(378)*
computer-aided manufacturing
   (CAM) *(380)*
computer animation *(382)*

digitized model *(380)*
graphics editor *(381)*
image editor (graphic
   illustrator) *(381)*
line graph *(372)*
multimedia presentation *(378)*
outliner *(376)*

pie chart *(373)*
pixel *(370)*
presentation graphics *(373)*
resolution *(371)*
scattergram *(372)*
solid model *(379)*
vector *(370)*

Test Your Knowledge

1. Define *pixel.*

2. How do pixel and vector graphics differ?

3. Define *resolution.*

4. What is bit-mapping?

5. List the types of graphics used to analyze information.

6. How does presentation graphics differ from analysis graphics?

7. What is clip art?

8. What types of visuals are used in multimedia presentations?

9. What is computer-aided design?

10. Explain solid modeling.

11. Describe CAD/CAM.

12. What is a graphics editor and how does it work?

13. How is an image editor different from a graphics editor?

14. Computer animation is used to produce what kinds of images?

15. Explain the two techniques commonly available to computer artists to create graphic images.

Expand Your Knowledge

1. Write a five-page paper on microcomputer CAD. Include a section explaining the differences between microcomputer CAD and the software that runs on larger systems.

2. Write a short paper (three to five pages) on Pixar graphics.

3. Using software reviews found in computer magazines such as *PC Computing,* compare three presentation graphics packages. Include current prices where available.

4. Using analysis software available at your school, design a graph or chart that compares your exam grades in a course. Use proper titles and labels.

5. Investigate computer animation. Write a short paper on the use of computer animation in the television and motion picture industry.

6. Research fractals. Write a short paper (three to five pages) describing what fractals are and how they are used to create graphic images.

15

Computer Communications and Networking

CHAPTER OUTLINE

An information explosion is occurring all around us. Keeping track of even critical information is increasingly difficult. More medical reports are generated, court cases decided, discoveries made, research published, and news reported in print and on the airwaves than can possibly be assimilated. Hotel, airline, and theater reservations are made without leaving home. Banking is available 24 hours a day. Computers are making just about all information more accessible.

The transmission of electronic information over long distances is called **telecommunication.** This information can be in the form of computer-generated data, the spoken word as in telephone conversations, or audio and video in the form of radio and television. The media used to transmit this information vary widely, including telephone wires, fiber optic cable, radio signals, and satellites.

Before computers became popular, the world was already "wired." Friends across the country or around the world could and still can be contacted by picking up and dialing the telephone. Television brings almost instantaneous images of events occurring on earth and in space. Telecommunication is usually thought of in terms of computers and telephones. However, the wiring of America began in the 1840s with the invention of the telegraph. The telegraph transmitted digital signals—sets of dots and dashes—like the zeros and ones used by modern computers. In the early 1900s, telegraph signals were replaced by voice signals with the invention of the telephone. Voice signals are not digital and for a while digital communications all but disappeared. Computers, however, have reintroduced digital communication.

The exchanging of information between computers and computing devices over communication lines is called **telecomputing.** These "conversations" can be simply the transfer of information from one place to another or they can involve considerable amounts of processing. The bulk of information transferred and processed does not come from computer professionals but from businesses, service organizations such as travel agents, and individuals.

After studying this chapter, you will be able to:

- Understand the different kinds of modems and their uses.

- Describe the different types of communication media.

- Define communication channels.

- Identify the role of software in computer communications.

- Describe local area networks.

- Identify the different types of wide area networks.

- Describe the services offered by academic networks.

- Identify the uses of wide area networks by business and industry.

- Describe the information utilities.

- Understand information networks.

MAKING THE CONNECTION

The simplest way to get computers and computing devices to communicate is to connect them directly by wires capable of transmitting digital signals (see Figure 15.1). Directly linking hardware is called a **point-to-point connection.**

Computers connected in this way can share both information and peripheral devices such as printers, disk drives, terminals, and color graphics equipment. Machine size is irrelevant. Large machines can be connected as easily as a microcomputer sitting on a desk is connected to a nearby printer.

Unfortunately, as the distance between computing devices increases, the reliability and strength of the signal decreases. While it is possible to have a memo printed on a printer down the hall, using one in the next building requires that the signal between the computer and printer be boosted, or enhanced. Even with the addition of such devices, direct-connection distances are limited.

As the demand to connect more and more computing devices over longer and longer distances grew, it became obvious that an alternative to wiring equipment together directly was needed. Users of different computers in distant locations wanted to exchange information and share ideas and resources. The telephone became the obvious solution. Information and ideas had long been shared in this way. Offices, businesses, and homes nationwide and even world-

Figure 15.1   Connected Computers: Computers and computing devices communicate with one another by transmitting digital signals over wires.

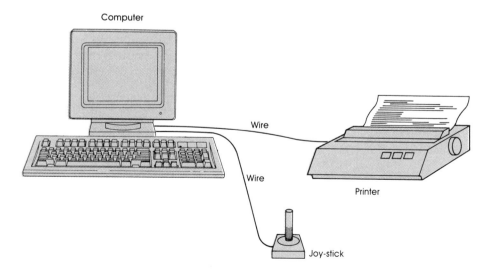

wide were already connected by millions of miles of copper wire. Repeaters and signal boosters were in place. Using the telephone to transmit computer-generated information seemed only logical.

Modems

Unfortunately, computers do not speak the same language as telephones. Computers and computing devices produce **digital signals,** or high and low electrical pulses representing ones and zeros. The telephone system, on the other hand, was designed to transmit the human voice as a continuous **analog signal.** For a computer to "talk" over traditional telephone lines, its digital signal had to be converted into an analog equivalent.

The solution came in the form of a device called a **modem** (MOdulate/DEModulate). A modem converts, or modulates, digital signals into corresponding analog signals so they can be carried over existing phone lines. The same device also converts incoming analog signals, or demodulates them, into their corresponding digital signals so they can be understood by a receiving computer. For two computers to "talk" over the telephone two modems are required—one connected to each computer—to code and decode the digital message (see Figure 15.2).

By combining the existing telephone infrastructure with modems, computers and computing devices anywhere in the world can communicate.

Just as there are different kinds of computers, different kinds of modems are available. The two most popular modems plug directly into telephone jacks and are called **direct-connect modems.** One type consists of a special circuit board that is inserted into an expansion slot in most desktop machines. These boards are included in many portable machines. Such modems are called **internal di-**

Figure 15.2   The Modem: Computers "talk" with one another over telephone lines through the use of modems.

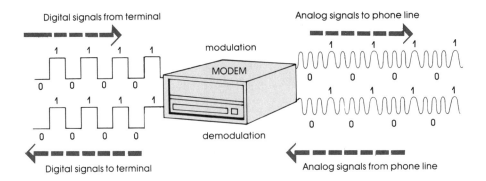

rect-connect modems because they are placed inside the box housing the computer and they use the computer's power supply.

External direct-connect modems are standalone modems housed in a self-contained box. They plug into both the computer (or terminal) and the phone jack. Such modems are not designed to fit into a particular computer model and are used with a wide variety of computers and terminals. However, they do require their own power supply and cost more than the internal variety.

Not all modems are direct-connect models. In an early modem design called an **acoustic coupler,** the telephone receiver (handset) was cradled in a pair of rubber cups located on the modem. The digital signals produced by the computer were converted into audible sounds that were then "spoken" into the telephone receiver. Similarly, the audible sounds produced by the telephone were converted by the modem into digital signals. Audible signals transmitted across the air space between the telephone receiver and the acoustic cups produced slow and often unreliable signals. Background noises could interfere with the data flow, producing transmission errors. Acoustic couplers are still used with telephones that do not have modular connections, such as pay phones and many hotel systems.

Since modems are computer devices, intelligent models with built-in microprocessors are very popular. These **intelligent modems** can be programmed to automatically dial and answer the telephone and disconnect from the phone system when a "conversation" is complete. The more intelligent a modem, the more it can do when combined with sophisticated communications software. Several different kinds of modems are represented in Figure 15.3.

The demand for the transmission of digital signals is rapidly increasing. Wherever possible, telephone companies are converting their lines to transmit digital signals directly. Such lines transmit data faster than their analog counterparts. This is critically important to organizations that transmit large amounts of computer data over long distances. Increasing transmission speeds decreases the cost of long-distance communication. In addition, when digital lines are used, modems are not required because no translation is necessary. However, since the bulk of residential conversations will continue to be via the spoken word, residential phone systems are unlikely to change. Computer conversations involving machines in homes and many offices will continue to require modems.

Channels

Computers can process data at incredible speeds. Transmission lines send and receive information at varying speeds, however, depending on their design. Transmission channels or data communication circuits are the roadways computers use to send data from place to place. Automobile roads vary in width from one-lane country roads to six-lane superhighways, reflecting the speeds our cars can go. Similarly, computer channels come in narrowband, voiceband, and

Figure 15.3   Types of Modems: (a) A Hayes internal direct-connect modem, (b) a Hayes external direct-connect modem, and (c) an acoustic coupler by Lexicon.

(a)

(b)

(c)

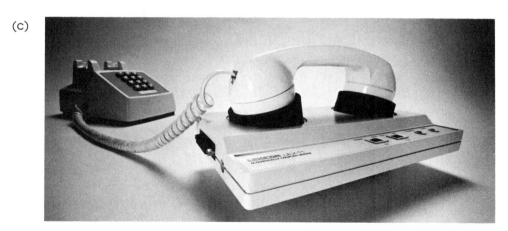

broadband varieties, reflecting data-transmission speeds. Just as roads, modern data circuits are usually bidirectional, with a sending and a receiving channel both open at the same time. A channel's **bandwidth** reflects the amount of data that can be transmitted in a given block of time. The wider the bandwidth the faster data can be transmitted, so more data can be sent in a shorter amount of time.

Computers transmit information in terms of bits, 10 of which usually are required to represent a single character (this includes parity checking bits). A modem transmitting at 1200 bits per second (bps) sends approximately 120 characters per second (cps). This is generally referred to as a **baud rate** of 1200. In general, the term baud rate is used interchangeably with bits per second. Most people read at approximately 120 cps. Despite this, faster communication is important. People often prefer to scan rather than read transmitted information. In addition, when using a desktop computer, data can be stored in memory for leisurely reading later. Transmission speeds of 2400 baud (bps) are common and 9600 are rapidly gaining in popularity as high-speed modems decrease in cost.

Narrowband channels transmit at rates less than 30 cps (300 baud) and are rarely used for the transmission of computer data. Telegraph and teletype machines transmit over narrowband channels. **Voiceband channels** were originally used for the transmission of sound. Standard telephone lines are voiceband channels. Such channels can transmit digital data at between 30 and 960 cps (9600 baud). Voiceband is frequently used to transmit computer-generated data. **Broadband channels** transmit at rates of more than one million cps. Such channels are used for transmitting large amounts of data and frequently use microwave systems or fiber optic cable.

COMMUNICATION MEDIA

Communication channels can use copper wire, radio waves, glass, and satellites to transmit data. Different media support different transmission speeds and therefore have different uses.

Twisted-Pair Copper Wire

A very common, inexpensive, and easy-to-install communication medium is **twisted-pair copper wire,** used with telephones. These standard telephone wires run throughout our homes, offices, and cities, and were designed to carry audio transmissions. Together with modems, they can be used for computer communications. Not being designed for digital transmission, twisted-pair copper wires are relatively slow and are easily affected by electromagnetic interference, which reduces the reliability of the transmission.

Coaxial Cable

Like twisted-pair copper wire, **coaxial cable** uses two conductors, but one of them is cast like a shell around the other (see Figure 15.4). This nearly eliminates electromagnetic interference. Although far more expensive than standard twisted-pair copper wire, coaxial cable can be used to transmit data at very high speeds. In most cases, the high transmission speeds offset the added cost of installation.

Microwave Signals

Microwave signals are extremely high-frequency (broadband) radio waves that can be used to transmit data at high speeds. Microwaves are used to transmit computer data and both television sound and pictures. Microwaves travel along straight lines or lines of sight. When used across the surface of the planet, repeater stations placed approximately 30 miles apart are required to compensate for the curvature of the earth. In large cities, microwave transmission dishes are

---

Figure 15.4   Coaxial Cable: Casting one conductor like a shell around another reduces electromagnetic distortion in coaxial cables. A cross-section is shown.

Figure 15.5   Satellite Transmissions: Microwave signals are transmitted from earth to a relay satellite, which then sends the signal back to earth.

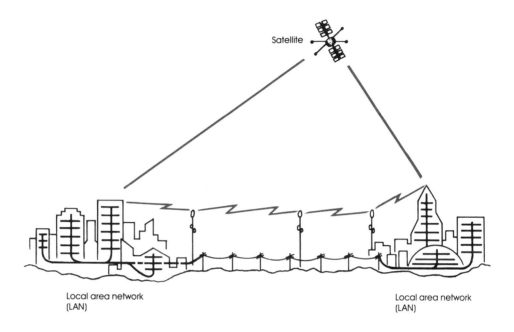

Local area network
(LAN)

Local area network
(LAN)

often placed on rooftops to capture data sent from one location to another within the city. Many universities use such dishes to send data between campuses.

Microwave signals are also beamed to orbiting satellites thousands of miles above the earth, which then relay the signals back to earth stations in distant locations (see Figure 15.5). Microwaves are high-volume, high-speed links in the communication system.

Fiber Optic Cable

The newest link in our communication system is **fiber optic cable.** Fiber optic cables are composed of hair-thin, perfectly clear glass or plastic fibers packed in a protective casing (see Figure 15.6).

These cables conduct laser light rather than electricity. Light provides an extremely broad channel for the transmission of data. Fiber optic cable can transmit vast amounts of data very quickly. Light sources can be turned on and off more rapidly than electricity, producing faster transmission speeds. In addition, fiber optic cable is lightweight and not subject to electrical interference, which causes transmission errors. It also breaks when wiretapped, an important data-

Figure 15.6 Fiber Optic Cable: Laser beams transmit data through fiber optic cables made of glass or plastic. A cross-section is shown.

security feature. This type of medium is so useful for the transmission of computer and voice data that the communications industry expects that as much as one-third of the nation's communications links will be fiber optic by the early 1990s.

SOFTWARE

Judging from the information discussed thus far, it might appear that computers and computing devices require nothing more than wires to communicate. Such is not the case. Although hardware connections are critical, software is required to organize and interpret the signals.

Protocols

When government leaders meet to discuss affairs of state, there are rules governing how the conversations between them will take place. These rules include who speaks and in what order, how one interrupts another speaker, and even how far apart participants stand. These rules are called **protocols.** Similar protocols are as necessary when computers communicate as they are when world leaders communicate. Computers that use different communication protocols cannot talk to each other. Protocols control transmission speeds, the direction of transmission, error detection and correction, and interruption techniques, for example. Both the hardware and the software are governed by communication protocols. As communication between machines becomes more and more important, standard telecommunication protocols are developing.

Microcomputer Software

Microcomputer communication software serves two purposes. First, the software allows the microcomputer and the modem to function in a coordinated way. Software provides the instructions for dialing telephone numbers, establishing connections, and breaking connections when "conversations" are complete. Second, the software lets the user set and change the protocols necessary for data communication. On the simplest level, microcomputer communication software converts a microcomputer into a dumb terminal capable only of sending and receiving information from another computer (see Chapter 5). More commonly, the software lets the microcomputer act both as a terminal and as a processor. By setting transmission speeds, direction, and establishing error-correction techniques, communication is established between devices. The software allows data to be captured on a disk from which, if required, they can later be sent to a printer. This process of capturing data is called **downloading.** Similarly, files stored on a microcomputer can be sent over the communications link to another machine, which is called **uploading.**

Without software, the links could not be established and data could not be transmitted between machines. Computers and computing devices can communicate at widely varying speeds, using a wide variety of media.

FAX TECHNOLOGY

A **fax,** or **facsimile** machine is a device designed to easily transmit images (graphics, text, or both) over standard telephone lines without using a computer. Faxes traditionally transform printed matter into a complex series of dots, similar to a bit-mapped graphic image (see Chapter 14). Using hardware very similar to a modem, these dot patterns are translated into analog signals and transmitted over phone lines to another fax that decodes the signal and prints out the image.

Faxes have taken the world by storm. Anyone who can dial the telephone and use a copy machine can send a fax. All that is needed is a fax machine at the sending and receiving locations, and something to send. Unfortunately, when a fax is received, what you see is what you get! The document, graphic, or photo cannot easily be read into a computer. Fax boards for computers are increasingly popular, and it is now possible to transmit computer-created images and text directly from the screen without first printing the image and placing the output in a fax machine. However, even with computer generated images received by a fax modem built into another computer, it is still not possible to capture the image in computer-usable form and process or edit the image in any way. Fax machines print their output on special thermal paper. However, a number of companies, including Hewlett-Packard, have developed standalone devices that enable faxed output to be printed on a laser printer. Fax modems for laptop computers are rapidly becoming popular expansion devices.

During the Persian Gulf War, fax machines took on new roles. The Kuwaiti resistance sent messages containing important military information to Allied commanders by using fax machines connected to cellular telephones. By frequently moving around, resistance members were able to avoid capture. On a more pleasant note, for short periods, AT&T offered free fax service between soldiers in the Gulf and their families at home. The service got far more use than expected with family members sending everything from letters and photos to hand-drawn love notes from small children. In a number of cases the hand or footprints of newborns were transmitted to fathers otherwise unaware of their birth.

By combining the communications power of the fax with the editing and processing abilities of the computer, the potential exists for making the sharing of text and graphics inexpensive, easy, and popular.

NETWORKING

A **computer network** is frequently defined as a group of computers and computer devices linked together over transmission lines so that information and resources can be shared. Computer networks, especially those that span the continent, are electronic "old-boy/girl networks," connecting people with similar interests in a given industry, field, or discipline. At the physical level, computer networks link machines. At the user level, computer networks link people to people, and people to the information they seek.

Computer networks link computers and peripherals for a specific purpose. These purposes can be very simple: a small office may have two microcomputers that need to share a printer or an extra hard disk. They can be as complex as a national airline reservation system or a research network for super-computer users such as the National Science Foundation Network (NSFnet). How the network is organized, what equipment is used, and how connections are made depend on the distances and devices involved as well as on the needs of the users. Let us examine how networks are designed.

Early Connections

Although the term *networking* has only been recently applied to computers, simple forms of computer networks have existed since the early 1950s. Prior to the microcomputer revolution, an organization would purchase a multiuser machine, either a mainframe or a minicomputer, and then connect terminals, printers, card readers, and other peripherals to it. Such a machine was called a **host computer.** The host computer and its associated devices were located close together. Distances between devices were limited, and connections consisted of coaxial cables. Transmission speeds were high. Both equipment and access were centralized, so the cost of resources was spread over a number of users. Within organizations, computing centers with specialized staffs were given the task of locating information stored in the central computer. Pertinent information was requested from the computing center, and the results were provided hours or days later.

In the early 1980s, the host-computer model was radically altered. With the introduction of the microcomputer, computing power became available to everyone. The model shifted from a highly centralized host computer to individual standalone machines. Nowhere was this more evident than in offices and on college campuses. In offices, microcomputers appeared where no computer connections existed before. On college campuses, rooms previously filled with terminals were replaced by rooms full of standalone microcomputers. The microcomputer model had several advantages over the centralized model:

- Distance was not a limitation. A microcomputer could be placed anywhere because it did not require a connection to anything else.

- Microcomputers were easier and "friendlier" to use than multiuser systems.

- Specialized software, such as spreadsheets and word processing programs, increased productivity.

Unfortunately, the standalone model had disadvantages as well.

- In the centralized model all information was shared and access was limited. In the decentralized model access was widespread but information was limited to what was stored on each individual machine.

- People working together on a project could not share their results as easily.

- Information was often duplicated on many machines, increasing the risk that one or more of these copies was inaccurate.
- The standalone model made it difficult to share expensive peripherals such as laser printers and plotters.

Computer networks are the outgrowth of these two divergent models. Along with the awareness that neither the host model nor the standalone model was ideal came technological advances. New connection devices and communication software made networking possible.

Local Area Networks

When computers, printers, storage devices, and other peripherals are linked together so they can communicate in any combination, a network is formed. The most common network, called a **local area network (LAN),** covers a limited geographic area such as a group of offices, an entire building, a number of nearby buildings, or a college campus. This limited or local area network shares resources and information among a variety of users. LANs connect many devices simultaneously over a common communications channel.

The connections between the devices in local area networks are continually undergoing change. Coaxial cable systems, for example, may be replaced by fiber optic systems. However, all LANs consist of communications channels and specialized systems software that enable the hardware to communicate. Currently, the most popular LANs use Ethernet. Developed by Xerox in association with Intel Corp. and Digital Equipment Corp., Ethernet is a high-speed LAN in which all computers and devices are connected to a single coaxial cable. Specially designed communications software is used to control transmission. Sharing a common high-speed channel results in rapid communication. Complex systems often require signal boosters to ensure accurate transmission of data. Slower-speed LANs, such as AppleTalk, can be operated on twisted-pair copper wire.

A variety of network layouts or **topologies** exist. The star network, the ring network, and the bus network are the most common. All of them are designed so that networked machines can share information and peripherals.

Star Network   A **star network** uses a central or host computer with all the attached computers and peripherals radiating out from this central machine. For any of the attached machines, called **nodes,** to communicate with another, information must flow to and through the central machine (see Figure 15.7). Unlike large centralized systems, each of the nodes is usually a desktop machine capable of independent processing.

This is the easiest network to organize because the central machine coordinates the systems interactions. If one of the nodes should fail to operate properly it can either be removed from the network or simply bypassed, without in-

Figure 15.7   Star Network: In a star network all attached machine (nodes) communicate through a central or host computer.

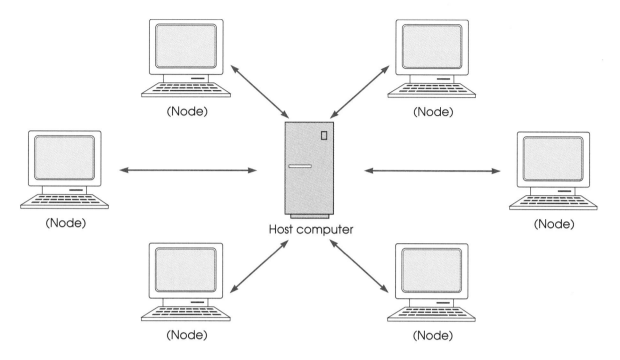

(Node)   (Node)

(Node)   Host computer   (Node)

(Node)   (Node)

terfering with the rest of the LAN. However, if the host computer should fail, the entire LAN fails.

Ring Network   In a **ring network,** a group of computers and peripherals are interconnected in a loop or ring. All nodes are linked together in a circle, one to the other (see Figure 15.8). Each member of the ring can process data directly as well as share applications and data along the network. If one node fails, the other members of the ring can continue to communicate because data can be passed in two directions. However, since data often pass through a number of cooperating machines before they reach their destination, communication can be somewhat slow.

Bus Network   Like the bus used to connect components of the CPU, a **bus network** contains a single, two-directional cable, capable of sending information between two attached devices very quickly (see Figure 15.9). Any two devices on the bus can send information back and forth by simply "taking control of the bus." Complex network protocols control the order in which nodes pass information.

Figure 15.8   Ring Network: In a ring network all nodes are linked together in a circle.

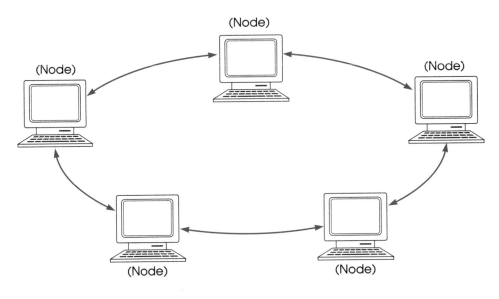

Figure 15.9   Bus Network: In a bus network all nodes are connected to a two-directional cable that can send data between devices.

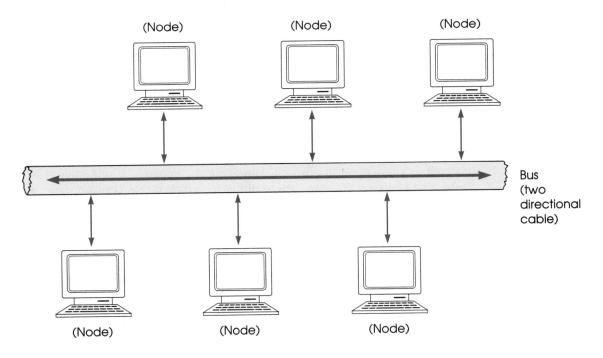

Wide Area Networks

We have seen that direct computer connections (point-to-point connection) can be made between two computing devices, regardless of distance, by using modems. In addition, we have seen that groups of computers and peripherals can communicate over limited distances using LANs. Computers linked together provide a unique environment for the sharing of resources, such as sophisticated laser and color printers, as well as the sharing of ideas.

Connecting LANs over long-distance communications lines with modems or other forms of digital communication creates **wide area networks.** In addition to the LANs, individuals using desktop computers can connect to these networks using modems and standard telephone lines. A wide area network environment enables computer users to share information, ideas, and computer resources. Through such networks, time and distance cease to separate people. This sounds like a futuristic vision, but it is not. It exists today.

A wide range of national and international wide area networks are currently available. Many of these are academic networks that connect colleges and universities throughout the world. Others, such as Dow Jones and MEDLINE, allow subscribers to search huge data bases for the latest up-to-the-minute information.

Electronic mail, introduced in Chapter 1, is the most commonly used service on *all* computer networks. Often called *E-mail,* it is a computerized version of surface mail and memo systems. Each user has an electronic mailbox on a host computer. Just as with a home or office mailbox, others can leave messages in the mailbox for later reading.

An E-mail user creates a message on a local computer. This message can range from a multipage report to a few lines such as: "Hello, I expect to be visiting your university in March. Can you make the necessary local arrangements for me?" The writer supplies the local electronic mail system with the computer address of the person to whom the message is going. This is an electronic address having any number of forms similar to *buffalo!kershner* or *kershner@cs.buffalo.edu.* The local mail system sends the message across the network to the address specified, where it appears in the appropriate electronic mailbox. The receiver then can respond when it is convenient.

Electronic mail is much faster and more reliable than postal services. Messages are transmitted in minutes rather than days. Since messages wait until the receiver has the opportunity to read them, they are not subject to the typical game of "telephone tag," often played when trying to reach busy people by telephone. (A phone call is made to a colleague who is not in. A message is taken. The colleague returns the call only to find the original caller is now not in. A message is left and the tag cycle continues.) E-mail is a rapid, easy way for people to communicate. Time zones and meetings no longer interfere with communication and the sharing of ideas.

On Line

"TALKING" OVER E-MAIL

Long-distance relationships are always difficult. Letter writing takes too long and sometimes people just aren't themselves on the telephone.

Electronic mail, or E-mail, has come to the rescue for many people. E-mail provides an entirely new mode of communication. Over long-distance networks, campuswide networks, and corporate electronic mail systems, people correspond, share secrets, ideas, and reports, trade gossip, and ask for information. To make the E-mail connection even easier, commercial E-mail networks including MCI Mail, AT&T mail, and IBM Information Network have created gateways among them so that users can more easily communicate. The largest nonacademic E-mail provider is CompuServe, and although not formally linked to the other systems, CompuServe has a link to MCI Mail and the Internet.

Although there are no formal rules governing what to write or what not to write using E-mail, an etiquette does exist. Users are warned not to "cc," or copy, messages to too many others so that the messages do not wind up on the wrong screens. Saturating the network with classified ads or political announcements is frowned upon.

Real communication involves emotion. The E-mail equivalent of yelling is typing in capital letters, and writing messages entirely in lower-case is considered mumbling. Most remarkable is the freedom people feel when using E-mail. Experts feel that E-mail can contain very open conversations where participants really let their hair down. E-mail has been used to make romantic dates, plan parties, and just blow off steam.

Many executives resist using E-mail because they feel that typing is for those lower on the corporate ladder. Brian Blackmarr, a Dallas-based office-automation expert, told *Newsweek* about one manager who was so frustrated at having to use a keyboard that he sent an obscene message to the information-processing director. The message was signed "Anonymous." Unfortunately for the executive, his E-mail system automatically attached information identifying him as the sender.

Privacy on E-mail is always a problem. While messages are supposed to be secret, it is easy enough to send a copy of another person's message. Federal law makes intercepting E-mail a crime, but many networks are rumored to have message graveyards where messages can be read by anyone with the correct access code. The sheer volume of E-mail on most systems may make this concern unnecessary.

The benefits of E-mail outweigh any of the risks. With E-mail, students can leave messages for instructors; reports, papers, and ideas can be shared over long distances; and friends can keep in touch whenever they have a moment. E-mail encourages people to share ideas. Workers who would never directly make suggestions to their bosses find E-mail an easy and comfortable outlet. Besides, sending and receiving E-mail is fun.

Sources: Don Steinberg, "Conquer the E-Mail Frontier," *PC Computing,* June 1991, pp. 190–196. Barbara Kantrowitz, Nadine Joseph, and Susan Agrest, "A New Way of Talking," *Newsweek,* March 17, 1986, p. 71.

In addition to academic networks, companies such as AT&T Mail, MCI Mail, Sprint Mail, and the IBM Information Network offer electronic mail (E-mail) services.

In addition to data base use and E-mail, wide area networks make our daily lives easier by allowing for worldwide air, hotel, and automobile reservations. Others permit the purchase of tickets to shows, concerts, and sporting events from our homes. Still others link academic institutions in the United States to their counterparts in dozens of countries around the world. Others, sponsored by the U.S. government, enable researchers to share ideas and equipment.

Sharing resources, ideas and information improves productivity and stimulates creativity. Distance and time zones cease to be problems for collaborative efforts, and expensive resources become available to those who need them.

Wide area networks fall into four general groups: bulletin boards, academic computer networks, corporate/business networks, and information networks.

Bulletin Boards

The simplest wide area network is the electronic bulletin board. Everyone is familiar with the concept of a bulletin board. At home they consist of important papers, phone numbers, coupons, and other items secured to some type of board for safe keeping. In grocery stores they are a place to announce garage sales, to advertise services such as house painting and babysitting, and to offer discount coupons on grocery items. The classified pages of college and local newspapers often have sections in which people can leave personal messages, such as "Happy Birthday Dad" or "Male 21 interested in blonde female," and advertise services and products. **Electronic bulletin board systems (EBBS or BBS)** serve the same purpose as their nonelectronic counterparts. Instead of thumbtacks and tape, electronic BBSs use computers, modems, and telephones. To connect to the bulletin board, the board's computer is called on the telephone by another computer. Messages are left and information is exchanged over this electronic connection.

Hundreds of thousands of computer owners use their computers as a means of developing electronic relationships. Bulletin boards facilitate the exchange of all kinds of information from stock quotes and telephone numbers to programs and user-written software called **shareware.** Chatting electronically with others, discussing hardware and software problems, or simply socializing with electronic friends are popular bulletin board pastimes.

Computer bulletin boards take two forms: public boards and commercial boards. Most public BBSs are free. They are maintained by an individual or a group, or they are sponsored by an organization such as a business or university. These systems are usually limited to one machine type (Apple, IBM, Amiga, Macintosh), although some can be reached by any microcomputer. Most systems have on-line help facilities to assist new users. Just as information posted with a thumbtack on a grocery store bulletin board is available to anyone who passes by, so information posted electronically is available to anyone who has access to a given electronic board.

Commercial bulletin boards are components of larger commercial data base services. Bulletin boards such as CompuServe are available only by paying a fee to become a subscriber. Fees are based on the length of time a subscriber is connected to the service. Commercial bulletin boards include news services, access to special publications or stock market reviews, and electronic mail services as well as entertainment, hotel, and restaurant information. Software can be exchanged, free classified ads posted, and electronic shopping or banking is available.

Bulletin boards provide users with an easy and convenient means of communicating. Through the telephone and microcomputers, they link interesting people throughout the country.

Academic Computer Networks

Within the last five years, every major American university has become connected to a variety of academic computer networks. All of these are interconnected on what is called the Internet, so that messages and files can be electronically sent anywhere within the academic community. The purpose of **academic computer networks** is to provide an environment where geographically separated faculty members, researchers, administrators, and students can communicate, share ideas and resources, and work jointly on projects. Access and use of computer networks has produced a noticeable increase in the productivity of computer scientists and other scientists and researchers.

Wide area academic computer networks offer a number of services. These include electronic mail, file transfer, and access to remote systems.

As we discussed under wide area networks, electronic mail is the most widely used of the services provided on academic networks. E-mail links users and hardware together providing an easy, comfortable way to share ideas and information.

With file transfer, files can be transferred between any two computers attached to the network. Files can contain papers, computer programs, computer graphics, and anything else that can be represented electronically. The ability to transfer such information makes collaborative efforts easy. A paper can be drafted in one location and reviewed, corrected, and commented on in another location on the same day. A program with a bug can be sent across the country to be debugged. Using a computer network, joint projects are not limited to a single location. They can involve individuals across the nation and in other parts of the world.

Through a network, a scientist can connect, or **log in,** to a distant computer without disconnecting from the local computer. In other words, using high-speed computer links, a scientist connected to a mainframe at one university can also connect and run programs, for example, on a supercomputer located at a distant university. Compared to using a modem and standard telephone lines, such a system provides a high-speed, relatively inexpensive means of communicating.

Although all academic networks provide similar services, their goals and constituencies are different. BITNET and NSFnet are two examples of academic computer networks.

> **BITNET** (Because It's Time NETwork) is a cooperative network that began between City University of New York and Yale University in 1981. It is a discipline-independent network serving hundreds of colleges and universities in the United States with connections in 21 countries, including Canada, Israel, Japan, and most European nations. The goal was to create a network connecting all higher educational institutions. Through BITNET, faculty members, administrators, and students can communicate, share ideas, exchange electronic mail, and transfer files. Everything from research papers and financial reports to personal chats and career advice is sent over the network. Connections are made over leased telephone lines paid for by individual institutions. Reasonable membership fees are charged to support services.
>
> **NSFnet** is a network in the process of creation. In 1984 the National Science Foundation (NSF) established the Office of Advanced Computing, whose task it was to provide both supercomputers and access to them to researchers nationwide. Two projects resulted. One project is charged with creating supercomputing centers across the country. The other originally established a national network connecting the scientists to the supercomputers. Currently, NSFnet has links to about a dozen midlevel networks in addition to the supercomputer centers. These midlevel networks have developed regionally or statewide with the support of the National Science Foundation, local governments, and universities.

The **Internet** is a collection of interconnected wide area academic and research networks running the same network protocol (TCP/IP). The Internet includes NSFnet, MILnet (an unclassified military network), and a number of academic and statewide networks. (Some people use the term *Internets* to convey the multi-network nature of the system.) Currently, there are over 100,000 organizations connected. Other academic and research networks, not formally part of the Internet, and including a number of European networks and BITNET, have special **gateways** or network-to-network connections. This makes it possible for researchers, educators, administrators, and students to communicate with ease worldwide.

This evolution from separate to interconnected networks (Internets) is leading toward the establishment, hopefully by the late 1990s, of NREN (National Research and Education Network). This is envisioned as a super high-speed national network.

Corporate/Business Networks

As might be expected, if the academic community has found networking to be an invaluable tool that increases productivity, the business community would find it useful in much the same way. Most of the networks used by businesses provide benefits in two areas:

1. *Intraorganizational services.* Local area networks are used to improve intraorganizational services and productivity. Using corporate networks, ideas, information, and resources can be shared within a company. Such networks improve decision making by giving executives the data needed to make decisions. In addition, networks improve access to the expertise available within an organization. Furthermore, expensive computer resources can be effectively shared at a substantial saving. Businesses indicate that the improved communication and easy access to hardware provided through local area networks enhance productivity.

2. *Consumer services.* Wide area networks provide new consumer services simply not available prior to their development. Such services include electronic banking, advanced hotel and transportation reservation systems, and improvements in customer service within large retail chains.

Although local area networks are playing an increasing role in the daily working of America's corporations, they have had relatively limited impact on the everyday lives of American citizens. On the other hand, wide area corporate networks are increasingly evident around us.

Transportation Industry   Anyone who has visited a travel agent; taken a trip by plane, ship, or train; or rented a car has seen firsthand the effect of computers on the transportation industry. Not so obvious is that the services provided are available because of wide area networks. The oldest of these networks is SABRE, the airline reservation system developed by American Airlines. Using such networks, agents can reserve and cancel seats, check flight schedules, print tickets and boarding passes, arrange for special meals, as well as provide services for the handicapped and children traveling alone. SABRE and similar networks operated by other airlines include information on all flights (see Figure 15.10).

System access is not limited to travel agents. Airline networks let individuals call the airlines and make reservations or check flights. The networks contain a large data base of information including weather reports, landing schedules, and pricing structures. Similar services are available on the networks serving other modes of transportation, such as trains and buses.

Hotel and Motel Industry   Just as individuals and travel agents can make transportation arrangements by connecting with industrywide reservation systems, so too can hotel and motel reservations and services be arranged. The

Figure 15.10   Computerized Travel: Using wide area networks such as SABRE, travel agents can make reservations, print tickets, and arrange for special airline services.

largest hotel and motel chains, including Holiday Inn (Holidex) and Hilton Hotels, have their own chainwide computer network. By calling a central number, usually toll free, and speaking with a reservation clerk or connecting to a microcomputer directly, rooms can be reserved, and special services such as cribs and handicapped facilities can be arranged. These systems also maintain customer billing, automated wakeup services, inventory controls, and forwarding of messages.

Electronic Banking   The largest, most comprehensive industrywide network exists in the banking industry. The motivation for establishing such a network came from the Federal Reserve System. Trillions of transactions are carried out annually between the Federal Reserve and its member banks. In order to handle the volume of transactions between banks, the Federal Reserve established FEDWIRE. Using this system, funds are transferred electronically between banks. Effective, accurate accounting is maintained without any cash or formal paperwork required among member banks. This system has proved so effective that independent cooperative systems have sprung up worldwide to serve other thrift organizations. These **electronic fund transfer (EFT)** systems have made national and international banking quicker, safer, easier, and substantially less expensive.

As banking became more computerized and networking became a more common procedure between banks, the idea of banking networks was extended to the bank customer as well. With the establishment of automated teller machines (ATMs), local area networks designed specifically for routine bank transactions became available to the public.

Retail Industry   As we discussed earlier, cash registers do not simply store money anymore. In most large retail stores and in an increasing number of smaller stores as well, cash registers are modified computer terminals or **point-of-sale (POS) systems.** Although these systems still handle cash transactions, they also print customer bills, check a customer's credit, and keep track of inventory. These terminals are the end-points of local area networks established within a given retail organization. The majority of these networks serve individual stores within a specific region, such as western New York or southeastern California. The large chain stores, such as Sears and J.C. Penney, have national networks connecting individual stores with centralized warehouse and credit facilities.

Information Networks

We use computer networks almost daily. These links provide access to information and services unheard of 10 years ago.

The information explosion has prompted the establishment of electronic data bases to store the massive amounts of information being generated. Some of these data bases are limited to specific types of information, such as journal articles and abstracts in the fields of medicine (MEDLINE) and law (LEXIS). Other data bases gather information and organize it for easy access. Sources include newspaper and magazine articles, movie reviews, stock quotes, and corporate reports. Initially, such information was available electronically only to a few selected organizations. Connections often required specialized equipment and software, and high membership fees where charged.

In recent years, however, many of these data base organizations or **information utilities,** have "gone public," making the information available to any microcomputer owner willing to subscribe to the service. Fees reflect the needs of the utilities' users. Just as with long-distance telephone charges, fees are higher during working hours than late at night or on weekends. Individuals and businesses that require up-to-the-minute information during the work day pay higher fees for the service. Those for whom time is not quite as critical make alternative arrangements.

Access to information utilities is a limited form of networking that is basically the sharing of resources. Through these networks, individuals across the nation and the world can tap into the information available.

A number of information utilities have taken the data base retrieval model and advanced it considerably, offering additional services to subscribers. These utilities, called **information networks,** offer subscribers the kinds of services that the academic networks provide their users. Information networks give users access to data base information and bulletin boards. They make electronic mail available and easy to use, and often provide travel and shopping opportunities. In a sense, they are full-service networks whereby subscribers share resources as well as ideas.

Many such networks now exist (see Figure 15.11). The most popular information networks are CompuServe, a division of H&R Block; Dow Jones News/Retrieval Service, operated by Dow Jones & Co., publishers of the *Wall Street Jour-*

Figure 15.11   Information Network: Subscribers to full-service networks such as CompuServe have access to data base information, bulletin boards, and electronic mail services.

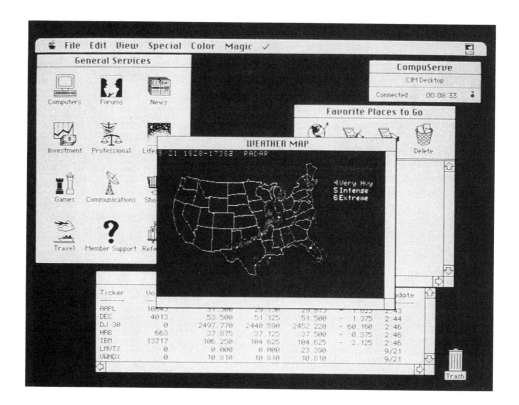

nal; and IBM Information Network, operated by IBM. Subscribers to these services can send electronic mail to other network subscribers; catch up on the day's news, weather, and sports; and search extensive data bases for information ranging from the condition of the dollar on international markets to computer crime. The most frequent search is for financial data, including information on stocks, bonds, and investments. Portfolio analysis is often available, and historical information on corporate America is maintained.

Special-interest groups use the bulletin boards provided by these information networks to share ideas ranging from medical treatments to the solutions to complex computer games. Subscribers can check airline schedules, buy tickets, and shop in electronic catalogs. Some services, such as Dow Jones, focus more on the needs of business people while still providing a full range of services.

Information networks provide their subscribers with access to ideas, information, and people to an extent never before imagined. Just as academic networks have reduced the barriers that separate researchers, students, and administrators, information networks are making time, distance, and location irrelevant to individual and corporate subscribers.

As computers have become more important in our lives, we have come to realize that while their individual use has its advantages, isolation in any form has disadvantages as well. Networking provides us with a means of sharing information, ideas, and resources without reducing the benefits standalone systems provide. Networking has the potential to help unify the planet and its people despite time and distance.

SUMMARY

The electronic transmission of information over long distances is called **telecommunication.** This information includes data transmitted by telephone and television, as well as computer-generated data. **Telecomputing** is the exchange of information between computers and computing devices over communication lines.

The simplest way to connect computers and computing devices together is to connect the equipment with wires. Such direct connections operate over only limited distances.

Computers can communicate over telephone wires through the use of a **modem.** Telephone wires transmit analog rather than digital signals. Modems are used to code (modulate) and decode (demodulate) messages and computer data for transmission.

Transmission channels are the pathways used to send computer data from one place to another. They are usually bidirectional. A channel's **bandwidth** reflects the amount of data that can be transmitted in a given block of time. The wider the bandwidth, the faster the transfer of data.

Communications channels use **twisted-pair copper wires, coaxial cables, microwave signals,** and **fiber optic cables** to transmit information.

Software is required to organize and interpret the signals transmitted between devices. Telecommunication **protocols** control transmission speeds, the direction of transmission, error detection and correction, and interruption techniques. Microcomputer communication software allows the microcomputer to act as both a terminal and a processor. **Uploading** and **downloading** of information are facilitated.

A **fax** is a modem-like device designed to transmit images over standard telephone lines without necessarily using a computer.

A computer **network** is a group of computers and computer devices linked together over transmission lines so that information, resources, and ideas can be shared. Computers linked in a limited geographic area are called a **local area network (LAN).** Common network **topologies** include the **star, ring** and **bus** designs.

Connecting LANs and other computers using long-distance communication lines and modems creates a **wide area network.** Wide area networks provide universities, industries, government, and individuals with access to data base information, **electronic mail (E-mail),** file transfer, and remote **log in.** Networking lets people share ideas, information, and resources despite time and distance.

Key Words

As an extra review of the chapter, try defining the following terms. If you have trouble with any of them, refer to the page number listed.

academic computer network *(410)*

acoustic coupler *(395)*

analog signal *(394)*

bandwidth *(397)*

baud rate *(397)*

BITNET *(411)*

broadband channels *(397)*

bus network *(405)*

coaxial cable *(398)*

computer network *(402)*

digital signal *(394)*

direct-connect modem *(394)*

downloading *(401)*

electronic bulletin board (EBBS or BBS) *(409)*

electronic fund transfer *(414)*

external direct-connect modem *(395)*

fax (facsimile) *(401)*

fiber optic cable *(399)*

gateway *(411)*

host computer *(403)*

information network *(415)*

information utility *(414)*

intelligent modem *(395)*

internal direct-connect modem *(394–95)*

Internet *(411)*

local area network (LAN) *(404)*

log in *(410)*

microwave signal *(398)*

modem *(394)*

narrowband channel *(397)*

node *(404)*

Test Your Knowledge

1. Define *telecomputing*.

2. How is telecommunications different from telecomputing?

3. What does a modem do?

4. List the three types of modems.

5. What is a communication channel?

6. How do narrowband, voiceband, and wideband channels differ?

7. List four kinds of communications media.

8. Why is fiber optic cable popular as a transmission medium?

9. What is a computer communication protocol?

10. Why is software important in microcomputer communications?

11. What is a fax machine? How does it work?

12. What is a computer network? What does LAN stand for?

13. Describe the three most common LAN topologies.

14. What is a wide area network?

15. What is the Internet?

16. How does E-mail work?

17. List the industries that are currently making extensive use of wide area networks.

18. What is an information utility?

19. How does an information network differ from an information utility?

20. Name the most popular information networks.

Expand Your Knowledge

1. Contact a representative of your computing center. Discuss your campus network. What transmission medium is most popular? Are all computers and computing equipment connected to the network? What academic networks are available to researchers on your campus? Can anyone use E-mail? Write a short (three- to five-page) paper detailing your information.

2. Automated libraries are gaining popularity on college campuses. Increasingly, such library automation systems are connected to campuswide networks. Research such library/campus-network connections. Write a short paper on the services such interconnections provide.

3. Write a short paper on the history and planned development of academic networks. Be sure to include CSnet, ARPAnet, NSFnet, the Internet, and the proposed NREN.

4. Investigate the public bulletin boards available in your local area. Compile a description of these bulletin boards. Include phone numbers, services, fees if any, and contacts. Sources can include books in your local or campus library, local computer-user groups, your local paper, and computer stores.

5. Research CompuServe. Write a short paper on how one gains access to this network and the services it provides. Include the costs involved in using the network.

16

Artificial Intelligence

CHAPTER OUTLINE

Since the mid-1950s, when the first computers, often called electronic brains, were invented, people have been fascinated with the possibility of creating intelligent machines. These machines not only would do the dull and boring tasks that fill so much of our time but also would assist us in tasks yet unimagined. Like us, they could learn and think, but they would do whatever we commanded. In the 1950s, as computers became more and more capable of performing complex mathematical tasks, scientists believed that it would be only a matter of time, a decade perhaps, until such artificial-thinking machines would be everywhere. In the ensuing 40 years computers have become ubiquitous. They are everywhere—in our homes, vehicles, schools, and businesses. They provide entertainment, help cook our food, and control our cars, aircraft, and spacecraft. In many instances computers *are* performing the dull, boring, and sometimes dangerous tasks people used to perform in our factories, laboratories, and power plants. Yet despite their powerful impact on our lives, they are mere tools. In general, they do not think, learn, or understand the world around them. The more we experiment with the development of intelligent machines, the farther off their reality appears to be.

After studying this chapter you will be able to:

- Define artificial intelligence (AI).

- Describe the two common approaches taken in AI research.

- Discuss expert systems and their development.

- Identify the different approaches used in the development of software to understand natural language.

- Identify the problem areas for natural language recognition systems.

- Understand computer vision.

- Describe commonsense reasoning.

- Distinguish between "blind" and "intelligent" robots.

DEFINING ARTIFICIAL INTELLIGENCE

Artificial intelligence (AI) is the study of how to make computers do things that in people require basic intelligence, and that people find easy. But what are the attributes that define intelligence? Are they the common everyday tasks we perform, often unconsciously, that make us intelligent? How will we know when we have an intelligent machine if we are not really clear what constitutes intelligence in human beings?

So, what is AI? "We all agree," observed AI researcher Albert Shank, "that we would like to endow machines with an attribute that we can't define." In 1950 Alan Turing (see Chapter 2) provided a definition for recognizing an artificially intelligent machine that remains in use today. He suggested that a person and a computer be placed in a setting so as to make possible a dialogue between them. The setting would require that the person be unable to see the machine and that they not be required to communicate verbally. As the result of their "chat," the device would be said to be artificially intelligent if the person did not know that the other party to the chat was a machine.

Computers are excellent at tasks such as number-crunching, sorting long lists, and recalling everything that is stored in memory. However, the everyday things that people do almost naturally, such as understanding language, learning, moving around in the world, and using common sense, are exceptionally difficult for computers. These everyday skills are exactly those things with which scientists in the field of artificial intelligence would like to endow computers.

AI: SCIENCE OR ENGINEERING?

The phrase "artificial intelligence" is an unfortunate title for so important a research area and does not accurately identify what the field is all about. AI would be better described as research into machine intelligence or simulated intelligence. It is the attempt to develop a series of computer programs that would act, when interacted with, as though human. These programs would behave essentially the way people would when presented with specific problems. In other words, the computer or the person would reach the same conclusion.

Toward this end, research into AI has taken two approaches. The first has been to use the computer as a tool for studying human intelligence. These researchers are concerned with the science of intelligence. They are interested in understanding how people think, and are using the computer to simulate cognition (thinking), natural language, and perception. They are less interested in developing computers that will act like humans than they are in learning what it is that makes us human and by consequence intelligent.

Scientists using the second, or engineering, approach are more interested in building machines that act as though they are people. These machines are easier to use because they behave more the way we do. The Japanese have taken this variant so seriously that they have created a state-run, multimillion-dollar research program, often called the fifth generation project, to endow computers with *practical* AI capabilities. Thus far, they have not succeeded.

Regardless of approach, advances in AI research affect the computers we deal with. Let us examine a number of the dominant fields within AI.

MACHINE LEARNING

As early as the late 1940s and 1950s, researchers had experimented with "teaching" computers how to play games with well-defined rules. This is called **machine learning.** Arthur L. Samuel, first at the University of Illinois and later with IBM, focused on programming a computer to play checkers by providing it not only with the rules of the game—the legal moves of the pieces—but with the rules of experience that a veteran player would have acquired. This is experience-based learning. Such rules are called **heuristics.** These rules modeled the way children initially "learn" to play the game. However, a child's initial attempts at a game are aimed simply at "getting a feel" for the game. With the computer, prior to each move, every rule stored in memory is checked to decide what to do. In addition, Samuel's program attached values to each possible move. By looking at possible future moves and calculating the probable success of any given move, the program seemed to act intelligently. This system is capable of **rote learning,** or learning by memorization. The computer follows a complex but essentially predetermined path to a solution. The learning is rule-based. This is not unlike a child's learning to multiply. The program played reasonably well. But Samuel was not a checkers expert, and the computer played only as well as he did.

Samuel realized that in order for his checkers program to act "intelligently," the system would have to learn from its mistakes. This kind of learning is called **learning by generalization.** To enable the program to learn in this way, Samuel built in code that recorded the successes or failures of each move. Later, when a move was repeated, the mathematical values assigned to each move were adjusted, up or down, to reflect earlier successes or failures. In other words, the program learned from past mistakes and adjusted its "behavior" accordingly. This combination of rule-based and experience-based learning enabled Samuel's checkers program to beat the reigning checkers champion.

Like checkers, AI researchers in the area of machine learning have successfully taught computers to play chess, backgammon, and GO (an Oriental board game that is popular, especially among college students in some areas). In all cases the systems combined the games' rules with "expert" advice and experience-based learning to produce effective competitive capabilities.

Many AI researchers question whether these sophisticated programs truly represent learning. In each case, the computer follows paths outlined by its programmer. Real, independent thought is not evident. Human learning involves more than just learning rules and experiential knowledge; it lets us make generalizations about objects, things, and rules. We invent new rules as necessary and modify or eliminate old rules that don't work. In an attempt to simulate human learning, researchers have designed programs that contain a number of different learning styles, which include:

- **rote learning**—"rules of thumb" (heuristics) and memorization
- **learning by generalization**—learning from mistakes; that is, trial-and-error
- **induction**—learning by example; by noting the similarities and differences between the current situation and previous ones
- **inference**—forming new rules from available information—"If X is like Y, then they are most likely the same"

A truly intelligent machine could start with an initial set of information, often called a **knowledge base.** This would include basic rules about the world that the computer will be involved with, and heuristics or experience rules provided to the computer by the programmer. Added to this are examples from which the system can generalize, and trial-and-error algorithms that let the system evaluate its mistakes. To learn, like a child playing a new game, the machine "takes a stab" at solving a particular problem or answering a question. Depending upon the result of this attempt, the knowledge base is modified. With enough trials and errors, the machine makes fewer mistakes.

Most current computer learning systems are unable to combine all of the learning styles at once. As a result, when presented with a series of events that require different methods and quick adjustments, current systems fail. People are able to use many different learning styles essentially simultaneously, moving effortlessly among them as required.

EXPERT SYSTEMS

Computer programs that attempt to duplicate the ways in which professionals make decisions are called **expert systems.** These are very advanced, highly sophisticated special-purpose software. Expert systems, sometimes called **knowledge-based systems,** have been used in medicine to analyze symptoms and diagnose diseases. They also have been used to design computer circuits and to write computer programs.

To develop an expert system, both the rules used by human experts and the human knowledge acquired in a narrow discipline must be collected and organized. Human experts use rules of thumb, or heuristics, that may or may not be written down when they evaluate situations or make decisions. These rules are combinations of formal learning, experience, and common sense. What makes human decision-making so difficult to predict is that our rules of thumb are often applied unconsciously; that is, they spring from our mind. Our logic often is based on imprecise information, intuition, or feeling. The decision-making process frequently looks something like this:

> If the car doesn't start and the lights don't work, then the battery is dead.

Such rules of thumb can be abstracted to the form:

> If *A* and *B* are occurring, then in all likelihood the problem is *X*.

An expert system records these rules of thumb as a series of if/then statements. Rules for combining these if/then statements also go into the system. This forms a knowledge base or a data base of knowledge questions. To create the data base, human experts are interviewed in detail and tracked as they go about their work so that the rules they have developed by experience can be recorded formally along with basic facts about the discipline. Each rule (if/then statement) reflects a specific piece of the human expert's knowledge. In addition to the rules that form the knowledge base, a set of programs is developed to manipulate the rules to make judgments or intelligent guesses in a humanlike fashion. This set of programs is called the **inference engine.** As the software is being developed, new rules may be added and previous rules modified based on continued observation and testing within the specific area of expertise.

Expert systems are usually designed for use by people working in a specific field, with little or no computer experience. Natural languages such as English, plus the specialized vocabulary of the particular discipline, are often used in the if/then statements. In systems designed to assist doctors, medical terms are used. Many systems let users ask the system for information about the rules used by the system to make decisions.

Expert systems exist in a wide variety of fields. In medicine they include CADUCEUS, which diagnoses 500 diseases by cross-referencing more than 3000 symptoms; PUFF, which is used to analyze breath samples in the diagnosis of cardiopulmonary disease; and MYCIN, which analyzes blood samples to diagnose blood diseases and recommends drug treatments. Other systems such as PROSPECTOR aid in the discovery and evaluation of mineral deposits (see Figure 16.1), and XCON is used by Digital Equipment Corp. to configure mini-computers and workstations for clients.

Figure 16.1   Expert Systems: PROSPECTOR, an expert system that predicts the potential for finding mineral deposits, was developed by interviewing expert prospectors.

On Line

THE AUTOMATED POST OFFICE

While automated cash registers and teller machines have been changing the way we shop and bank, a quiet revolution has been occurring in post offices around the country.

If you look at the bottom of many of the envelopes you receive, you will find bar codes printed on them. In an effort to process the mail more quickly and economically, the U.S. Postal Service is supporting the development of special equipment to scan an envelope optically, find and interpret the address and zip code, and use this information to sort the mail automatically.

While reading an address on an envelope may seem a simple task, it is really quite complex. Researchers at the State University of New York at Buffalo are designing a group of expert systems that can (1) distinguish the mailing address from other material printed on the envelope, no matter where the address is located, (2) analyze the shape of typed or handwritten characters, and (3) use a complex dictionary of addresses to print the zip code's bar code equivalent on the envelope for further processing.

For people, locating the address on an envelope is straightforward. For computers this task is very difficult. Computers must first "learn" to locate the address before they can make any attempt to decipher it. Magazine covers, junk mail fliers, and shiny plastic windows that often obscure addresses complicate the process. People seem to be able to "zoom in" on the address. "We don't look at just one thing" when decoding the information on an envelope, says Sargur Srihari, director of the research group. Rather, we use a large number of visual cues. The research team's goal is to identify and teach these "clues" to the computer.

The "clues" include, for example, locating blocks of text that have the correct shape as a standard address. The SUNY computer can locate the address correctly 90 percent of the time. The computer has then been taught to identify the zip code and has rules for deciphering even handwritten numbers. Numbers have predictable shapes, and the computer can learn to use cues such as curves, sharp angles, and straight lines to identify numbers. The researchers are quick to explain that more than 130 rules are used by the computer in recognizing numbers. The SUNY research computer can read approximately 75 percent of all handwritten zip codes. Current postal service technology, in contrast, can manage no more than 5 percent. However, the new process requires as much as a minute to decipher each envelope. Research into a faster system is ongoing.

Eventually, bar codes reflecting this process will appear on all mail and will be used to route mail to the post office nearest its destination. At present, businesses and individuals use the five-digit zip code, and final address-by-address sorting is done by hand. When the nine-digit zip code becomes common, it is hoped that mechanical sorters will use the bar code to sort mail by individual street block or office building. The system may eventually even be able to place the mail in the carrier's bag automatically.

Source: "Research on Reading Machines," *Laboratory for Document Image Understanding,* Department of Computer Science, State University of New York at Buffalo, October 1990.

A U.S. Coast Guard system analyzes distress signals sent out by ships in danger and provides assistance in locating them. Expert systems played a vital role in the air campaign during the Persian Gulf War in 1991.

The decision-making ability of well-designed expert systems is quite high. However, people are often reluctant to use such systems. As with all computer programs, expert systems are tools that can help people make faster, easier, and, it is hoped, wiser decisions.

HUMAN/COMPUTER COMMUNICATION

Natural Language Understanding

As discussed in Chapter 8, research into **natural language understanding** is progressing toward the development of systems that comprehend and then act upon human language. One of the earliest research areas involved natural language–designed programs that aimed to translate information quickly, efficiently, and automatically from one language to another. This became known as **machine translation.**

It was reasoned that if the computer had all of the grammatical and organizational or **syntax** rules of a language and a complete dictionary, then the computer would be able to translate information between languages easily. These systems were able to translate simple, unambiguous sentences, similar to those found in a child's early reader. Natural language, as written and spoken, however, is filled with words and phrases that have multiple meanings, contain ambiguities, and are idiomatic. Natural language is more than rules of grammar and structure (syntax). The meaning of words and phrases, or **semantics,** is critical for understanding.

One of the classic stories of an early attempt at machine translation, using a system that did not include semantics, is the following. The researcher wanted to translate the sentence "The spirit is willing but the flesh is weak" from English to Russian and then back again to confirm a valid translation. The computer had been programmed with all the necessary vocabulary and syntax rules. The resulting English translation was, "The vodka is good but the meat is rotten." Unfortunately, although the words translated correctly, the meaning was totally lost. For translation to be successful, the computer must understand the meaning of the words and phrases that make up the sentence.

With the recognition that machine translation requires an understanding of natural language, research moved away from the practical into the realm of pure science. Research into how the mind learns natural language and how to represent language and all of its diverse meanings has become the focus of much of the AI research in the field. With the creation of LISP (see Chapter 8),

AI researchers had a computer language capable of representing the complexity of natural language.

Research into natural language understanding has taken two approaches. Some computer scientists have joined forces with researchers in linguistics and psychology to investigate how natural language is acquired, deciphered, and comprehended by people. They then develop computer models of natural language to better understand how we use language. In Figure 16.2, we see a **se-**

Figure 16.2   A *semantic network* is a structure for storing data that uses links or nodes that specify facts, concepts, and their relationships.

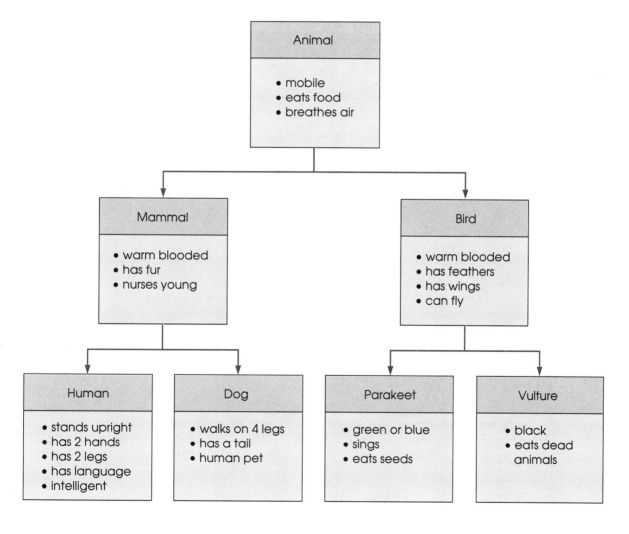

mantic network. This is a structure for storing data using links or nodes that specify the facts and concepts, as well as their relationships.

Another popular representation is called the **frame,** found in Figure 16.3. A frame is a collection of data and associated rules that, taken as a unit, provide a natural language system with the information it needs to understand a fact or concept. The more closely the computer model mimics natural language and human concepts, the more clearly language and the human learning process is understood. For these researchers, the focus is on understanding language and the human mind.

Other researchers are working on the development of **natural language interfaces.** In such systems, a person can query a data base for information, or input instructions to the computer in ordinary sentences, and receive appropriate answers. For example, the user may "ask" that a data base "List the names of all clients whose permanent residence is Alaska" or ask "How many students received a grade lower than C on the first exam?"

Although such systems accept queries written in what appears to be natural language, the scope of the questions, the structure of the sentences, and the al-

---

Figure 16.3   A *frame* is a collection of data, associated rules, and procedures that relate them, that describe a fact or concept.

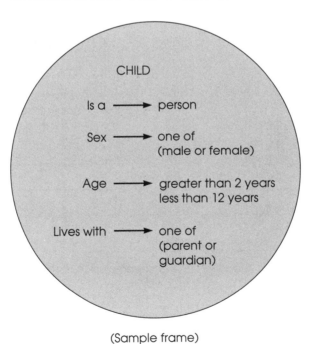

(Sample frame)

lowable vocabulary are by necessity very limited. They do provide a more natural, "friendly" interface. Within limitations, natural language systems can work effectively. Unfortunately, users may get a false sense of the capabilities of the system, and they may lose sight of its limitations. Novice users may begin to expect the system to behave much like the computers on "Star Trek"—able to answer almost any question. When these systems fail to answer questions outside their sphere of knowledge, users can become confused and frustrated.

The development of programs that truly understand natural language is not really around the corner. These systems will require a far greater understanding of human learning and use of language than currently exists. However, the use of natural language systems for specific purposes will continue to expand as the need for easy access to computerized information becomes more and more important.

Universal Language Recognition Systems

Progress in the research and development of devices that recognize spoken language has been even more difficult than designing systems that understand natural language that is input at a keyboard. Work on "universal" **speech recognition** or **natural language recognition** systems—systems that understand human languages as *spoken* by anyone, continues at many universities and corporations. There is as yet no general voice-processing system. In Chapter 5, we found that speech recognition systems taught to understand the speech of one individual are gaining in popularity. However, systems that understand natural language as spoken by anyone face many problems. Researchers are focusing on these problem areas:

- *Context.* Computers must be able to recognize that words take on different meanings depending upon the context in which they are used.

- *Idioms.* Languages are idiomatic and words do not always have their literal meaning. The computer must understand that "My car broke down on me" does not mean that the automobile came apart on top of my body.

- *Pronunciation.* A given word must be recognized consistently despite variations in its pronunciation. Words spoken with a dialect or an accent would still have to be understood. The computer must recognize the word *coffee* whether it is spoken by a New York City native or a Texan.

- *Noise.* Computers must be able to distinguish the speaker from background noise.

- *Emphasis.* Computers must correctly interpret the speaker's word emphasis and adjust the word's meaning accordingly.

Although researchers are making progress on universal recognition systems, neither the hardware nor the software presently exists that is necessary to make the essential fine discriminations for deciphering spoken language.

PERCEPTION

People perceive their environment through the five senses. As with other areas of AI, computers that can perceive their environment are extremely useful. AI research has experimented with the use of computerized sensing devices to simulate sight, touch, and smell. Simulated sight has proven the most successful.

Computer Vision

A computer and a program that can process visual information is called **computer vision.** Initially, computer vision was conceived as a component of robotics; for robots to take on complex tasks within the real world some ability to see would be necessary.

Programs using computer vision are no longer limited to robotics. In addition, these programs can recognize objects within a fixed scene despite shadows, distance, and overlapping images. When comparing two images, as in photographs, these systems can recognize slight variations. This ability is extremely valuable in analyzing satellite photos for military and weather purposes. A number of electronics firms use similar systems to check computer chips for flaws or missing circuits so small that they could be found no other way. Systems using artificial sight are employed to look for abnormal chromosomes, to scan printed documents, and (by the U.S. Postal Service) to sort the mail.

But computer vision cannot yet distinguish objects in the real world regardless of their location, position, color, or surrounding environment. Any one of us can identify our parents regardless of the clothing they are wearing, their distance from us, or their position—seated, standing, or bending over, for example. No computer program can produce this level of discrimination. Computer vision systems can:

- *Digitize images.* Pixel-like gradations of color or gray are used to record and exhibit images in what appear to be three dimensions.

- *Detect lines and boundaries.* By looking for changes in light patterns, objects can be distinguished from their surroundings. This lets the systems identify where one "object" begins and another ends.

- *Use depth perception.* Through the use of two camera images presenting slightly different views, a program can mathematically determine the depth and distance of an object.

- *Use pattern recognition (texture).* Objects have distinct surface patterns or textures. These patterns can be stored in memory, and the computer can compare scanned images with stored patterns in an attempt to identify new objects.
- *Use color.* Recording and distinguishing between colors assists in object identification, as well as supplying clues to the three-dimensional shape of objects.

In general, no computer vision system is able to incorporate all of these features into a single system. Developing an expert system style program that employs one or two of these techniques has proved useful in simulating vision. Combining multiple expert systems that make use of all the techniques, and developing the inference engine needed to access all the knowledge, is as yet impossible. It has been suggested that neural nets, computer programs whose designs seem to simulate the synapses in the brain, may be fruitful. Computer vision researchers are trying to unravel how the mind works by understanding how we interpret what we see. Again, science and engineering are combining their efforts to produce systems that act intelligently.

A "Sense" of Touch

Robotics and artificial limb construction are the two areas where computer systems that make use of the sense of touch are gaining popularity. In robotics, machine touch is enabling mechanical robots to have a better "sense" of their surroundings. Robots used to pick fruit, for example, need to "understand" how much pressure to apply to the fruit so it can be picked without being crushed. Similarly, providing factory robots with both computer vision and a sense of touch expands their abilities to perform assembly line tasks (see Figure 16.4).

Until recently, prosthetic devices that replaced a missing limb were unable to replace the sensations—the signals to the brain—that the limb produced. These devices enabled people with missing legs, for example, to move around without crutches or a wheelchair but were at best partial replacements. Without the sensation of touch and pressure, the users of artificial limbs have no way of knowing how heavily they are stepping and have difficulty adjusting to inclined surfaces. An additional problem is the body's continued "belief" that the limb is still present, even though it is not. People with artificial limbs often suffer aches and pains in places where the limb used to be.

Through the use of "intelligent" touch sensors, all this is changing. A number of companies have developed artificial limbs that contain touch- and pressure-sensitive pads. These pads are connected to computer components built into the artificial limb (see Figure 16.5).

Where the limb is connected to the body, transmitter pads are attached that transmit signals to nerves. The signals vary depending upon the computer's analysis of the sensory information. With training, the user can be trained to

Figure 16.4   Touch Sensitive Robots: Robots with touch sensors can more accurately and carefully respond to the world around them. Shown is a computer-controlled experimental industrial robot being used to handle artillery ammunition.

utilize these signals as if they were coming from a natural limb. Recently, individuals testing these devices have participated in marathon races and dance competitions and are learning to play musical instruments. Many report that the phantom pains previously associated with the missing limb have disappeared.

COMMONSENSE REASONING

Expert systems are extremely effective in simulating the decisions of human experts. When the rules can be clearly specified, they work extremely well. Unfortunately, even the most sophisticated expert systems cannot make the simple decisions that we make every minute of every day. For computers to understand the world around them, they have to possess knowledge of the everyday world. An expert system is only as effective as its knowledge base. Give it an unexpected, unpredictable, or incomplete query and the system will give an incorrect answer and have no insight whatsoever that an error was even possible.

Some have argued that what gives us our humanity is not so much the mysterious spark of creativity but our ability to assimilate information about the world (often unconsciously), organize it, "digest it," and transform it into the simple commonsense knowledge we have about the world and how it works. It is this ability to deal with the unexpected in a commonsense way, they claim, that is the basis of intelligence.

In an effort to build a computer program capable of using common sense to understand the world, AI researcher Douglas Lenat is building a system called Cyc (short for Encyclopedia). Outwardly, Cyc looks like an incredibly complex expert system. Cyc contains a knowledge base and an inference engine. Where expert systems contain the accumulated knowledge of experts in a very limited field, and the associated inference engines are able to manipulate this knowledge in useful ways, Cyc contains (or will eventually contain) all the ordinary knowledge that human beings take for granted. Instead of the expert's rules of thumb, Cyc is being given a basic understanding of the world—common sense.

To give Cyc knowledge of the world, Lenat's research group expects to enter over 100 million items of information into Cyc's knowledge base. Gathering the

---

Figure 16.5   Artificial limbs increasingly contain touch sensors that act like nerves, making the devices more natural to use.

knowledge is relatively easy—newspapers, magazines, and standard encyclopedias provide the information—but it has been extremely difficult to represent the knowledge in a form that the machine can understand and use. That is, designing the inference engine has been the problem. Lenat's team has developed a unique "programming language" designed to manipulate the "fuzzy," incomplete, and often unpredictable concepts that people deal with every day. When the project began, Lenat realized that before any information could be entered into the knowledge base, life's fundamental concepts such as time, space, the nature of physical objects, and how these objects interact had to be defined. Using frames (see Figure 16.3), objects and concepts had to be explained and coded. Cyc did not even start out with the innate reflexes of a human infant. Cyc's inference engine includes more than twenty types of reasoning so that it can draw conclusions about different types of problems. Complex problems use if/then rules much like standard expert systems. But inference, learning by example, and generalization also have been designed into the system.

Equally important, Cyc's search process has given it a technique for discounting irrelevant pieces of knowledge, a very humanlike ability. When we process information, we ignore large amounts of accumulated knowledge. Cyc's programming includes default logic, where Cyc is told to assume that certain things are "usually" true even though exceptions exist. This is how people think. "If I asked you where your car was," responds Lenat, "you would assume that it was where you left it." It "may have been stolen," but you would not have initially assumed so.

As part of this multiyear project, the AI team has come to recognize the incredible complexity of our commonsense knowledge base. "Teaching a computer all the ordinary things human beings take for granted is not an easy job," according to Lenat (in David H. Freedman, "Common Sense and the Computer," *Discover*, August 1990, pp. 68–69). Simple questions and concepts such as "What is a tree?" and "If you paint a chair blue, is it still the same chair?" require a remarkable understanding of the world.

Even with only 2 million of the 100 million items of information Cyc eventually will contain, its limited commonsense reasoning ability is impressive. For example, if Cyc knows that two people live near each other, and that one of them resides in New York, the system will correctly conclude that the other individual lives in New York. Similarly, if Cyc knows that World War II was fought between 1939 and 1945, and that Iraq's invasion of Kuwait occurred in 1990, then Cyc will correctly conclude that the invasion of Kuwait did not occur during World War II.

Researchers agree that for Cyc to operate effectively, it must not only contain the millions of entries necessary to explain and classify the real world, but Cyc would also need to understand natural language. Lenat expects that within five years, Cyc will understand, and will demonstrate, a moderate ability at both commonsense reasoning and natural language. Other experts find such a timetable unrealistic. But even if this project does not meet Lenat's expectations, it will have provided researchers with a much better understanding of the reasoning process and the ways in which humans assimilate information. The envelope of knowledge will be expanded even if Cyc never attains more than rudimentary common sense.

ROBOTICS

Science fiction, whether in the form of books, movies, or television, has given us a sensational picture of a robot. For most of us, a robot instantly brings to mind C3P0 and R2D2 of *Star Wars* fame. Our imaginary robots are mobile and dexterous. They move freely in their environment. Equally important, they can communicate and make decisions independently when they need to. In the case of C3P0, they even look a lot like us.

Real robots, however, look little like our imaginary models. **Robots** are mechanical devices, often armlike machines, that can be programmed to do a number of tasks (see Figure 16.6). **Robotics** is the division of AI concerned with creating machines capable of recognizing and effectively reacting to changes in their environment.

Figure 16.6   Robots are programmable armlike machines that do not resemble the robots of science fiction lore.

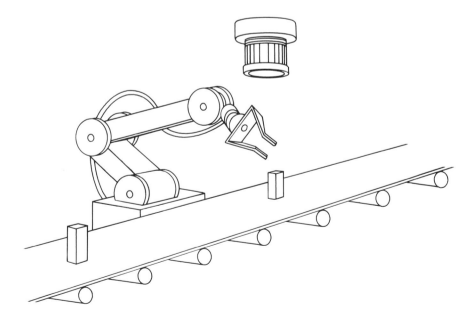

Industrial robots are complex programmable tools designed to do highly repetitive tasks within a very limited environment. They are used, for example, in the following:

- *Environments that pose health hazards to humans*—nuclear power plants, high-temperature facilities or operations, places where dangerous chemicals are in use, and specialized military missions

- *Highly repetitive, boring, mechanical jobs*—welding, screwing things together, painting assembly-line products

- *Mechanical tasks that require precision*—pattern-cutting, picking fruit

- *Environments that must be kept dust- and pollutant-free*—semiconductor industry, disk-drive industry

- *Settings that involve very heavy lifting*—automated warehouses

Most robots in use today are said to be "blind"; that is, they cannot make use of visual information. They have been programmed or "taught" to perform a specific task. Although they do this task with precision they can make no visual adjustments for even minor changes in their environment. They are multipurpose machines in that in most cases they can be reprogrammed to perform an alternative although similar task. They are unable to adjust to changes in their environment. As an example, a welding robot will continue to weld in the prescribed arc even if there is no object to weld.

Robots with "intelligence" will be able to adjust visually to changes in their physical environment. Such systems require significant computing resources and complex programs to sense, interpret, and understand the world around them. This involves use of pattern recognition techniques, learning algorithms, and computerized vision (see Figure 16.7).

A number of manufacturers have combined "blind" robots with those containing state-of-the-art AI systems. The General Motors Saturn plant has combined assembly line robots, which perform the repetitive tasks of welding and painting now common throughout the auto industry, with robots that contain computer vision and limited touch. "Seeing" robots place the sheet metal used to make car roofs in the correct location so that it can then be welded into place by other "blind" robots. Robots with vision can identify a required part and then install it. These systems are used to install windshields, car doors, and other modular parts in the Saturn car line. Such high-tech plants are expected to act as models for the rest of the American automobile industry.

IBM has created a robot-based manufacturing system called ALPS (Automated Logistics and Production System). Using ALPS, IBM laptop computers are assembled without human intervention. This fully integrated robot system includes robots that bring components from the loading dock and then assemble, test, and package the laptop machines.

Figure 16.7   Robots with computer vision can react to the world around them. This robot can draw an image within its visual field.

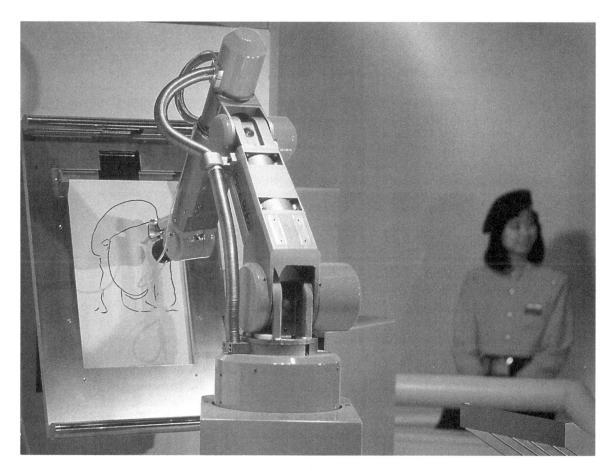

The potential for robot systems seems endless, yet the programs required to transform them from complex machine tools to "intelligent" devices requires the best that AI has to offer.

Research into artificial intelligence may not be able to produce truly "intelligent" machines. But this research is enabling us to write programs that make computers easier to use and affords greater insight into what it is that makes us human.

SUMMARY

Artificial intelligence (AI) is the study of how to make computers do things that in people require basic intelligence and that people find easy. AI is better described as research into machine intelligence or simulated intelligence. AI attempts to develop a series of computer programs that act, when interacted with, as though human.

Computers are excellent at tasks such as number-crunching, sorting long lists, and recalling everything that is stored in memory. However, computers find it difficult to do such simple everyday tasks as understanding language, learning, moving around in the world, and using common sense.

AI research has taken two directions. The first is an investigation of intelligence; learning what it is that makes us human and by consequence intelligent. The second approach focuses on building machines that act as though they were people—machines that are easier to use because they act more the way we do.

Computer **machine learning** is the process by which games, such as checkers and chess, are "taught" to computers in an effort to simulate the learning process. To simulate human learning, researchers have designed programs that contain a number of different learning styles including **rote learning, learning by generalization, induction,** and **inference.**

Computer programs that attempt to duplicate the ways in which professionals make decisions are called **expert systems.** To develop an expert system, the basic facts of a discipline, and the rules used by human experts within that discipline or specialty, are collected. The data base containing the facts and the rules of thumb **(heuristics)** is written as a series of if/then statements. This forms a **knowledge base.** Rules for combining the facts and the if/then statements, called the **inference engine,** also go into the system.

Natural language understanding is the area of AI that focuses on the development of systems that comprehend and then act upon human language. **Machine translation** systems investigate the translation of information quickly, efficiently, and automatically from one language to another. Much natural language research combines the efforts of individuals in computer science, linguistics, and psychology. These researchers investigate how natural language is acquired, deciphered, and comprehended by people. Other researchers work on the development of **natural language interfaces** where a query to a data base is made using ordinary sentences. Researchers in **speech recognition** are working on systems that eventually will be able to understand spoken human languages.

Designing a computer program that can process visual information is called **computer vision.** Computer vision systems are able to digitize images, detect lines and boundaries, and use depth perception, pattern recognition, and color.

Touch-based computer systems are being developed for use in robotics and in effective humanlike prosthetic devices.

Research into **commonsense reasoning** is attempting to build a computer program capable of using common knowledge about the world. It is a specialized expert system that will contain over 100 million items of information reflecting the ordinary knowledge that human beings use daily.

Robotics is the division of AI concerned with creating machines capable of recognizing, adjusting to, and effectively reacting to changes in their environment. **Robots** are mechanical devices, often armlike machines, that can be programmed to do a number of tasks. Industrial robots are complex programmable tools designed to do highly repetitive tasks within limited or dangerous environments.

Key Words

As an extra review of the chapter, try to define the following terms. If you have trouble with any of them, refer to the page number listed.

artificial intelligence *(422)*	machine learning *(423)*
commonsense reasoning *(434)*	machine translation *(426)*
computer vision *(432)*	natural language interface *(430)*
expert system *(425)*	natural language understanding *(426)*
frame *(430)*	robot *(437)*
heuristics *(424)*	robotics *(437)*
induction *(424)*	rote learning *(424)*
inference *(424)*	semantic network *(429–30)*
inference engine *(426)*	semantics *(428)*
knowledge base *(425)*	speech recognition (natural language
knowledge-based system *(425)*	recognition) *(431)*
learning by generalization *(424)*	syntax *(426)*

Test Your Knowledge

1. Define artificial intelligence.

2. Describe the two different directions that AI research has taken.

3. What is machine learning?

4. List the learning styles that machine learning has investigated.

5. Within an expert system, what is its knowledge base? What is the inference engine?

6. List four expert systems currently in use. Briefly describe each.

7. What is machine translation?

8. What is the difference between syntax and semantics?

9. Why are both syntax and semantics important in natural language understanding and machine learning?

10. List two techniques used to model natural language.

11. Describe a natural language interface. Why is it useful?

12. List the problem areas that researchers in speech recognition are investigating.

13. Describe computer vision.

14. List three areas where computer vision systems have been successfully employed.

15. List the five techniques that computer vision systems employ to successfully discriminate an object from its surroundings.

16. What are the two areas where touch-sensitive computers have found applications?

17. Who is Cyc? How is Cyc involved in commonsense reasoning research?

18. What is robotics?

19. What are the capabilities and limitations of industrial robots?

20. Describe the situations where robotics has proved useful.

Expand Your Knowledge

1. As discussed in this chapter, the U.S. Postal Service is developing an "intelligent" system designed to locate and read the addresses on envelopes. After researching this topic, write a brief three- to five-page paper on it.

2. Robots and intelligent computers are popular in science fiction movies. Watch two such movies. Write a short three- to five-page paper describing the use of "intelligent" computers in these movies. Include the features of these devices that make them appear "intelligent." What qualities of "intelligence" do they lack?

3. Douglas Lenat does not consider Cyc an expert system. After doing additional research, write a short three- to five-page paper examining Lenat's viewpoint. Describe the similarities and differences between Cyc's programming and traditional expert systems.

4. In 1988 a chess-playing program called Deep Thought tied for first place in a chess tournament against international master Igor Ivanov. Since then other master chess programs have been written. Research chess programs and describe the features of these systems that enable them to play successfully against human chess masters.

5. Research natural language interfaces. Many AI scientists scoff at the development of such systems. In a three- to five-page paper describe natural language interface systems and explain their limitations.

6. Write a three- to five-page paper on Japan's "fifth generation" project. What "intelligent" features do researchers hope such systems will contain?

17

Management Information Systems

CHAPTER OUTLINE

445

Thus far, we have examined all aspects of computing, from history and ethics, to networking and artificial intelligence, to hardware and software. The focus throughout has been on using computers as a tool for problem solving. In this chapter, we will look at the use of computers in business and organizations as tools to provide the information needed for decision making.

In general, organizations such as businesses, government, charities, and schools have complex and varied information needs. A small company that sells peripheral devices has different information needs from General Motors. An **information system** consists of the people, methods, and the machines that transform data into information. A **management information system** provides the information needed by all managers to make effective decisions and solve problems. Before the computer, organizations used paper files, calculators, and clerical workers to provide management with the required information. With the invention of the computer, many organizations have automated their systems, making information easier and more efficient to obtain.

After studying this chapter, you will be able to:

- Understand how organizations and computer systems are related.

- Describe the systems development life cycle.

- Describe the types of information systems.

- Identify the different approaches to managing an organization.

- Describe the different information needs of managers.

- Understand the evolution of computer use in business.

- Revisit problem solving from a managerial point of view.

- List the strategic planning questions associated with information technology.

ORGANIZATIONS AND COMPUTER SYSTEMS

A **system** is a collection of people, machines, and methods organized to accomplish a set of specific functions. You can think of General Motors as a system organized to manufacture and sell cars. A college is a system organized to provide students with a postsecondary education. Systems are complex, having interrelated parts. Each part or **subsystem** can be viewed as a system within a system. Therefore, a system can also be viewed as a set of interrelated subsystems. General Motors, for example, has a manufacturing subsystem, a sales subsystem, and a distribution subsystem, which combine with other subsystems to form the whole corporation.

Organizations, including businesses, government, charities, and schools are all systems. They bring together people and resources such as land, facilities, money, equipment, materials, and information to accomplish specific goals. Organizational systems, like computer systems, transform raw materials (input) into finished products (output). For example, the goal of a college is to educate students. Individuals who are seeking education are the raw material or input to the college. At a minimum, the college combines faculty, buildings, books, laboratories, computers, and libraries to educate (process) students. The desired output of the college is well-educated individuals. The faculty and administration control or direct the college. The college keeps track of information (memory) on all of the students who apply, attend, and graduate.

A manufacturing firm like General Motors is also a system. The goal of General Motors is to design and produce motor vehicles such as automobiles and trucks. The input to General Motors includes customer orders, raw materials, and components from suppliers. Then General Motors uses its factories, equipment, and employees to build (process) the input into completed vehicles and spare parts (output) that are ready to be sold. Corporate executives and stockholders control or direct the firm. General Motors must retain information (memory) about its customers, suppliers, parts, vehicle designs, and equipment to be successful.

A **computer system** combines hardware and software to solve problems and attain specific goals. A computer system's input devices, processor, memory unit, control unit, and output devices fit naturally into organizations since the computer system's general structure appears to mirror the way people conduct business and solve problems. An information system is created when a computer system is used by people, in combination with stored data, to transform those data into information so that people can make better, more informed decisions.

SYSTEMS DEVELOPMENT LIFE CYCLE

Fully functional information systems do not just appear within a business. The development and use of information systems goes through a six-phase process that can be compared to the human life cycle. A system is "born" when the organization realizes that the current approach to accomplishing a task is no longer effective. The system grows as people organize and develop the necessary hardware, software, and staff to make the new system effective. Once the system is fully developed and in use, it is said to be in production. Over time, the system does not keep up with the changing needs of the organization; it becomes obsolete. In "death," the system outlives its usefulness and the life cycle is about to begin again as new ideas are generated to improve the information environment. The name for this process is **systems development life cycle** (see Figure 17.1).

The six phases in the systems development life cycle are identified as follows:

Figure 17.1 The systems development life cycle has six phases: (1) feasibility study, (2) systems analysis, (3) systems design, (4) systems development, (5) systems implementation, and (6) systems evaluation.

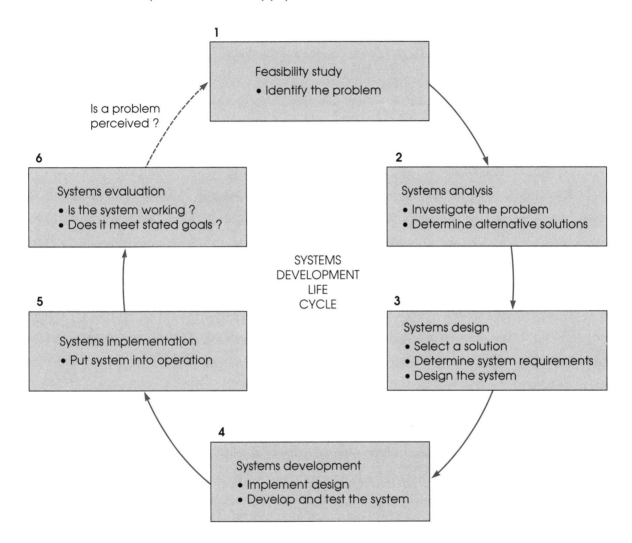

1. **Feasibility study** or Preliminary investigation. During this phase the current system (whether manual or automated) is briefly analyzed to determine if it should be developed, enhanced, or replaced.

2. **Systems analysis.** In this phase, the operation of the present system is carefully examined. All possible information relating to how the current system operates is gathered and analyzed. This is sometimes called **fact finding.**

Through data gathering and analysis, system requirements and objectives are identified. Once the current system's strengths and weaknesses are clearly understood, systems analysis determines the changes that need to be made. Alternative approaches to designing a new or improved system are identified.

3. **Systems design.** Once an approach is selected, a statement of objectives, cost/benefit analysis, and a design report are developed. This report considers the input, output, and processing requirements of the system and includes the definition of data files, systems control, and procedures.

4. **Systems development.** This next phase involves the purchase of appropriate computer hardware and software as well as the development and testing of new software, should such be required.

5. **Systems implementation.** In this phase, the designed system becomes fully operational. User training, conversion of data from the old system to the new, and installation of the new system are accomplished.

6. **Systems evaluation.** Systems do not always work as expected. The final phase in the systems development life cycle is evaluation. The system is reviewed to determine whether it is meeting its objectives and is performing the tasks as expected. This is also an opportunity to identify potential enhancements that can make a system more effective.

Effective organizations regularly evaluate their systems. Systems that work may be made more efficient; those that fail to perform are replaced. In this way, over time, a system is born and reborn as the organization's needs and expectations change.

INFORMATION REQUIREMENTS

Different organizations have different requirements for information. Typically, the larger the organization, the more complex and varied its information needs. Before the computer, organizations relied exclusively on people and paper to record information and perform computations. In the early years of computers (the 1950s and early 1960s), only large organizations could justify and afford their use. The federal government and large corporations such as General Motors, for example, had both the need for information and the money to be able to develop computerized information systems. As we saw in Chapter 2, during this period not only was hardware very expensive, but organizations had to write most of their own software. Therefore, the automation of information systems required both a large, expensive computer system and a large programming staff to develop systems and applications software. In contrast, today, even small businesses are able to automate their information needs. Hardware has become affordable and user friendly. Efficient software is readily available off-the-shelf.

The information collected and created by an organization can be used in two ways: internally and externally. Within an organization information is used to manage the staff and operate the business on a day-to-day basis to meet corporate goals. But beyond these internal functions, information can also be provided to external organizations. For example, at a local college, a grade report is generated each semester reflecting each student's grades. Grade reports are provided only to students and to those individuals within the college who need this information. Grades evaluate students' progress. Students doing well may be placed on the Dean's List. Those doing poorly may be placed on probation. These are all *internal* uses of grade information. If a student is close to graduation, the student may request that transcripts be sent to graduate schools or prospective employers. This is an *external* use of grade information.

Types of Information Systems

An information system is often classified by the number of areas of a business it supports. For example, a manufacturing firm like General Motors has many different departments. Each department supports a particular business function such as designing products (engineering design), buying raw materials (purchasing), manufacturing the products (production), managing the storage of parts (inventory), selling products (marketing), managing money (finance, accounting, payroll), managing people (human resources), and keeping customers happy (customer service). There are a large number of applications where computers can assist the running of a manufacturing firm. Some of the systems can operate independently, but others work better if information is shared among a number of departments.

Function-Based Information Systems   An information system that provides support for a specific application area, such as payroll or accounting, is known as a **function-based information system.** It supports one specific area or function within the organization.

In many ways it is easier to write a function-based system because one department has control over the information. Each function-based system maintains its own data base or files. However, problems can occur when different groups within an organization require similar information. For example, both the marketing department and the customer service department need to maintain customer addresses. A customer who has recently moved calls the customer service staff to inform them of the change. If the information in the customer data base is not shared between the marketing department and the customer service department, it is possible that the marketing department may not be informed of this address change. Unnecessary problems result. Billing errors may occur, and sales and service representatives may go to the incorrect address.

Integrated Information Systems When an information system expands so that more than one area in a business is supported, usually through a shared data base, it is known as an **integrated information system.** Integration facilitates decision making and assures that all interconnected departments have access to accurate, up-to-date information. In this way, the data base's *integrity* is maintained. An integrated information system helps to eliminate the possibility of redundant or duplicated information. In the above example, an integrated system would provide a single customer data base that is shared among all departments that require customer information. An address update made by one department automatically would be available to all departments.

Manufacturing Resource Planning (MRP) Expanding the integration approach further, **manufacturing resource planning (MRP)** is an integrated information system that allows the different areas of a manufacturing company such as engineering, production, purchasing, inventory, and marketing to have access to a common data base of information. One of the difficult tasks faced by a manufacturer is how to schedule and produce its product. Coordinating interrelated activities among many departments can be difficult. The correct raw materials and inventory parts must be available at the right time in the right amount in the proper order. Workers must be trained and ready to work, and the appropriate machinery must be available and working.

In the late 1960s, IBM introduced integrated software to support the special needs of manufacturing firms using IBM hardware. This system eventually became known as manufacturing resource planning. MRP originally was used to schedule the manufacturing work force, raw materials, and machines based on actual and anticipated orders. MRP evolved over time, and many vendors now offer similar systems. Current systems enable users to control the total manufacturing process, thus improving a firm's profitability. A good MRP package is integrated with the organization's accounting and personnel subsystems.

Computer Integrated Manufacturing (CIM) When all phases of a product's design, manufacturing, and distribution are supported through a common data base environment, this is called **computer integrated manufacturing (CIM).** In many cases, organizations that start off using manufacturing resource planning (MRP) move to computer integrated manufacturing (CIM) with the assistance of systems analysts. The GM Saturn Car Plant is an example of implementing CIM (see Figure 17.2).

Figure 17.2 Computer integrated manufacturing (CIM): The GM Saturn car is produced in a plant that uses CIM, the process of electronically generating designs and electronically applying them to manufacturing operations.

MANAGERIAL STRUCTURES WITHIN AN ORGANIZATION

A Top-Down Approach

There are several levels of management in a traditional organization, each having different kinds of problems to solve. Top-level managers plan the long-range activities that define the nature of an organization and its ability to continue operating in the future. Middle-level managers implement this long-range plan by breaking it down into manageable pieces. First-line managers and employees handle the day-to-day operations and details of an organization. Specific tasks such as manufacturing and providing a service are carried out at this level.

Top-level managers set an organization's goals for the long term. They develop a long-range plan and determine what the organization will look like and be doing over the next 5 to 10 years. This goal setting is called **strategic planning.** They look at the current state of the organization and plan the growth and development needed so that the organization can meet its long-range objectives. Since new facilities, new buildings, and new equipment are expensive and take a long time to acquire and install, strategic planning for them must be done in a timely and careful manner.

Once top-level managers have set goals and planned a corporation's direction, they delegate to the middle management the responsibility of turning plans into action. Middle-level managers worry about the details of building a new factory or acquiring the appropriate equipment to do a specific job. At this level, managers are concerned with the midterm planning (up to one year) needed to implement the organization's objectives. This is called **tactical planning.** Once the factory is built and available for use, it is the role of first-line managers to maintain its day-to-day operation. The first-line managers assign people to jobs and supervise the production of the products or services.

Many different organizational structures exist. Some organizations have a hierarchical or pyramid-type structure (see Figure 17.3) with one or more individuals at each sublevel. Other organizations may have a single individual at each management level, or one person may have responsibilities that span the various levels of management. A company like General Motors is very hierarchical. The president and executive committee determine the corporation's goals. Middle-level managers (division heads) implement these goals, and first-line managers run the day-to-day operations within individual plants by hiring and scheduling workers to get the job done (see Figure 17.4).

In a college, a faculty member performs activities associated with all levels of management. When serving on the curriculum committee, this individual

Figure 17.3   Different levels of management perform different functions and have varying information needs.

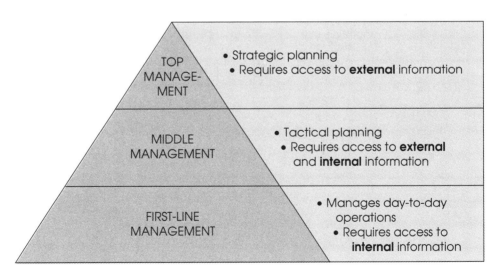

Figure 17.4 First-line managers run the day-to-day operations.

helps to determine degree requirements and the range of course offerings. In this capacity, the faculty member helps set departmental goals and acts as a top-level manager. When serving on committees that allocate resources and develop specific course guidelines, he or she acts as a middle-level manager and implements the goals set by the curriculum committee. When teaching a course, a faculty member is a first-line manager dealing with the day-to-day instruction of students.

The Team Approach

The latest trend in management emphasizes the team approach. Workers and first-line managers are empowered with more individual responsibility than has been customary. In this approach, managers are coming to view their role as one of *facilitators* for workers rather than simply direction givers.

The team approach, Japanese in origin, reflects the philosophy of **just-in-time manufacturing.** In a traditional organization structure, only the managers have the authority to interrupt production. In general, quality control is maintained by end-product inspection. When manufacturing is complete, products are inspected, and products that do not meet quality control standards are discarded. A worker in this environment who detects an error has no ability to effect a change. The first-line manager must be located, the suspected error must be explained, and only when the manager is sufficiently convinced can the production process be stopped. In contrast, in just-in-time manufacturing, quality control is the responsibility of everyone—managers and workers alike. If a worker sees something wrong on the production line, that person has the responsibility to stop production and correct the problem *just-in-time*; in other words, as it occurs and before it is repeated and becomes a much larger problem. The goal is to replace end-of-the-line inspections with continual product inspection by all workers throughout the production process. "Work" has been restructured. Individual workers assume more of the responsibility for the quality of the product. Workers make suggestions on how to improve the production process. Because workers are the closest to production, management takes their suggestions seriously and adjusts production where appropriate.

DIFFERENT MANAGERS, DIFFERENT INFORMATION NEEDS

Just as different levels of management perform different functions, they have different information needs. Information is critical for the fulfillment of an organization's goals. With adequate information, decisions can be based on careful reasoning and detailed analysis (see Figure 17.3). Although intuition has its place, effective intuition is based on information, history, and understanding, not on pure guesswork.

Strategic Information

As we have seen, top-level managers are involved in the long-range planning of organizations. **Strategic information** focuses on external data, including customer feedback, employee relations, government regulations, information about competitors, and economic predictions. Top-level managers weigh external information when setting goals and identifying problems (see Figure 17.5).

Although most strategic information is externally based, some comes from within the organization. This internal information, usually in summary form for easy use, includes forecasts and projections from individual departments. For managers to plan, they must have an accurate picture of how the organization operates without getting too involved with the details of its operation. Top executives need information that enables them to see the "big picture." Examples of strategic information include long-range financial projections containing investment and revenue estimates, relevant legal information, employee contracts, research and development plans, new product ideas, and information on competitors.

Figure 17.5   Top-level managers need external information to help them set long-term goals.

Tactical Information

Middle-level managers use information to plan and operate an organization for up to a year. Such tactical planning requires both external and internal information and is used to implement the goals set by top-level management. External information such as one-year economic forecasts, product development reports, and changes to existing laws are as important as budget reports, sales estimates, and quarterly inventory summaries. Such **tactical information** gives middle-level managers an understanding of the organization in the midterm (see Figure 17.6).

Operational Information

First-line managers, responsible for the day-to-day operation of an organization, require information that gives a detailed picture of what is happening within departments, to products, employees, and customers. They need to measure daily progress against established goals and determine ways to improve effi-

Figure 17.6   Middle-level managers need internal and external information for short-term planning.

ciency and quality. Such short-term, day-to-day, or **operational information** focuses on the internal operation of the organization and includes sales orders, customer complaint reports, payroll records, personnel records, product orders, and inventory records. This information enables first-line managers to oversee the daily functioning of a firm.

EVOLUTION OF INFORMATION SYSTEMS

The terms used to describe computer systems and applications in business often overlap. As the technical ability of the hardware and managerial use of computer systems have changed, so too have information systems and the terms devised to describe them.

Data Processing

During the 1950s and 1960s, computers were used to maintain an organization's daily operation. Computers reduced costs by performing many routine and repetitive tasks such as accounting, inventory, and payroll. These day-to-day activities were well defined and structured, leading to easy computerization. Such automation focused on the processing of "ordinary" data and was called **electronic data processing** or simply **data processing.**

At this time, computer hardware was extremely expensive, a fact that made processing or computer time very costly. To reduce computer time, early data processing systems required that data be collected offline (when not directly connected to the computer) and submitted in batches or groups to the computer. This technique is referred to as **batch processing** or **off-line processing** (see Figure 17.7).

Although batch processing reduces computer time, thus saving money, a significant amount of clock time elapses between the time the data are entered into the machine and the time they are processed. This lag varies from hours to days. Batch processing minimizes computer time at the expense of accessibility to information.

Figure 17.7   The card reader was one of the most popular I/O devices in a batch processing environment.

Interactive Processing

As managers realized the value of rapid access to information, they demanded more responsive systems. Immediate access to information and rapid processing of data became a management priority. Coincident with this, the cost of hardware began to plummet. Disk-based storage and software that supported interactive human/machine communication gained popularity. Such communication is known as **interactive processing** or **on-line processing.** On-line systems have the capability of processing transactions almost immediately and of giving very rapid access to information. Furthermore, batch systems are potentially inaccurate, because pending updates may not yet have been processed. With on-line systems, changes are immediately reflected in the system's files, providing accurate information when queries are made.

Management Information Systems

As software expanded, the tasks that computers performed expanded as well. Software was developed to meet the changing information needs of organizations. Computer systems moved beyond the accumulation of the raw facts (data) and increasingly were used to analyze information. As we have seen, the sharing of information among different departments within an organization became common, and software evolved from single-purpose information systems to integrated information systems. These integrated information systems took on the name management information systems (MIS).

Decision Support Systems

Despite access to integrated information systems, management's often insatiable need for more information, faster, can exceed an MIS department's ability to supply the information in a timely manner. These increasing demands resulted in the development of a new type of information system called **decision support systems (DSS).** Decision support systems allow managers to personally make special one-time requests directly to the system without using the MIS department. This is called an **ad-hoc query** and often takes the form of what-if questions.

   For example, a college's alumnus has decided to donate money for a one-time scholarship. This scholarship is limited to a single academically outstanding sophomore or junior who, although ineligible for standard financial aid, has financial need. In addition, the student must come from the donor's home state. Depending on the flexibility of the college's information system, identifying students who meet these criteria can be a complex task. With a decision support system, the appropriate dean could use an ad-hoc query to determine which students are eligible for consideration. Such a query might look like the following:

```
LIST ALL STUDENTS FOR (GPA > 3.8) AND
(CLASS = 'Junior' OR CLASS = 'Sophomore') AND
(APPLIED_FOR_FINANCIAL_AID = 'Yes') AND
(RECEIVED_FINANCIAL_-AID = 'No') AND
(HOME_STATE = 'NY')
```

The student will be selected by the dean after the candidates are interviewed. The dean's decision will be supported by information gleaned from the computer. Access to information is the power of a decision support system.

Decision support system queries often take the form of what-if questions. For example, a General Motors manager is trying to decide how to price a new automotive product. The manager develops a spreadsheet model to examine the costs associated with vehicle's production. One significant factor in the cost of the car is employees' wages. The union contract is due to expire shortly, so the manager does not have accurate figures on how much labor will cost. The only information known is that in the future, wages will be changing. To estimate costs, the manager could ask the following what-if questions: "What if the union gets a 5-percent increase in wages?" "What if the union gets a 10-percent increase in wages?" "What if negotiators can persuade the union to give back 2 percent in wages or benefits?" In this way, the manager can examine the effect of wages on prices without waiting months for the MIS department to provide the information.

Executive Information Systems

Historically, information systems have tended to emphasize the internal activities of an organization. Since the organization has control over its own activities, access to such information is easy to obtain and control. However, for long-range planning, top-level management increasingly needs access to external as well as internal information. External information can include data about an organization's competition, the effect of government regulations, and changes within the financial community such as the effect of inflation, bond prices, and interest rates.

Executive information systems (EIS) are designed with top-level managers in mind. A key feature of good executive information systems is the ability to integrate both internal and external information. Information utilities such as Dow Jones (see Chapter 15) or other outside data sources are often included. To be effective, such systems must be flexible and easy to use. Since managers are often uncomfortable with keyboards, user-friendly software is critical. A number of major corporations are expanding their computer systems to include executive information systems in an effort to gain a competitive edge.

Information Centers

Information has become so valuable that a MIS department cannot meet all of a business's needs. Important projects are sometimes backlogged waiting for the

MIS department to get to them. It is not unheard of for MIS departments to have projects that wait three to five years for attention.

These delays may interfere with an organization's healthy operation. To solve this problem, some organizations are establishing **information centers.** An information center provides technical support and computing resources for short-term projects. Users are coached and given hands-on access to resources. In addition to hardware and software, the information center offers training, consulting, and some support in the development of specialized software.

THE POWER OF MANAGEMENT INFORMATION SYSTEMS

Rapid access to information gives a firm an advantage over its competition. By being better able to anticipate and meet the needs and wants of its customers, businesses can increase their profitability. An organization does not invest in technology to satisfy a whim or simply to have the most current technology. Technology is simply too expensive. Rather, purchase of new technology reflects management's expectation that more rapid access to information will be reflected in higher profits.

Setting and Meeting Organizational Goals

For computer technology to be justified, its benefits must outweigh its costs. Computerized information systems must help an organization reach its goals and must assist management in developing productive and profitable strategies for the organization's future. Unfortunately, because the advantage of rapid access to information cannot directly be measured in dollars, such cost versus benefit analysis is not easy.

Information systems provide information. In operations such as office administration, inventory management, and billing and accounting, they can directly increase productivity and reduce costs. In other situations, they are corporate tools for decision making. For example, customer service departments keep records of customers' comments and complaints. Engineers can use this information to improve existing products or to design new products that meet needs not previously anticipated.

To be effective, an information system must support the organization in achieving its goals. Computing should be utilized to provide the greatest benefit to the organization as a whole. Effective information systems deliver the correct amount of accurate information in a timely and useful form to the right decision maker. Care and attention must go into the development of information systems to ensure their quality. Such systems are reliable and provide information that managers can trust. In the event of a problem, well-defined information systems are easy to fix and maintain. When designers make efforts to anticipate future needs, the resulting systems are adaptable to changes in corporate expectations.

Anticipating Problems

As an organization grows increasingly dependent on technology, it becomes critical to have contingency plans in the event of a system breakdown. Before the advent of computers, an organization depended entirely on its staff and paper files for information. Computers changed the way organizations operate. The computer became indispensable to an organization's day-to-day operations, making the organization "dependent" on its information system. Banks, for example, manage money. If a bank's computer system "goes down," its everyday operations rapidly deteriorate. Most bank functions can no longer be done without computers. As a result, banks make precise contingency plans to have alternative computer systems available should their primary system fail.

An organization's information system can become so important that its failure affects the organization in much the same way that an injury and the subsequent removal of a starting quarterback affects a football game. How much influence the quarterback's removal has on the outcome of the game reflects on how dependent the team is on that individual. Similarly, how a company is affected by the failure of its computer system depends on how pervasive the computer is within the organization. For an airline, a computer system failure means that the airline cannot make reservations, update arrival and departure times, and adjust flight schedules. Depending upon the degree of integration within its system, the airline might be unable to pay its employees or vendors. Essentially, the airline cannot maintain its business.

Anticipating system interruption and acting to ensure continued access to an organization's information system is critical. For routine support, backups of information should be stored close to the computer site. Off-site storage of backups, along with arrangements for substitute computing facilities, is essential in the event of a disaster (see Figure 17.8). In highly critical applications such as air traffic control systems and military surveillance, an organization may even have round-the-clock access to a duplicate computer system. Some organizations purchase insurance policies to protect and compensate them in the event that a disaster disables their computing environment.

PHASES OF MANAGERIAL PROBLEM SOLVING AND TYPES OF PROBLEMS

We are always problem solving. Problems range in difficulty from very simple to very complex. In Chapter 6, we discussed problem solving steps. Top-down analysis and design can be applied to an organization by its management. Although it is management's role to identify an organization's goals, management must also recognize and identify the "problems" that stand in the way of success.

Figure 17.8   Making arrangements for substitute computer facilities, in cases of disasters, can be essential to organizations.

Management is said to be *proactive* when it plans for and anticipates potential problems, such as a parts shortage. If alternative suppliers have been identified, just in case the usual supplier experiences a shortage, management is being proactive. When management deals with unanticipated problems that arise, it is problem solving in a *reactive* way. An organization's survival depends on its ability to anticipate, identify, and solve problems.

Although corporate problem solving follows the same basic steps described in Chapter 6, its outward appearance is different. Whether managers are proactive or reactive, their recognizing that a problem exists characterizes the definition stage. Making the problem's resolution a goal means setting appropriate expectations. For example, by making parts acquisition a priority, the organization defines the solution of the problem. Managers examine the current situation and brainstorm to invent and analyze alternative courses of action. A number of options will be examined to determine the best action plan.

After management has gathered and analyzed adequate information, the most appropriate solution is selected. If automation is involved, a computer program will have to be written to implement all or part of the solution.

We can look at managerial problem solving as a three-phase activity, involving (1) identifying the problem; (2) identifying alternative solutions; and (3) selecting a particular solution path and seeing that it is followed to completion.

Easily identifiable problems for which alternative solution paths can be designed, and for which it is possible to identify a "best" solution, are called **structured problems.** Structured problems are the easiest to solve because they are so well defined. Examples of structured problems include keeping track of who owes money to you (accounts receivable) and to whom you owe money (accounts payable), calculating how much to pay an employee (payroll), analyzing costs for a project, and determining the best location for building warehouses or factories. Structured problems are often the first applications to be computerized by an organization. Because they are well defined, they are relatively easy to automate.

A problem in which one or two of the phases is unstructured is known as a **semistructured problem.** Examples of semistructured problems include scheduling equipment and people to build products, managing the cash flow in an organization (how money is received and spent), preparing budgets, and new product planning.

A problem for which none of the three phases is well defined is an **unstructured problem.** This kind of problem is difficult to identify, much less to solve. Examples of unstructured problems include deciding what type of products to make, determining how many units of a particular product to make so that an adequate supply is available to the customer without having too many left unsold, and deciding what is the most important area to research so as to best improve products or develop new products.

Problems in which one or more solution phases are not well defined or in which available information is incomplete are extremely difficult to solve. Although managers are comfortable having computers solve structured problems, allowing computers to make decisions on problems that seem to require "judgment" makes managers uncomfortable. Managers recognize that computer systems can consider only available, specified information. Since computers have no intuition, managers are leery of trusting computerized results to semi- and unstructured problems. Advances in data base query languages, artificial intelligence, and expert systems are enabling the development of advanced computerized systems that assist managers with these types of problems. Considerable research and development remains to be done when dealing with problems that have incomplete information.

MANAGING MANAGEMENT INFORMATION SYSTEMS

Information systems must be managed within an organization. There are two distinct types of control. The MIS department, with its hardware, software, and people, must be managed. Independently, the flow of information within the company must be controlled. The perceived importance of information systems to an organization, as well as the particular staff members who need the information, will influence how the MIS services are organized and controlled. The MIS department typically provides *services* to other departments in the organization. Usually, there is a midlevel manager known as the director of management information systems who is responsible for management of the MIS department. Although the MIS department serves the information needs of the organization, it does not itself generate the information. Other departments are responsible for the contents and flow of information. For example, the customer service and accounting departments "create" information by gathering it from customers. The MIS department is responsible for ensuring that information is available on the computer. Decisions regarding who needs to see information and in what form usually are made by managers above the MIS department.

Recently, as information technology has assumed a more important role in the overall success and strategy of various firms, information management has become a concern of top-level management. **Information resource management (IRM)** refers to the concept that information is as much a corporate resource as people, materials, equipment, and facilities. With the advent of computer networks, all the computers and communications facilities of an organization are coming under the control of a single department. The **chief information officer (CIO)** is responsible for managing all of an organization's computer, communications, and information resources. This individual interacts directly with the organization's senior executives.

PLANNING QUESTIONS FOR INFORMATION TECHNOLOGY

Planning for technology, including the development and use of information systems, requires long-range planning. The level of detail and sophistication of such an information plan will vary based on the objectives of the organization, its current level of technology, the type of "work" the organization does, and what technology the organization's competitors are using.

Top-level management must answer the following questions and communicate the results to everyone within the organization if planning is to be useful and effective.

1. What business are we in versus what business should we be in? What kind of information technology is appropriate for our business? These questions may seem overly simplistic. However, it is important for top-level management to specify the mission of the organization flexibly. An organization that cannot properly focus its energies and effectively compete will not survive.

2. What problems and opportunities do we have in this business? What environmental forces — for example, government regulations, available work

force, other competitors, suppliers, and customers—affect our business? What factors are critical to our success?

3. What "game plan" do we intend to follow to make our business successful?

4. How can we effectively apply information technology to help us achieve success?

5. Can we or should we apply information technology to improve our business plan? How can we use information technology to add new products, customers, or markets?

6. What is the best organizational structure to allow us to achieve our goals, business strategy, and plans? How does this structure influence the organization of information service activities so that we can best accomplish our business objectives?

Information is the currency of the future. Effective planning for access to information for an organization will determine its success. Computerized access to information enables managers at all levels to make effective, efficient, and competent decisions. Successful organizations are making information technology a priority.

On Line

APPLE AND IBM REACH AN HISTORIC AGREEMENT

Traditionally, both IBM and Apple have been loners. They both have pursued the development of their computers independently and have emphasized their own proprietary products. They have been arch-competitors. However, during June and July of 1991, top-level management at both firms sat down together to discuss the possibility of sharing technology and working together on projects in the future.

The letter of agreement between these two computer giants indicates the direction of future research and product development.

- Apple has agreed to use a new single-chip version of IBM's RS/6000 processor in future Macintosh products.

- Together IBM and Apple will develop and market the new *Power PC* computer that will be designed and built by Motorola and IBM.

- Together they will create an new object-oriented operating system environment that will run on Intel, Motorola, and IBM RISC processors and support a wide range of systems software, including IBM's version of UNIX, IBM's OS/2, and the Macintosh operating system.

- This new "platform" will let Intel-based systems (those designed by IBM and other vendors) run Macintosh applications.

- They will codevelop networking and communication products that will enable Macintoshes to connect easily to IBM-based networks and communciate with IBM host computers.

- There are also plans to create a common multimedia platform to give both companies an entry into this new technology.

The direction being taken by these on-time competitors is clearly described in their agreement. Their dramatic decision to join forces reflects the changing marketplace. Although by name IBM and Apple are probably the best known, they hold only a relatively small share of the personal computer market. Each has much to gain by their joining forces.

Apple gains access to the corporate market as a partner with IBM. In addition, the proposed hardware development will enable Apple products to become fully integrated into IBM networks and accessible from IBM host computers. IBM gets help in development of an object-oriented operating system, increasing its independence from Microsoft Corporation. Additionally, IBM systems gain access to the user-friendly Apple interface and a vast collection of Macintosh-based applications software. Motorola may be the unsung winner in this agreement since

success will make it a more dominant player in the microcomputer and workstation processor field.

If the winners are clear, so are the losers. Clearly Microsoft Corp. is concerned that this cooperative venture could negatively impact both MS-DOS and Windows. In addition, if the products materialize as described, IBM with Apple, and not Microsoft, will determine the future direction of the microcomputer industry. The other major potential loser in the venture is Intel Corporation. Intel is presently one of the world's leading manufacturers and developers of microprocessor chips. The Apple/IBM venture, based on IBM and Motorola processors, would clearly hurt the sale of Intel processors.

If Apple and IBM make good on their stated plans, the original movers and shakers of the microcomputer industry again will be the dominant players in the market.

Sources: Robert L. Scheier, "Sweeping Accord Pits Ex-Rivals Against Industry," *PC Week,* July 8, 1991, pp. 1, 6. Patricia Keefe and J. A. Savage, "Who'll win in alliance game?" *COMPUTERWORLD,* July 8, 1991, p. 104.

SUMMARY

A **system** is a collection of people, machines, and methods organized to accomplish a set of specific functions. Systems are complex, having interrelated parts. Each part or **subsystem** can be viewed as a system within a system. Organizations are systems that combine people, resources, and information to achieve specific goals.

A **computer system** combines hardware and software to solve problems and attain specific goals. An **information system** is created when a computer system is used by people, in combination with stored data, to transform those data into information so that people can make better, more informed decisions.

An information system goes through six phases: (1) a **feasibility study,** (2) **systems analysis,** (3) **systems design,** (4) **systems development,** (5) **systems**

implementation, and (6) **systems evaluation.** This is the **systems development life cycle.**

An information system that provides support for a specific application area is known as a **function-based information system.** An **integrated information system** supports more than one area in a business through a shared data base. **Manufacturing resource planning (MRP)** is an integrated information system that allows the different areas of a manufacturing company to have access to a common data base of information. **Computer integrated manufacturing (CIM)** is achieved when all phases of a product's design, manufacturing, and distribution are supported through a common data base environment.

In a traditional organizational structure, there are several levels of management. Top-level managers plan the long-range activities that define the nature of an organization and its ability to stay in business and prosper in the future. Middle-level managers implement this long-range plan. The day-to-day operations and details of an organization are the responsibility of first-line managers and employees.

Some organizations have a hierarchical or pyramid-type structure with one or more individuals at each sublevel. Other organizations may have a single individual at each management level, or one person may have responsibilities that span the levels of management. A new trend in management, **just-in-time manufacturing,** emphasizes teamwork, in making quality control the responsibility of everyone, managers and workers alike.

Top-level managers require information that will help them plan a corporate strategy. **Strategic information** focuses on external data. **Tactical information** gives middle-level managers an understanding of the organization in the short term. **Operational information** focuses on the internal operation of the organization and is used by first-line managers.

Data processing is the use of computers exclusively to maintain an organization's daily operation. **Interactive processing** gives users immediate access to information. **Management information systems** are systems designed to allow different departments within an organization to share common data. **Decision support systems** allow managers to make special one-time requests directly to the system without using the MIS department. **Executive information systems** are designed with top-level managers in mind and effectively integrate both internal and external information. **Information centers** provide technical support and computing resources for short-term projects.

Managerial problem solving has three phases: (1) identifying the problem; (2) identifying alternative solutions; and (3) selecting a particular solution path and seeing that it is followed through to completion.

Easily identifiable problems for which alternative solutions paths can be designed and for which it is possible to identify a "best" solution are called **structured problems.** They are the easiest to solve. A problem in which one or two of the phases is unstructured is known as a **semistructured problem.** A problem in which none of the three phases is well defined is known as an **unstructured problem.** These problems are difficult to identify and solve.

Information resource management (IRM) refers to the concept that information is as much a corporate resource as people, materials, equipment, and facilities. The **chief information officer (CIO)** is responsible for managing all the computer, communications, and information resources of the organization.

Key Words

As an extra review of the chapter, try defining the following terms. If you have trouble with any of them, refer to the page number listed.

ad-hoc query *(459)*
batch processing *(458)*
chief information officer (CIO) *(465)*
computer integrated manufacturing (CIM) *(451)*
computer system *(447)*
decision support systems (DSS) *(459)*
electronic data processing *(458)*
executive information system (EIS) *(460)*
fact finding *(448)*
feasibility study *(448)*
function-based information system *(450)*
information center *(461)*
information resource management (IRM) *(465)*
information system *(446)*
integrated information system *(451)*
interactive processing *(459)*
just-in-time manufacturing *(454)*

management information system (MIS) *(446)*
manufacturing resource planning (MRP) *(451)*
off-line processing *(458)*
on-line processing *(459)*
operational information *(457)*
semistructured problem *(464)*
strategic information *(455)*
strategic planning *(452)*
structured problem *(464)*
subsystem *(446)*
system *(446)*
systems analysis *(448)*
systems design *(449)*
systems development *(449)*
systems development life cycle *(447)*
systems evaluation *(449)*
systems implementation *(449)*
tactical information *(456)*
tactical planning *(453)*
unstructured problem *(464)*

Test Your Knowledge

1. Define a management information system.

2. What is a system?

3. Why are computer systems so useful to business?

4. List the six phases of the systems development life cycle.

5. Describe a function-based information program.

6. Describe an integrated information system.

7. What is manufacturing resource planning?

8. Identify and describe the three levels of management.

9. List the three phases of managerial problem solving.

10. How does batch processing differ from interactive processing?

11. Describe a decision support system.

12. Describe an executive information system.

13. Describe an information center.

14. What is the difference between proactive and reactive problem solving?

15. What is information resource management? Who is the CIO?

Expand Your Knowledge

1. Go to the library and investigate the information systems requirements for a specific industry, such as banking, automobile manufacturing, or another industry of interest. Write a short paper on the systems requirements of the industry you picked.

2. Investigate the issues and technology used in computer integrated manufacturing. Write a short, three- to five-page paper on computer integrated manufacturing.

3. Examine one of the following systems development methodologies: Warnier-Orr Methodology, Yourdon Methodology, Structured Design, Data Flow Diagrams, Entity Relationship Diagrams, Hierarchical plus Input-Process-Output (HIPO), or other methodology of interest. Write a short, three- to five-page paper on how and when the methodology you selected is used.

4. Pretend you are a middle-level manager in a firm that is considering additional information technology. Describe the scenario that represents your current environment. Make a proposal to top management to invest in additional information technology.

5. Write a five-page paper that discusses how the personal computer has affected and changed the modern organization.

18

Evaluating Computers and Software

CHAPTER OUTLINE

Buying a Computer—Know Your Needs
   Steps in Purchasing a Computer • Purchase Sources • *On Line: Never Pay Full Price*

Protecting Your Purchase
   Surge Protectors • Insurance Riders

Buying Software
   Necessary Software • Steps for Purchasing Software

Learning and Support
   Documentation • Information and Self-Education • Courses and Training • User Groups

So, you want to buy a computer! What do you need it for? While this may seem like a strange introduction to a chapter dealing with the purchase of computers and software, it is a singularly important question. Buying a computer with all of its associated peripherals and software is expensive. Research indicates that computers are often the third most expensive purchase you will make. The gold and silver medals go to the purchase of a house and a car. If you cannot instantly identify your reasons for purchasing a computer, you may not need one. Answers to this basic question such as, "It will help me in school," "It will make me more organized," or "I'll use it to balance my checkbook and pay bills" are not sufficiently compelling reasons to purchase a computer.

During the 1980s, most of the cheapest computers (costing less than $500) disappeared from the market. The computer market evolved rapidly. Consumers became more sophisticated as they turned from toys to real computers that are easy to operate, run a wide variety of software, and can produce graphics.

If you are interested in buying a computer, do not let me discourage you. They are valuable tools and can be a lot of fun. They are expensive, however, and their varied use makes them different from other consumer purchases. When you buy a toaster, you know what it does. When you buy a car, assuming you know how to drive, you expect to be able to sit down and immediately drive the car away. Although a new car does come with an owner's manual, it is infrequently used, unlike the manuals that accompany a new computer.

After studying this chapter, you will be able to:

- List the steps required to purchase a computer successfully.

- Describe the primary sources of computer purchases.

- Identify the types of protection computers require.

- List the steps in purchasing appropriate software.

- Discuss the methods available to learn how to use hardware and software.

- Understand the purpose of user groups.

BUYING A COMPUTER—KNOW YOUR NEEDS

The new owner of a computer can expect to spend many often frustrating hours sitting in front of the machine learning how it operates. Learning to use a computer can be compared to owning and learning to drive a pre–Model T automobile. A lazy drive down a country lane implied hours of driving in circles before the vehicle was actually under human control.

Since computers are not like other consumer products, a more careful, informed approach to their purchase is required. The same care that is used when purchasing a house or a car should be used when purchasing a computer. Examine your needs carefully. A measured approach is necessary when buying a computer. Just as with a home, a computer should serve your needs for some time.

Steps in Purchasing a Computer

There are nine important steps involved in a successful computer purchase.

Step 1: Analyze your needs. The more carefully you determine what you are going to do with the computer, the more satisfied you are going to be with the machine you eventually buy. Microcomputers are used for widely varying tasks from entertainment to serious research, from word processing to electronic shopping. The most common uses include:

- word processing
- entertainment
- business finance
- personal finance
- record keeping
- general education
- telecommunications
- programming

Buying a computer requires considerable homework. Make a wish list in general terms of the kinds of tasks you expect to do with your computer (see Figure 18.1a, b). Next refine your list. Be specific. Your list might look like this: (1) Write papers and reports and check spelling, (2) Maintain detailed information on record or slide collections, (3) Play computer games or chess, (4) Communicate with other computers from home or work.

Make sure to consider *who* will use the computer. Is it an individual or family purchase? If it is a family machine, everyone should be involved in developing the wish list. If the computer is expected to perform multiple tasks, order your list. The most pressing needs will have the highest priority and be at the top of the list.

Step 2: What can I afford? Deciding how much you can afford to spend is not trivial. A complete computer system, including software and a printer, can cost thousands of dollars. A system that is too small to meet your needs cannot perform the tasks you require. On the other hand, funds are always limited. If you cannot afford a system that meets your primary needs, purchasing a computer is not appropriate. Although you can rethink your priorities, you may regret purchasing a machine under adjusted priorities, because it might not meet expectations, especially later on.

Figure 18.1   (a) Home record keeping and (b) entertainment (shown is a computer game screen) are just two of the many uses of computers today.

(a)

(b)

Step 3: Analyze your software needs. Determine the software (the specific computer tools) that will meet the needs identified in Step 1. Information is critical. Most consumer products perform a single task. Computers, given the proper software, can perform multiple tasks. Software can be used as a classification tool, because each program performs a specific task or group of tasks. Some software focuses on very specific problems, such as calculating income taxes or maintaining a business inventory. Other packages, such as word processors, data base systems, and communications software, are more general. Carefully identified needs are required if appropriate software is to be located. While it is possible to write your own software, this should be considered only by very experienced programmers.

As an initial phase in your software analysis, match the goals you identified in Step 1 with the available software. For example, writing papers and checking for spelling errors requires a word processor. Maintaining and accessing information about a record or slide collection can easily be performed by data base software, and communicating with other computers requires communications software.

Step 4: Research the available software. You need to identify the specific packages or the specific features a software package must contain to suit your needs. Remember, not all software packages or languages are available for all microcomputer systems. For example, Apple has the best selection of precollege educational software, and the financial, record-keeping, and word processing software most frequently used by businesses run on IBM and compatible equipment. Many of the most sophisticated and easy to use desktop publishing software runs on the Macintosh.

The task of researching software can seem overwhelming, but it need not be. Start by talking to people who own computers. What kinds of software and hardware do they have? Are they satisfied with their purchases? What software is used at your school? What packages have you heard about? The software you need must be determined *before* hardware can be selected. Many software packages, including games, spreadsheets, data base systems, and desktop publishers, require specialized hardware. Many packages have memory requirements.

Now, go to the library. The library is an outstanding source of information about computers and software. Increasingly, public and university libraries are providing access to computers and software. Such computer sites provide an ideal unpressured way to experiment with computers and software. Public and college libraries carry a wide variety of computer magazines, many of which regularly review computer products. Magazines such as *Byte*, *PC Computing*, and *Consumer Reports* give advice to the consumer about computer hardware and software (see Figure 18.2).

In addition to using friends, neighbors, and the library as information resources, computer courses are available at schools and community centers.

Figure 18.2   Computer Magazines: Numerous computer magazines are on the newsstands to help buyers choose a computer and software.

Learning about computers and software makes intelligent consumers. Once you know what kind of software you need, you are ready to visit computer stores.

Step 5: Shop for software and identify hardware requirements. Software will determine the amount of memory and peripheral equipment you need. Plan on visiting a number of computer stores. Individual stores will sell different brands of computers and have salespeople with varying hardware and software experience. Use the salespeople as resources. Let them try to sell you a machine by demonstrating software packages that suit your needs. However, you are "just shopping." At this stage you are not yet prepared to buy anything. Leave your checkbook at home. Some stores will pressure you to "buy a computer today!" Do not let the salespeople snow you with computer buzzwords. Be skeptical. If the salesperson is confusing you or refuses to answer your questions, shop elsewhere. Computer stores abound and most have staffs that are competent, easy to work with, and understanding.

While identifying software packages that satisfy your needs, take careful notes. What hardware and peripherals do the packages require? For example, communication packages require a modem, word processors require a printer if you intend to get a hard copy of your written product, and many games require a color monitor to be effective. Many packages have memory requirements.

Ask questions—the more you ask, the happier you will be with the product you eventually buy. Consider these questions: On what machines do the packages you are interested in run? When the package you liked was demonstrated, did the machine have any special hardware? Will you need that hardware to use the program? What does the software cost? What does the hardware cost? If you buy everything together in a package, can you get a discount?

Step 6: Identify the computer that suits your individual needs. Think carefully about the software packages you have seen demonstrated. List the packages you preferred in one column. Next to each package list the hardware it requires. Weigh the following:

1. **Compatibility.** Is compatibility important to you? Do you want to share files with others? If so, you must have a compatible machine.

2. **Expandability.** Is the computer system you've identified expandable? As your computing needs and expectations grow can your computer grow with you? As your needs change you may need to add more memory or peripherals. For example, future software may require a voice synthesizer, a CD-ROM drive or more RAM in main memory.

Adjust your lists to reflect these considerations. Be sure to include in your software list packages you have used in school or in the office. The more familiar you are with software packages the quicker you will put your purchase to effective use. Prioritize both lists and check to see that the packages and hardware you have outlined satisfy the needs listed in Step 1.

Step 7: Go shopping again. You have undoubtedly seen more than one machine that could satisfy your needs (see Figure 18.3). This should not make you nervous. If you were shopping for a car you would expect to find more than one suitable vehicle. A car would be selected, at least in part, on price, overall design, and available options. Select your computer the same way. Comparison shop, but price should not be the sole factor in your selection. Service and customer support, including setup, instruction, and a willingness to answer questions before and after your purchase should play a considerable role. Just as you would test drive a car, "test drive" your selection. Make sure it works the way you expect and that you are comfortable with the look and feel of the machine. To some degree, you get what you pay for. Computers can be purchased through the mail. Although such purchases can save you money, customer support is essentially unavailable. It is very difficult to explain a problem to a sales representative over the telephone. Similarly, if you purchase your computer from a local organization, select one that will help you "get up and running." While you should not expect weeks of one-on-one instruction, some hand-holding is reasonable.

Figure 18.3   Computer Shopping: Selecting a computer from the vast array available, including these from Apple, can be difficult.

Step 8: Purchase your machine and arrange for support and service. When you've located the machine you want, spend some time with the sales representative arranging for support. Many computer stores will assemble the computer and provide some initial instruction on its operation. Be sure to understand all warranties and guaranties. Computers do break down. Discuss service with the salesperson. Different levels of repair services are available. Repairs done in your home or business, called **on-site service,** can be very expensive. Repair service pick up or customer drop off are more reasonable alternatives for microcomputers. Ask about the availability and cost of loaner equipment while your machine is being repaired. As with a car, once you've gotten used to having a computer around, its absence can prove very inconvenient.

Step 9: Enjoy your machine. Take time to learn how to use your machine effectively. Lessons may be appropriate. Initially, learning to use a computer can be frustrating. But it will also be a source of fascination and fun. If you shopped carefully, your computer will satisfy your needs and you will find uses for your computer system that you neither considered nor envisioned.

Purchase Sources

Computers can be purchased in a number of different ways. The three most popular are computer stores, university and college buying programs, and mail-order sales.

Computer Stores Local computer stores sell a wide variety of hardware and software (see Figure 18.4). Some specialize in specific brands and others sell machines from many manufacturers. Sales representatives are usually knowledgeable and helpful. Unfortunately, staff turnover is high, and not all representatives are equally trained. Many computer stores have a service department and can troubleshoot hardware problems. They also provide advice and some instruction on hardware and software products they sell. The cost of these services is included in the price charged for hardware and software. Such local support can be invaluable to new and experienced customers alike.

University and College Buying Programs Many colleges and universities have arrangements with major microcomputer manufacturers to sell computers to students, faculty, and staff at substantial savings. Manufacturers find such arrangements attractive because they can count on a large number of sales to a constantly changing population. The university community benefits because up-to-date equipment is available at a considerable discount. Standard manufacturer warranties apply to such sales, and many schools pretest the hardware

---

Figure 18.4   The Computer Store: Some computer stores sell specific brands, others offer a variety of products.

On Line

NEVER PAY FULL PRICE

Computers are expensive, advertised prices are often high, salespeople can be poorly informed, and some stores operate on the legal fringe. As a consumer two rules apply: *buyer beware*—know what you are buying; and *never pay the full sticker price.* Just as with a car purchase, haggle and negotiate. Use the sticker price as a starting point.

Unlike car dealerships, today's computer stores may not actually have the microcomputer you want in the store. Many stores have converted display space into sales cubicles, so you should not expect to see more than a picture of the machine you are buying. Don't let the sales representative sell you more than you need. Just as with a car, computer extras can substantially raise the final purchase price. Visit a number of stores and let them compete for your business. Most retailers will match the price quoted by a competitor, but many will require that you produce a formal price quote on a rival's official stationery.

The following tips can help you negotiate the best deal while protecting your investment:

1. **Check up on your local dealer.** Contact local user groups and the Better Business Bureau to confirm that the dealer is reputable. Look for an authorized IBM, Apple, or Compaq dealer. Such businesses have had to submit financial documentation to the manufacturers in return for the right to be an authorized dealer.

2. **Check out the dealer's repair facilities.** Dealers that repair the products they sell are more likely to stand behind them. Ask about turnaround time on repairs. Repair times of a few days are reasonable to expect.

3. **Ask about the store's return policy.** Don't buy a computer from a dealer that insists all sales are final. Be wary of shops that give credit rather than cash for returned merchandise. Many stores have a 30-day money-back guarantee policy.

4. **Negotiate the best price.** Most stores will reduce the quoted price when pressed. Visit a number of stores and use competing quotes to further reduce prices.

5. **Once you've negotiated the best price, see what else you can get the dealer to include.** Many dealers will include products such as DOS, Windows, or extra memory with your purchase to "sweeten" the deal. It pays to ask.

6. **Beware of unusually low prices.** A deal that is too-good-to-be-true usually indicates a "shady" deal. Products sold without the manufacturer's authorization may be inexpensive, but the manufacturer's warranty is often voided by the sale.

7. **Don't buy a service contract.** Unless your machine will be in constant use, or is used as part of a business, a service contract is not needed. If your computer should break down, and you do not have a service contract, you will have to wait a few days to have your machine repaired. But avoiding this inconvenience is not worth the price of the service contract. Computers are very reliable machines. If they break, they usually do so while under the manufacturer's warranty and will therefore be repaired for free with or without a service contract.

8. **Pay with a credit card.** Most of the major

credit card companies double the length of the manufacturer's warranty. In addition, they give you 60 days to stop payment if the dealer refuses to let you return an item or you have problem with the product.

Computers can be expensive, but good deals are available. Buy carefully and negotiate.

Source: "Never Pay the Sticker Price," *PC Computing,* February 1991, pp. 110–122.

prior to delivery. Some schools provide inexpensive and convenient on-campus repair facilities. Although such programs are economical, most schools cannot provide the type of user support found at local computer stores.

Mail-Order and Catalog Sales Computers, software, and peripheral devices, like most other products, can be purchased through the mail. Mail-order purchases are usually the least expensive way to buy computers and associated products. Mail-order purchases can reduce costs by as much as 50 percent, although buyers should watch for extra fees connected to shipping and handling that may significantly increase the purchase price. Although manufacturers' warranties remain in force with such purchases, customer support is nonexistent. A product that does not operate properly under warranty must be returned to the manufacturer in the original box. Once the warranty has expired, users are on their own. However, items that require no user support, such as ribbons, paper, disks, and computer games, are excellent mail-order purchases.

PROTECTING YOUR PURCHASE

Today when a microcomputer is purchased, all of the components necessary for operation, such as a keyboard, a monitor, internal and external memory, and some sort of operating system, are included. All that is needed to turn this machine into a problem-solving tool is carefully selected software. But two other factors are important as well—surge protectors and insurance riders.

Surge Protectors

No desktop computer should be purchased without a **surge protector.** This inexpensive and easily overlooked device can save the computer owner hundreds if not thousands of dollars in repairs. A surge protector, costing between $25 and $100, restricts or limits the amount of electrical current passing through an electrical outlet. If line current were constant and never interrupted, a surge protector would be unnecessary. After power failures and, to a lesser degree,

Figure 18.5   The Surge Protector.

when a device is turned on, power surges through lines into electrical devices. Such power surges can be so strong that chips burn out. Surge protectors safeguard electrical equipment from such burn-outs at a relatively insignificant cost (see Figure 18.5).

Although surge protectors should always be used with computers, they can provide protection for other devices as well. TVs, VCRs, and microwave ovens contain computer chips that can be damaged by power surges.

Insurance Riders

Another form of protection recommended for computers is insurance. Many homeowner and renter insurance policies do not cover repairs to or replacement of damaged or stolen computers. This is especially true if the computer is partially used for business purposes. Special computer riders available from insurance companies can be added to standard homeowners and renters policies at a nominal cost.

Given the cost of computers, peripherals, and software, surge protectors and policy riders are worth the expense.

BUYING SOFTWARE

When buying a computer system, it is difficult if not impossible to separate the purchase of software from the purchase of hardware. As stated earlier, the more carefully you analyze your computer needs and the more carefully you search for appropriate software to satisfy those needs, the happier you will be with your computer selection. Searching for appropriate software is not trivial. Within each application area, there can be hundreds of packages performing essentially the same task but in somewhat different ways. Many packages are well written and easy to use, but this is not always the case. Success in using a program is often a reflection of your computer experience. Packages such as *PFS: First Choice,* and *Microsoft Works* are designed for the new user. Other packages, such as Lotus and dBASE, require more experience.

Necessary Software

Chapter 10 identified the five building-block programs: (1) word processing, (2) spreadsheet, (3) file or data base management, (4) communication, and (5) graphics.

Although these packages constitute a fairly complete set of problem-solving computer tools, everyone does not need to purchase software from each of these groups. A spreadsheet program is an inherently useful program. However, it is valueless to the computer owner who has no interest in using the computer for personal or business finance. A data base program is an extremely valuable tool for organizing information, whether recipes, information about a stamp collection, or tax records. However, entering the data into a data base is a very time-consuming task. Without the necessary time commitment to data entry, a file or data base program is worthless.

Steps for Purchasing Software

Software needs and interests change, and computer owners purchase additional software to satisfy these needs. Just as careful planning is needed when purchasing a computer, so planning is necessary whenever software is purchased. The following six steps contribute to successful software purchases. They are applicable for both initial and future software purchases.

Step 1: Analyze your needs. Determine the type of software necessary to meet these needs. Create a list of the features you require. Imagine yourself using the package. What are your expectations? Adjust your list to reflect your expectations.

Step 2: Identify packages that suit your needs. Since software packages vary considerably in the features they contain and their ease of use, learn as much as possible about what is available. Read software reviews. Talk to other users. Test available software. Experiment with the software used by your friends, available at school, or in the library. Do not overlook local computer stores. They often have software you can test prior to purchase.

When reading software reviews, remember that, just like a movie, software appeals differently to different individuals. Just as a movie critic can pan a movie you absolutely loved, a software reviewer can praise a package you find hard to understand and difficult to use. It is often helpful to read several different reviews. Different reviewers will focus on different package features. By reading a number of reviews, a clearer picture of a package's advantages and disadvantages will emerge.

Although it is possible to develop software to satisfy your needs, good software requires considerable programming skill and is very time-consuming to write. Programmers can be hired to write software tailored to specific needs, but such programs are very expensive.

Step 3: Assess your hardware. Different packages often have different memory and hardware requirements. Before purchasing any program, be sure it will run on your machine or be prepared to purchase the additional hardware required.

Figure 18.6   Software: Comparison shopping for software can result in savings for the customer.

Step 4: Determine what you can afford. Price differences between packages can be significant. Be careful to purchase a package that will satisfy your present and anticipated needs. Avoid software extras you will never use.

Step 5: Comparison shop. Once you've determined which package you want, compare prices. Shop around. Just as you would look for the best price for a TV or VCR, do the same for software. Different computer stores sell the same software packages at different prices. Do not overlook mail-order software firms. Ordering software by mail can result in considerable savings. However, do not shop by price alone. Just as with the purchase of hardware, user support can mean the difference between a package that meets your needs and one that is worthless. When you are learning to use a new package, being able to show an experienced user a problem and to ask specific questions can be vital. Many manufacturers provide toll-free customer support telephone lines. Although price is important, user support can turn confusion into insight (see Figure 18.6).

Step 6: Purchase only what you need. Learning to use software effectively requires time. It is easiest to learn one package at a time. New packages are constantly being developed, and existing software is always being improved, refined, and made easier to use. Prices change. Buy only what you need at the moment. Don't buy software that may sit on the shelf and gather dust.

Carefully selected software will transform the computer from a confusing machine to a problem-solving tool.

LEARNING AND SUPPORT

Learning to use a computer requires time and attention. Unlike a television set, it cannot simply be plugged in and turned on.

Documentation

All hardware and software come with use and operating instructions called **documentation.** In most cases, documentation consists of written instruction manuals that try to explain everything from installation and general use to the troubleshooting of errors. Unfortunately, most documentation is written by the people who developed the hardware or software and understand its operation. Pages are often filled with buzzwords and jargon that the novice has yet to learn. Most new users find documentation anything but user-friendly. It is a valuable resource once you know how a package works, but as an initial learning tool it often leaves much to be desired.

Information and Self-Education

It is very difficult for a novice to learn to use a computer and make effective use of software simply by reading the accompanying documentation. For some, learning by experimentation, sometimes called **useful hacking,** is a rewarding experience. For most, more formal techniques are required. Computer books designed to assist in understanding software can be found in most bookstores. These are not textbooks. Rather, they are how-to guides written by people who are writing about software they have mastered. Such books are filled with examples and sample problems readers can follow as they work on their computers. Error messages are explained, common errors are examined, and possible solutions provided.

In addition to books, dozens of computer magazines are available at newsstands. Many of these include reviews and reports explaining how to make better use of both software and hardware. Many local newspapers and computer magazines include question-and-answer columns in which experts provide solutions to computer problems.

Courses and Training

For many, however, such self-help approaches are inadequate. Computers require hands-on instruction. Two forms of hands-on instruction are popular—tutorials and courses.

A number of manufacturers include self-teaching materials, or **tutorials,** along with their printed documentation. This material includes a series of lessons a user can follow while sitting at the computer. Each lesson is designed to provide instruction on the operation of a small portion of the software. *Hands-on* is the key. Such learning is self-guided and self-paced. Lessons can be provided on disk, as part of the printed documentation, or both.

Self-teaching material can be very useful, but it does not let the learner ask questions. Furthermore, it is often inflexible. For many, the quickest and easiest way to learn to use hardware and software is to enroll in a short course. Such courses are widely available. Some are provided by computer stores to assist and encourage customers. Short and semester-long computer courses are offered by local colleges and school districts. Although the costs of such courses vary, most are quite reasonable.

On the more expensive side, private organizations offer weekend classes designed to teach a specific software package very quickly. These courses can be very effective and very expensive. In addition, private lessons can provide an effective way to learn to use computers and software.

User Groups

All over the nation and in many foreign countries, computer users have formed clubs or groups called **user groups.** User groups form around particular types or models of computers. For example, Apple groups are distinct from Macintosh groups even though both machines are built by Apple Computer Corp. Groups exist for IBM PCs and compatibles, Apples, Ataris, Amigas, and many others, including machines that are no longer manufactured. (Machines are called **orphans** if they are no longer being manufactured.) These groups provide their members with many types of support ("No, you are not crazy if you think the documentation for that package was written by a Martian") as well as hardware and software information. Members share ideas and problem-solving tips.

User-written programs, or **shareware,** are made available to members. Shareware is public-domain software that is available for free distribution and has not been protected under U.S. copyright laws. Many groups maintain large software lending libraries where members can try out software prior to purchase. Examples of good shareware include PC-Write, PC-File, and PC-Talk.

Public-domain software can also be purchased directly from the author. Many are made available through catalogs. All are very inexpensive and the author is usually is willing to provide some support.

Some individuals join users groups for the hands-on support available from more experienced users. Others appreciate the social atmosphere where ideas and information can be easily shared. Many user groups have monthly or weekly meetings and include speakers and discussion on hardware and software.

Buying computers and software requires planning and a careful assessment of one's needs. Support, information, and training are readily available to those who seek them out. Carefully chosen and supported, a computer can be a fascinating, fun, and extremely valuable tool.

SUMMARY

Nine steps are important in making a successful computer purchase. They are: (1) analyze your needs, (2) determine affordability, (3) analyze software needs, (4) research available software, (5) shop for software and identify hardware requirements, (6) identify the appropriate computer, (7) shop again, (8) purchase the machine, and (9) put the machine to use.

The most popular ways to purchase computers are through computer stores, university and college buying plans, and mail order.

Surge protectors and insurance riders added to homeowner or renter policies are important safeguards for desktop computers.

Careful planning is needed when purchasing software. Six steps contribute to successful software purchases. They are: (1) analyze your software needs, (2) identify packages that suit your needs, (3) assess your hardware needs, (4) determine what you can afford, (5) comparison shop—look for the best price, and (6) purchase only what you need.

Documentation is the use and operating instructions that manufacturers provide with hardware and software.

Books, magazines, and newspapers provide people with information and advice on hardware and software use. **Tutorials** and courses can provide hands-on experience with computers and software.

User groups are clubs formed around a particular model or type of computer. These groups provide their members with support; access to software, including **shareware;** and problem-solving tips.

Key Words

As an extra review of the chapter, try defining the following terms. If you have trouble with any of them, refer to the page number listed.

compatibility *(477)*   shareware *(487)*
documentation *(485)*   surge protector *(481)*
expandability *(477)*   tutorial *(486)*
on-site service *(478)*   useful hacking *(486)*
orphan *(487)*   user group *(486)*

Test Your Knowledge

1. What is the first step needed for the successful purchase of both hardware and software?

2. Name the nine steps in buying a computer system.

3. Briefly describe each of the nine steps involved in buying a computer system.

4. Why is it necessary to identify software needs prior to a hardware purchase?

5. What role does the library play in buying a computer?

6. Why should compatibility and expandability be considered when purchasing a computer?

7. List the three popular sources for computer purchases.

8. What is a surge protector? Why is it useful?

9. Name the five building-block software packages.

10. Name the six steps in buying software.

11. Define *documentation.*

12. What types of self-education materials are available to computer owners?

13. Explain the two types of hands-on instruction available to educate users about computers and software.

14. What is a user group?

15. Define *shareware.*

Expand Your Knowledge

1. Contact your computing center and learn if your school participates in a computer buying program. If it does, gather material about the plan, including the hardware available and current price lists. Write a short paper instructing fellow students how to purchase a computer through your school.

2. Identify your computer needs. Using available resources, identify the software you would require and the hardware needed. In three columns list your needs, available software, and required hardware.

3. Using a local computer store and three computer magazines, compare prices for three printers and five software packages of your choice. How much can you save buying by mail? In your opinion, is buying by mail worth it?

4. Contact a local user group. Attend a meeting and write a short paper on the organization. Include the kind of support the group provides, meeting days and times, and location.

Photo Credits

Chapter 1

1.2(a) Apple Computer, Inc.; 1.2(b) Cray Research; 1.3(a) Boeing Company; 1.3(b) NASA; 1.4(a) COMPAQ Computer Corporation; 1.4(b) International Business Machines Corporation (IBM); 1.5 Raytheon Company; 1.6 Motorola; 1.8(a) IBM; 1.8(b) Apple Computer, Inc.; 1.9 Apple Computer, Inc.; 1.10 Radio Shack, Division of Tandy Corporation; 1.11 Toshiba America, Inc.; 1.12 Digital Equipment Corporation; 1.13 IBM; 1.14 Sun Microsystems; 1.15 IBM; 1.16 Cray Research.

Chapter 2

2.2 Dr. E.R. Degginger; 2.3(a) Portrait by Philippe de Champaign / The Bettmann Archive; 2.3(b) Smithsonian Institution Collection; 2.4(a) The Bettmann Archive; 2.4(b) IBM Archives; 2.5(a) The Granger Collection; 2.5(b) IBM Archives; 2.6(a) Smithsonian Institution Collection; 2.6(b) Courtesy Joan and David Slotnick; 2.7 BBC Hulton Picture Library / The Bettmann Archive; 2.8(a) IBM Archives; 2.9(a) IBM Archives; 2.9(b) Burroughs Corporation; 2.10(a) Iowa State University Information Service; 2.11 Topham / The Image Works; 2.12 Cruft Photo Lab, Harvard University; 2.13 University of Pennsylvania Archives; 2.14 The Institute for Advanced Studies, Princeton, N.J.; 2.15 Sperry Corporation; 2.16 IBM; 2.17 IBM; 2.18 Bettmann Archive; 2.19 IBM; 2.20 IBM; 2.21(a,b) IBM; 2.22 Digital Equipment Corporation; 2.23 Motorola Inc.; 2.25 Greg Weithman / Fotokammer; 2.26(a,b) UPI / Bettmann; 2.27 COMPAQ Computer Corporation; 2.28 Apple Computer Inc.; 2.30 NeXT.

Chapter 3

3.5(a,b) IBM; 3.6 IBM; 3.7 The Thinking Machine Corporation; 3.8 AT&T.

Chapter 4

4.2(a,b) 3M Company; 4.6 Seagate Technology; 4.9(a,b) BASF Corporation Information Systems; 4.10 Seagate Technology; 4.11 SONY Corporation of America.

Chapter 5

5.2(a,b,c) Apple Computer, Inc.; 5.3 Apple Computer Inc.; 5.4(a) Apple Computer, Inc.; 5.4(b) Microsoft Corporation; 5.5 WICO Corporation; 5.6 IBM; 5.7 Applicon; 5.8(a,b) IBM; 5.9 IBM; 5.10 IBM; 5.11 Panasonic Industrial Company; 5.14 Panasonic Industrial Company; 5.15 IBM; 5.16 Hewlett-Packard Company; 5.17 Hewlett-Packard Company; 5.18 Hewlett-Packard Company; 5.19(a,b,c) Hewlett-Packard Company; 5.20 Unisys Corporation; 5.21 Sun Microsystems; 5.22 Apple Computer, Inc.; 5.23 Hank Morgan / Rainbow; 5.24 Texas Instruments; 5.27 Recognition Equipment Incorporated; 5.29 Logitech; 5.30 Epson; 5.31 Kurzweil Computer Products, A Xerox Company; 5.32 Gridpad; 5.33 Spencer Grant / Picture Cube; 5.34 American Petroleum Institute; 5.35 NCR Corporation; 5.36 NCR Corporation.

Chapter 9

9.1 AP / Wide World Photos; 9.3 IBM.

Chapter 10

10.3 National Oceanic and Atmospheric Administration; 10.4 Boeing Aerospace; 10.5 IBM; 10.6 Chrysler Corporation; 10.7 IBM; 10.8 WordPerfect Corporation; 10.9 Microsoft; 10.11 Apple Computer, Inc.; 10.12 Microsoft.

Chapter 11

11.6 Microsoft; 11.7 Microsoft; 11.11 Aldus Corporation.

Chapter 13

13.10 Spencer Grant / The Picture Cube.

Chapter 14

14.1 NASA; 14.5 Microsoft; 14.6(a,b,c) IBM; 14.7 Microsoft; 14.8 IBM; 14.9 IBM; 14.10 Apple Computer, Inc.; 14.11 Image-In; 14.12 Compaq.

Chapter 15

15.3(a,b,c) Hayes Microcomputer Products, Inc.; 15.4 AT&T; 15.6 AT&T; 15.10 Microsoft; 15.11 Compuserve, Inc.

Chapter 16

16.1 SRI International; 16.4 Cary Wolinsky / Stock, Boston; 16.5 Otto Bock; 16.7 Peter Menzel / Stock, Boston.

Chapter 17

17.2 Saturn; 17.4 IBM; 17.5 IBM; 17.6 IBM; 17.7 IBM; 17.8 Billy E. Barnes / Stock, Boston.

Chapter 18

18.1(a) Apple Computer, Inc.; 18.1(b) Sierra On-Line; 18.2 Greg Weithman / Fotokammer; 18.3 Apple Computer, Inc.; 18.4 Spencer Grant / The Picture Cube; 18.5 Tandy Corporation; 18.6 Greg Weithman / Fotokammer.

Glossary

abacus an ancient calculating device invented in China around 5000 B.C. on which calculations are performed by manipulating strings of beads (Ch. 2)

ABC acronym for *Atanasoff Berry Computer* (Ch. 2)

aborted (bombed) a program that does not produce the desired results (Ch. 7)

academic computer network a computer network that enables geographically separated faculty members, researchers, administrators, and students to communicate, share ideas and resources, and work jointly on projects (Ch. 15)

access to call up a document or file on the computer (Ch. 11)

access arms movable arms, similar to the playing arm of a phonograph, that read information from disks (Ch. 4)

acoustic coupler an early modem that cradled a telephone receiver in rubber cups and translated digital signals into audible signals that could be transmitted over telephone lines (Ch. 15)

Ada a computer language named after Ada Lovelace that was commissioned by the Department of Defense to be an all-purpose computer language capable of doing all computer-related tasks, is highly structured, and is capable of communicating directly with computer hardware (Ch. 8)

address a number or code that describes the location in memory where data or instructions are stored (Ch. 3)

addressable a characteristic of data stored on magnetic disks; each data record has its own unique address or location in memory (Ch. 4)

ad-hoc query when a manager uses a decision support system to directly make special one-time requests without using the MIS department (Ch. 17)

AI acronym for *artificial intelligence* (Ch. 16)

ALGOL a computer language designed for scientific programming (Ch. 8)

algorithm a problem-solving procedure consisting of a step-by-step set of instructions (Ch. 6)

ALU acronym for *arithmetic and logic unit* (Ch. 3)

American Standard Code for Information Interchange see *ASCII* (Ch. 3)

analog computer a computer that manipulates measurable data such as voltage, pressure, and rotation (Ch. 1)

analog signal a continuous signal used in telephone line transmissions (Ch. 15)

analysis graphics visuals, such as graphs or charts, used to analyze large amounts of data by revealing relationships and trends (Ch. 14)

Analytical Engine a steam-powered, general-purpose computing device designed in 1833 by Englishman Charles Babbage that included the five components found in modern digital computers (Ch. 2)

applications software programs that allow the computer to perform particular tasks or solve specific problems (Ch. 10)

arithmetic and logic unit (ALU) the part of the CPU that contains circuitry responsible for performing addition, subtraction, multiplication, and division and can make simple decisions by choosing between two alternatives using the

arithmetic and logic unit (ALU) *(continued)* mathematical operations of less than (<), greater than (>), and equal to (=) (Ch. 3)

artificial intelligence (AI) the study of how to make computers do things which, in people, require basic intelligence, and which people find easy (Ch. 16)

ASCII (American Standard Code for Information Interchange) a seven-bit code used to store computer characters that is the standard code for most minicomputers and microcomputers (Ch. 3)

assemblers see *assembly languages* (Ch. 8)

assembly languages (assemblers) mnemonic, low-level computer languages whose individual instructions correspond directly with machine language instructions and that must be translated into machine-readable form; each type of computer has its own individual assembly language (Ch. 8)

Atanasoff Berry Computer (ABC) an early prototype for an electric computer invented in 1942 by John V. Atanasoff with the help of student Clifford Berry that included a memory drum and arithmetic unit (Ch. 2)

ATM acronym for *automated teller machine* (Ch. 5)

automated teller machines (ATMs) computerized banking machines that are available 24 hours daily and can be used to make deposits and withdrawals and to transfer funds between accounts (Ch. 5)

back-slash commands format commands in many text editor/text formatter systems that sit on a line by themselves in the screen's left margin and usually begin with a back-slash (Ch. 11)

backup duplicate copies of information stored in memory (Ch. 4)

backward compatible when an operating system has the ability to run earlier versions of software (Ch. 10)

bandwidth the amount of data a communication channel can transmit in a given block of time; the wider the bandwidth the faster the data can be transmitted (Ch. 15)

bar codes groups of black bars of varying thickness, such as those found on supermarket products, used in optical character recognition (Ch. 5)

bar graph a graph used to show the differences within a single set of data or to compare the relationships between different sets of data (Ch. 14)

BASIC a computer language invented as a tool to teach programming (Ch. 8)

batch processing off-line processing; data is collected off-line, when not directly connected to the computer, and submitted in batches or groups to the computer (Ch. 17)

baud rate transmission speed; generally refers to the number of bits that can be transmitted in a second. (Ch. 15)

binary number system a number system using base 2 (Ch. 1)

bit the symbol 0 or 1 (Ch. 1)

bit mapping using graphics software to link each pixel to a specific memory bit or set of bits (Ch. 14)

BITNET (Because It's Time NETwork) a cooperative, discipline-independent network begun between City University of New York and Yale University in 1981; it currently serves hundreds of colleges and universities worldwide (Ch. 15)

block see *physical record* (Ch. 4); also portions of text to be moved in a word processing system (Ch. 11)

bombed see *aborted* (Ch. 7)

broadband channels communication channels that transmit at rates of more than one million characters per second (Ch. 15)

bug any error in a computer program (Ch. 7)

Burroughs' Adding/Listing Machine the first practical adding and listing machine, unique because it used a paper printing device for output; patented in 1888 by William Burroughs (Ch. 2)

bus a group of shared wires that link the components of a computer; instructions, operational commands, and data pass along it (Ch. 3)

business graphics analysis graphics used in business (Ch. 14)

bus network a network that connects computing devices using a single, two-directional cable, capable of sending information between attached devices very quickly (Ch. 15)

byte a group of bits (usually eight) that represents one character of data (Ch. 1)

C a modern form of assembly language that has syntax structures of a high-level language along with the ability to communicate directly and easily with computer hardware (Ch. 8)

CAD acronym for *computer-aided design* (Ch. 14)

CAD/CAM acronym for *computer-aided design/ computer-aided manufacturing* (Ch. 14)

CAI acronym for *computer-assisted instruction* (Ch. 10)

CAM acronym for *computer-aided manufacturing* (Ch. 14)

CD-ROM (Compact Disc Read Only Memory) a highly compact, removable, *read-only*, optical storage medium, storing up to 660 MB (megabytes) per disk (Ch. 4)

cell the intersection of a given column and a specific row on a spreadsheet (Ch. 12)

central processing unit (CPU) the electronic circuitry within the computer that changes or processes data (Ch. 1)

CGA see *color graphics adaptor monitor* (Ch. 5)

character-based user interface a user-interface where words, or symbols are typed in at a *prompt* (Ch. 10)

chief information officer (CIO) individual responsible for managing all the computer, communications, and information resources of the organization (Ch. 17)

CIM acronym for *computer integrated manufacturing* (Ch. 17)

CIO acronym for *chief information officer* (Ch. 17)

clip art pictures, symbols, and drawings that can be inserted into graphic displays (Ch. 14)

clones IBM look-alikes that can use IBM hardware and software (Ch. 2)

coaxial cable a high-speed data-transmission medium that consists of two conductors, one cast like a shell around the other, and virtually eliminates electromagnetic interference (Ch. 15)

COBOL a high-level language invented during the second generation of computers and designed exclusively to assist businesses; well-suited for creating and processing large files and generating reports (Ch. 8)

color graphics adaptor (CGA) monitor a low-resolution color monitor that has a pixel density of 640 by 200 (Ch. 5)

color graphics (multi-color) monitors monitors that can produce multicolored displays (Ch. 5)

COLOSSUS the first practical single-purpose electronic computer, developed by the British during World War II with the help of Alan Turing and used exclusively to break German codes (Ch. 2)

command-driven an operating system or software package for which the user must remember and input a set of characters (commands) to get the system to perform the desired tasks (Chs. 10, 13)

command files files that contain groups or lists of commands frequently used together (Ch. 13)

commonsense reasoning the ability to assimilate, organize, and transform everyday knowledge into information used in problem solving (Ch. 16)

compatibles computers that can do most of what an IBM PC can do, including run its software (Ch. 2)

compatibility the ability of computers to run the same software and share data (Ch. 18)

compiler a program that takes a high-level language as input and translates it in a single operation, producing a machine-readable code as output (Ch. 7)

computer animation the use of computers to create moving images ranging from cartoon-like drawing to those that simulate or imitate reality (Ch. 14)

computer-aided design (CAD) the application of computer graphics to the design, drafting, or modeling of devices or structures (Ch. 14)

computer-aided design/computer-aided manufacturing (CAD/CAM) the combination of computer-aided design and computer-aided manufacturing into an automated manufacturing process (Ch. 14)

computer-aided manufacturing (CAM) is the use of advanced technology to manage and control manufacturing (Ch. 14)

computer-assisted instruction (CAI) self-paced instructional software that gives students immediate reinforcement when learning or reviewing material (Ch. 10)

computer (punched) card an 80-column paper card for storing computer data and instructions that uses one or more holes punched in each

computer (punched) card (*continued*) column to represent digits and uppercase letters (Ch. 4)

computer integrated manufacturing (CIM) a system where all phases of a product's design, manufacturing, and distribution are supported through a common data base environment (Ch. 17)

computer matching a procedure in which a computer is used to compare two files or lists of information, seeking the same item on both lists (Ch. 9)

computer network a group of computers and computer devices linked together over transmission lines so that information and resources can be shared (Ch. 15)

computer system a combination of hardware and software to solve problems and attain specific goals (Ch. 17)

computer virus a seemingly innocuous program disguised as normal software whose sole purpose is to destroy programs and data on the computers of unsuspecting users (Ch. 9)

computer vision a computer program that can process visual information (Ch. 16)

control unit a component of the CPU whose circuitry controls the internal activities of the computer and that manages the flow of data throughout the machine based on the instructions it receives from programs (Ch. 3)

copy (replicate) commands spreadsheet commands that make it possible to duplicate the contents of a cell or group of cells elsewhere on the spreadsheet (Ch. 12)

copy and paste technique used by many word processing and graphics packages to copy text or graphic objects from one location to another (Ch. 11)

core see *magnetic core memory* (Ch. 3)

CPU acronym for *central processing unit* (Ch. 1)

crash a breakdown of computer equipment (Ch. 4)

cursor a flashing light most often in the shape of a rectangle, underscore, or arrow that indicates on the screen where the next character will appear (Ch. 5)

cut and paste technique used by many word processing and graphics packages to move text or graphic objects from one location to another (Ch. 11)

daisy wheel the typing element on a letter-quality printer closely resembling spokes on a bicycle wheel that transfers characters onto paper when a hammer strikes each spoke (Ch. 5)

data raw facts collected from any number of sources that are the basis of information (Ch. 1)

data base raw facts usually organized around a topic, account number, or key to make specific items easy to find (Chs. 10, 13)

data base management systems (DBMS) complex data base systems able to search, sort, and report easily; used to manipulate multiple files at once (Chs. 10, 13)

data integrity reliability, directly related to the ability of the data base to remain current (Chs. 10, 13)

data item a single unit of data; a piece of data representing a single value (Ch. 4)

data processing see electronic data processing (Ch. 17)

DBMS acronym for *data base management systems* (Chs. 10, 13)

debugging finding and correcting errors in programs (Ch. 7)

decision support systems (DSS) computer system designed to provide managers with timely nonroutine information (Ch. 17)

default parameters (default settings) settings that a computer system will use unless directed otherwise (Ch. 11)

default settings see *default parameters* (Ch. 11)

delete to remove unwanted characters (Ch. 11)

deletion commands spreadsheet commands that make it possible to remove columns and rows that are no longer necessary (Ch. 12)

desk checking see *hand simulation* (Ch. 7)

desktop portable a personal computer designed like a small suitcase that has the capabilities of a standard desktop microcomputer (Ch. 1)

desktop publishing the production of camera-ready documents on a microcomputer that can be directly duplicated either on a copier or a phototypesetting machine (Ch. 11)

development software   programs used to create, update, and maintain other programs (Ch. 10)

diagnostic messages   error messages produced when a program is being translated; assist the programmer in diagnosing program problems by locating syntax errors that made statements impossible to translate (Ch. 7)

Difference Engine   a special-purpose computing device designed in 1822 by Englishman Charles Babbage to solve polynomial equations (Ch. 2)

digital computer   a device that manipulates data, performs arithmetic, and assists in problem solving by organizing data into countable units or digits (Ch. 1)

digital signal   high and low electrical pulses used to represent ones and zeros produced by computers and computing devices (Ch. 15)

digitized model   a binary version of a computer-aided design that is stored in memory (Ch. 14)

digitizer (graphics tablet)   an electronic drawing device that employs a special pen to sketch directly on the surface of a tablet and transmits the sketch simultaneously onto the screen (Ch. 5)

digitizing camera   a camera-like device that scans a diagram or picture and converts the image into digital form (Ch. 14)

direct-connect modem   a modem that connects directly into a telephone jack (Ch. 15)

direct OCR   see *direct optical character recognition* (Ch. 5)

direct optical character recognition (direct OCR)   a system that can read printed characters that are not written with special ink (Ch. 5)

diskette   see *floppy disk* (Ch. 4)

disk pack   2 to 12 disks stacked together on a single spindle, in a fashion similar to phonograph records (Ch. 4)

documentation   a written description of how a program or software package is to be used (Chs. 7, 12, 18)

DOS   acronym for *disk operating system,* the character-based operating system shipped with all IBM PC and compatible computers

dot commands   format commands in many text editor/text formatter systems that sit on a line by themselves in the screen's left margin and usually begin with a period or dot (Ch. 11)

dot matrix printer   printers whose characters are made up of a pattern or matrix of dots (Ch. 5)

download   to transmit a file as a unit from a larger computer to a smaller one (Chs. 5, 15)

drum plotter   a plotter that positions the paper over movable drums that rotate as the pens move (Ch. 5)

DSS   acronym for *decision support systems* (Ch. 17)

dumb terminal   a terminal that can be used only for entering data or viewing output and must be connected to a large computer (Ch. 5)

EBBS or BBS   see *electronic bulletin board* (Ch. 15)

EBCDIC (Extended Binary Coded Decimal Interchange Code)   an eight-bit code used to store characters on IBM mainframes (Ch. 3)

editing   changing or manipulating text (Ch. 11)

EDSAC   the first computer to incorporate a stored program, using letters as input and converting them to binary digits by means of a primitive assembler; built in 1949 at Cambridge University in England (Ch. 2)

EDVAC   a stored-program machine built in 1951 that used a unique binary code developed by John von Neumann (Ch. 2)

EFT   acronym for *electronic fund transfer* (Ch. 15)

EGA   see *enhanced graphics adaptor monitor* (Ch. 5)

EIS   acronym for *executive information systems* (Ch. 17)

electronic bulletin board (EBBS or BBS)   the simplest wide area network, which is called on the telephone by another computer so users can leave messages and exchange information (Ch. 15)

electronic data processing   the processing of ordinary or routine data such as payroll, inventory, and accounting (Ch. 17)

electronic fund transfer (EFT)   transferring funds electronically between banks (Chs. 10, 15)

electronic mail (E-mail)   the process by which computer users exchange electronic messages over telecommunication media (Ch. 1)

electronic spreadsheet   software designed to be an automated accountant's pad or ledger that can manipulate rows and columns of numbers (Chs. 10, 12)

electrostatic printers non-impact printers whose tiny wires, when electrically charged, induce a chemical reaction in the paper's chemical composition and produce dot matrix characters (Ch. 5)

E-mail see *electronic mail* (Ch. 1)

embedded computers computers built into other devices, including missiles, automobiles, and hospital intensive care unit equipment (Ch. 8)

enhanced graphics adaptor (EGA) monitor a high-resolution color monitor with a pixel density of 640 by 350 and useful in processing text and graphics (Ch. 5)

ENIAC the first general-purpose electronic computer, which was room-sized, contained 18,000 vacuum tubes, could perform several mathematical operations at once, and had limited memory capacity; developed in 1946 by John Mauchly and Presper Eckert at the Moore School (University of Pennsylvania) (Ch. 2)

EPROM acronym for *erasable and programmable read only memory* (Ch. 3)

erasable and programmable read only memory (EPROM) PROM chips that can be erased by removing them from the computer and specially treating them (Ch. 3)

Ethernet a LAN in which all computers and devices are connected to a single coaxial cable and that uses specially designed communications software to control data transmission (Ch. 15)

E-time see *execution time* (Ch. 3)

execute to process a program using a computer (Ch. 3)

execution time (E-time) the time required to execute an instruction (Ch. 3)

executive information systems (EIS) systems designed for top-level managers with the ability to integrate both internal and external information (Ch. 17)

expert system (knowledge-based system) a collection of rules used by human experts, written as a computer program that attempts to duplicate the ways in which professionals make decisions (Ch. 16)

Extended Binary Coded Decimal Interchange Code see *EBCDIC* (Ch. 3)

external direct-connect modem a stand-alone modem housed in a self-contained box that plugs into both the computer (or terminal) and the phone jack (Ch. 15)

expandability ability to increase the capacity of a computer system by adding memory, boards, and peripheral devices (Ch. 18)

families of software software that is integrated by designing groups of stand-alone programs that store information in a common format and use a common set of operating commands (Ch. 10)

fax (facsimile) a modem-like device designed to transmit images over standard telephone lines without requiring a computer (Ch. 15)

feasibility study preliminary investigation; first phase of the system life cycle where the current system is briefly analyzed to determine if it should be developed, enhanced, or replaced (Ch. 17)

fiber optic cable thin, clear plastic or glass wires that use lasers to transmit vast amounts of data very quickly (Ch. 15)

field a *data item* (Ch. 4) or a column in a data base that contains a specific type of information, such as last name or first name (Ch. 13)

file combinations of records that are read and processed as a single unit (Ch. 4)

file managers the simplest kind of data base packages, usually menu-driven, able to process only one file at a time and to search and sort records on any of the fields in the record (Ch. 13)

firmware another name for read only memory (Ch. 3)

first-generation computers the first commercial computers, which contained vacuum tubes, used computer (punched) cards for input and output of data and instructions, had magnetic core memory, and were programmed using machine language; included UNIVAC I and the IBM 650 (Ch. 2)

flatbed plotter a plotter in which the paper is held in one place while the pens move across the page (Ch. 5)

flatbed scanner an optical device used to capture and duplicate into a computer pages of text and images larger than a standard sheet of paper (Ch. 5)

floppy disk (diskette) a small, removable magnetic disk used mostly with microcomputers (Ch. 4)

flowchart a pictorial method of depicting an algorithm in which the focus is on the program's logical flow (Ch. 6)

font a character shape or type style (Chs. 5, 11)

footer information at the bottom of a page (Ch. 11)

format the layout of text (Ch. 11), or spreadsheet commands that allow the user to justify (right, left, or center) cell data (Ch. 12)

format commands commands that allow the user to justify data as necessary within a spreadsheet cell, display numbers in their most meaningful form, and adjust the width of columns to allow for data of varying length (Ch. 12)

formulas mathematical statements or sets of instructions associated with a spreadsheet cell and used to calculate the value of that cell (Ch. 12)

FORTRAN a high-level language invented during the second generation of computers for processing complex mathematics that is still popular in mathematics and engineering (Ch. 8)

fourth-generation computers modern digital computers based upon large-scale integration and microprocessors (Ch. 2)

frame a collection of data and associated rules that, taken as a unit, provides a natural language system with the information it needs to understand a fact or concept (Ch. 16)

full backup a complete copy of all the data stored in memory at a given time (Ch. 4)

function special spreadsheet software routines that perform frequently needed tasks, including sum, average, standard deviation, and square root (Ch. 12)

function-based information systems an information system that provides support for a specific application area (Ch. 17)

function keys special additional keyboard keys found on intelligent terminals and personal computers that can be programmed to perform special tasks (Ch. 5)

gateway a computer that connects two different computer networks; a network-to-network connector (Ch. 15)

general-purpose applications software software programs that focus on particular areas but can be adapted to individual needs (Ch. 10)

general-purpose computer a computer designed to solve a variety of problems (Ch. 1)

global search and replace a word processing command that tells the computer to replace every occurrence of a particular word or phrase with a specified correction (Ch. 11)

graphical-user interface (GUI) a user-interface that combines a pointing device *(mouse)*, icons, and window-oriented software with multitasking (Ch. 10)

graphics board a set of chips that allow a graphics monitor to run on a computer (Ch. 5)

graphics editors graphics software that includes preprogrammed graphics primitives, such as circles, squares, points, curves, and lines, that can be entered on the screen and manipulated along with freehand drawings; also called paint packages or computer easels (Ch. 14)

graphics tablet see *digitizer* (Ch. 14)

GUI acronym for *graphical-user interface* (Ch. 10)

hacker someone who intentionally, maliciously or not, breaks into other computer systems (Ch. 9)

hand-held portable a tiny, light, portable computer with limited memory, cassette-tape storage, and a one-line display (Ch. 1)

hand scanners a hand-held optical device measuring three to four inches in width used to capture images and text for desktop systems (Ch. 5)

hand simulation (desk checking) using pencil and paper to go through each program instruction to identify the step or steps that are producing errors (Ch. 7)

hard copy computer output printed on paper (Ch. 5)

hard disk see *magnetic disk* (Ch. 4)

hardware the set of physical components that combine to make up a computer system (Ch. 1)

Harvard MARK I a general-purpose computing device developed by Harvard professor Howard Aiken, in association with IBM, that used electromagnetic telephone relays, punched paper tape, and could perform addition or subtraction in 0.3 second, yet is not often considered a com-

Harvard MARK I (*continued*)
puter because it did not have a memory (Ch. 2)

header information at the top of a page (Ch. 11)

Hercules board a monochrome graphics board that produces high-resolution characters and shaded display graphics on a monochromatic monitor (Ch. 5)

heuristics written or unwritten rules of thumb used when people evaluate situations or make decisions (Ch. 16)

high-level languages English-like programming languages, such as Pascal, BASIC, FORTRAN, COBOL, Modula 2, and Ada, designed for easy problem solving that do not require an in-depth knowledge of the computer's internal structure but need a *compiler* (Ch. 7) to translate instructions into machine readable form (Ch. 8)

Hollerith's Census Machine an early calculating device that automated the tabulating of census information and could be used to keep track of large amounts of similar data (Ch. 2)

holography a method of storing data by making a two- or three-dimensional photograph on a crystalline storage medium (Ch. 4)

home computer a microcomputer designed for use in the home (Ch. 1)

host computer a multiuser machine, either a mainframe or a minicomputer, with terminals, printers, card readers, and other peripherals connected to it (Ch. 15)

hybrid computer a computer that combines the input/output design of an analog computer with the digital computer's ability to store instructions and perform highly accurate mathematical calculations (Ch. 1)

hypermedia hypertext whose links include sound, video, and graphics, as well as text (Ch. 11)

hypertext software that allows users to browse through linked information in any order (Ch. 11)

IBG acronym for *interblock gap* (Ch. 4)

IBM 650 the first computer designed specifically for the business community (Ch. 2)

IC acronym for *integrated circuits* (Ch. 2)

icons on-screen pictures that represent common computer tasks (Chs. 2, 10)

image editor (graphic illustrator) high-end, advanced graphic editors that support the use of color scanners (Ch. 14)

impact printers printers whose characters are formed by tiny hammers striking paper through an inked ribbon (Ch. 5)

index file a file containing key data and record numbers that is used in indexing to improve sorting speed (Ch. 13)

indexing a data base feature in which the index file is sorted rather than the original file (Ch. 13)

inference engine a set of programs within an expert system's knowledge base that manipulate the if/then rules to make judgments or intelligent guesses in a human-like fashion (Ch. 16)

information the result of changing data in some way so that meaningful conclusions can be drawn (Ch. 1)

information centers location within an organization where technical support and computing resources are provided for short-term projects (Ch. 17)

information networks private computer networks that offer subscribers access to data base information, bulletin boards, and electronic mail service, as well as travel and shopping opportunities (Ch. 15)

information resource management (IRM) the concept that information is a corporate resource just like people, materials, equipment and facilities (Ch. 17)

information utilities electronic data bases, some of which offer specific information such as medical journal articles, available to any microcomputer owner willing to subscribe (Ch. 15)

inheritance a characteristic of object-oriented programming languages in which a new *object*, unknown to the computer, is defined for the computer in terms of objects that the computer already knows as defined properties (these defined properties are called the new object's "parents") (Ch. 8)

inkjet printers non-impact printers that squirt microscopic dots of ink on the surface of paper to form dot matrix characters; frequently used to produce color graphics (Chs. 5, 14)

input the initial, or raw, data entered into the computer for processing (Ch. 1)

input device a piece of computer hardware designed to transmit data to the CPU (Chs. 1, 5)

insertion command a spreadsheet command used to place new columns or rows wherever needed (Ch. 12); also a wordprocessor command for adding characters to text (Ch. 11)

instruction time (I-time) the time required to interpret an instruction (Ch. 3)

integrated circuits (IC) chips of a semiconductor material, usually silicon, etched with miniaturized electronic circuitry (Ch. 2)

integrated information systems an information system that supports more than one area in a business through a shared data base (Ch. 17)

integrated packages powerful software tools such as word processors, spreadsheets, data base managers, and graphics combined into a single package (Ch. 10)

intellectual property the concept that the ideas upon which software is based are considered to be the property of their author (Ch. 9)

intelligent modems modems that contain a multiprocessor chip and can be programmed to automatically dial and answer the telephone and disconnect from the phone system when a conversation is complete (Ch. 15)

intelligent terminal a computer terminal with its own built-in microprocessor that is capable of performing limited processing tasks independent of the computer to which it is attached (Ch. 5)

interactive processing on-line processing; processing that supports interactive human/machine communication. (Ch. 17)

interblock gap (IBG) a section of blank tape that separates blocks on magnetic tape (Ch. 4)

intermediate results partial or incomplete results calculated by a program during processing; the printing of these results is used to locate logic and syntax errors (Ch. 7)

internal direct-connect modem a modem inside the computer housing that uses the computer's power supply (Ch. 15)

Internet a collection of interconnected wide-area academic and research networks running the TCP/IP network protocol; includes NSFnet, MILnet, and a number of academic and state-wide networks (Ch. 15)

interpreter a special program that translates and executes a program one statement at a time (Ch. 7)

interrecord gap (IRG) a piece of blank tape used to separate logical records for processing on magnetic tape (Ch. 4)

IRG acronym for *interrecord gap (Ch. 4)*

IRM acronym for *information resource management* (Ch. 17)

I-time see *instruction time* (Ch. 3)

JIT acronym for *just-in-time manufacturing* (Ch. 17)

Josephson Junction an electronic switch invented in the early 1980s that could change states from 0 to 1 at least 10 times faster than devices in use at the time (Ch. 3)

joystick a keyboard alternative used almost exclusively with home computers and video games to move the cursor around the screen (Ch. 5)

justified margins that are even or straight (Ch. 11)

just-in-time manufacturing (JIT) manufacturing that emphasizes the team approach where quality control is the responsibility of managers and workers (Ch. 17)

key see *key field* (Ch. 13)

key field (key) a field shared by different files in a data base (Ch. 13)

keyboard the traditional means of putting information into a computer from a terminal; contains standard typewriter keys, a number pad, and special keys such as CTRL, ESC, and BREAK used to communicate with the computer (Ch. 5)

knowledge base the facts and the rules of thumb (heuristics) written as a series of if/then statements that provide an AI program with information about the world in which the computer will be involved (Ch. 16)

knowledge-based system see *expert system* (Ch. 16)

labels words, titles, or text within a spreadsheet that are used to form row and column headings (Ch. 12)

LAN acronym for *local-area network* (Ch. 15)

laptop portable a computer designed to fit com-

laptop portable (*continued*)
fortably into a briefcase and having a type-writer-sized keyboard and monitor (Ch. 1)

large-scale integration (LSI) the technology by which thousands of circuits are squeezed onto computer chips, reducing machine size and improving speed (Ch. 2)

laser printers non-impact printers that combine lasers with copy-machine technology to produce dense dot matrix characters (Ch. 5)

learning by generalization learning from mistakes; using generalizations from one experience to interact with another similar experience (Ch. 16)

Leibniz's Multiplier a calculating device invented in 1673 by Gottfried Wilhelm von Leibniz that expanded upon Pascal's calculator and could add, subtract, multiply, and divide (Ch. 2)

letter-quality printers printers that produce type indistinguishable from that formed by an electric typewriter by printing a completely formed character with each strike of a hammer (Ch. 5)

light pen a hand-held pen with a light-sensitive point, connected to the computer by a narrow cable, and used as an input device in association with a keyboard and CRT (Chs. 5, 14)

line graph a graph that reflects trends by the upward or downward direction of its lines (Ch. 14)

line printer a printer that types an entire line of output at once (Ch. 5)

linkage editor (link/load program) a program that automatically links programs being translated for use by a computer (Ch. 7)

link/load program see *linkage editor* (Ch. 7)

LISP the dominant language for artificial intelligence programming that is designed to manipulate lists of non-numeric information (Ch. 8)

local area network (LAN) a computer network that covers a limited geographic area, such as a series of offices or an entire building, and is owned or operated by a single organization or college (Ch. 15)

logical records combinations of related fields on magnetic tape (Ch. 4)

logic error a program error produced when a program executes completely but either no output or incorrect output results because the algorithm or logic of the program is incorrect (Ch. 7)

log in to connect to a computer (Ch. 15)

LOGO an interactive programming language designed to teach programming to children through the use of on-screen graphics to develop and reinforce problem-solving skills (Ch. 8)

LSI acronym for *large-scale integration* (Ch. 2)

machine-dependent usable by only one brand of computer (Ch. 8)

machine-independent a computer language or program that operates on any computer for which an appropriate *translator program* exists (Ch. 8)

machine languages the lowest level of computer languages, uses instructions in the form of combinations of 1's and 0's and can be understood and interpreted directly by the machine's internal circuitry; each type of computer has its own individual machine language (Ch. 8)

machine learning programs that "teach" computers how to play games with well-defined rules in an effort to simulate the learning process (Ch. 16)

machine translation the area of AI involved with designing natural language programs to translate information quickly, efficiently, and automatically from one language to another (Ch. 16)

magnetic core memory (core) a nonvolatile storage medium used with early computers that consisted of tiny ($\frac{1}{100}$ inch) iron oxide (ferrite) rings with several wires threaded through each ring that could be magnetized to represent 1 or 0 (Ch. 3)

magnetic disk (hard disk) a direct access storage device first marketed by IBM in 1956, both sides (surfaces) of which are coated with a magnetizable compound able to store data and instructions as magnetized dots (Ch. 4)

magnetic ink character recognition (MICR) a system designed to automate check processing in which a machine similar to a card reader reads numbers containing iron oxide particles printed at the bottom of a check (Ch. 5)

magnetic tape a strong plastic tape coated on one side with an iron oxide on which computer data and instructions can be stored as microscopic magnetized dots (Ch. 4)

magneto-optical disk   a rewritable, removable, optical storage medium that combines lasers with a magnetic recording medium (Ch. 4)

mainframe   a large, very fast, 32- to 64-bit multiuser computer (Ch. 1)

mail-merge   a word processing feature that combines a list of names and addresses with a form letter (Ch. 11)

management information systems (MIS)   systems designed so that different departments within an organization can share common data (Ch. 17)

manufacturing resource planning (MRP)   an integrated information system that allows the different areas of a manufacturing company such as engineering, production, purchasing, inventory, and marketing to have access to a common data base of information (Ch. 17)

massively parallel computer   a parallel computer that distributes a problem's calculations across a very large number of independent, low-cost, carefully coordinated processors (Ch. 3)

megabyte   the equivalent of one million bytes (Ch. 1)

memory (storage)   the electronic circuits that store data and the results of processing (Ch. 1)

menu   a list of options (Ch. 11)

message   a means by which objects communicate with each other; instructs an object to carry out its operations (Ch. 8)

MICR   acronym for *magnetic ink character recognition* (Ch. 5)

micro   see *microcomputer* (Ch. 1)

microcomputer (micro)   a single-user computer whose CPU is a microprocessor (Ch. 1)

microprocessor   a chip containing a central processing unit (CPU) and its associated memory, often called a computer on a chip (Ch. 1)

microwave signals   very high-frequency radio waves that can be used to transmit data at high speed, including computer data and television sound and pictures (Ch. 15)

mini   see *minicomputer* (Ch. 1)

minicomputer (mini)   a multiuser digital computer that is smaller, less expensive, and has less data-handling capability than a mainframe but is more expensive and more powerful than a microcomputer (Ch. 1)

MIS   acronym for *management information systems* (Ch. 17)

modem   a device that converts, or modulates, computer-generated digital signals into corresponding analog signals so they can be carried over phone lines (Ch. 15)

Modula-2   an improved version of Pascal, with the ability to control system hardware, that is designed to support the development of large programs through the careful use of subprograms (Ch. 8)

monochrome monitor   a computer monitor designed to display high-resolution text using lighted pixels of a single color to produce images on a dark background and whose characters have a pixel density of 720 by 350 (Ch. 5)

mouse   a palm-sized pointing device for a computer used in association with a keyboard (Ch. 5)

MRP   acronym for *manufacturing resource planning* (Ch. 17)

multimedia presentation   presentations that use video displays, on-screen animation, projections of interactive computer displays in addition to traditional transparencies, slides, and handouts (Ch. 14)

multiprocessor   a CPU designed to perform multiple tasks simultaneously (Ch. 1)

multitasking   the ability for multiple software applications to run at the same time (Ch. 10)

multiuser system   a computer system designed to handle more than one user at a time (Ch. 1)

narrowband channels   communication channels that transmit at rates of less than 30 characters per second and are rarely used for the transmission of computer data (Ch. 15)

natural language interface   a query language where input instructions are entered in ordinary sentences in a natural language and receive appropriate natural language answers (Ch. 16)

natural language processing   a research area within artificial intelligence investigating the ability of computers to process information re-

natural language processing (*continued*) ceived by the computer in a natural (human) language such as English (Ch. 5)

natural language understanding a research area within artificial intelligence working towards the development of systems that comprehend and then act upon human language (Ch 8, 16)

node any computer, computing device, or peripheral connected to a computer network (Ch. 15)

non-impact printers printers that use heat, electricity, lasers, photography, or ink sprays to print dot matrix characters (Ch. 5)

notebook portable a light, portable computer approximately the size of an $8\frac{1}{2}$ by 11 inch notebook, with a typewriter-sized keyboard and a small monitor (Ch. 1)

NSFnet a wide area network created by the National Science Foundation, initially intended to provide both supercomputers and access to them to researchers nationwide (Ch. 15)

number crunching the solving of complex problems that involve vast amounts of mathematical manipulations (Ch. 1)

object a self-contained unit of data and its associated operations (Ch. 8)

object code see *object program* (Ch. 7)

object-oriented programming a recent programming technique that combines data with the operations that act on the data into a single unified structure (Ch. 8)

object program (object code) the translated machine-language version of a program (Ch. 7)

OCR acronym for *optical character recognition* (Ch. 5)

offline processing see batch processing (Ch. 17)

OMR acronym for *optical mark reader* (Ch. 5)

online processing see *interactive processing* (Ch. 17)

on-site service computer repairs done at the location of a computer (Ch. 18)

operating environment a graphic user-interface and operating system where pictures, or icons, indicate basic functions (Ch. 10)

operating system software that coordinates or oversees the tasks performed by the computer by integrating the instructions of a specific pro-

gram with the actual wiring of the computer's hardware and that also provides communication between the user and the programs (Ch. 10)

operational information short-term, day-to-day information that focuses on the internal operation of the organization (Ch. 17)

optical character recognition (OCR) computer recognition of printed information in the form of bar codes or the direct recognition of printed characters (Ch. 5)

optical mark reader (OMR) an input device designed to read hand-written pencil marks on specially designed forms; commonly used to analyze multiple choice tests and survey questions (Ch. 5)

optical processor a prototype computer processor comprised of light-based optical switches or transistors (Ch. 3)

orphans computers that are no longer being manufactured (Ch. 18)

outliner software which provide fill-in-the-blanks outline formats to help users plan and organize talks (Ch. 14)

output information that is the result of computer processing (Ch. 1)

output device computer hardware that communicates computer output to people (Chs. 1, 5)

overwriting typing over letters in word processing (Ch. 11)

parallel computing computers containing more than one CPU that can execute multiple instructions simultaneously (Ch. 3)

parity (check bit) an extra bit added to ASCII and EBCDIC codes to ensure accurate transmission of data (Ch. 3)

partial backup a copy of data items that have changed over a given period of time (Ch. 4)

Pascal a computer language named after the mathematician Blaise Pascal that is a general-purpose teaching language emphasizing top-down design (Ch. 8)

Pascal's Calculator the first adding machine, invented in 1642 by Frenchman Blaise Pascal and consisted of a series of gears or wheels that could perform addition and subtraction when manipulated (Ch. 2)

PC acronym for *personal computer* (Chs. 1, 2)

pen-based system a pen or stylus-based computer system that allows users to print characters on a touch sensitive screen; the hand printed characters are then converted into computer readable form by complex handwriting recognition programs (Ch. 5)

peripheral devices see *peripherals (Ch. 5)*

peripherals (peripheral devices) the physical devices attached to the computer's CPU (Ch. 5)

perpendicular recording a storage technique that realigns the magnetized dots of data stored on disks, greatly increasing storage capacity (Ch. 4)

personal computer (PC) a flexible and memory-rich microcomputer (Ch. 1), and the name coined by IBM for its single-user microcomputer (Ch. 2)

phreaking free telephoning using phone numbers that hackers have obtained by illegally breaking into computer systems (Ch. 9)

physical record (block) a group of logical records that are read and processed at once (Ch. 4)

pie chart a graph used to show proportional relationships in a given set of data (Ch. 14)

Pixar a computer graphics system that produces computer-generated visual effects that cannot be distinguished from natural photography (Ch. 14)

pixels points of light on a computer screen used to create graphic images (Chs. 5, 14)

point-of-sale (POS) systems computer systems that process business transactions at the location (point) where the sale occurs and are commonly found in supermarkets, department stores, and restaurants (Ch. 5)

point-to-point connection the direct connection of two computing devices via a transmission medium (Ch. 15)

portable the ability to move programs from machine to machine with only minor changes required (Ch. 8)

portable computer a complete microcomputer designed to be carried from place to place (Ch. 1)

preprogrammed having program instructions directly built-in (Ch. 1)

presentation graphics analysis graphics designed to assist in presenting insights to others (Ch. 14)

previewing the ability to examine a document on the screen as it will appear on paper (Ch. 11)

primary memory memory associated with the CPU that stores instructions and data while a file or program is being processed (Ch. 3)

privacy the right to be left alone (Ch. 9)

program the step-by-step set of instructions, written in a computer language, that directs the computer to perform specific tasks and solve specific problems (Ch. 1)

programmable read only memory (PROM) special ROM chips on which user-written programs can be stored and that can be programmed only once (Ch. 3)

programming language a language that people use to communicate with computers (Ch. 8)

PROM acronym for *programmable read only memory* (Ch. 3)

prompt a symbol or set of symbols on the screen that indicate that the computer is waiting for a command to be entered (Ch. 10)

protocols computer communication rules that control transmission speeds, the direction of transmission, error detection and correction, and interruption techniques (Ch. 15)

pseudocode a written method that uses English phrases and formulas in outline form to indicate the step-by-step instructions necessary for solving a problem (Ch. 6)

punched paper tape a one-inch-wide continuous strip of paper on which computer data instructions can be stored as a unique pattern of holes punched across the tape's width (Ch. 4)

RAM see *random access memory* (Ch. 3)

random access memory (RAM) user-programmable, general-purpose memory that stores program instructions, initial data, and intermediate and final results from programs (Ch. 3)

read only memory (ROM) pre-programmed or manufacturer-defined memory that utilizes non-volatile, primary memory chips and contains vital operational instructions for the computer (Ch. 3)

read/write head a tiny electromagnet that can create, read, or erase the magnetic dots that store information on the surface of a magnetic disk (Ch. 4)

recalculate the ability of a spreadsheet to immedi-

recalculate *(continued)*
ately recompute all formulas when a data value is changed (Ch. 12)

records combinations of fields that form larger units of meaningful information (Ch. 4), or a row in a data base that contains related information such as a student's name and address (Ch. 13)

register very fast, mini-memory device directly embedded in the CPU that is used to hold a data item, an instruction, or a piece of information (Ch. 3)

report paper or disk copy of summaries of data found in a data base; grouping of related data items so that they can be easily understood by the reader (Ch. 13)

resolution a measure of pixel density on a computer screen (Chs. 5, 14)

RGB the red-green-blue format used by most color monitors (Ch. 5)

ring network a network connecting a group of computers and peripherals in a loop or ring (Ch. 15)

robot a mechanical, often arm-like, device that can be programmed to do a number of tasks; computer-controlled device equipped with sensors for detecting input and environmental changes; able to make simple decisions (Ch. 16)

robotics an area of AI involved with the design and programming of robots; concerned with creating machines capable of recognizing, and effectively reacting to changes in their environment (Ch. 16)

ROM acronym for *read only memory* (Ch. 3)

rote learning learning by memorization (Ch. 16)

ruler line see *status line* (Ch. 11)

run-time error error message produced when a program is executed and stops processing (Ch. 7)

scattergram a graph that shows the distribution among a set of values (Ch. 14)

search a procedure in which the computer will examine stored data to find items that satisfy particular criteria (Ch. 11)

search and replace the process by which a computer searches for a designated word or phrase and replaces it with another word or phrase (Ch. 11)

secondary memory memory outside the processor that is used for semi-permanent storage (Chs. 3, 4)

second-generation computers computers based on the transistor that could be programmed in either assembly language or a higher-level language such as FORTRAN or COBOL and whose solid-state technology made them smaller, faster, and more reliable than first-generation machines (Ch. 2)

seek time the time it takes to find information on a disk (Ch. 4)

semantic network a computer model of natural language to aid researchers in better understanding how people use language; a structure for storing data using links or nodes that specify the facts and concepts, as well as their relationships (Ch. 16)

semantics the meaning of words and phrases (Ch. 16)

semiconductor memory the current memory technology in which thousands of microscopic integrated circuits are etched on a silicon chip (Ch. 3)

semi-structured problem a problem where some of the problem solving phases are well defined (Ch. 17)

shareware user-written or public-domain software that is available for free distribution and is not protected under U.S. copyright laws (Chs. 15, 18)

silicon chips tiny integrated circuits packed onto chips of silicon (Ch. 2)

slide rule a calculating device invented in 1621 by William Oughtred that has two rulers that slide against one another and are marked so that the distances of the markings from the ends are mathematically proportional (Ch. 2)

soft copy computer output sent to a video screen (Ch. 5)

software programs used for problem solving or that direct the operations of the computer (Ch. 1)

solid model a seemingly three-dimensional model produced by CAD software (Ch. 14)

solid state a tiny electronic switch built with no moving parts (Ch. 2)

sorting a data base procedure that reorders or rearranges the records in a data base file either alphabetically, numerically, or chronologically (Ch. 13)

source code see *source program* (Ch. 7)

source program (source code) the high-level language version of a program (Ch. 7)

special-purpose computer a computer that is designed to solve a specific problem and has program instructions built directly into its hardware (Ch. 1)

specialized applications software applications software that focuses on a very specific task or group of tasks (Ch. 10)

speech recognition (natural language recognition) a computer input device that focuses on specific voices or understands natural language (Ch. 5)

star network network that connects computers and peripherals to a central or host computer with all the attached devices radiating out from the central machine (Ch. 15)

status line (ruler line) the line on a word processing screen where information about the file appears, including cursor location, the amount of text entered, and the file name (Ch. 11)

storage see *memory* (Ch. 1)

stored program concept a theoretical program design developed by mathematician John von Neumann in the late 1940s in which program instructions are stored as numeric codes directly in the machine's memory (Ch. 2)

strategic information information used by top level managers that focuses on external data (Ch. 17)

strategic planning planning done by top level managers that set an organization's goals for the longterm (three to five years) (Ch. 17)

subprogram a division of a large, complex program that solves a specific part of the problem (Ch. 8)

subsystem part of a complex system; a system within a system (Ch. 17)

supercomputers ultra-fast computers designed to process hundreds of millions of instructions per second and store and retrieve millions of data items (Ch. 1)

superconduction the condition in which the resistance and heat associated with the flow of electricity is virtually eliminated (Ch. 3)

supermini minicomputers that perform like mainframes (Ch. 1)

superVGA monitors a super high resolution color monitor with a pixel density of between 800 × 600 pixels and 1280 × 1024 pixels; most complex models have photographic quality and require graphic boards that contain dedicated microprocessors and large amounts of memory to control the pixels and their output

surge protector a peripheral device designed to safeguard electrical equipment by restricting or limiting the amount of current passing through an electrical outlet (Ch. 18)

syntax the set of rules that define how words and mathematical expressions can be combined within a computer language (Ch. 7)

syntax errors errors made in the use and structure of programming language (Ch. 7)

system a collection of people, machines, and methods organized to accomplish a set of specific functions (Ch. 17)

system analysis second phase in systems development life cycle where the operation of the present system is carefully examined and analyzed; fact-finding (Ch. 17)

systems design third phase in systems development life cycle, which is the process of constructing a plan for a system based on systems analysis (Ch. 17)

systems development fourth phase in systems development life cycle, which is the process of developing, programming, and testing a new system (Ch. 17)

systems development life cycle a systems cycle consisting of a feasibility study, systems analysis, systems design, systems development, systems implementation, and systems evaluation (Ch. 17)

systems evaluation sixth phase in systems development life cycle, in which the system is evaluated to determine if it meets its objectives and is performing expected tasks (Ch. 17)

systems implementation fifth phase in systems development life cycle in which the designed system is placed in operation (Ch. 17)

systems software software that controls the operation of the computer, receives input, produces output, manages and stores data, and carries out

systems software (*continued*)
or executes the instructions of other programs (Ch. 10)

tactical information information used by middle level managers to plan and operate an organization for up to a year (Ch. 17)

tactical planning planning done by middle level managers that is needed to implement an organization's objectives for up to one year (Ch. 17)

telecommunication the transmission of information, including computer-generated data, telephone conversations, or video in the form of television, over long distances using communication lines (Ch. 15)

telecomputing the exchanging of information between computers and computing devices over communication lines (Ch. 15)

template the outline of a spreadsheet with only the key labels and formulas set in the appropriate places (Ch. 12)

text editor/text formatter software two-phase word processing software whose text contains special formatting or dot commands that provide instructions to the formatter; to see what a document looks like, the user must leave the editor portion of the program and run the formatter portion (Ch. 11)

thermal printers non-impact printers whose tiny, heated wires react chemically with special paper to produce dot matrix characters (Ch. 5)

third-generation computers computers that used integrated circuits with electronic circuitry etched onto small silicon chips and were smaller, more reliable, and less expensive than second-generation machines (Ch. 2)

toggling hitting a key more than once to turn it on and then off (Ch. 11)

tools libraries of utility programs used in UNIX that implement common tasks such as copying and listing files (Ch. 10)

top-down analysis a technique for breaking down problems into subtasks that can be further divided until each subtask can be solved directly (Ch. 6)

topology the physical layout of a computer network (Ch. 15)

touch screen a user-friendly computer terminal designed so that the user makes choices or activates commands by pointing to and touching information displayed on the screen (Ch. 5)

touch tablet an input device with a $4\frac{1}{2}$-inch square pad that combines features of a mouse with a touch screen and was developed by Koala Technologies Corp. for use with home and personal computers (Ch. 5)

trackball a stationary mouse that is a rectangular pointing device measuring 4–5 inches on each side with a one-inch in diameter ball in the center; the ball is moved by the fingers (Ch. 5)

transistor a tiny electronic switch or semiconductor device that controls the flow of electricity between two terminals (Ch. 2)

translator program a computer program that translates computer code into machine-readable form, as in compiler, interpreter, and assembler (Ch. 7)

transmission channels data communication circuits that computers use to send data from place to place (Ch. 15)

tutorials self-teaching materials that include a series of lessons a user can follow while sitting at the computer (Ch. 18)

twisted-pair copper wire the most common, least expensive, and easiest-to-install communication medium (Ch. 15)

UNIVAC I the first computer built for data processing rather than military or research use (Ch. 2)

Universal Product Code (UPC) a bar code adopted by the grocery industry in 1973 whose bars contain information uniquely identifying each grocery item (Ch. 5)

UNIX a machine-independent minicomputer and mainframe operating system originally developed at AT&T's Bell Labs (Ch. 10)

unstructured problem a problem where none of the problem-solving phases are well defined (Ch. 17)

UPC acronym for *Universal Product Code* (Ch. 5)

upload to transmit a file as a unit to a larger computer (Ch. 15)

user-friendly a term used to describe software or

computer hardware that is designed to be easy to use and is intended for people with little technical expertise (Ch. 5)

user groups computer clubs formed around particular types of computers to provide members with software and hardware support (Ch. 18)

utility programs programs that control input, output, and critical processing tasks such as disk access (Ch. 7)

vacuum tube a tube-like device used to control the flow of electric current; basic component in first generation computers (Ch. 2)

values the numbers placed directly in a spreadsheet's cells (Ch. 12)

VDT acronym for *video display terminal* (Ch. 5)

vectors closely placed, lighted straight-line segments used to create screen images and characters (Ch. 14)

very large-scale integration (VLSI) the technique whereby hundreds of thousands of transistors and circuits are packed onto silicon chips (Ch. 2)

video display terminal (VDT) the most common means of communicating with a computer, consisting of a keyboard attached to a monitor (Ch. 5)

video graphics adaptor (VGA) monitor a very high-resolution color monitor that produces remarkably lifelike images and has a density of 640 by 480 pixels (Ch. 5)

virtual reality complex graphical software which takes input from a specially-designed mask and glove, enabling users to enter into an artificial 3-D drama as an active participant (Ch. 14)

VisiCalc the first electronic spreadsheet, developed by Dan Bricklin and Robert Frankston in 1979 to run on an early Apple II computer (Ch. 2)

VLSI acronym for *very large-scale integration* (Ch. 2)

voiceband channels communication channels that were originally used for the transmission of sound (telephone lines) and that can transmit computer data at between 30 and 960 characters per second (Ch. 15)

voice synthesis a computerized voice output device that either records words and phrases, stores them in the computer's memory, and later builds sentences from them, or records phonemes (the finite sounds that comprise a spoken language) and uses them to construct words and sentences (Ch. 5)

volatile requiring continuous current to retain stored information (Ch. 3)

von Neumann Computer a theoretical computer designed in the early 1950s by John von Neumann that was based on the concept of storing a program in memory, that received instruction entered as a numeric code, and whose hardware was organized into components, each of which performed a specific task and could be called upon in series repeatedly to perform its function (Ch. 2)

what you see is what you get (WYSIWYG) word processing software in which entered text can be immediately corrected and adjusted, formatting commands are immediately acted upon, and the text on the screen is moved around to reflect the command (Ch. 11)

wide area network computers and computing devices connected over long-distance communications lines (Ch. 15)

Winchester disk a magnetic disk system invented by IBM in which the disks, access arms, and read/write heads are sealed in an airtight container (Ch. 4)

windows overlapping screen images in which the computer user can view multiple computer operations at once (Chs. 1, 10)

word the number of bits that can be processed at one time (Ch. 1)

word wrap an automatic carriage return feature in which the software sets up margins marking the maximum length of every line, and when a word crosses this invisible boundary, it automatically moves to the next line (Ch. 11)

word processing writing with a computer; characters, words, and phrases can easily be added, removed, and changed within a document (Chs. 10, 11)

workstation the physical layout of furniture and computer equipment designed to make using computers both comfortable and efficient, or a

workstation (*continued*)
highly sophisticated desktop minicomputer including a large graphics monitor, a pointing device, and software that enables the user to run several programs at the same time (Ch. 1)

WORM optical computer disks employing the same technology as CD-ROM, with which user writes once and then can read many times (Ch. 4)

WYSIWYG acronym for *what you see is what you get* (Ch. 11)

Index

The letter *i* following a page number indicates the information will be found in an illustration and/or its caption. The letter *b* following a page number indicates the information will be found in an On Line box.

511